For Reference

Homophones and Homographs

Homophones and Homographs

An American Dictionary

SECOND EDITION

Compiled by

James B. Hobbs

McFarland & Company, Inc., Publishers
Jefferson, North Carolina, and London

British Library Cataloguing-in-Publication data are available

Library of Congress Cataloguing-in-Publication Data

Hobbs, James B., 1930–
  Homophones and homographs : an American dictionary / compiled by
James B. Hobbs. – 2nd ed.
    p.   cm.
  Includes bibliographical references.
  ISBN 0-89950-776-X (lib. bdg. : 50# alk. paper) ∞
  1. English language – United States – Homonyms – Dictionaries.
  2. Americanisms – Dictionaries.   I. Title.
  PE2833.H63   1993
  423′.1 – dc20   92-56651
                                                             CIP

Manufactured in the United States of America

McFarland & Company, Inc., Publishers
  Box 611, Jefferson, North Carolina 28640

Table of Contents

Preface

It all began as an absorbing if impromptu diversion during supper one spring evening in 1982, an effort to assist a seven-year-old friend win his class challenge project of generating the largest number of homophones — words that sound the same but differ in spelling and meaning, like **moose** and **mousse**. Although his 279 words fell 77 short of victory, the heat of that contest infected several of us with a long-lasting compulsion to identify such words. From that affliction arose the 1986 edition of this dictionary containing 3,625 homophones and 602 homographs, the latter being words that are spelled the same but differ in sound and meaning, like **lead** (to guide or precede) and **lead** (a heavy metallic element). Believing that collection to be the most comprehensive accumulation of such words in the English language, I set the task aside as being finished.

But additional words continued to emerge from such places as *The New York Times* crossword puzzles, friends and acquaintances who became aware of my offer to pay a dollar for each pair of new homophones or homographs, and periodic meanderings through various dictionaries. Eventually I undertook a complete reexamination of the some 460,000 entries in *Webster's Third New International Dictionary of the English Language Unabridged,* and a thorough review of the 600,000 and 315,000 entries in *Webster's New International Dictionary of the English Language 2nd Edition Unabridged* and *The Random House Dictionary of the English Language,* 2nd edition unabridged, together with an inspection of each item cited in the present volume's annotated bibliography. All told, probably in excess of two million entries were explored during these intervening seven years — an adventure that has resulted in what is now almost certainly the most comprehensive and accurate compilation of its kind, containing 7,149 homophones and 1,469 homographs, which is about two times the number reflected in the first edition.

Still, no claim can be advanced that this is the final word on the subject, for several reasons. First, the language undergoes continual change, with new words arriving, old ones departing, and some lying dormant pending revival or burial. Second, pronunciations occasionally change. Third, several homophonic and homographic words were omitted from this compilation because they failed to conform to the rather rigid criteria outlined herein. Finally, several words have almost certainly been overlooked during the eyestrain and physical exertion connected with examining several 13-pound tomes and a couple of million entries. Again, readers are cordially invited to notify the publisher or author of errors of omission or commission.

Several individuals assisted in bringing this volume to fruition:

David Weisman, the now college undergraduate who brought home the 2nd-grade assignment from his teacher Robie Barga at Swain School in Allentown, Pennsylvania. Also Melody Weisman, his mother, who discovered several homophones, originally suggested the inclusion of homographs, and safe-kept the entire manuscript at critical junctures.

Peg, my wife, who uncovered several homophones and homographs associated with her craft of weaving, such as **sley, we've,** and **sliver.** Her cheerful tolerance of a spouse whose nose was too often buried between dictionary pages deserves acknowledgment here.

Colleagues at Lehigh University, who supplied helpful suggestions and findings: Dr. Frank S. Hook, professor emeritus of English; Drs. Eli Schwartz and Robert J. Thornton, professors of economics with backgrounds in classical languages and etymology; and Dr. Albert Wilansky, distinguished professor of mathematics and contributor of several homographs including **cover** from his native Nova Scotia.

John D. Hitchcock of Laramie, Wyoming; Felicia Lamport of Cambridge, Massachusetts; Sybil P. Parker, publisher in the professional and reference division of McGraw-Hill Book Company; and John L. Turner of Scotts Valley, California, whose insights and contributions in correspondence with me and in their published writings were of considerable great help.

Drs. William Davis of Newark, Delaware, and Bevan J. Clarke, professor of accountancy and management information systems at the University of Christchurch, New Zealand, who both evidence insatiable curiosity in a variety of human endeavors. Plus Jule Shipman, whose eagle eye uncovered several errors in the manuscript.

René Hollinger and Diane Oechsle, who provided invaluable and patient assistance in word processor manipulations.

Finally, each of the authors cited in the annotated bibliography appearing at the end of this dictionary.

My sincerest and warmest appreciation to each.

J.B.H.
Bethlehem, Pennsylvania

Overview of Homophones
and Homographs

This brief orientation addresses the following areas so as to provide a context and perspective on homophones and homographs: definitions; the "Conflict of Homophones" controversy; criteria for including and excluding words; notational devices, arrangements, and phonetic symbols; and the organization of the dictionary.

Definitions

This dictionary focuses on American homophones and homographs and is based on pronunciations that prevail in most sections of the United States. Briefly, a homophone is a word that is pronounced the same as another (a "sound-alike") but which differs in spelling and meaning, such as **cite, sight,** and **site.** On the other hand, a homograph is a word that is spelled the same as another (a "look-alike") but which differs in sound and meaning, such as **tear** (to separate or pull apart) and **tear** (a secretion from the eye).

The relationship and significance of these two classes of words in the English language may be better understood by referring to the following diagram, which divides all English words into eight categories according to the three characteristics of sound, spelling, and meaning. For example, a homonym is a word that has the same sound and spelling but has several meanings, such as **set,** which may possess the largest number of different meanings of any word in the English language.

The sharp distinction between the first three categories in the diagram is adopted in this dictionary because the following definitions that are reflected in *Webster's Third New International Dictionary of the English Language Unabridged* for these three categories are ambiguous and overlapping:

Homonym: One of two or more words spelled and pronounced alike, but different in meaning. Includes homophones and homographs.

1

Category	A word having the same (+) or different (−) following characteristic as another:			Comment or example
	Sound	*Spelling*	*Meaning*	
1. **Homonym**	+	+	−	A large number of words fall into this category, such as **plane**: a tool for smoothing, a type of tree, to skim across water, or to soar in air
2. **Homophone** ("sound-alike")	+	−	−	A considerable number of words make up this category, such as **right, rite, wright,** and **write.**
3. **Homograph** ("look-alike")	−	+	−	Several words are in this category, such as **bass** (a fish) and **bass** (a low voice).
4. **Synonym**	−	−	+	A large number of words are in this category, such as **pig, hog,** and **swine.**
5. **Heterograph** (not a universal definition)	+	−	+	Very few words fall into this category, such as **comptroller/controller, czar/tsar,** and **drachm/dram.**
6. **Heterophone** (not a universal definition)	−	+	+	This category contains few, if any, words.
7. **No formal designation**	−	−	−	A vast number of words fall into this category, each of which is unique with respect to sound, spelling, and meaning.
8. **No formal designation**	+	+	+	This category is probably empty, since it is doubtful that any two words have all three characteristics in common.

Homophone: One of two or more words pronounced alike but different in meaning or derivation or spelling. Also called homonym.

Homograph: One of two or more words spelled alike but differing in meaning or derivation or pronunciation. Also called homonym.

In short, these three categories are sharply separate and distinguishable, and will be considered as such throughout this dictionary. (Please note that the two "no formal designation" categories at the bottom of the diagram are included merely for completeness to describe all eight possibilities that arise because of three characteristics.)

The "Conflict of Homophones" Controversy

Many languages are blessed or burdened, depending on one's point of view, with homophones and homographs. The world champion for number of homophones is probably Chinese, partially resulting from its subtle voice inflections and almost imperceptible nuances. But the English language has more than many others, for several reasons. First, English has borrowed liberally from other languages. For example, **air, err,** and **heir** stem from Middle English, Old French, and Latin. Second, the English and Americans have a penchant for shortening words thereby creating numerous homophones, such as **plane** (from airplane) which is homophonous with **plain,** or **ads** (from advertisements) which is homophonous with **adds** and **adze.** Third, some homophones are created by converting proper names to specific things, like (James) **Joule,** which is homophonous with **jewel.** Fourth, the prevalence of acronyms in America and many modern societies generates numerous homophones, such as **WAACS** (Women's Army Auxiliary Corps) which is homophonic with **whacks.** Finally, sound changes occur through a process known as assimilation, such as the "d" in **chased** evolving toward the "t" in **chaste.** This last phenomenon frequently results in the creation of puns or double entendres. For example: "The seriously chased are seldom chaste very long. (Or might it be the other way 'round?)"

Several linguistic and language scholars have addressed a more sophisticated question: Do homophones, whether in English or any language, tend to self-destruct because of their apparent tendency to create confusion and ambiguity? A doctrine advanced by Jules Gilliéron from 1902 to 1921 stated that two words of different origin which become homophones by regular sound-changes may, because of ambiguity and confusion, interfere with each other to such an extent that one is ultimately driven from the vocabulary of a particular dialect. This doctrine or principle is referred to as the "Conflict of Homophones."

Professor Robert Menner of Yale University addressed this concept in 1936, arguing that if a word that had become homophonous with another were lost, the loss should not be attributed solely to homophonic conflict without observing two rules of caution. First, two homophones are unlikely to interfere unless they belong to the same part of speech. A verb is unlikely to conflict with a noun, or a noun with an adjective. Second, the words must fall within the same sphere of ideas and be likely to appear in similar contexts. If these two conditions are fulfilled, Menner asserted, it is possible for a combination of sounds representing two different words to become ambiguous, and the resultant confusion may be so marked as to lead to the elimination of one of the words. Menner maintained further that even if a homophone were lost under these circumstances, it would be difficult to prove that homophony was the sole determining cause. Other and more usual causes of obsolescence (such as changes in popularity, style, or constancy of use) must first be ruled out—a process that is difficult because such changes are often obscure and elusive.

Julian Franklyn (see his citation in the annotated bibliography) made the summary point in 1966 that homophony tends to be local in time as well as in space. "Homophones of 1764 are not quite the same as those of 1964; and homophones north of Trent differ from those recognized south of that select boundary." In short, **aunt** and **ant** may be homophonous for some, while others insist that **aunt** must properly rhyme with **font** or **taunt**, but never with the insect.

Professor Edna Williams of Smith College reinforced many of these key points in her doctoral dissertation, which was written in 1936 with Professor Menner chairing her dissertation committee. Dr. Williams argued that words become subject to mutual confusion and conflict due to homophony only when the words concerned: (a) are alike in sound, (b) are in common use in the same social and intellectual circles, and (c) perform the same syntactical functions in the language within a common sphere of ideas. She observed that the conflict of homophones is only one of many alleged causes of the loss of words, and one of the least frequent relative to the vast number lost in English. Seldom, she summarized, are circumstances so simple and obvious that we may say without debate that one cause was solely responsible for the loss of a word. The most that can be said is that homophony may have been a contributing factor, or in some cases almost certainly the main factor, causing the unpopularity of certain terms and the disappearance of others.

Criteria for Including and Excluding Words

The following three unabridged dictionaries served as the principal authorities for entries contained in this dictionary: *The Random House Dictionary of the English Language,* 2nd edition, 1987; *Webster's New*

International Dictionary of the English Language 2nd Edition Unabridged, 1949; and *Webster's Third New International Dictionary of the English Language Unabridged,* 1981. *Webster's Third* played the central role with respect to spelling, pronunciation, and definitions. In particular cases, other dictionaries cited in the annotated bibliography were consulted to arbitrate differences and discrepancies, particularly the twenty volumes of *The Oxford English Dictionary, 2nd Edition.*

With respect to homophones, at least one pronunciation had to be common to two or more homophonic candidates for them to be included in this dictionary as bona fide homophones. With respect to homographs, on the other hand, at least one pronunciation of homographic candidates had to be dissimilar for words to be listed as bona fide homographs. In general, r's were not "dropped" from spellings to create homophones or homographs, such as dropping the r from **car** to make it homophonic with **caw.** Nor were r's added to spellings, such as **idea(r),** to create a homophone or homograph. Neither were h's dropped to make words homophonic or homographic, such as dropping the "h" from **heady** or **hitch** to make them homophonic with **eddy** or **itch.**

Words that are deemed near-but-unacceptable homophones or homographs are those whose meanings are similar or stem from the same basic word-root, but differ primarily in grammatical usage, such as **absence/absents** or **absent** (the adjective)/**absent** (the verb). These words are classified as Group I homophones or homographs in subsequent listings. Also classified as near-but-unacceptable homophones are words with close but perceptibly different pronunciations, such as **loose** ('lüs) and **lose** ('lüz). These words are classified as Group II homophones. A few homophones are classified as near-but-unacceptable because they fall into both Group I and II categories, such as **mystic** and **mystique.** The observant reader will note that an exhaustive listing of all meanings and nuances of a particular homophone or homograh is not included in that word's definition, such as the approximately 113 different definitions for **set,** depending on whether it is used as a transitive or intransitive verb, as a noun, or as an adjective. And normally suffixes are not added to homophones merely to lengthen listings, such as **sew** (then **sewed, sewing, sews**) or **sow** (then **sowed, sowing, sows**).

In general, the following words are excluded from this dictionary: obsolete, archaic, and very rarely used words; words associated primarily with regional dialects, especially those of England, Scotland, and the Southern United States; most colloquialisms, although several slang terms are included; proper names, such as **Claude** (homophonic with **clawed**), **Jim (gym)**, and **Mary (merry)**; and most foreign units of money, weights, and measures, except such familiar ones as the French **franc** and the Italian **lira.**

Unlike the first, this second edition does include many countries, provinces, major cities, nationalities, and races — the rationale being that recognition of such notable characteristics might serve to broaden a too-frequent parochial/provincial American perspective.

Notational Devices, Arrangements, and Phonetic Symbols

Homophones and homographs are arranged alphabetically within their respective categories. All homophones are cross-referenced in alphabetical order, although the definition of each is given only once where it is first mentioned. For example, **Aaronic** and **ironic** are grouped together and defined at their original appearance in the A section. **Ironic** then reappears without definition after **ire** in the I section, with parenthetical reference to **Aaronic**. An <u>underlined word</u> is both a homophone and a homograph.

To repeat, Group I homophones and homographs (which follow bona fide homophone and homograph entries) are near-but-unacceptable homophones and homographs whose meanings are similar or stem from the same basic word-root, differing primarily in grammatical usage. Group II homophones are also near-but-unacceptable homophones because of close but perceptibly different pronunciations. Some homophones are both Group I and II.

The following pronunciation symbols and notations are adapted from *Webster's Third New International Dictionary of the English Language Unabridged* and used throughout this dictionary. (The symbols and modifiers adopted by the International Phonetic Alphabet are not used in this dictionary due to their complexity, formidableness, and general unfamiliarity to most general readerships.)

a	...	cat
à	...	cart, as pronounced by "r-droppers"
ä	...	cot
ā	...	fade
ar	...	care
aù	...	**out**
e	...	bed
ē	...	feed
i	...	silver or **ear**
ī	...	side
ŋ	...	si**ng**
ȯ	...	saw
ȯi	...	oil
ȯ(ə)r	...	orb
ō	...	tone
th	...	ether

th	...	ei**th**er
ə	...	c**u**rb, Am**e**rica, or immediately preceding l, m, n, and ŋ, p, or s—as in kitt**e**n
ə̇	...	unstressed variant, as in hab**i**t
u̇	...	w**oo**d
ü	...	t**oo**l
œ	...	French **ue**
yu̇	...	c**u**rable
yü	...	f**ew**
ⁿ	...	the preceding vowel is pronounced with the nasal passages open, as in French vi**n** blanc
′	...	the mark preceding a syllable with the primary (stronger) stress, as in ′**book**ˌkeeper
ˌ	...	the mark preceding a syllable with the secondary (weaker) stress, as in ′bookˌ**keeper**
:	...	the mark preceding a syllable whose stress can vary between primary and secondary
|	...	indicates the placement of a variant pronunciation, such as **quart**, ′kwȯr|t or ′kwȯrt|
•	...	the mark of syllable division that is inserted in a sequence of sounds which can have more than one syllable division, such as **nitrite**, ′ni•trit or ′nit•rit

Accent marks are used at appropriate points, although some linguists might argue that these marks are an integral part of the spelling, such that **charge** and **chargé** represent two distinct spellings, rather than being simply variant pronunciations of the same spelling. The reader may choose to allow or disallow words as bona fide homographs with the following accent marks: acute (á)—the vowel is pronounced with a rise in pitch; grave (à)—the vowel is pronounced with a fall in pitch; and circumflex (â)—the vowel is pronounced with a rising-falling tone.

Organization of the Dictionary

Alphabetized homophones are presented first, followed by alphabetized homographs. The table on page eight summarizes by alphabetic character the number of homophones and homographs. For example, a total of 367 homophones begin with "a," of which 56 are one-syllable, 151 two-syllable, etc.; and 119 homographs begin with "a." The extreme right column indicates the number of words that are both homophonic and homographic. Mathematically inclined readers will observe that the ratio of total homophones to total homographs in this edition is 5:1 (compared to 6:1 in the first edition).

	Total words	Homophones				Homographs	Homophones and Homographs
		1-syllable words	2-syllable words	3-syllable words	4-6-syllable words		
A	367	56	151	111	49	119	13
B	542	287	229	22	4	98	27
C	902	291	428	136	47	198	33
D	273	87	151	29	6	47	9
E	135	31	49	41	14	34	2
F	289	152	116	21		34	13
G	300	165	120	13	2	54	13
H	239	113	106	14	6	40	6
I	117	9	41	45	22	18	
J	68	43	21	2	2	22	
K	184	88	87	8	1	18	4
L	299	151	126	18	4	69	17
M	394	144	194	42	14	117	25
N	134	65	64	5		25	9
O	117	25	43	45	4	20	3
P	594	212	274	78	30	139	23
Q	50	26	24			8	2
R	353	147	171	35		100	16
S	728	348	307	53	20	141	38
T	454	190	217	31	16	98	26
U	173	7	96	58	12	22	
V	82	24	43	11	4	24	5
W	293	201	84	6	2	18	5
X	12	2	7	3			
Y	34	28	6			4	
Z	16	6	7	3		2	
Total	7149	2898	3162	830	259	1469	289

An appendix of unusual word groupings follows the homographs, consisting of the following:

- Homophones — four or more one-syllable words
                  — three or more two-syllable words
                  — three or more three-syllable words
                  — all four-, five-, and six-syllable words. Two pairs of six-syllable homophones (the largest number detected thus far) are identified in this dictionary: **synechological/synecological** and **uncomplimentary/uncomplementary**
- Homographs — three or more words.
- All words that are both homophobic and homographic

The final section is the annotated bibliography, which reflects almost 100 references that were consulted in compiling this dictionary.

Homophones

A

a an indefinite article
ay an expression of sorrow or regret
eh an expression of inquiry or slight
surprise

Aaronic belonging to the lesser order
of the Mormon priesthood
ironic relating to a result opposite to
and as if in mockery of the appropriate or expected result

ab in Egyptian religion, the spirit of
the physical heart and the seat of
the will and intentions
abb coarse wool from the inferior
parts of a fleece

aba A loose sleeveless Arabian garment
abba an honorific title given to the
Deity, bishops, partriarchs, and
Jewish scholars

abaisse a thin undercrust of pastry
abase to lower or reduce in rank or
esteem

abb (see **ab**)

abba (see **aba**)

abele a white poplar tree;
able possessing resources needed to
accomplish an objective

abeyance temporary inactivity or
suppression
obeyance an act or custom of obey-
ing

able (see **abele**)

absinthin a bitter white crystalline
compound constituting the active
ingredient of wormwood
absinthine a moderate yellow green
color

Acacian relating to a schism occurring A.D. 484-519 between Eastern
and Western Christian churches
acaciin a crystalline glycoside found

in the leaves of a common North
American locust tree

Acadian a native or inhabitant of
Acadia; a French colony consisting
principally of what is now Nova
Scotia; a Louisianian descended
from French-speaking immigrants
from Acadia
Akkadian a Semitic inhabitant of
Mesopotamia before 2000 B.C.

acanthin the substance, consisting of
strontium sulphate, forming the internal skeleton of radiolarians
acanthine a basic compound obtained from the livers and embryos
of the spiny dogfish; resembling the
leaves of an acanthus plant

acanthous bristling, sharp, or thorny
Acanthus a genus of prickly herbs of
the Mediterranean

Acarus a genus of arachnids including a number of small mites
Acorus a genus of rushlike herbs
with the flowers in a close spadix

accede to express approval or give
consent
axseed a sprawling plant native to
Europe, and naturalized in the
eastern U.S. as crown vetch

accede to express approval or give
consent
exceed to surpass, excel, or outdo

accept to take without protest
except to omit something

accepter a person who takes without
protest
acceptor a substance or particle capable of combining with another
substance or particle; a circuit that
combines inductance and capacitance in series so as to resonate to
a given impressed frequency

access a way to approach or reach
excess an amount exceeding the usual
or normal

accidence a part of grammar that
deals with inflections
accidens any fortuitous or nonessen-
tial property, fact, or circumstance
accidents sudden events that occur
without intent

acclamation a loud eager expression
of approval, praise, or assent
acclimation a physiological adjust-
ment to a change in the environment

accouter to equip or fit out
acuter a sharper point or angle

ace a playing card ranking highest in
its suit; a person who excels at
something
Ais a people in the Indian river
valley, Florida
ase an enzyme

acephalous having the style issuing
from the base instead of from the
apex of the ovary
acephalus a headless fetal monster

Aceria a large genus of eriophyid
mites including several parasites of
economic plants
Assyria an ancient empire of western
Asia

acetic related to acetic acid or
vinegar
ascetic extremely strict in religious
exercises
Ossetic relating to or characteristic of
the Ossets, a tall Aryan people of
central Caucasus

acher a person who suffers a dull
persistent and throbbing pain
acre a unit of measure in the U.S.
and England equal to 43,560
square feet or 160 square rods

achy afflicted with aches
aikie to lay claim to something; to

demand equal division of something found

Acorus (see Acarus)

acouchi a resin similar in nature to
elemi and obtained from various
South American trees
acouchy a small species of agouti

acre (see acher)

acrogenous increasing by growth
from the summit or apex
acrogynous having the archegonia
at the apex of the stem and involving the apical cells in their formation

acron the unsegmented part of the
body in front of a segmented
animal's mouth
Akron a city in northeastern Ohio

actin a protein of muscle
actine a star-shaped spicule, as of a
sponge
acton a jacket plated with steel

acts performs
ax(e) a cutting tool

acuter (see accouter)

Adam the unregenerate nature of
man; a style of furniture designed
in the late 18th century
atom a minute particle of matter

adder a snake
attar a perfume obtained from
flowers

addition a result of increasing or
augmenting
edition a form in which a literary
work is published

addle to throw into confusion or
disorder
attle in mining, waste rock

adds joins or unites
ads notices to attract attention to a
product or business
adz(e) a cutting tool

adduce to bring forward for consideration in a discussion or analysis
educe to evoke or extract

Adelea a large genus of protozoans that are parasitic on arthropods
Adelia a genus of tropical American shrubs with toothed leaves

ades sweetened drinks
aides assistants
AIDS acquired immunodeficiency syndrome (an acronym)
aids helps

adherence steady or faithful attachment; continued observance
adherents persons who adhere to or follow; persons 14 years or older who are listed on the records of the Salvation Army but have not yet become soldiers

adieu an expression of farewell
ado bustling about

adjutant a staff officer acting as a general and administrative assistant to the commanding officer
agitant a person who is active in or furthering a course of action

ado (see **adieu**)

Adoptian relating to the doctrine that Jesus became the son of God by exaltation to a status that was not by his birth
adoption the taking of an outsider into a family, clan, or tribal group

ads (see **adds**)

adventuress a woman who schemes to win social position or wealth by unscrupulous or questionable means
adventurous inclined to engage in exciting or very unusual experiences

adz(e) (see **adds**)

aer a large veil in the Eastern Orthodox church which covers the chalice or paten
air the atmosphere
are 100 square meters
e'er a contraction of ever

ere before
err make a mistake
eyre a journey
heir an inheritor

aerial related to the air
areal relating to an area or an extent of space
ariel a small Australian flying marsupial; an Arabian gazelle

aerie a high eagle's or hawk's nest
aery having an aerial quality
airy resembling or related to air; having an affected manner
Eire the republic of Ireland

aerie a high eagle's or hawk's nest
eerie weird
Eire the republic of Ireland
Erie an Iroquoian people of northern Ohio, northwestern Pennsylvania, and western New York; a city in northwestern Pennsylvania; the next smallest of the five Great Lakes

aerose brassy
erose having the margin irregularly notched, as if gnawed

aery (see **aerie**)

aes in Roman antiquity, anything made of bronze or copper
ease relaxation; naturalness

affect to influence or make an impression on
effect a resultant condition

affective relating to feelings or emotions
effective productive of results; efficient

affiance solemnly promise to marry
affiants those that swear to an affidavit

affluence an abundance of property
affluents tributary streams

affusion the act of pouring a liquid upon, as in baptism
effusion unrestrained expression of feeling

afterward subsequently; the future
afterword an epilogue

Agamae a class or subkingdom embracing all plants reproducing by means of spores rather than flowers or seeds
agamy the absence, nonregulation, or nonrecognition of marriage

agitant (see **adjutant**)

ah an expression of delight, relief, regret, or contempt
aw an expression of mild incredulity or disgust
awe reverence or wonder with a touch of fear

Aht a Wakashan people of Vancouver Island and the Cape Flattery region in northwestern Washington
aught zero or a cipher (also **ault**)

ai a three-toed sloth; an expression of grief, despair, or anguish
ay an expression of sorrow, regret, or surprise
aye an affirmative vote
eye an organ of sight
I a personal pronoun

aides (see **ades**)

AIDS and **aids** (see **ades**)

aiel a writ by which an heir enters a grandfather's estate and dispossesses a third party who attempts to gain possession
ail to affect with pain or discomfort
ale a beverage

aikie (see **achy**)

ail (see **aiel**)

air (see **aer**)

airable capable of being aired
arable fit for tillage and crop production

airan an Altaic and Turkish drink prepared from fermented milk
Iran a country in southwestern Asia

airless lacking air or movement of air
heirless having no inheritor

airship a lighter-than-air aircraft with propelling and directional control systems
heirship the right of inheritance

airy (see **aerie**)

Ais (see **ace**)

aisle a passage between seats
I'll a contraction of I will or I shall
isle a small island

Aissor a people in parts of Asiatic Turkey and Persia calling themselves Syrians
icer a worker who covers food with ice before shipment; a worker who mixes icing or ices baked goods

ait a little island
ate consumed food
eight a number between seven and nine

Aka a hill tribe north of Assam
aka any of several species of New Zealand woody vines
Akha the most southerly group of Lolo-speaking Tibeto-Burman people forming a large part of the hill tribes of Shan State, Myanmar; a Pygmy people of the Vele basin in the Belgian Congo

Akhs the spirits of deceased persons conceived as gloriously transferred so as to reflect the deeds of the persons in life
ox an adult castrated male bovine

Akka (see **Aka**)

Akkadian (see **Acadian**)

Akron (see **acron**)

Alascan a foreign Protestant in England during the reign of Edward VI
Alaskan relating to or characteristic of the state of Alaska

albumen   egg white
albumin   a large class of simple proteins

alcanna   a color varying from reddish brown to strong brown
Alkanna   a genus of herbs native to southern Europe
alkanna   an Old World tropical shrub or small tree

alcatras   a large water bird, such as the pelican or frigate bird
Alcatraz   the island in San Francisco Bay, California formerly a high-security prison

ale   (see **aiel**)

Alectrion   the type of genus of Nassariidae comprising various typical basket shells
Alectryon   a monotypic genus of New Zealand trees with alternate compound leaves and showy paniculate flowers

aleph   the first letter of the Hebrew alphabet
alif   the first letter of the Arabic alphabet

alfa   either of two Spanish and Algerian grasses of which cordage, shoes, baskets, and paper are made
alpha   the first letter of the Greek alphabet; the first in a sequence

alif   (see **aleph**)

alison   a plant of the genus Alyssum
allicin   a liquid compound with a garlic odor and antibacterial properties

Alkanna and **alkanna**   (see **alcanna**)

alkenyl   any univalent aliphatic hydrocarbon radical derived from an alkene by removal of one hydrogen atom
alkynyl   a univalent aliphatic hydrocarbon radical containing a triple bond

alkide   a binary compound of an alkyl, especially with a metal

alkyde   any of a large group of thermoplastic or thermosetting synthetic resins that are essentially polyesters

alkynyl   (see **alkenyl**)

all   the entire amount
awl   a pointed tool

allay   to reduce in intensity
allée   a formal avenue or mall

allegation   something asserted
alligation   the action of attaching or the state of being attached; a process for the solution of problems concerning the mixing of ingredients that differ in price or quality

allegator   a person who asserts, affirms, or states without proof
Alligator   the genus of Crocodylidae comprising the American and Chinese alligators
alligator   either of two crocodilians; a machine with strong jaws, one of which opens like a movable jaw of an alligator

allicin   (see **alison**)

alligation   (see **allegation**)

Alligator and **alligator**   (see **allegator**)

allision   the running of one ship upon another ship that is stationary
elision   the act of dropping out or omitting something
Elysian   sweetly blissful

alliterate   characterized by the repetition, usually initially, of a sound that is usually a consonant in two or more adjacent words or syllables
illiterate   showing a lack of familiarity with language and literature; having little or no education

allocator   a person that distributes according to some predetermined ratio or agreed measure
allocatur   a court order granting something requested

allowed permitted
aloud audible

all ready everybody
already by this time or soon

all together everyone together
altogether in total or entirely

alluded referred to indirectly
eluded evaded
eluted removed from an absorbment
by means of a solvent; washed out
or extracted
illuded deceived

allure the power of attraction or
fascination
alure a gallery or passage along par-
apets of a castle, around the roof
of a church, or along a cloister

allusion an indirect reference
elusion an evasion
illusion a misleading image

all ways in every way
always at all times

aloe a pale green color
alow in or to a lower part

aloud (see **allowed**)

alow (see **aloe**)

alpha (see **alfa**)

already (see **all ready**)

altar a place of worship or sacrifice
alter to become different or cause to
become different

altogether (see **all together**)

alumen alum; either of two colorless
or white isomorphous crystalline
double sulfates of aluminum having
a sweetish-sourish astringent taste
illumen illuminate

alure (see **allure**)

always (see **all ways**)

am the present first person singular
of be
em a unit of measure in printing

ama a Japanese woman diver who
works usually without diving gear;
a vessel for eucharistic wine
amah a female servant typically
Chinese, especially a nurse
amma an abbess or spiritual mother

amaretto an almond-flavored liqueur
amoretto a naked usually infantile
figure representing the god of love
and often holding a bow and arrow

amatol an explosive consisting of
ammonium nitrate and TNT
amytal a crystalline compound used
as a sedative and hypnotic

Ambassadeur a bearded iris with
maroon and bronze flowers
ambassador an official representative
of a sovereign or state

ameen a minor official of the judicial
and revenue departments in India
amine a compound containing one
or more halogen atoms
ammine a molecule of ammonia

amend to reform oneself or become
better
emend to correct a literary work

amerce to punish by a monetary
penalty
immerse to dip into liquid

America of or from North, Central,
or South America; of or from the
United States
Amerika the fascist or racist aspect
of American society

amine (see **ameen**)

amma (see **ama**)

ammine (see **ameen**)

amoretto (see **amaretto**)

amorous strongly moved by love;
manifesting love
Amyris a genus of tropical American
trees and shrubs with compound
leaves and white flowers

amorphous without definite form or shape

amorphus a fetus with head, heart, or limbs

amotion removal of a specified object or person from a place or position

emotion feeling or an expression of feeling

ample more than adequate

ampul a small bulbous glass vessel

amtrac an amphibian flat-bottomed vehicle that moves or tracks over land and which can be propelled through water

Amtrak the government-subsidized public intercity passenger railroad system in the U.S.

amygdalin a white crystalline glucoside that occurs in the kernels of the bitter almond

amygdaline pertaining to a tonsil

Amyris (see **amorous**)

amytal (see **amatol**)

an an indefinite article

en a unit of measure in printing

analyst a person who weighs or studies to arrive at an answer

annalist a writer of annals

ananym a pseudonym consisting of the real name written backward

anonym an idea that has no exact term to express it

Anas a type of widely distributed freshwater ducks

anise an herb with aromatic seeds

anchor a device to hold an object in place

anker a U.S. unit of measure equal to ten gallons

anchored secured firmly

ancred a cross with each arm divided into two recurving points

anchorite a person who lives in seclusion, usually for religious reasons

ankerite a variety of dolomite containing considerable iron

ancred (see **anchored**)

and a conjunction, meaning also or in addition

end a cessation or terminus

androgenous pertaining to the production of or tending to produce male offspring

androgynous in astronomy, sometimes hot and sometimes cold with respect to planets

androgynus an individual possessing characteristics of both sexes

ands conjunctions, meaning also or in addition

ends terminations; leftover scraps

ens a thing's being or essence; in typesetting, en quads

anger a strong feeling of displeasure and usually of antagonism

angor extreme distress or mental anguish, usually of a physical origin

anils Schiff bases derived from aromatic amines

annals historical records

anise (see **Anas**)

anker (see **anchor**)

ankerite (see **anchorite**)

annalist (see **analyst**)

annals (see **anils**)

annunciate to announce

enunciate to utter articulate sounds

anonym (see **ananym**)

ansae parts of a celestial body having the appearance of handles; structures resembling loops

antsy eager, impatient, or restless

Anser a genus of birds comprising geese

answer a reply

ant   an insect
aunt   a sister of either of one's parents

antae   piers produced by thickening a wall at its termination
ante   a poker stake; before
anti   one who is opposed
auntie   an aunt, often used endearingly

antecedence   an apparent motion of a planet toward the west; retrogradation
antecedents   significant events, principles, or activities of one's earlier life; predecessors in a series

anti   (see antae)

antsy   (see ansae)

Aor   one of a group of related peoples inhabiting the Naga hills in eastern Assam along the Myanmar frontier
hour   a time measurement equal to 60 minutes or 1/24 of a day
our   belonging or related to us

Aoul   a member of any of several small peoples living in the malarial swampy lowland districts of Nepal
aoul   an Abyssian gazelle
aul   a Central Asiatic tent made of felt or skin fastened over a circular wooden framework
owl   a nocturnal bird of prey

apatite   a group of calcium phosphate minerals containing other elements
appetite   a natural desire

apian   relating to bees
apiin   a crystalline glycoside obtained from parsley

aplanatism   freedom from spherical aberration
aplanetism   the state of producing nonmotile asexual spores

apophasis   denial of one's intention to speak of a subject that is simultaneously named or insinuated

apophysis   a swelling, such as a process of a bone or the cone scale of certain conifers

aport   toward the left side
apport   the production or motion of an object by a spiritualist medium without physical activity or contact

apothegm   a terse aphorism
apothem   a perpendicular from the center to one of the sides of a regular polygon

appetite   (see apatite)

apport   (see aport)

appressed   pressed close
oppressed   weighed down

apses   projecting parts of churches
apsis   the point in orbit at which the distance of a body from the center of attraction is either greatest or least

aquation   the replacement of a coordinated atom by water molecules
equation   a statement of equality between two mathematical expressions

Ara   a genus of macaws containing the blue-and-yellow macaw
Eire   of or from the republic of Ireland

arable   (see airable)

araneous   covered with or composed of soft loose hairs or fibers
Araneus   a genus of orb-weaving spiders

Arau   a Papuan people of western New Guinea
arrau   a large turtle found in the Amazon river and valued for its edible eggs and as a source of oil

arcs   portions of a curved line
arks   boats or ships
arx   a citadel, in Roman antiquity

are   (see aer)

are   exist, the present 2nd singular and present plural of be
our   belonging or related to us

area   the extent of space
aria   a melody or tune
eria   the Assam silkworm which feeds on the castor-oil plant

areal   (see **aerial**)

arear   to the rear
arrear   behind in discharging one's obligations

argal   therefore, used chiefly to imply that the reasoning is specious or absurd; a grayish or reddish crystalline crust deposited in wine casks during aging; dry cattle or camel dung used for fuel
argel   either of two related African plants whose leaves have been used to adulterate senna

Argas   a genus of ticks including the cosmopolitan chicken tick
Argus   a vigilant guardian
argus   any of several large brilliantly patterned East Indian pheasants; any of several butterflies

argel   (see **argal**)

argon   a colorless odorless inert gaseous element
Argonne   a wooded region in northeast France noted for battles in World Wars I and II

Argus and **argus**   (see **Argas**)

aria   (see **area**)

Arianism   a theological movement initiated by Arius in opposition to Sabellianism that won strong support during the 4th century A.D. chiefly in the Eastern churches
Aryanism   the doctrine popularized by Nazism that Aryan peoples possess superior capacities

ariel   (see **aerial**)

aril   a covering of certain seeds

aryl   a univalent radical (as phenyl) derived from an aromatic hydrocarbon

Arion   a genus of slugs including a common European black slug
orion   Holland blue or a dark blue color

Arkansas   a state in the south central U.S.
arkansaw   to kill in an unsportsmanlike manner; to cheat or take advantage of

Arkie   a native of Arkansas; a rustic or insignificant person
arky   old-fashioned or out of style

arks   (see **arcs**)

arky   (see **Arkie**)

armer   a person or device that arms a weapon
armoire   a usually large and ornate cupboard or wardrobe
armor   defensive covering for the body

aroar   roaring or bellowing
aurore   an hydrangea pink color

arrant   notoriously bad or shameless
errant   quixotically adventurous; aimlessly moving about

arras   a wall hanging or hanging screen of tapestry
arris   the sharp edge formed by the meeting of two surfaces
heiress   a female heir to property

arrau   (see **Arau**)

array   to set in order; a regular grouping or arrangement
arret   a judgment of a court or sovereign

arrear   (see **arear**)

arret   (see **array**)

arris   (see **arras**)

arrosive　of the nature of gnawing
erosive　tending to erode or affecting erosion

arses　the bottom ends of wooden pulley blocks
arsis　an unaccented part of a musical measure

arusa　a small shrub found in India with leaves yielding a yellow dye
arusha　an Indian shrub yielding a flaxlike fiber

arx　(see **arcs**)

Aryanism　(see **Arianism**)

aryl　(see **aril**)

As　a chief god of pagan Scandinavia
ass　a beast of burden; a simple-minded fool
asse　a fox of southern Africa

asale　for or on sale
assail　to attack with violence or vehemence

ascent　rising
assent　concurrence

ascetic　(see **acetic**)

ascian　an inhabitant of the torrid zone where the sun is vertical at noon for a few days each year such that no shadow is cast
ashen　deadly pale or pallid in color

ase　(see **ace**)

ashen　(see **ascian**)

askar　a native infantryman in an Arabic-speaking country
asker　one who poses or asks questions

asperate　to make rough, harsh, or uneven
aspirate　to pronounce with an h-sound as the initial element; to draw or withdraw by suction

ass　(see **As**)

assail　(see **asale**)

assay　to judge the worth of
essay　a short literary composition

asse　(see **As**)

assemblé　a ballet movement
assemblée　a social gathering

assent　(see **ascent**)

Assyria　(see **Aceria**)

Aster　a large genus of chiefly fall-blooming leafy-stemmed herbaceous plants native to temperate regions
aster　any plant of the genus Aster
Astur　a genus consisting of goshawks
astur　a goshawk

astray　into a wrong or mistaken way of thinking or acting; off the correct route
estray　something that has wandered or gone out of its normal place, as a domestic animal found wandering

Astur and **astur**　(see **Aster**)

Ata　a member of an Indonesian tribe of Mindanao
atta　unsorted wheat flour or meal, in India

ate　(see **ait**)

ate　blind impulse or reckless ambition
Ati　a predominantly pagan Negritoid people on Panay, Philippines

atom　(see **Adam**)

atta　(see **Ata**)

attar　(see **adder**)

attar　a perfume obtained from flowers
odder　more unusual
otter　an aquatic fish-eating mustelid mammal

attle　(see **addle**)

aube　an often Provençal love lyric usually dealing with a parting of lovers at dawn
obe　a subdivision of a phyle or clan in ancient Laconia

audience a group or assembly of listeners

audients catchumens in the early stages of instruction for admission to the church but not yet as applicants for baptism

auger a boring tool
augur to predict

aught (see **Aht**)

aught zero
ought should

augur (see **auger**)

aul (see **Aoul**)

aunt (see **ant**)

auntie (see **antae**)

aural of the ear
oral of the mouth
orle in heraldry, a border within a parallel to but not touching the edge of the field

aureole the luminous area surrounding bright light
oriole a colorful American bird

aureolin cobalt yellow
aureoline golden in color

auricle the upper chamber of the heart; an earlike lobe
oracle a divine revelation

aurore (see **aroar**)

aurous relating to or containing gold
orris the Florentine iris, or its fragrant rootstalk; gold or silver braid or lace used on 18th century clothing

austenite a solid solution in gamma iron of carbon and sometimes other solutes
austinite a mineral consisting of a basic calcium zinc arsenate

Austria a country in central Europe
Ostrea the type genus Ostreidae including oysters that retain eggs in the parent's gills during early development

ostria a warm southern wind on the Bulgarian coast
Ostrya a small widely distributed genus of trees having fruit resembling cones, including the hop hornbeam

autarchic relating to absolute sovereignty
autarkic relating to self-sufficiency

autograft a tissue or organ transplanted to another part of the same body
autographed wrote one's signature

autonomous possessing self-government
autonymous naming itself

autosight an automatic sighting device
autosite that part of a double fetal monster that nourishes both itself and the parasitic twin

avert to turn away or aside, especially in order to escape something dangerous or unpleasant
evert to overthrow or upset; to turn outward or inside out

avulsion a tearing away of a structure of a part accidently or surgically
evulsion a rooting, casting, or plucking out

aw (see **ah**)

away distant in space or time
aweigh hanging perpendicular just clear of the ground

awe (see **ah**)

aweigh (see **away**)

awful extremely unpleasant
offal waste material

awl (see **all**)

awn   a slender bristle that terminates the bract of a spikelet, such as in wheat
on   a preposition denoting position atop something

ax(e)   (see **acts**)

Axel   a one-and-a-half-turn jump in skating
axil   the angle between a branch or leaf and the axis from which it arises
axle   a shaft on which a wheel revolves

axes   cutting tools
Axis   a genus of Cervidae comprising the hog deer and axis
axis   a straight line around with something rotates; a deer of India and southern Asia

axil   (see **axel**)

Axis and **axis**   (see **axes**)

axle   (see **axel**)

axseed   (see **accede**)

ay   (see **a** or **ai**)

aye   (see **ai**)

ayin   the 16th letter of the Hebrew alphabet
ion   an atom or group of atoms when combined in a radical or molecule that carries an electrical charge

azimene   in astrology, a weak deficient degree which when ascendant at birth causes a physical defect
azimine   an azimono compound

Group I

aberrance - aberrants
absence - absents
abstinence - abstinents
acceptance - acceptants
acinous - acinus
adolescence - adolescents

adulteress - adulterous
affirmance - affirmants
all over - allover
amino - ammino
amphibian - amphibion
angulous - angulus
announce - enounce
an(o)estrous - an(o)estrus
anorchous - anorchus
anthropogeny - anthropogony
anthropophagous - anthropophagus
appendance - appendants
appurtenance - appurtenants
ascendance - ascendents
assistance - assistants
assonance - assonants
astringence - astringents
attendance - attendants
attractance - attractants

Group I and II

ambience $ä^nby ä^ns$
ambients $'ambēəns$

Group II

abac $'ābak$
aback $ə'bak$

abbe $a'bā$
abbey $'abē$

abhorred $əb'hȯrd$
aboard $ə'bȯrd$

accrue $ə'krü$
ecru $'ekrü$

adduce $ə'düs$
educe $i'düs$

adduct $'a.dəkt$
educt $'ē.dəkt$

aesthetic $es'thedik$
ascetic $ə'sedik$

affluent $'aflüənt$
effluent $'eflüənt$

afflux 'ɑ,fləxs	**aperitif** ə'perə'tēf
efflux 'e,fləxs	**aperitive** ə'perədiv
Africans 'ɑfrikənz	**aphagia** ə'fōjēə
Afrikaans 'ɑfrə̇,känz	**aphasia** ə'fōzhēə
agar 'ägər	**apiin** 'āpēən
auger 'ȯgər	**Apion** 'āpē,än
ager 'ōjər	**Apios** 'āpē,äs
agger 'ojər	**apiose** 'āpē,ōs
aggression ə'greshən	**aplomb** ə'plȯm
egression ē'greshən	**aplome** 'ɑ,plȯm
agust 'əgəst	**appel** ɑ'pel
august ə'gəst	**apple** 'ɑpəl
ahl 'öl	**appose** ɑ'pōz
all 'ȯl	**oppose** ə'pōz
aigrette ō;gret	**apprise** ə'prīz
egret 'ēgrə̇t	**uprise** 'əp,rīz
aition 'īdē,än	**argil** 'är,jə̇l
idaein ī'dēən	**Argyle** 'är,gīl
alight ə'līt	**Armenian** är'mēnēən
alite 'ɑ'līt	**Arminian** är'minēən
align ə'līn	**artist** 'ärdə̇st
A-line 'ā,līn	**artiste** är'tēst
allure ə'lür	**astir** ə'stər
Alur 'ä,lu̇r	**Astur** 'ostər
alluvium ə'lüvēəm	**atlantes** ɑt'lɑntēz
eluvium ē;lüvēəm	**Atlantis** ɑt'lɑntis
illuvium i;lüvēəm	**attrited** ə'trītəd
amandin 'äməndə̇n	**attritted** ə'tritəd
amandine 'ämən,dēn	**auks** 'ȯks
amor 'ä,mȯr	**ox** 'äks
amour ,ä'mu̇r	**aura** 'ȯrə
amula 'ɑmyələ	**ora** 'ōrə
amulla 'ɑmələ	**aurate** 'ȯ,rāt
Anabas 'ɑnɑbɑs	**orate** ȯ'rāt
anabasse ,ɑnɑ'bɑs	**Auster** 'ȯster
Andean 'ɑndēən	**ouster** 'au̇stər
indienne 'ɑndē,en	**auxin** 'ȯksə̇n
anil 'ɑnᵊl	**oxen** 'äksən
anile 'ɑ,nīl	**awed** 'ȯd
annual 'ɑnyəl	**odd** 'äd
annule 'ɑnyül	**awner** 'ȯnər
anthropophagi ,ɑnthrə'päfəjī	**honor** 'änər
anthropophagy ,ɑnthrə'päfəjē	**axile** 'ɑk,sil
	axile 'ɑk,sīl

B

ba   an eternal divine soul in Egyptian religious belief
baa   a sheep's bleat
bah   an expression of disdain
bas   a bet in roulette on one of the vertical columns paying 2 for 1

baa   (see **ba**)

baaed   bleated, as sheep
bad   unfavorable or derogatory
bade   made an offer

baaed   bleated, as sheep
baud   a unit to measure signaling speed in telegraphic code
bawd   a person who keeps a house of prostitution
bod   the body (by shortening)

Baal   any of several Canaanite and Phoenician chief dieties
baal   a false god
bael   a thorny citrus tree of India
bail   to deliver from arrest; to clear water from a boat
bale   a large bundle of goods; pain or mental suffering

Baatan   a province of the Philippines
bataan   a valuable Philippine timber tree
Batan   a people inhabiting the Batan islands of the Philippines
baton   a stick with which a conductor leads a musical group

babble   to utter meaningless sounds as though talking
Babel   a lofty or towering structure; an excessively grandiose or visionary scheme or project
babel   a confusion or medley of sounds, voices, or ideas

bac   a vat or cistern
back   in the rear; endorse or support

bacc(h)ar   a plant of grasslands variously identified as Cyclamen euro-
paeum
backer   a supported

bacchanal   a drunken revelry
bacchanale   a ballet marked with voluptuous dances

bach   to live as a bachelor
batch   a quantity of persons or things considered as a group

back   (see **bac**)

backer   (see **bacc[h]ar**)

bad   (see **baaed**)

badder   more unfavorable or derogatory
batter   a mixture of flour, liquid, and other ingredients; to beat repeatedly

baddy   a hoodlum or other malefactor; an undesirable or negative event (slang)
batty   resembling a bat; mentally unstable

bade   (see **baaed**)

bael   (see **Baal**)

bael   a thorny citrus tree of India
bile   a yellow or greenish viscid alkaline fluid excreted by the liver

baetyl   a roughly shaped stone worshipped as of divine origin
beadle   a messenger in the service of a law court
beetle   an insect of the order Coleoptera
betel   a climbing pepper plant
bietle   a deerskin jacket worn by Apache women

baffed   made a stroke with a golf club so the sole of the club strikes the ground and lofts the ball
baft   a coarse stuff originally made of cotton

bag to catch; a container made of flexible material, usually closed on all sides except for an opening that may be closed

bague in architecture, the ring or plate of an annulated column

bah (see **ba**)

bahr a body of water

bar a straight piece of metal or wood; to confine or shut out

barre a handrail ballet dancers use during exercises

Bhar a caste of agricultural laborers in India

bai a yellow mist composed of airborne loess or fine sand that is prevalent in China and Japan during the spring and fall

buy to purchase

by next to

bye the positin of a tournament participant who has no opponent in a particular round

'bye goodbye (by shortening)

bail (see **Baal**)

bailee a person who receives goods under a bailment contract

bailey a medieval castle's outer wall

bailie a magistrate of a Scottish barony similar to a sheriff

bailer a person who attaches handles to pails or buckets

bailor a person who delivers goods to another in trust

baler a person or machines that bales

bailey (see **bailee**)

bailie (see **bailee**)

bailor (see **bailer**)

bait a lure to attract fish, animals, or persons

bate to reduce the force of intensity

bete in certain card games, to subject to a penalty for failure to fulfill one's contract

beth the second letter of the Hebrew alphabet

baiting heckling, hounding, or attacking in speech or writing, usually with malice

bating with the exception of; cleaning depilated leather hides with tryptic enzymes

baize a coarsely woven woolen or cotton napped fabric

bays compartments in a bar; wall openings or recesses; barks at

beys district governors in the Ottoman Empire

balas a ruby spinel of pale rose-red or orange color

ballas a nearly spherical aggregate of diamond grains used as an industrial diamond

bald lacking all or a significant portion of hair

balled formed into a round mass

bawled cried out loudly

baldie a small double-ended fishing boat used on the east coast of Scotland

baldy a white-headed pigeon of Australia; a person that is bald

bale (see **Baal**)

baleen a horny substance growing in the mouth of whales that forms a fringelike sieve to collect and retain food

baline a coarse woolen or cotton material used in packing

Bilin the Cushitic language of the Bogos

baler (see **bailer**)

baline (see **baleen**)

ball a round mass

baule the theoretical amount of nitrogen or a mineral necessary to produce ½ the maximum possible crop yield

ballas (see **balas**)

balled   (see **bald**)

ballet   a part-song often in stanzas with a refrain
ballot   a ticket or sheet of paper containing a list of names for use in casting a vote

balm   a healing ointment
bomb   a projectile carrying an explosive charge
bombe   a frozen molded dessert

banat   a province under the jurisdiction of a ban
bonnet   a woman's head covering of cloth or straw usually tied under the chin with ribbons

banc   a bench on which court judges sit
bank   a portion of earth above the surrounding level; a business establishment that accepts deposits of and loans money

band   an item which confines or constricts movement; organized groups of people
banned   prohibited

bands   items that confine or constrict movement; organized groups of people
banns   a notice of proposed marriage proclaimed in church or a public place
bans   prohibits

bank   (see **banc**)

banket   the auriferous conglomerate rock of the Transvaal
banquette   a raised way along the inside of a trench on which soliders and guns are posted to fire on the enemy

banned   (see **band**)

banns   (see **bands**)

banquette   (see **banket**)

bans   (see **bands**)

bans   former provincial governors in Hungary, Croatia, or Slavonia having military powers in time of war
bonds   agreements binding one or more parties' devices for holding or tying something together
bons   broad beans; kidney beans
bonze   a Buddhist monk of the Far East

baos   African board games usually played by moving pebbles along two rows of holes
boughs   tree branches
bouse   to haul by means of tackle
bows   bends down; the forward parts of ships or boats

bar   (see **bahr**)

barb   a sharp projection extending backward, as from a fishhook or arrowhead
barbe   a short lace scarf worn at the throat or on the head

Barbary   a coastal region in North Africa
barberry   a prickly shrub of the genus Berbis
barbery   a barber's craft

barbe   (see **barb**)

barbel   a slender tactile process on the lips of certain fishes; a large European freshwater fish with four barbels on its upper jaw
barble   one of the small projections of the mucous membrane that marks the opening of the submaxillary glands under the tongue in horses and cattle

bard   a poet
barred   shut or kept out

bare   exposed to view
bear   a large heavy mammal; to carry a load
ber   an edible drupaceous fruit from the tree of the genus Ziziphus; a Chinese date

baretta a rutaceous evergreen shrub of Texas
biretta a square head covering worn by ecclesiastics

barf vomit
barff to protect iron or steel with a coating of iron oxide

baric pertaining to atmospheric pressure, especially as measured by a barometer
barrack a building to house military service personnel

baritone a male singing voice between bass and tenor (seldom barytone)
barytone (a word) having an unaccented final syllable, especially in Greek grammar

barney a small car attached to a cable and used on slopes in a mine
barny suggesting a barn especially in size or characteristic smell

baron a member of the peerage; a man of great power in some activity
barren devoid or lacking something, as vegetation; sterile

barrack (see **baric**)

barre (see **bahr**)

barred (see **bard**)

barrel a round bulging vessel of greater height than breadth usually made of staves bound with hoops
beryl a hard mineral consisting of a silicate of beryllium and aluminum

barren (see **baron**)

barret a small cap
barrette a bar-shaped clip for holding hair in place

barrier an obstruction
berrier a person who picks small pulpy edible fruit
burier a person or animal that buries or conceals something

barry a baritone saxophone
berry a small pulpy edible fruit

bury to inter a corpse; to conceal

barytone (see **baritone**)

bas (see **ba**)

basal fundamental; relating to the foundation, base, or essence
basil any of several aromatic plants

base a foundation
bass a low pitched sound
beth the second letter of the Hebrew alphabet

based formed a foundation
baste to sew with long loose stitches; to moisten with liquid during cooking

baseman a person stationed or positioned at a base, as in baseball
bassman a person who plays a bass viol or sings a bass part

bases foundations
basis a fundamental ingredient or essence
basses persons or instruments able to create the lowest pitched sounds

basi a valuable Philippine timber tree
bossy inclined to domineer; a cow or calf; studded

basil (see **basal**)

basilican resembling a basilica by having a nave and aisles with clerestory
basilicon an ointment composed of rosin, yellow wax, and lard

basin an open usually circular vessel
bason a bench, with a plate heated by a fire underneath, on which felt is formed

basis (see **bases**)

bask to derive pleasure or enjoyment
Basque one of the people inhabiting the western Pyrennes region on the Bay of Biscay in Spain
basque a woman's tight-fitting bodice

bason (see **basin**)

Basque and basque (see bask)

bass (see base)

basses (see bases)

bassman (see baseman)

baste (see based)

bat a stout solid stick; a flying
mammal
batt a sheet of material for use in
making felt or insulation (seldom:
bat)

bataan (see Baatan)

Batan (see Baatan)

batch (see bach)

bate (see bait)

bating (see baiting)

baton (see Baatan)

baton to beat or strike with a club
or cudgel
batten a board used for flooring; to
fasten, as hatches; to feed glutton-
ously

batt (see bat)

battel the account for college expenses at Oxford University
battle to engage in combat

batten (see baton)

batter (see badder)

batterie a ballet movement consisting of beating together the feet or
calves of the legs
battery the act of battering or beating; the pitcher and catcher of a
baseball team; a device for producing electric current

battle (see battel)

battu in ballet, to strike repeatedly
in dance
battue driving or drawing out game
from cover by beating woods and
bushes

batty (see baddy)

bauble a trinket, geegaw, or play-
thing
bobble to make an error or mistake;
to fumble

baud (see baaed)

baule (see ball)

baule the theoretical amount of nitrogen or a mineral necessary to
produce ½ the maximum possible
crop yield
bole any cylindrically shaped object
or mass
boll a plant's pod or capsule, as cotton or flax
Bolle a cultivated variety of white
poplar with a pyramidal habit
bowl a rounded hollow vessel; to
throw a ball down a green or alley,
as in tenpins

bawd (see baaed)

bawled (see bald)

bawn a fortified court of a castle; a
fold for livestock
Bon a pre–Buddhist animist religion
of Tibet; a popular Japanese festival
Bonn a city in western Germany
bonne a French maidservant

bayou a minor waterway that is
tributary to a river or another body
of water
bio biography (by shortening)
byo a cradle

bays (see baize)

bazaar a place for the sale of
merchandise
bizarre odd, extravagant, eccentric,
or weird

bb a shot pellet about .18 inches in
diameter
beebee the youngest member of a
family or brood
bibi a Hindu mistress of a house

be to exist
bee a social colonial hymenopterous insect; a gathering of people to accomplish some purpose

beach a shoreline of ocean, sea, or lake
beech a smooth gray-barked tree

bead a small often round piece of material that is pierced for threading on a string or wire
bede a miner's pick

beader a device or person that makes a bead or strings beads
beater a device or person that beats or whips something

beadle (see **baetyl**)

beady resembling beads
bidi a cheap locally made cigarette, in India

bean the seed of a climbing leguminous plant
been existed
bin a four-stringed musical instrument of India with a long bamboo fingerboard

beany a small round tight-fitting skullcap worn especially by schoolboys and collegians; marked with an oil-flavor suggestive of beans
bene well

bear (see **bare**)

beardie a small vigorous shaggy collielike sheepdog of Scottish origin
beardy having a growth of facial hair, particularly about the chin and jaws

beast a creature
beest a specialized secretion of a cow's mammary glands after calving

beastie a small creature
bheesty a water carrier for a household or regiment in India

beat to strike repeatedly

beet a biennial plant with a bulbous root

beater (see **beader**)

beau a man who goes steadily with a woman; an escort
bo a hobo; a fig tree of India
boo marijuana (slang)
bow a weapon used to propel an arrow; an implement used to play a stringed musical instrument

Beaune a red table wine
bone the hard part of a vertebrate's skeleton

beaut a beautiful thing
bute phenylbutazone, a potent crystalline drug used to reduce pain and inflammation in rheumatic diseases and gout
Butte a city in southwestern Montana
butte an isolated hill or mountain with steep sides

becken large concave brass plates that produce clashing musical tones, (cymbals)
beckon to extend attraction, interest, allure, or appeal

bedded deposited in layers or stratified
betted wagered

bedder a person who fixes beds; a plant grown in a bed
better to improve; in a more excellent manner

bedding bed clothes; a bottom layer
betting wagering

bede (see **bead**)

bee (see **be**)

beebee (see **bb**)

beech (see **beach**)

been (see **bean**)

been existed
ben a seed of an East Indian or African tree

been existed
bin an enclosed storage place

beer a fermented beverage made from malted grain and hops
bier a stand on which a corpse or coffin is placed

beery influenced by beer drinking; convivial
biri a cheap locally made cigarette, in India

bees social colonial hymenopterous insects; gatherings of people to accomplish a purpose
bise a cold dry wind of southern Europe

beest (see **beast**)

beet (see **beat**)

beetle (see **baetyl**)

beflour to dust with powder made of ground grain
beflower to adorn with blossoms

bel a thorny citrus tree of India
bell a hollow spherical metallic device that resonates when hit with a clapper
Belle a variety of white-fleshed peach of outstanding beauty
belle a popular or attractive girl or woman

ben (see **been**)

bench a long seat
bensh to say a blessing or recite prayers

bene (see **beany**)

Beni a Negro people of southern Nigeria
ben(n)e an East Indian annual erect herb
benny an amphetamine tablet used as a stimulant (slang); a close-fitting benjamin overcoat (slang)

bensh (see **bench**)

benzene a flammable, volatile, toxic aromatic liquid hydrocarbon
benzine a flammable, volatile petroleum distillate consisting chiefly of aliphatic hydrocarbons

benzil a yellow crystalline diketone made by oxidizing benzoin
benzyl the univalent radical derived from toluene by removing one hydrogen atom from the side chain

benzine (see **benzene**)

benzyl (see **benzil**)

ber (see **bare**)

berg an iceberg
burg(h) a village

berley bait scattered on the water to attract fish
burley thin-bodied air-cured tobacco
burly strongly built; a burlesque

Bern(e) the capital of Switzerland
birn a socket on a clarinet into which the mouthpiece is fitted
burn to consume fuel

berrier (see **barrier**)

berry (see **barry**)

berth a sleeping accommodation on a ship, plane, or train
birth the act of being born

beryl (see **barrel**)

bete (see **bait**)

betel (see **baetyl**)

beth (see **bait** or **base**)

betted (see **bedded**)

better (see **bedder**)

betting (see **bedding**)

beurre buttered, as "peas au buerre"
birr an onward rush, as of a wind or onslaught in battle
buhr a projection resembling a tooth on a millstone

bur(r) a prickly envelope of some fruits and plants

beys (see **baize**)

Bhar (see **bahr**)

bhat a member of an Indian caste of bards and entertainers
bot(t) the larva of the botfly

bheesty (see **beastie**)

Bhora a modern Shi'ite sect of western India retaining some Hindu elements
bora an occasional violent cold north to northeast wind that blows over the northern Adriatic sea; a rite in which Australian aborigine boys are initiated into manhood

bhut an especially malevolent spirit or ghost in India
boot a covering for the foot and leg that is usually made of leather or rubber

bib a cloth worn around the chest
Bibb a variety of dark green lettuce with a small head
bibb a piece of timber bolted to the hounds of a ship's mast to support the trestletrees

bibi (see **bb**)

bichir a large primitive fish found in the upper Nile
bitcher a person who complains, gripes, or grouses about something

bichy a kola nut
bitchy suggestive of malice or arrogance

bidder the maker of a bid, as in contract bridge; a person who invites or issues a mild order
bitter a strong, pungent, or unpleasant taste; acrid; grievous

bidding an offer of a price; an invitation or summons
bitting the shape of the bit of a key that causes it to actuate the lock

biddy an elderly housemaid or cleaning woman in a dormitory; an adult female domestic fowl
bitty made up of bits; scrappy; small or tiny

bider a person who waits, tarries, or awaits one's pleasure
biter a person that seizes with the teeth or mouth

bidi (see **beady**)

bier (see **beer**)

bietle (see **baetyl**)

bight a curve or loop in a rope, hose, or chain
bite to seize with the teeth
byte a group of adjacent binary digits that a computer processes

bile (see **bael**)

Bilin (see **baleen**)

billed charged a customer for merchandise; offered on a program
build to construct

billian a valuable timber tree of Borneo having heavy hard ant-proof wood
billion a thousand millions

bin (see **bean** or **been**)

bio (see **bayou**)

bird a warm-blooded egg-laying feathered vertebrate, usually able to fly
burred rough and prickly

birdie a golf score one under par on a hole
birdy abounding in birds

biretta (see **baretta**)

biri (see **beery**)

birl to revolve
burl a hard woody tree growth

birma the Santa Maria tree, an evergreen tropical American tree

Burma a country in southeast Asia that changed it official name to the Union of Myanmar in 1989

birn (see **Bern[e]**)

birr (see **beurre**)

birth (see **berth**)

Biscayan a native or resident of Biscay province, Spain
biscayen a military musket or the ball used in it

bise (see **bees**)

bit a small quantity; the part of a steel bridle that is inserted in a horse's mouth
bitt a post fixed on a ship's deck around which lines are made fast

bitcher (see **bichir**)

bitchy (see **bichy**)

bite (see **bight**)

biter (see **bider**)

bitt (see **bit**)

bitter (see **bidder**)

bitting (see **bidding**)

bitty (see **biddy**)

bizarre (see **bazaar**)

blays a small European cyprinid fish
blaze a bright flame or intense light

bleater an animal or person that makes a sound suggestive of the call of sheep; any of several game birds that resemble the woodcock
bleeder a person that draws or gives blood

blend to mix or combine
blende any of several minerals with somewhat bright nonmetallic luster

blew produced an air current
blue a color between green and violet, as a clear sky or deep sea

blewits an edible agaric (fungus) that is pale lilac when young
bluets a light blue color; any of several North American plants of the madder family

blight a plant disease or injury; to cause to deteriorate
blite any of several herbs, as the strawberry blite

bloc a combination of persons, groups, or nations for a common interest
block a solid piece of wood, metal, or stone

blooey out of order or awry (slang)
bluey a blue crab; any of several Australian lizards; a legal summons

blue (see **blew**)

bluets (see **blewits**)

bluey (see **blooey**)

bo (see **beau**)

boar an uncastrated male swine
Boer a South African of Dutch or Huguenot descent
bore to pierce or drill a hole

board a piece of sawed lumber; to enter a ship, plane, bus, or train; a group of persons
bord a straight passageway driven at right angles to the main cleavage of coal in a mine
bored pierced or drilled a hole; devoid of interest

boarder a person provided with regular meals and or lodging
bordar a feudal tenant bound to menial service to a lord
border an outer part or edge

boardroom a room designated for meetings of a board which usually contains a large conference table
bordroom a space off a passageway from which coal is being or has been mined

boat a small vessel propelled by oars, paddles, sail, or engine
bote compensation for injury to a person or honor

boating the act or sport of one who uses small watercraft
boding an omen or ominous premonition about the future

bobble (see **bauble**)

boca a river mouth or harbor entrance
bocca a vent at the side or base of an active volcano from which lava flows

bocce or **bocci(e)** a bowling game of Italian origin
botchy full of defects: poorly done

boce a brightly colored European fish of the family Sparidae
Bos a genus of ruminant mammals including wild and domestic cattle
bose to test the ground by noting the sound of percussion from the blow of a heavy hammer

Boche a German, usually used disparagingly
bosh pretentious nonesense or silliness; the lower sloping part of a blast furnace

bocks bookbinding leathers made from sheepskin
box a square or oblong container

bod (see **baaed**)

bode to indicate by signs or be an omen of
bowed bent or curved

boding (see **boating**)

Boer (see **boar**)

Boer a South African of Dutch or Huguenot descent
booer a person who shouts disapproval or contempt
boor a rude, clumsy, insensitive, or boring person

bogey in golf, to shoot a hole in one stroke over par; a small stone
bogie tobacco in small twisted ropes

bolar resembling clay
bowler a player who delivers the ball to the batsman in cricket; a person who plays tenpins

bolas weapons consisting of two or more stone or iron balls attached to the ends of a cord which are used to ensnare animals
bolus a large rounded mass in the form of a pill or chewed food

bold fearless in meeting danger or difficulty
boled having a cylindrical shape
bolled having or producing pods or capsules, as in a plant
bowled played the game of bowls or tenpins

bolder more fearless in meeting danger or difficulty
boulder a detached mass of rock

bole (see **baule**)

boled (see **bold**)

boll (see **baule**)

Bolle (see **baule**)

bolled (see **bold**)

bollix to involve in bewildering entanglements
bollocks young or castrated bulls

bolter an animal that is given to suddenly breaking away
boulter a line to which many hooks are attached for deep water bottom-fishing

bolus (see **bolas**)

bomb (see **balm**)

bombard to attack with explosive projectiles or other explosive weaponry
bombarde a powerful reed stop of 32- or 16-foot pitch in a pipe organ

Bombay a city in India
bombé having an outward swelling curve in furniture

bombe (see **balm**)

Bon (see **bawn**)

bon the broad or kidney bean; the stiff dried hand-cleaned but not completely degummed fiber of ramie
Bonn a city in western Germany

bonds (see **bans**)

bone (see **Beaune**)

bon(e)y skinny or scrawny; full of bone
Boni a Bush Negro people of the interior of French Guiana

Boni (see **bon[e]y**)

Bonn (see **bawn** or **bon**)

bonne (see **bawn**)

bonnes French maidservants
bunds embankments used to control the flow of water; politically oriented associations of people
buns round or oblong breadrolls; knots or coils of hair

bonnet (see **banat**)

bons (see **bans**)

bonze (see **bans**)

boo (see **beau**)

boo-boo a stupid or careless mistake
boubou any of several large African shrikes; a long, loose fitting brightly colored garment worn by both sexes in parts of Africa

booby an awkward foolish person; any of several gannets of tropical seas
Bubi a Bantu-speaking people of the island of Fernando Po, West Africa

booer (see **Boer**)

boogie to dance the boogie-woogie; negro, usually used disparagingly

Bugi an Indonesian people of the southern part of Sulawesi island

bookie a person who determines odds and receives and pays off bets; a person who makes books
booky inclined to rely on knowledge obtained from books; bookish

bool a hoop for rolling
boule a game similar to roulette
buhl inlaid decoration using tortoise shell, yellow metal, and white metal in cabinet work

boon an often timely and gratuitous benefit received and enjoyed; the woody portion of the stem of flax or hemp after the removal of fiber by retting
Boone a chert formation of the Mississippian geological series in the western Ozarks

boor (see **Boer**)

boos shouts of disapproval or contempt
booze an intoxicating drink

boot (see **bhut**)

bootee an infant's sock of knitted or crocheted wool (also bootie)
booty plunder or spoils of war
buddhi the faculty of intuitive discernment or direct spiritual awareness in the beliefs of Hinduism and Buddhism

booze (see **boos**)

bora (see **Bhora**)

bord (see **board**)

bordar (see **boarder**)

border (see **boarder**)

bordroom (see **boardroom**)

bore (see **boar**)

bored (see **board**)

born brought into existence
borne endured or tolerated
bourn(e) an intermittent stream

borough a village, township, or town
burro a small donkey
burrow a hole in the ground

Bos (see **boce**)

Bos a genus of ruminant mammals including wild and domestic cattle
boss raised ornamentation; a superintendent or overseer
boose an African tree

bose (see **boce**)

bosh (see **Boche**)

boss (see **Bos**)

bosse (see **Bos**)

bossy (see **basi**)

botany the science of plants
botonny a cross having a cluster of three balls or knobs at the end of each arm

botchy (see **bocce**)

bote (see **boat**)

botonny (see **botany**)

bot(t) (see **bhat**)

boubou (see **boo-boo**)

bouché stopped with the hand, as in French horn playing
bouchée a small patty or creampuff filled with creamed meat or fish
boucher a hand axe or crude stone implement used by paleolithic man

Bougainvillaea a genus of ornamental tropical American woody vines
Bougainvillia a widely distributed genus of marine hydrozoans

boughs (see **baos**)

boulder (see **bolder**)

boule (see **bool**)

boule a game similar to roulette; a pear-shaped mass of some substance formed synthetically in a Verneuil furnace

boulle inlaid cabinetwork decoration developed under Louis XIV

boullion a broth made by slowly boiling meat in water
bullion gold, silver, or other metal in the shape of bars or ingots

boulter (see **bolter**)

bourdon the drone bass, as in a bagpipe or hurdy-gurdy
burden something carried

bourn(e) (see **born**)

bouse (see **baos**)

bow (see **beau**)

bowed (see **bode**)

bowl (see **baule**)

bowled (see **bold**)

bowler (see **bolar**)

bows (see **baos**)

box (see **bocks**)

boy a male child
buoy an object floating in water and moored to the bottom to serve as a channel marker

bracked sorted or inspected merchandise
bract a somewhat modified leaf associated with the reproductive structures of a plant

brae glacier or ice cap
braies breeches or trousers worn during medieval times
bray a loud harsh cry characteristic of a donkey
brey a conventionalized heraldic representation of a pair of barnacles

braes glaciers or ice caps
braise to cook slowly in fat and little moisture in a tightly closed pot
brays utters a loud harsh cry characteristic of a donkey
braze to solder with an alloy

breys conventionalized heraldic representation of pairs of barnacles; softens skins or leather by working with the hands
brys buttermilk paps usually made with barley and eaten with sugar and syrup

Brahman any of several breeds of Indian cattle
Bremen a city in northwest Germany

braid a cord or ribbon, usually with three or more interwoven strands
brayed uttered a loud harsh cry characteristic of a donkey
breyed softened skins or leather by working with the hands

braies (see **brae**)

brail the feathers at a hawk's rump; a rake-like tool to harvest clams
Braille the system of tactile symbols by which blind persons read and write
brale a conical diamond indenter with an angle of 120 degrees that is used in the Rockwell hardness test

braise (see **braes**)

brake a device to arrest motion of a mechanism, often by friction; to apply such a device
break to split into pieces

brakie a member of a train crew whose duties include operating hand brakes (slang)
braky abounding with brambles, shrubs, or ferns

brale (see **brail**)

brand a mark made with a stencil or hot iron; to apply such a mark
branned cleansed of oil, especially with bran

brands marks of simple easily recognized pattern made by a hot iron, stencil, or strap; a class of goods associated with a single or manufacturer or firm

brans broken coats of the seeds of wheat, rye, or other cereal grain separated from the kernels

branned (see **brand**)

brans (see **brands**)

brass an alloy of copper and a base metal, usually zinc or sometimes tin
brasse a European bass

brassie a wooden golf club soled with some metal
brassy resembling brass; coarse and impudent

bray (see **brae**)

brayed (see **braid**)

brays (see **braes**)

braze (see **braes**)

breach an infraction or violation of some standard or law
breech short pants covering the hips and thighs; the buttocks

bread food made of flour dough or grain meal
bred reared or inculcated with certain traditions

break (see **brake**)

bream a European freshwater cyprinoid fish
brim the edge or rim of a cup or hat

breast the front of the chest
Brest a seaport and city at the western extremity of France

bred (see **bread**)

breech (see **breach**)

breed to propagate sexually
bride a small joining that resembles a bar and is used to connect various parts of a lace pattern

brees girls or young women
breeze a steady light or moderate air current
Bries soft perishable cheeses ripened by mold

Bremen   (see **Brahman**)

brew   to produce or bring about by mixing ingredients
bruh   a pigtailed macaque of the East Indies

brewed   produced or brought about by mixing ingredients
brood   the young of animals hatched concurrently; to incubate eggs; to dwell moodily on a subject

Brest   (see **breast**)

brews   produces or brings about by mixing ingredients
bruhs   pigtailed macaques of the East Indies
bruise   an injury caused by a blow not breaking the injured surface

brey   (see **bray**)

breyed   (see **braid**)

breys   (see **braes**)

bricks   a building or paving material made of molded clay
brix   the percentage of sugar concentration by weight according to the Brix scale

bridal   a nuptial festival or ceremony
bridle   a headgear by which a horse is controlled

bride   (see **breed**)

bridle   (see **bridal**)

Bries   (see **brees**)

bril   a unit of subjective luminance
brill   a European flatfish related to the turbot

brilliance   sparkling with luster
brilliants   old sizes of type (approximately 3½ point) smaller than diamond

brim   (see **bream**)

brisk   moving quickly; alert, lively, or sprightly
brisque   an ace or ten in certain card games, as in bezique

Britain   Great Britain (by shortening)
Briton   a member of one of the peoples inhabiting Britain prior to the Anglo-Saxon invasions
britten   the red-necked grebe, a shorebird

brix   (see **bricks**)

bro   brother (slang)
broh   a pigtailed macaque of the East Indies

broach   to turn dangerously broadside to the waves; to introduce a subject for discussion
brooch   a fastening device now used chiefly for ornamental jewelry

brocard   an elementary principle or maxim
brokered   functioned as negotiator or intermediary

broch   a prehistoric circular stone tower found on the Orkney and Shetland islands and the Scottish mainland
brock   a badger

broh   (see **bro**)

brokered   (see **brocard**)

brome   a grass of the genus Bromus, as awnless bromegrass
brougham   a vehicle similar to a carriage or automobile with the driver's seat outside

bromous   pertaining to an unstable acid believed to be formed in solution by action of bromine water on silver nitrate
Bromus   a large genus of grasses native to temperate regions

bronks   unbroken or imperfectly broken range horses of western North America
Bronx   a borough of New York City

brooch   (see **broach**)

brood   (see **brewed**)

brookie a brook trout
brooky full of creeks

broom a sweeping implement; any of various leguminous shrubs
brougham a vehicle similar to a carriage or automobile with the driver's seat outside
brume mist, fog, or vapor

brougham (see **brome** or **broom**)

brownie a good natured goblin; a member of the Girl Scouts between ages seven through nine
browny verging on the color brown

brows foreheads
browse to gaze; to look over casually

bruh (see **brew**)

bruhs (see **brews**)

bruise (see **brews**)

bruit abnormal sounds heard on auscultation; to publicize
Brut a medieval chronicle of Britain
brute utterly lacking in sensitivity or higher feelings

brume (see **broom**)

Brut (see **bruit**)

brute (see **bruit**)

brys (see **braes**)

Bubalis a genus of African antelopes including the hartebeest
Bubalus a genus of Bovidae comprising mud-wallowing buffaloes of Asia

Bubi (see **booby**)

buccal relating to the cheeks
buckle an ornamental fastening device; to warp, bend, or heave

bucco the dried leaves of certain plants of the genera Barosma and Diosma used as a diuretic and diaphoretic
bucko a person who is domineering and bullying, especially officers of sailing ships

buckie an alewife fish that is smoked for food
bucky exhibiting characteristics of the male animal

buckle (see **buccal**)

bucko (see **bucco**)

bucky (see **buckie**)

bud an undeveloped shoot on a tree, bush, or flower
but except for that
butt to strike with the head or horns

budder a person who inserts buds in plant stocks
butter a creamy spread; to cover with lavish praise or flattery

buddhi (see **bootee**)

buddle an inclined trough or platform on which crushed ore is concentrated by running water which washes out the lighter and less valuable portions
buttle to serve or act as a butler

buddy full or suggestive of buds; a close friend
butty a worker or middleman who takes an allotment of work by contract at so much per ton of coal or ore for execution; an archer's shooting companion

buffo a male singer or comic roles in opera
Bufo a large genus of toads that contains the common toads of America and Europe

Bugi (see **boogie**)

buhl (see **bool**)

buhr (see **buerre**)

build (see **billed**)

bullion (see **bouillion**)

bunds (see **bonnes**)

buns (see **bonnes**)

buoy (see **boy**)

burden   (see **bourdon**)

burger   a flat cake of ground or chopped meat fried or grilled and served between slices of bread
Burgher   a Ceylonese of mixed blood, specifically of Dutch descent
burgher   a resident of a town

burg(h)   (see **berg**)

burghal   relating to a municipal corporation
burgle   to burglarize

Burgher and **burgher**   (see **burger**)

burgle   (see **burghal**)

burier   (see **barrier**)

burl   (see **birl**)

burley   (see **berley**)

burly   (see **berley**)

Burma   (see **birma**)

burn   (see **Bern[e]**)

burny   inclined to burn
byrnie   a coat of mail

burred   (see **bird**)

burro   (see **borough**)

burrow   (see **borough**)

bur(r)   (see **buerre**)

bury   (see **barry**)

bus   a large motor-driven vehicle designed to carry passengers
buss   to kiss; a rugged square-sailed fishing boat

bussed   kissed; transported by bus
bust   a sculptured representation of the upper part of the human figure; to punch or break open

but   (see **bud**)

bute   (see **beaut**)

butt   (see **bud**)

Butte and **butte**   (see **beaut**)

butter   (see **budder**)

buttle   (see **buddle**)

butty   (see **buddy**)

buy   (see **bai**)

by   (see **bai**)

bye   (see **bai**)

'bye   (see **bai**)

byo   (see **bayou**)

bypassed   detoured around
bypast   something that is past or bygone

byrnie   (see **burny**)

byte   (see **bight**)

Group I

---

bar - barre
bargainer - bargainor
belligerence - belligerents
bivalence - bivalents
blender - blendor
boosy - boozy
brunet - brunette
bulbous - bulbus
bureau - buro

Group I and II

---

biographee   bī'ögrə,fē
biography   bī'ögrəfē

bourg   'bůrg
burg(h)   'bərg

Group II

Bacchae	ˈbak͵ē
baccy	ˈbakē
balks	ˈbȯks
box	ˈbäks
ballad	ˈbaləd
ballade	baˈläd
bal(l)on	baˈlōⁿ
balloon	bəˈlün
balun	ˈba͵lən
banzai	ˈbänˈzī
bonsai	ˈbän͵sī
bar	ˈbär
barré	bäˈrā
baratte	bəˈrat
barret	bəˈret
barbel	ˈbärbəl
barbell	ˈbär͵bel
barbet	ˈbärbət
barbette	bärˈbet
baren	ˈbä͵ren
baron	ˈbarən
baritone	ˈbarə͵tōn
baryton	ˈbarə͵tän
baroness	ˈbarənəs
barenness	ˈbarənnəs
barre	bäːrā
beret	bəˈrā
baton	baˈtȯn
beton	bāˈtȯn

Baumer	ˈbȯmər
bomber	ˈbämər
bawdy	ˈbȯdē
body	bädē
Begar	ˈbā͵gär
beggar	ˈbegər
below	bēˈlō
bilo	ˈbēlō
beryl	ˈberəl
birl	ˈbərl
besot	bəˈsȯt
besought	bəˈsȯt
binnacle	ˈbinəkəl
binocle	ˈbinokl
blowen	ˈblōən
blown	ˈblōn
Boran	bōˈrän
boron	ˈbō͵rän
bot(t)	ˈbät
bought	ˈbȯt
bourse	ˈbu̇rs
burse	ˈbərs
brickle	ˈbrikəl
bricole	briˈkōl
brut	ˈbru͞et
brute	ˈbrüt
buffi	ˈbüfē
buffy	ˈbəfē
Bulgar	ˈbu̇l͵gär
bulgur	bu̇lːgu̇r
bustee	ˈbə͵stē
busty	ˈbəstē

C

caam the heddles of a loom
calm stillness or quietude

caama a southern African fox
cama a cowboy's bedroll
comma a punctuation mark
kaama a large African antelope

Kama the Hindu god of love
kama in Hinduism, enjoyment of the world of the senses as an end of humanity

caaming setting the reed in weaving by properly placing the warp yarns
calming quieting or soothing

caapi a vine of northwestern South America

copje a small hill, especially on the African veld

copy a reproduction of original work

caatinga a stunted rather sparse forest in northeastern Brazil that is leafless in the dry season

Cotinga the type of genus of birds called Cotingidae that are related to the manakins

cotinga a bird of the family Contingidae

cache a hiding place

cash ready money

cachou an aromatic pill or pastille made of licorice, various aromatics, and gum that is used to sweeten the breath

cashew a tropical American tree important chiefly for its nut

cashoo an extract of the heartwood of an East Indian acacia; a variable color averaging auburn

cacky sticky or muddy; to void excrement

khaki a durable cotton or woolen cloth used for military uniforms; a light yellowish brown color

cacoon a tropical American plant

cocoon an envelope that larvae of many insects form about themselves prior to changing to a pupa

cadalene a colorless liquid hydrocarbon obtained by dehydrogenating cadinene

Catalan a native or inhabitant of Catalonia, an eastern region of Spain

Catalin a thermosetting plastic made of a cast phenol-formaldehyde resin

caddish like a person without gentlemanly instincts

cattish like a cat; spiteful

caddy a person who assists a golfer; any container for storing frequently used things when they are not in use

catty having characteristics resembling those of a cat; stealthy; agile

cadet a pupil in a military school; a grayish blue color

cadette a member of the Girl Scouts aged 12–14

Caecilian a member of the family Caeciliidae, which includes small slender wormlike burrowing amphibians

Sicilian a native or inhabitant of Sicily

Caesar a Roman emperor; a powerful ruler

seizer a person or animal that takes by force

caffa a rich silk cloth with printed or woven designs popular in the 16th century

Kafa a native of the Kafu region in southwestern Ethiopia

Kaffa a grayish reddish brown color

Cain a red or reddish yellow color; trouble, disturbance, or uproar

cane a hollow or pithy jointed stem; a walking stick

caique a light skiff used on the Bosporus

kike a Jew, usually taken to be offensive

Cairo the capital of Egypt

Chi-Rho a Christian monogram and symbol formed by the first two letters of the Greek word for Christ

cala a picnic ham, a shoulder of pork with much of the butt removed commonly smoked and often boned

Calla a genus of bog herbs

calla a familiar house plant or greenhouse plant

calabar the gray fur of a Siberian squirrel (also **calaber**)

calabur a tropical American shrub or small tree

caliber a tube's internal diameter

calc   a branch of mathematics (by shortening); a small portable calculator (by shortening)
calque   a linguistic borrowing from another language

calculous   affected with gravel or stone
calculus   a branch of mathematics dealing with the limit concept; a concretion of salts around organic matter

calendar   a tabular chronological register of events, things, or persons
calender   to press material between rollers or plates to make or smooth into sheets

calf   the fleshy hind part of the leg below the knee; a young of domestic cattle
calve   to give birth to a calf
kaph   the eleventh letter of the Hebrew alphabet

caliber   (see calabar)

caliginous   misty, dark, or obscure
kaligenous   forming alkalies

calix   an ecclesiastical chalice
calyx   the outer set of floral leaves making up a flower's external part

calk   a pointed device worn on a shoe to prevent slipping (seldom caulk)
cauk   to secure by a tenon
caulk   to make a seam watertight or airtight (seldom calk)
cawk   an opaque compact variety of the mineral barite

call   to summon
caul   a covering network

Calla and calla   (see cala)

caller   a person who announces or summons
choler   a ready disposition to anger and irritation
collar   a neckband; a ring placed on an object, as a pipe

callous   unfeeling; a protective condition of mental or emotional insensitivity
callus   a hardened layer of skin

calm   (see caam)

calmer   more tranquil, serene, or placid
colmar   a fan fashionable during Queen Anne's reign

calming   (see caaming)

calmly   in a calm, quiet, or composed manner
comely   having a pleasing appearance

calot   a close-fitting cap without brim or visor
calotte   a large glacier not confined to a single valley

calque   (see calc)

calques   linguistic borrowings by one language from another
calx   friable residue left when a mineral or metal has been subjected to roasting

caltrap   a heraldic representation of a military caltrop
caltrop   any of several plants having stout spines on the fruit or flower heads

calumniation   slandering
columniation   the use of arrangement of columns in a building

calve   (see calf)

calve   to give birth to a calf
cave   the sum which each player puts on the table at the beginning of play in such card games as brelan and bouillette

calvous   lacking all or most of the hair on the head
calvus   a cumulonimbus cloud having its upper portion changing from a rounded cumuliform shape to a

diffuse, whitish, cirriform mass with vertical striations

calx (see **calques**)

calyx (see **calix**)

cam a rotating or sliding piece of machinery
cham a local chieftan, especially in Afghanistan, Iran, and some areas of central Asia

cama (see **caama**)

camara the hard and durable wood of the tonka-bean tree
camera a chamber, room, or hall; a lightproof box fitted with a lens for taking photographs

camas(s) an American plant of the genus Camassia of the western U.S.
camus a short and flat or concave nose; pug-nosed

came moved toward something; arrived: a slender grooved rod of cast lead used to hold glass panes in a window
kame a short ridge of stratified drift deposited by glacial meltwater

camera (see **camara**)

campaign a connected series of determined operations or systematic efforts designed to bring about a particular result
campane in heraldry, a bell

Camptosaurus a small unspecialized bipedal duck-billed dinosaur
Camptosorus a fern having lanceolate fronds that root at the tips

camus (see **camas[s]**)

can know how to; a container
cann a bulbous drinking mug
Cannes a city and resort area in southeast France on the Mediterranean sea
khan a local chieftain in some areas of central Asia; a rest house in some Asian countries

can know how to
Chen a genus of geese, including the snow goose
ken the range of comprehension or perception

Canada a country in northern North America; a Canada goose
Kannada the major Dravidian language of Mysore, south India

canapé an appetizer consisting of savory food atop a cracker or bread
canopy a covering for shelter or protection

cancellous having a spongy or porous structure
cancellus a screen or rail typically of stone grating or latticework used to enclose or separate a part of a church and the altar or choir

cand the transparent or translucent mineral fluorite
canned enclosed or preserved in a container; put a stop or end to

cane (see **Cain**)

canions close-fitting ornamental kneepieces joining the upper and lower parts of the leg covering worn by men in Elizabethan England
canyons deep narrow valleys with steep sides

cann (see **can**)

cannable suitable for canning or preserving
cannibal an animal that devours its own kind

canned (see **cand**)

Cannes (see **can**)

cannon a metal tubular weapon for firing projectiles
Canon an ecclesiastical decree, regulation, or code
canon one of the clergy of a medieval cathedral or large church

cannibal (see **cannable**)

cannonry cannonading or artillery
canonry a body of canons

Canon and **canon** (see **cannon**)

canonry (see **cannonry**)

canopy (see **canapé**)

cant jargon; an inclination or slope; to cut at an angle
can't contraction of cannot
quinte a protective parry in fencing

canter a three-beat gait that is smoother and slower than a gallop
cantor a choir leader; a singer of Jewish liturgical music

Cantharis a brilliant green blister beetle common in southern Europe
cantharus a basin or stoup containing holy water; a deep cut of ancient Greece with a high stem and loop-shaped handles

cantor (see **canter**)

canvas to cover or furnish with canvas
canvass a personal solicitation of votes or opinions; a full discussion

canyons (see **canions**)

capa a fine grade of Cuban tobacco
cappa a cape that is part of ecclesiastical or academic garb
kappa the tenth letter of the Greek alphabet

cape a judicial writ, now abolished, relative to a plea of lands or tenements
kepi a military cap with a close-fitting band, a round flat top sloping toward the front, and a visor
KP kitchen police, enlisted personnel detailed to assist cooks in a military mess

capelin a small salmonoid marine fish
capeline a woman's hat with a small crown and a wide, soft brim

Capella a genus of birds containing the snipes
kapelle the choir or orchestra of a royal or papal choir

capital a stock of accumulated goods; money; a column's uppermost member
Capitol the building in which a legislative body meets

cappa (see **capa**)

caprin any of the esters of glycerol and capric acid
caprine suggestive of a goat

captain a military officer; a leader or chief
captan a white to cream colored powder used as a fungicide on food plants and flowers

caput a knoblike protuberance, as on a bone or muscle
kaput utterly defeated or destroyed; finished; ruined

carab a beetle
Carib an Indian people of northern Brazil extending northward to Belize
carob a leguminous tree of the Mediterranean that yields edible pods

carat a unit of weight for precious stones
caret a mark on written material indicating where something is to be inserted
carrot a biennial plant with a tapering root used as a vegetable
karat a unit of fineness for gold equal to 1/24 part of pure gold (seldom **carat**)

carate a disease endemic in tropical America that is characterized by the presence of various colored spots
karate a Japanese martial art of self defense

carbeen   an Australian eucalypt
carbene   a component of bitumen soluble in carbon disulfide
carbine   a short-barreled lightweight rifle

carbinyl   the univalent radical corresponding to any alcohol derived from methanol
carbonyl   the bivalent radical CO occurring in aldehydes, ketones, esters, and amides

card   to cleanse, disentangle, and collect together animal or vegetable fibers; a flat thin piece of paperboard
carred   carried or placed in an automobile

carded   mounted on a card; disentangled and prepared fibers for spinning
carted   carried or conveyed in a cart

carder   a person that attaches cards to articles for display or sale
carter   a person who is engaged in vehicle transport; a teamster

caret   (see **carat**)

Carian   a native or inhabitant of ancient Caria, a division of southwest Asia Minor
carrion   the dead and putrefying flesh of an animal

Carib   (see **carab**)

caries   tooth decay
carries   transports while supporting or holding
Carys   substages of the Wisconsin glacial stage
karris   large gum trees of western Australia

carman   a car driver
carmen   a song, poem, or incantation
carmine   a vivid red color

carob   (see **carab**)

carol   to sing joyously; a song

carrel   a small alcove in a library for individual study
Karel   relating to Karelia, a region of northwestern Russia adjoining eastern Finland
kerril   a sea snake of the Asiatic coast from the Persian Gulf to Japan
keryl   a mixture of alkyl radicals derived from kerosene

carom   to rebound; a rebound at an angle
Carum   a genus of biennial aromatic herbs

carom   a billard shot in which the cue ball strikes each of two object balls; a glancing off
cherem   one of three forms of ecclesiastical excommunication pronounced by a rabbi

carpal   pertaining to the wrist
carpel   a structure in a seed plant comprising the innermost whorl of its flower

carred   (see **card**)

carrel   (see **carol**)

carries   (see **caries**)

carrion   (see **Carian**)

carrot   (see **carat**)

car(r)ousel   a merry-go-round
karrusel   an escapement designed to reduce position errors in a watch

carry   to transport while supporting or holding
Cary   a substage of the Wisconsin glacial stage
karri   a large gum tree of western Australia
kerrie   a knobkerrie, a rather short wooden club with a heavy round knob at one end that may be thrown as a missile or used in close attack
Kerry   an Irish breed of small, hardy, long-lived black cattle noted for their milk

cart   a small, usually lightweight wheeled vehicle
carte   a chart, map, or diagram; a bill of fare; a playing card
kart   a miniature motorcar used for racing
quart(e)   a fencer's parry or guard position; a sequence of four playing cards of the same suit

carted   (see carded)

carter   (see carder)

Carum   (see carom)

Cary   (see carry)

Carys   (see caries)

cash   (see cache)

cashew   (see cachou)

cashoo   (see cachou)

cask   a barrel-shaped container made of staves, headings, and hoops
casque   head armor; a process or structure suggesting a helmet

casket   a coffin or repository
casquet   a light piece of armor covering the head
casquette   a cap with a visor

casque   (see cask)

casquet   (see casket)

casquette   (see casket)

Cassia   a genus of herbs, shrubs, and trees native to warm regions (usually 'kasēə)
cassia   any of the coarser varieties of cinnamon bark
Kasha   a softnapped twilled fabric of fine wool and hair

cast   to throw; to form in a mold; a group of actors
caste   a social division or class

caster   a person who throws; a wheel or wheels mounted in a frame and free to swivel

Castor   a genus of mammals comprising the beavers
castor   a beaver skin

cat   a shrub cultivated by the Arabs for its leaves which act as a stimulant narcotic when chewed or used in tea
cot   a bed made of canvas stretched on a frame
cotte   a tight-fitting garment resembling a cotehardie, a long-sleeved thigh-length medieval garment
Kot   an extinct people once living along the Agul river in Siberia
xat   a carved pole erected as a memorial to the dead by some Indians of western North America

Catalan   (see cadalene)

Catalin   (see cadalene)

catarrh   inflammation of a mucous membrane characterized by congestion and secretion of mucus
katar   a short dagger

catch   to capture or seize
ketch   a fore-and-aft-rigged boat

cate   a dainty or choice food
kate   a pileated woodpecker

cattish   (see caddish)

catty   (see caddy)

caucus   meeting of an organization's leaders to decide plans
coccus   a spherical bacterium

caudal   relating to the tail or toward the hind part of the body
caudle   a drink made of warm ale or wine and mixed with other ingredients

caught   captured or seized
cotte   a tight-fitting garment resembling a cotehardie, a long-sleeved thigh-length medieval garment
Kot   an extinct people once living along the Agul river in Siberia

cauk   (see calk)

caul (see **call**)

caulk (see **calk**)

cause something that affects a result
caws utters a harsh, raucous cry characteristic of a crow

causes brings into existence
Causus a genus of nocturnal venomous African snakes

cave (see **calve**)

cavel a cudgel or staff
cavil to object or criticize adversely for trivial reasons

caw a harsh raucous throaty outcry, such as a crow's call
Kaw a Siouan people of the Kansas river valley

cawk (see **calk**)

caws (see **cause**)

cay a small low island or emergent reef
kay something having the shape of the letter K
quai a person lying along the Seine river in Paris; a landing on the left bank of the Seine river in Paris noted for its bookstalls
quay a landing place alongside navigable water for loading and unloading

cay a small low island or emergent reef
key a device inserted in a lock or bolt to open it
quay a landing place alongside navigable water for loading and unloading

cay a monkey of the genus Cebus
chi the 22nd letter of the Greek alphabet
Kai a people on the Huon Gulf of the Territory of New Guinea

cedar a coniferous tree
ceder one who yields or withdraws
cedor an assigner of a debt or claim
cedre a moderate olive green color

seater a person who puts in seats; a tool for adjusting something (as a valve) into its seat
seeder an implement used to plant seeds

cees things having the shape of the letter C
C's $100 dollar bills (slang)
psis plural of the 23rd letter of the Greek alphabet
seas bodies of salty water
sees perceives with the eye
seize to confiscate; to grasp or clutch
sis plural of the seventh tone of the diatonic scale
Szis members of a people found mainly in the Sadon area of the Myanmar-China frontier

ceil to line a ship's bottom and sides with planking; to make a ceiling
ciel a light blue color
seal an aquatic carnivorous mammal; to make secure
seel to close a hawk's eyes by drawing threads through its eyelids

cell a single room; a microscopic mass of protoplasm; a transparent sheet of celluloid
sell to exchange goods or services for money or the equivalent

cella the frequently hidden part of a Greek or Roman temple housing a deity's image
sella the mid-line depression on the surface of the phenoid bone in the skull

cellar a storage room or rooms below ground level
sellar involving the midline depression on the surface of the sphenoid bone in the skull
seller a person who offers a good or service for sale

Celt a member of a division of early Indo-European peoples in Iron-age and pre-Roman Europe
kelt a salmon or sea trout that is weak and emaciated after spawning

Celtis a genus of trees and shrubs, as the hackberry
celtuce a celerylike vegetable derived from lettuce

cense a perfume
cents units of monetary value each equal to 1/100 of the U.S. dollar
scents smells; fills with or yields an odor
sense something to be grasped; a mechanism or faculty of perception, as seeing, hearing, tasting, feeling, or smelling

censer a vessel for burning incense
censor a person who scrutinizes communications to delete unauthorized material
senser a person who perceives something
sensor a device designed to respond to a physical stimulus

censo in Spanish law, an annuity or ground rent
senso a Chinese medicine for dropsy consisting of the dried secretion of a native food

censor (see **censer**)

censorial exercising a censor's function
sensorial preoccupied with or primarily responsive to sensations

censual related to a census
sensual related to or affecting sense organs or the senses

census a count of population, vital statistics, or other information
senses things to be grasped; mechanisms or faculties or perception

cent a unit of monetary value equal to 1/100 of the U.S. dollar
scent a fragrance; to smell; to fill with or yield odor
sent dispatched or transmitted

centare a metric unit of area equal to 1/100 of an are; a square meter

centaur one of an ancient mythical Greek race dwelling in the mountains of Thessaly and imagined as men with the bodies of horses

center a point around which things revolve or pivot; the middle, core, or nucleus
scenter a person or animal that perceives or detects by smell

cents (see **cense**)

cepe an edible mushroom
cyp either of two tropical American timber trees called princewood
seep to enter or penetrate slowly; to ooze
sipe a small traction-producing hook or bracket-shaped groove in an auto tire

'cept aphetic form of accept or except
sept a branch of a family

ceras one of the often brightly colored and branching integumentary papilliae that serve as gills on the backs of nudibranches
cerris the European Turkey oak

cercal relating to a tail
circle a closed plane curve every point of which is equidistant from its center

cercus a pair of segmented appendages near the posterior end of many insects
Circus a genus of hawks comprising the harriers
circus a spectacular public entertainment consisting of acts of skill, trained animals, and clowns

cere a protuberance at the base of a bird's bill
sear to scorch with a sudden application of intense heat
seer a person with extraordinary intuitive or spiritual insight
sere a dried up or withered condition

cereal   prepared foodstuff or grain
serial   arranged in a spatial or temporal succession of persons or things; appearing in successive parts

ceres   a moderate orange color; protuberances at the base of bird bills
Seres   a people of eastern Asia mentioned by Greeks and Romans as making silk fabrics
series   a spatial or temporal succession of persons or things

ceresin   a white or yellow hard brittle wax used as a substitute for beeswax
Saracen   a nomadic people of the deserts between Syria and Arabia
sericin   a gelatinous protein that cements the two fibroin filaments in a silk fiber

Cereus   a genus of cacti of the western U.S. and tropical America, including saguaro
serious   grave in appearance
Sirius   the Dog Star, in the constellation Canis Major, and the brightest star in the heavens

ceria   an oxide of cerium
Syria   a country in southwestern Asia

cerise   a moderate red color
siris   any of several trees of the genus Albizzia, such as the silk tree

cerous   relating to or containing the element cerium
cirrus   a wispy white cloud
scirrhus   a hard cancerous tumor
serous   resembling serum

cerris   (see **ceras**)

cerulean   of sky blue color
c(o)erulein   a xanthene dye obtained by heating gallein with concentrated sulfuric acid

Cervus   a genus of deer
service   performance of work ordered or paid for by another

cession   yielding to another
session   a period devoted to a certain activity

cessionary   an assignee or grantee of property, claim, or debt under a deed of conveyance
sessionary   recurring or renewed at each session

cetaceous   relating to the Cetacea which comprises whales, dolphins, and porpoises
setaceous   consisting of, or resembling bristles

cete   a group of badgers
seat   something to sit in; an assigned sitting place

cetin   a crystalline fat
seton   a suture

cetyl   a univalent radical that occurs in waxes
setal   relating to slender, typically rigid or bristly and springy organs or parts of animals and plants

Ceylon   an island south of India which became the independent republic Sri Lanka in 1972
salon   a usually spacious or elegant living room

cha(a)c   one of the Mayan gods of rain and fertility
chock   a wedge or block for steadying a body or holding it motionless; as completely as possible

chafer   any of various beetles, including the June beetle
chaffer   to discuss terms or haggle over the price

chair   furniture to accommodate a sitting person
chare   an odd job or task

chaise   a light carriage or pleasure cart
shays   slow, wood-burning, geared locomotives used for hauling logs to a mill

cham   (see **cam**)

Chamaeleon   a large genus of lizards including most of the Old World chameleons

chameleon   a fickle person who is given to expedient or facile change in ideas or character

chamar   a fan typically made of a yak's tail or peacock feathers
chummer   a person that scatters chum in fishing

chameleon   (see Chamaeleon)

champagne   a white sparkling wine that undergoes the first fermentation in a cask and the second in a bottle
champaign   an expanse of level open country
champain   in heraldry, a broken or deflected line in an ordinary

chance   an activity or event that occurs unpredictably
chants   hymnlike repetitive melodies

chancre   a primary sore or ulcer
shanker   a person who makes or fastens on shanks

chant(e)y   a song sung by sailors, often in rhythm with their work
shanty   a small poorly built dwelling

chants   (see chance)

chap   a fellow; sore roughening of the skin
chape   the metal piece at the back of a buckle that fastens it to a strap

chap   a jaw or the fleshy covering of the jaw
chop   to cut into with an implement

chape   (see chap)

chaps   a pair of joined leather leggings worn over trousers
(s)chappes   yarns or fabrics of spun silk

chard   a beet with large yellowish-green leaves
charred   converted to charcoal or carbon by exposure to heat

chare   (see chair)

charpie   lint

sharpie   a long narrow shallow-draft sailboat; an exceptionally keen alert person

charque   jerked meat
sharky   infested with elasmobranch fish (sharks)

charred   (see chard)

chartreuse   a variable color averaging a brilliant yellow green; several vegetables arranged and cooked in a mold
Chartreux   any of a breed of short-haired domestic cats of French origin

chary   hesitant and vigilant about dangers and risks
cherry   a fruit-bearing tree or shrub; a small smooth-skinned edible fruit

chased   followed rapidly and intently
chaste   abstaining from sexual intercourse

château   a large country house
Chatot   an extinct Muskogean people of Florida west of the Apalachicola river

chatelain   a governor or warden of a castle or fort
chatelaine   an ornamental chain, pin, or clasp worn at a woman's waist

Chatot   (see chateau)

chauffeurs   persons employed to operate motor vehicles
chauffeuse   a low-seated French fireside chair
shofars   ram's horn blown at high Jewish observances

cheap   inexpensive
cheep   to make a small birdlike sound or to chirp

cheapie   something that costs very little money or effort to produce
cheepy   inclined to make small birdlike sounds

check to impede progress; a bank draft
Czech a native of the Czech Republic

checker a person who marks, counts, tallies, or examines materials or products
chekker a stringed keyboard instrument of the 14th and 15th centuries

cheeky having well-developed cheeks; impudent or brazenfaced
chikee a stilthouse of the Seminole Indians that is open on all sides and thatched

cheep (see **cheap**)

cheepy (see **cheapie**)

cheer lightness of mind and feeling; gaiety
chir an East Indian resinous timber pine

chekker (see **checker**)

Chen (see **can**)

cherem (see **carom**)

cherry (see **chary**)

chevee a flat gemstone with a smooth depression
chevet the apsidal eastern termination of a church choir

chew to crush or grind in the mouth
Chuje an Indian people of northwestern Guatemala

chews crushes or grinds in the mouth
choose to select with free will
tchus expressions of distaste

chez in the home or business place
shay a slow, wood-burning, geared locomotive used for hauling logs to a mill
shea a sea butter tree

chi (see **cay**)

chiaus a cheat or swindler; a Turkish messenger or sergeant
chouse to drive or herd livestock

roughly; to chase, harass, or stir up

chic artistic cleverness
sheik(h) a head of an Arab family, tribe, or village
Shik a people of Turkmenistan regarded as of Arabian origin

chic(c)ory a thick-rooted, usually blue-flowered perennial herb
chickery a poultry hatchery

chickee a small or young chicken
chikee a stilthouse of the Seminole Indians that is open on all sides and thatched

chickery (see **chic[c]ory**)

chigger a six-legged larval mite that attaches itself to various vertebrates to suck blood
jigger to jerk up and down; a measure used in mixing drinks

chikee (see **cheeky** or **chickee**)

chil an Indian kite (a bird)
chill to make cold

Chile a South American country
chili a thick sauce made principally of meat, tomatoes, and hot peppers (chilies)
chilly noticeably cold

chill (see **chil**)

chilly (see **Chile**)

Chilo a genus of small slender dull colored nocturnal moths
Kyloe a breed of small very hardy beef cattle from the Highlands of Scotland having thick shaggy hair

ching a Chinese scripture
jing a mild oath, as in the phrase "by jing"

chins lower portions of the face lying beneath the lower lip
chintz a firm glazed cotton fabric of plain weave
chintze to caulk temporarily

chir   (see cheer)

Chi-Rho   (see Cairo)

chirr   the short especially vibrant or trilled and repetitive sound characteristic of certain insects, like grasshoppers and cicadas
churr   a whirring noise characteristic of some birds such as the nightjar or partridge

chitin   the amorphous horny substance forming part of the hard outer covering of insects
Chiton   a genus of mollusks
chiton   the basic garment of ancient Greece; a mollusk of the order Polyplacophora

chlor   a yellowish green color
chlore   to treat with a dilute solution of bleaching powder

chlorin   any of several derivatives of chlorophyll obtained by hydrolysis
chlorine   a common nonmetallic gaseous element

chlorogenin   a steroidal sapogenin obtained from a soap plant
chlorogenine   an alkaloid found in a tree bark

chock   (see cha[a]c)

choir   an organized group of singers
quire   four sheets of paper folded into eight leaves

cholate   a salt or ester of cholic acid
collate   to assemble according to an orderly system; to bring together for close comparison

choler   (see caller)

choler   a ready disposition to anger and irritation
coaler   something (as a railroad or ship) chiefly employed in transporting or supplying coal

choline   a crystalline or syrupy liquid base widely distributed among animal and plant products

colleen   an Irish girl

choose   (see chews)

chop   (see chap)

choral   of or belonging to a chorus or choir
chorale   a hymn or song sung by a choir or congregation
coral   a skeletal deposit produced by certain anthozoan polyps

chorale   a hymn or psalm sung by a choir or congregation
corral   an enclosure for confining livestock

chord   a combination of two or more tones sounded together
cord   a slender flexible cylindrical construction of several threads or yarns spun together
cored   removed the axial portion, as of an apple

chordate   having a notochord
cordate   shaped like a heart

chorea   any of various nervous disorders having marked uncoordination of various parts of the body
Correa   a small genus of Australian shrubs
correa   any plant of the genus Correa
keriah   a Jewish ritual of rending one's garment at the funeral of a near relative as a symbol of mourning
Korea   a country in eastern Asia, divided into North Korea and South Korea since 1948

chorion   the highly vascular outer embryonic membrane of higher vertebrates
Korean   a native or inhabitant of North or South Korea

chose   a piece of personal property
shous   Chinese characters signifying longevity that are often used in decoration

shows puts on view or displays

chott a shallow saline lake of northern Africa (also **shott**)
shot directed the propelling of a missile
shott a young hog of either sex, especially less than one year old

chough an Old World bird, as the jackdaw
chuff a miser; a brick cracked by rain during burning

chouse (see **chiaus**)

choux darlings, used as a term of endearment
shoe an outer covering for the foot
shoo to scare or drive away
shu in Confucianism, reciprocity or mutual considerateness in all actions

choux soft cabbage-shaped ornaments or rosettes of fabric used in women's wear
shoes outer coverings for the foot
shoos scares or drives away

Chow a heavy-coated blocky powerfully built dog
chow a mixed balanced animal ration of food; military food (slang)
ciao hello or goodbye, in Italian

christcross a personal cipher used in place of a signature
crisscross a ploy in football in which the paths of two offensive players cross, as in a pass pattern

chrome to surface with chromium
crome to catch or kill something by hooking or hitting it with a stick or implement; to overpower or subdue

chromogen a pigment-producing microorganism
chromogene a gene, used to sharply distinguish the nuclear gene from the cytogene

chronical of long duration or frequent recurrence

chronicle an historical account of facts or events arranged chronologically; to prepare such an account

chrysal a transverse line of crushed fibers in the belly of an archery bow beginning as a pinch
crissal having feathers that cover a bird's cloacal opening

Chrysis a type genus of brilliantly colored wasps
crisis a decisive moment

Chrysochloris a genus of African golden moles
chrysochlorous of a golden green color

chucker a person who throws with a short arm action
chukker a playing period in a polo game

chuff (see **chough**)

Chuje (see **chew**)

chukker (see **chucker**)

chummer (see **chamar**)

Chün relating to a type of Chinese pottery produced in a great variety of colors in Honan province during the Sung period
June the 6th month of the Gregorian calendar

churr (see **chirr**)

chute a narrow walled passageway
shoot to set off an explosive charge or discharge a weapon

ciao (see **Chow**)

cibol a Welsh onion or shallot
sibyl a female prophet

cicely any of several herbs of the family Umbelliferae
Sicily an island in the Mediterranean sea west of Italy

Cidaris the type genus of Cidaridae, a family of sea urchins

cidaris the royal tiara of ancient Persian kings
siderous relating to or containing iron

cider a beverage made from apples
citer a person who calls upon or quotes by way of evidence
sider a person living in or on a specified side, as an east-sider
sighter a person who tests the accuracy of sights on small arms

ciel (see **ceil**)

cig a cigarette (slang)
sig a signature, as a newspaper's logotype

cilia minute hairlike processes
Psyllia a genus of jumping plant lice

Cilicia an ancient region in Asia Minor
Silicea a class of Porifera including all sponges not placed in Calcarea

cilicious made of hair
siliceous related to silica

cilium an eyelash; a minute hairlike process
psyllium fleawort, an Old World plantain

cinch to guarantee or assure; a strong girth strap for a pack or saddle
sinh the hyperbolic sine

cingular shaped like a ring
singular relating to a single or individual unit; uncommon

cinque the number five in dice or cards
sank became submerged

cinque the number five in dice or cards
sink to become submerged
sync(h) synchronized

cipher a symbol denoting the absence of quantity or magnitude
sypher to overlap the chamfered

edges of planks or make a flush joint, as for a bulkhead

circle (see **cercal**)

circulus one of the usual concentric ridges on a fish scale, each representing an increment of growth
surculus a shoot originating from the roots or lower part of a plant's stem; a sucker

Circus and **circus** (see **cercus**)

cirral relating to a curllike tuft
seral relating to an ecological dry period

cirrhosis a chronic progressive disease of the liver
psorosis a virus disease of citrus trees
sorosis a women's club

cirrhus a mucusbound ribbonlike mass of spores that is exuded from a fungus
cirrus a white filmy variety of cloud usually formed in the highest cloud region at altitudes of 20,000 to 40,000 feet
seeress a female prophet

cirrus (see **cerous**)

cis having certain atoms or groups on the same side of the molecule
sis sister (by shortening)
siss a prolonged sibilant or hissing sound

cisor an incisor tooth (by shortening)
sizer a person who determines or sorts by sizes or checks for sizes

cist a wicker receptacle for carrying sacred utensils in ancient Rome
cyst an abnormal closed sac in a body
sissed hissed

cist a neolithic grave lined with stone slabs
kissed touched with the lips
kist a clothes or linen trunk

cit   a city inhabitant
sit   to rest in a position in which the body is essentially vertical and supported chiefly on the buttocks

cite   to bring to mind; to call to attention
cyte   a maturing germ cell
sight   something seen
site   a location or space of ground

cited   brought to mind; called to attention
sided   having right or left lateral parts
sighted   having vision or being able to see

citer   (see cider)

citrene   a right-handed hydrocarbon occurring in celery-seed oil
citrin   a crystalline water-soluble flavonoid concentrate originally prepared from lemons
citrine   a semiprecious yellow stone resembling topaz; resembling lemon or citron

citrin   a crystalline water-soluble flavonoid concentrate originally prepared from lemons
citron   a citrus fruit resembling a lemon but larger and without a terminal nipple

citrine   (see citrene)

citron   (see citrin)

citrulin   a purgative yellow resinous preparation of the colocynth apple
citruline   a crystalline amino acid formed as an intermediate in the conversion of ornithine to arginine

clack   loud confused talk
claque   a group hired to applaud at a performance

claimant   a person who asserts a right or title
clamant   crying out

claire   a small enclosed pond for growing oysters
Clare   a nun of an order founded by Assisi in the 13th century

clamant   (see claimant)

clamber   to crane, struggle, or climb
clammer   a person who digs for clams
clamor   a continuous loud noise

clan   a social unit, smaller than a tribe but larger than a family, claiming descent from a common ancestor
Klan   an organization of Ku Kluxers

clang   a loud resounding sound like that of a trumpet or pieces of metal struck together
Klang   in music and acoustics, a fundamental with its overtones

claque   (see clack)

Clare   (see claire)

clarety   a color resembling the dark red of claret wine
clarity   clearness

classed   divided or distributed into categories or classifications
clast   a grain of sediment, sand, or gravel, especially as a constituent fragment of an older rock formation

classes   social ranks; denominations
classis   an ecclesiastical governing body of a district

clast   (see classed)

clatch   a clod; a daub of something; a mess
klatch   a gathering characterized by informal conversation

clause   a section of discourse or writing
claws   sharp nails or talons on an animal's toes

clavis a glossary which aids interpretation

clavus a rounded or fingerlike part or process, as the club of an insect's antenna; a vertical purple band on a Roman tunic

claws (see **clause**)

cleek a narrow-faced iron golf club

clique a narrow exclusive circle of persons

cleft a space made as if by splitting; partially split

Klepht a Greek belonging to the independent armed community formed after the Turkish conquest of Greece

clews the lower corners of a square sail (rarely **clues**)

clous points of chief interest or attraction

clues evidence tending to lead a person toward a problem's solution (rarely **clews**)

cluse a narrow gorge cutting transversely through an otherwise continuous ridge

click a slight sharp noise

clique a narrow exclusive circle of persons

klick a kilometer

climb to rise or go upward

clime a climate

cling to hold to each other cohesively and firmly

Kling a Dravidian probably of Tamil origin of the seaports of southeastern Asia and Malaysia

clip a device which grips or clasps; to cut as with a shears

klip(pe) an outlying isolated remnant of an overthrust rock mass due to erosion

clique (see **cleek** or **click**)

clivis a musical symbol denoting the first of two tones being the higher in pitch

clivus a smooth sloping surface on the sphenoid bone in the skull that supports the broad mass of transverse nerve fibers

cloche a woman's small helmetlike hat; a translucent cover for a young plant

closh a post on a whaling ship fitted with hooks for hanging blubber to be sliced

clomp to tread clumsily and noisily; a heavy tramping sound

klomp a gathering characterized by informal conversation; a wooden shoe worn in the Low Countries

close to shut or terminate

clothes clothing

cloze related to a reading comprehension test

closh (see **cloche**)

clothes (see **close**)

clouded obscured; mentally confused

clouted mended with patches; hit forcefully

clouter a person who covers with cloth, leather, or other material; a person who hits a baseball, especially long and hard

clowder a group of cats

clough a narrow valley

clow a floodgate

clous (see **clews**)

clouted (see **clouded**)

clow (see **clough**)

clowder (see **clouter**)

cloze (see **close**)

clucker a person who makes the sound of a brooding hen

Klucker a Ku Klux Klansman

clucks makes the noise of a brooding hen

Klux to maltreat or terrorize in the

way thought typical of the Ku Klux Klan

clues (see **clews**)

cluse (see **clews**)

clyster an enema
klister a soft wax used on skis

coach a large, usually closed four-wheeled carriage; a railroad passenger car
Koch a member of a hinduized Mongoloid people of Assam

coacts acts or works together; forces or compels
coax a coaxial transmission line in which one conductor is centered inside and insulated from an outer metal tube that serves as a second conductor

coaks dowels placed in timbers to unite them or keep them from slipping
coax to persuade or influence
cokes residues from carbonized coal

coal a hot ember; a black solid combustible mineral
cole a plant of the cabbage family
Ko(h)l a people of Bengal and Chota Nagpur, India
kohl a preparation used in Arabia and Egypt to darken the edges of eyelids

coaled converted to charcoal by burning; supplied with coal
cold having a temperature notably below an accustomed norm

coaler (see **choler**)

coaly covered or impregnated with coal; a coal heaver
coly any of a small group of fruit-eating African birds comprising the genus Colius
Koli a low-caste people of Bombay, Punjab, and other parts of India

coaming a raised frame around a

floor or roof opening to keep out water
combing arranging or adjusting hair with a toothed instrument

coarse ordinary, unrefined, or inferior
course a particular path between two points

coarser more unrefined or inferior
courser a swift or spirited horse

coat an outer garment
cote a shed for small domestic animals

coated covered or impregnated with a durable chemical or rubber compound
coded put into the form of symbols for meaningful communication

coater a person or machine that coats surfaces
coder a person or device that puts information into coded form

coax (see **coacts** or **coaks**)

cob a male swan; a corncob; to break into small pieces prior to sorting
cobb the great black-backed gull
kob an African antelope related to the waterbuck

cobble to mend or make, as shoes; to pave with cobblestones
coble a flat-floored fishing boat
Kabul the capital of Afghanistan

coccal relating to a plant having berries or seeds; a berry-shaped organism; relating to the type genus of Coccidae that includes certain typical scales
cockal a game played with knucklebones
cockle a plant growing in grain fields, as cowherb or cocklebur; a bivalve mollusk

coccus (see **caucus**)

cockal (see coccal)

cocker in archery, a ground quiver; a person who handles fighting roosters; a cocker spaniel
kakar a small deer of southeastern Asia and the East Indies

cockle (see coccal)

cocks adult males of domestic fowl; positions the hammer of a firearm for firing
coques loops of ribbons or feathers used in trimming hats
cox to steer and direct, as does a coxswain

cockscomb a plant with red, purple, or yellow flowers
coxcomb a vain conceited foolish person who is falsely proud of personal achievements

cocky pert, arrogant, or jaunty
kaki a Japanese persimmon
khaki a light yellowish brown color

cocoa a beverage of milk or water, sugar, and powdered cacao seeds
Koko a group of numerous aboriginal peoples of northern Queensland, Australia
koko an araceous plant, such as taro, cultivated in tropical western Africa

coconut a fruit of coconut palm
cokernut an edible seed of the coquito palm

cocoon (see cacoon)

cocoon any of various protective coverings produced by animals, such as silkworms and spiders
kokoon a brindled gnu

coda a final or concluding musical section
cota a fort formerly common in parts of the Philippines
Kota an artisan and buffalo-herding people of the southwestern India

coddle to pamper; to cook in a liquid just below its boiling point
cottle a clay wall encircling an object to be molded
katel a wooden hammock used in Africa as a bed in a wagon

coddling slowly cooking in a liquid just below its boiling point
codling a young codfish

coded (see coated)

coder (see coater)

codling (see coddling)

coeler pertaining to the sky
sealer a machine or person who makes secure or seals

coenocyte a multi-nucleate mass of protoplasm
coenosite a free or separable symbiotic ecological arrangement

c(o)erulein (see cerulean)

coffer a strongbox for safely storing valuables
cougher a person who expels air from the lungs suddenly and explosively

Cognac a brandy distilled from white wine from the French departments of Charente and Charente-Maritime
cognac a moderate brown color
Konyak a people of the Assam-Myanmar frontier area

coif a manner of arranging hair
quaff to drink freely or copiously

coign the corner of a crystal formed by the intersection of three or more faces
coin a piece of metal issued by a government to circulate as money
quoin a wedge used on ships to keep casks from rolling

coil an arrangement of something in a spiral or concentric rings

koel any of several cuckoos of India, the East Indies, and Australia

coin (see **coign**)

coir stiff coarse coconut husk fiber
coyer more modestly rejecting approaches or overtures

coke the infusible hard residue from carbonized coal
colk a bowl-shaped, cylindrical, or circular hole formed by a stone's grinding action in the rocky bed of a river or stream

cokernut (see **coconut**)

cokes (see **coaks**)

cokie a cocaine addict
coky resembling coke

colation removal of solids from liquid by straining, especially through filter paper
collation assembly of paper or forms into an orderly system

cold (see **coaled**)

cole (see **coal**)

colin the bobwhite or any of several related New World game birds
colleen an Irish girl

colk (see **coke**)

collar (see **caller**)

collard an edible hardy plant of the cabbage family
collared wearing a neckband

collate (see **cholate**)

collation (see **colation**)

colleen (see **choline** or **colin**)

college a building or group of buildings used in connection with some educational or religious purpose
kalij any of the crested India pheasants that are related to the Chinese silver pheasant

collin a prepared form of gelatin used in tanning analysis
colline any of the ridges of a brain coral

collum a neck or necklike part or process
column a vertical arrangement of items; a supporting pillar or shaft

colmar (see **calmer**)

Cologne a city in western Germany
cologne a perfumed liquid composed of alcohol and an aromatic
colon a colonial farmer, planter, or plantation owner

Colombia a country in northwestern South America
Columbia the capital of South Carolina; a Salishan people of eastern Washington

Colombian relating to or characteristic of Colombia
Columbian having a black-white color pattern characteristic of the plumage of certain varieties of poultry

colombous related to or containing the metallic element niobium
Colombus the capital of Ohio

colon (see **Cologne**)

colonel a military officer ranking between a brigadier general and a lieutenant colonel
kernel a seed's inner portion; a central or essential part

color a hue, as red, yellow, or blue
culler a person who picks out imperfect items, as defective poultry

Columbia (see **Colombia**)

Columbian (see **Colombian**)

column (see **collum**)

columniation (see **calumniation**)

coly (see **coaly**)

comb an instrument for adjusting, cleaning, or confining the hair
come the dried rootlets produced in malting grain
kolm a Swedish shale exceptionally high in uranium oxide

combing (see **coaming**)

comby resembling a comb in structure
Komi a people of north central Russia

come (see **comb**)

come the dried rootlets produced in malting grain
cum along with

comedia a Spanish regular-verse drama
commedia an Italian comedy, as performed in the 16th and 18th centuries

comedic like comedy
cometic relating to or like a comet

comedy a drama of light and amusing character, typically with a happy ending
comity kindly courteous behavior

comely (see **calmly**)

comely having a pleasing appearance
cumbly a blanket made of wood or goat's hair

comet a celestial body with a fuzzy head surrounding a bright nucleus and long tail
commit a card game

cometic (see **comedic**)

comics comedians
comix comic art, often luridly sexual or political in character
kamiks Eskimo sealskin boats

comity (see **comedy**)

comix (see **comics**)

comma (see **comedia**)

commedia (see **comedia**)

commerce the buying and selling of commodities
commers a social gathering of German university students

commie a playing marble made of clay; a communist
kami a sacred power or force in the Shinto religion

commissariat the organized system by which armies and military posts are supplied with food and daily necessaries
commissariot a county or sheriff's court in Scotland that appoints estate executors

commit (see **comet**)

compellation an act of addressing someone
compilation the gathering together of written material; an accumulation of many things or ideas

complacence secure self-satisfaction
complaisance a pleasing ingratiating deportment

complementary supplementing
complimentary expressing regard or praise

comptroller a public officer who supervises the propriety of expenditures
controller an electric device to govern how electric power is delivered

con an argument on the negative side; to swindle; a convict
conn the control exercised by a person who directs a ship's movements
khan a local chieftain in some areas of central Asia; a rest house in some Asian countries

conceded allowed, admitted, or acknowledged
conceited having an unjustifiably high opinion of oneself

concenter to bring together at a focus or point; to concentrate
consenter a person who agrees with, permits, or concurs

conch a large spiral-shelled marine gastropod mollusk
conche a machine in which chocolate is worked and kneaded

conch a large spiral-shelled marine gastropod mollusk
conk to hit, especially on the head; to break down

conche (see conch)

concord a state of agreement
Concorde a supersonic passenger aircraft manufactured and operated jointly by England and France

cond to superintend the steering of a ship or airplane
conned swindled
Khond any of several Dravidian peoples of Orissa, India

confectionary a place where elaborate, complex, or ornate items are kept
confectionery sweet edibles

confidant a person with whom one feels free to discuss private or secret matters
confidante a sofa divided by arms into separate seats
confident characterized by a strong belief in oneself
confitent a person who confesses, especially to a priest

confirmation the process of substantiating a factual statement with empirical evidence
conformation the form or outline; shaping

confitent (see confidant)

Congaree a Sioux people in the Congaree valley, California
congeree a large, strictly marine, entirely scaleless eel that is an important food fish

congery a collection or mass of entities
conjury the practice of magic

Congo a territory surrounding the Congo river in West Africa; a dark grayish yellowish brown
congo a ballroom dance of Haitian origin
congou a black tea from China

conics the theory of conic sections
connex closely connected; constituting one syntactical unit

conjury (see congery)

conk (see conch)

conker a popular English game in which each player swings a horse chestnut threaded on a string to try to break one held by an opponent
conquer to acquire by force or gain dominion over

conn (see con)

connects joins, fastens, or links together
connex in mathematics, the infinity of points and lines

conned (see cond)

connex (see conics and connects)

conquer (see conker)

consensual involving or caused by involuntary action or movement correlative with a voluntary action, as the contraction of the iris when the eyelid is opened
consentual involving or carried out by mutual agreement

consenter (see concenter)

consentual (see consensual)

consequence something that is produced by a cause or follows from a set of conditions
consequents musical restatements of the subject in the canon and fugue; a stream or valley that has developed in harmony with the general slope of an existing land surface

consonance   harmony of parts
consonants   speech sounds characterized by constriction at one or
more points in the breath channel

consulter   a person who counsels or
advises
consultor   an advisor who assists a
Roman Catholic bishop

continence   self-restraint from yielding to desire
continents   divisions of land on Earth

contingence   contact or touching
contingents   chance occurrences;
representational groups

continuance   remaining in the same
condition or place
continuants   ones that continue;
determinants of which all the elements are zero except those of a
principal diagonal and the two adjacent minor diagonals; consonants
that may be prolonged without
change of quality

controller   (see comptroller)

convects   transfers heat by convection
convex   curved, as the exterior of a
sphere

conventical   relating to a convent or
nunnery
conventicle   an assembly, meeting,
or convention, especially of a
society or body of persons

convex   (see convects)

coo   the call of a pigeon or dove
coup   a successful stratagem; a blow
or stroke

cookee   a cook's helper, especially in
a logging camp
cookie   small sweet cake

coolamon   an Australian vessel of
bark or wood resembling a basin
and used for carrying and holding
water
Kulaman   a people inhabiting southern Mindanao, Philippines

coolie   an unskilled laborer, usually
in the Far East
cool(l)y   without passion or ardor;
with indifference
coulee   a small stream

cool(l)y   (see coolie)

coom   grease exuding from axle
boxes or bearings
cwm   a deep steep-walled basin high
on a mountain, usually shaped like
half a bowl and often containing a
small lake

coonie   a cowhide stretched under a
wagon as a carrying device, especially for fuel; a person of Acadian
French heritage
coony   showing astuteness and cleverness

coop   a small enclosure for animals
coupe   a two-door automobile with
one seating compartment; a dessert

cooped   deprived of free motion by
cramped quarters
couped   in heraldry, cut off short at
the ends so as not to extend to the
edges of the field

cooper   one who makes or repairs
barrels or casks
couper   a lever in a loom for lifting
a harness

Coos   a Kusan people of Oregon
coos   soft low cries or calls, as of a
dove or pigeon
cooze   a female considered as a sexual object (slang); a vagina (slang)
coups   highly successful stratagems

copje   (see caapi)

coppa   an Italian pork sausage
seasoned with cayenne pepper
koppa   a letter in the early Greek
alphabet

copped   rising to a top or head; acquired; stolen, especially on the
spur of the moment; captured
Copt   an Egyptian of the native race
descended from ancient Egyptians,

especially a member of the Coptic
church

cops policemen; a conical mass of
yarn wound on a tube
copse a thicket or grove of small trees

Copt (see **copped**)

copy (see **caapi**)

copyright the exclusive, legally
secured right to write, print, pub-
lish, and sell artistic works
copywrite to create and write advertising or publicity copy

coques (see **cocks**)

cor the heart (in prescriptions)
core the central part of a body
corps an organized subdivision of a
military establishment; a group
having a common activity
khor a watercourse or ravine

Cora a genus of basidiolichens
widely distributed on soil and trees
in Central and South America; a
Taracahitian people of the states of
Jalisco and Nayarit, Mexico
cora a gazelle found from Iran to
North Africa
corah plain undyed India silk
kora a large gallinule of southeastern Asia and the East Indies; a 21-
string musical instrument of African origin resembling a lute

coral (see **choral**)

corbeille a basket of flowers or fruit
corbel an architectural member
which projects from within a wall
and supports weight

cord (see **chord**)

cordate (see **chordate**)

cordobán cordovan leather
Cordovan a native or resident of
Córdoba, Spain
cordovan a dark grayish brown color

core (see **cor**)

cored (see **chord**)

Cork a county and city in Ireland
cork the outer tissues of the stem of
the cork oak
corke any of the colors imparted by
the dye archil varying from moderate to dark purplish

cormous bearing or producing thick
rounded modified underground
stem bases, as the gladiolus
cormus the entire body or colony of
a compound animal, as coral

corni French horns
corny relating to corn; trite; mawk-
ishly sentimental

cornice a decorative band conceal-
ing curtain fixtures
Cornus a genus of shrubs and small
trees of the family Cornaceae

corniche a road built along the edge
of an overhanging precipice or
along the face of a cliff
Cornish an English breed of domestic fowl; a Celtic language of Corn-
wall, England, extinct since the late
18th century

Cornus (see **cornice**)

corny (see **corni**)

corollate having a corolla, the inner
set of floral leaves immediately surrounding the sporophylls
correlate one of two related things
viewed in terms of its relationship
to the other

corps (see **cor**)

corral (see **chorale**)

Correa and **correa** (see **chorea**)

correlate (see **corollate**)

Cortes a Spanish parliament or par-
liaments
cortez any of several Central American timber trees of the genus
Tabelula

corydalis   an herb native to north temperate regions and southern Africa
Corydalus   a genus of large megalopterous insects, as dobsons

coscet   a class of peasant landholders
cosset   to treat as a pet; a lamb reared without a dam's aid
cossette   a strip or slice, as of potato

cose   to make oneself cozy
coze   to chat

cosign   to jointly sign a document
cosine   a trigonometry term

cosset   (see coscet)

cossette   (see coscet)

cot   (see cat)

cota   (see coda)

cote   (see coat)

Cotinga and cotinga   (see caatinga)

Coto   a Tucano people of eastern Ecuador; a Chibchan people of Costa Rica
coto   the bark of a tree of northern Bolivia formerly used as an astringent and stomachic
koto   a long Japanese zither having 13 silk strings

cotte   (see cat or caught)

cotter   a wedge-shaped or tapered piece used to fasten together parts of a machine or structure; a cotter pin
Kadir   a primitive somewhat negroid jungle-dwelling people inhabiting the Deccan plateau in southern India
quatre   the four at cards or dice

cottle   (see coddle)

cotty   entangled or matted
Kati   a Kafir people of easternmost Kafiristan in the Hindu Kush mountains of Afghanistan

couac   a strident tone sometimes produced by a reed instrument when the reed is out of order or the instrument is blown incorrectly
quack   the characteristic duck cry or call; a medical charlatan

couche   in heraldry, inclined
couchee   a reception given in the late evening, especially by nobility

cough   to expel air from the lungs suddenly with a harsh noise
Kaf   a mountain range in Moslem mythology that encircles the earth and where lives a mythical bird of wisdom
kaph   the eleventh letter of the Hebrew alphabet
koff   a two-masted vessel with spritsails used by the Dutch and Danes

cougher   (see coffer)

coulé   in music, a slur; a gliding dance step
coulee   a small stream

coulee   (see coolie)

council   a deliberative assembly
counsel   opinion, advice, or direction

councillor   a council member
counselor   an adviser

counsel   (see council)

counselor   (see councillor)

counter   a device used in keeping accounts and in playing games
counto(u)r   a pleader in an English court; a sergeant-at-law

coup   (see coo)

coupe   (see coop)

coupe   a ballet step
cupay   a common tropical American tree (the pitch apple) having coarse evergreen leaves

couped   (see cooped)

couper   (see cooper)

coups (see **Coos**)

courant a newspaper name
currant a small seedless raisin; an edible acidic fruit of several plants of the genus Ribes
current occurring in the present; a continuously flowing part of a fluid or electricity

courier a messenger
currier a person who works tanned hides into salable form; a person who combs a horse

course (see **coarse**)

courser (see **coarser**)

courtesy well-mannered conduct or consideration for others
curtesy the future potential interest that a husband has in real estate in which his wife has an estate of inheritance

cousin a child of one's aunt or uncle
cozen to deceive by artful wheedling or tricky dishonesty

covariance the arithmetic mean or the expected value of the product of the deviations of corresponding values of two variables from their respective mean
covariants the functions of both coefficients and variables of quantities that retain their form when the quantities are transformed linearly

coven an assembly of witches
covin a collusive agreement between persons to the detriment of another

cow a mature female of wild or domestic cattle
kou a tree of the Pacific islands whose wood is used for making household utensils

coward a person who shows ignoble fear
cowered cringed in abject fear of something

cowl a hood or hooded sleeveless garment
cowle a written grant or engagement in India, especially of safe-conduct or amnesty

cox (see **cocks**)

coxcomb (see **cockscomb**)

coy shy; showing marked, often playful or irritating reluctance to make a definite or committing statement
koi a carp, a soft-finned freshwater fish

coyer (see **coir**)

coyote a small wolf native to western North America extending to Alaska and New York
coyotey mangy-looking

coze (see **cose**)

cozen (see **cousin**)

crackie a broken or chipped playing marble
cracky having cracks; a mild oath; odd or eccentric

cracks narrow breaks or thin slits; loud earsplitting roars
Crax the type genus of Cracidae, which includes long-legged birds such as curassows and guans

cracky (see **crackie**)

Cracow the former capital of Poland
crakow 14th and 15th century European footwear made with an extremely long pointed toe

craft artistic dexterity
kraft a strong paper

crakow (see **Cracow**)

crampette the chape of a sword scabbard
crampit a sheet of iron on which a player stands to deliver the stone in curling

crance a band on the outer edge of a bowsprit to which the bobstays and bowsprit shrouds are fastened
krantz a sheer cliff or precipice in southern Africa

crankie a bend, turn, twist, or crinkle
cranky out of working order; given to fretful fussiness

crape a band worn on a hat or sleeve as a sign of mourning
crepe a small very thin pancake; a lightweight fabric with wrinkled surface

crappie a North American sunfish
crappy markedly inferior in quality; lousy

crappie a North American sunfish
croppy an Irish rebel in 1798 who wore short hair as a token of sympathy with the French Revolution; a long iron rod used in making cylinder glass to transfer the cylinder to a flattening stock

crappy (see **crappie**)

craton a relatively immobile area of the earth's crust that forms the nuclear mass of a continent or the central basin of an ocean
kraton a region that has remained undisturbed while an adjacent area has been affected by mountain-making movements

crawk a sound-effects person who imitates animals
croc crocodile (by shortening); a hook-shaped iron projection fastened to the stock of a harquebus
crock a thick earthernware pot or jar

crawl to move slowly with the body close to the ground; to draw along
kraal a village of southern Africa; an enclosure for keeping turtles or lobsters alive in shallow water
kral a title or early rulers of Slavonic countries equivalent to a king

crawley a coralroot of dry woodlands in eastern and central North America
crawlie a small burrowing crayfish
crawly creepy

Crax (see **cracks**)

crays spiny lobsters of Australia
craze a transient infatuation or fad

creak a high, typically subdued rasping or grating noise
Creek the Creek Confederacy, an American Indian confederacy organized around the Muskogee people of Georgia and eastern Alabama before their removal to Oklahoma
creek a natural stream of water normally smaller than a river

cream the yellowish part of milk that rises to the surface
crème a sweet liqueur

crease a line, groove, or ridge made by folding a pliable substance
creece watercress or garden cress

creases ridges made by folding pliable material
krises Malay or Indonesian daggers often with scalloped cutting edges and serpentine blades

creat an East Indian herb having bitter juice variously used in medicine
create to bring into existence

crécy prepared with carrots
cressy abounding in cresses, such as watercress

Cree an Indian people ranging from James Bay in Ontario, Canada, to Montana
qre a traditional Jewish mode of reading the Hebrew bible that is substituted for one actually standing in the consonantal text

creece   (see crease)

Creek and creek   (see creak)

creek   a natural stream of water normally smaller than a river
cric   the ring which turns inward and condenses the flame of a lamp
crick   a painful spasmodic muscular condition

Crees   an Indian people ranging from James Bay south to Montana
crise   a moment of risk or stress; a crisis

crème   (see cream)

crepe   (see crape)

cressed   abounding in cress, such as water cress
crest   the top of a structure or a natural formation

cressy   (see crécy)

crest   (see cressed)

Cretan   a native or inhabitant of the island of Crete in the eastern part of the Mediterranean sea
cretin   a person showing marked mental deficiency, often because of a thyroid deficiency

crevasse   a wide and deep opening or chasm; a breach in a river's levee
crevice   a narrow recess or slit

crewed   acted as a member of a group engaged in a common endeavor
crude   a natural or raw state; marked by uncultivated simplicity

crewel   worsted, slackly twisted yarn used for embroidery
cruel   sadistic; stern, rigorous, or grim

crewman   a member of a group engaged in a common activity
crumen   a suborbital gland in deer and antelope that secretes a waxy substance

Kruman   a member of the Kru people

crews   serves as a crew member
cruise   a journey for the sake of traveling without destination
crus   French vineyards that produce wine grapes
cruse   a small vessel for holding liquid
krewes   private social clubs that sponsor balls and parades as part of the Mardi Gras festivities
Krus   members of an indigenous Negro people of Liberia skilled as boatmen

cric   (see creek)

crick   (see creek)

crise   (see Crees)

crisis   (see Chrysis)

crispen   to become crisp or brittle
crispin   a shoemaker or cobbler

criss   a wooden stand with curved top on which crest tiles are shaped
kris   a Malay or Indonesian dagger, often with scalloped cutting edges and a serpentine blade

crissal   (see chrysal)

crisscross   (see christcross)

croc   (see crawk)

crock   (see crawk)

croes   in early Scottish law, satisfactions in an amount for killing a person
Cros   persons of mixed Indian, white, and black ancestry, especially in southeastern North Carolina and eastern South Carolina
Crows   members of a Siouan people inhabiting the region between the Platte and Yellowstone rivers
crows   large glossly black birds; makes a sound characteristic of a cock
croze   a groove near either end of a

barrel stave into which the barrel-head is inserted

crome (see **chrome**)

crooks implements having a bent or hooked form
crux a determinative point at issue; a main or central feature

crool to make a repeated low, liquid, or gurgling sound
cruel sadistic; stern, rigorous, or grim

croppy (see **crappie**)

Cros (see **croes**)

cross a structure consisting of an upright with a transverse beam; to intersect
crosse the stick used in the game of lacrosse

crotal a small spherical metal rattle on a harness
crotale one of a pair of small cymbals or rods used like castanets by dancers in antiquity
crotyl the butenyl radical

crotals reddish brown colors
crottels excrement, especially of hares

crotin a mixture of poisonous proteins found in the seeds of a small Asiatic tree
Croton a genus of herbs and shrubs, as spurges
croton a plant of the genus Croton

crottels (see **crotals**)

crotyl (see **Crotal**)

Crows and **crows** (see **croes**)

croze (see **croes**)

crucks the two curved timbers forming a principal roof support in primitive English house construction
crux a determinative point at issue; a main or central feature

crude (see **crewd**)

cruel (see **crewel** and **crool**)

cruise (see **crews**)

crumen (see **crewman**)

crus (see **crews**)

cruse (see **crews**)

crustacean belonging to the class of Arthropoda comprising lobsters, crabs, and shrimp
crustation the process of forming crust

crux (see **crooks** or **crucks**)

crystallin either of two globulins in the crystalline lens of the eye in vertebrates
crystalline composed of crystals or fragments of crystals; resembling crystal

ctene a ciliated swimming plate of a phylum (Ctenophora) of marine animals resembling jellyfish
teen relating to persons between ages 12 and 20

cubical a shape with six equal square sides
cubicle a small room or compartment

cuckoo a European bird; to repeat monotonously, as does a cuckoo
cucu either of two American shore birds, the greater or lesser yellow-legs
kuku a New Zealand fruit dove

cud the portion of food regurgitated by a ruminating animal from its first stomach to be chewed a second time
khud a ravine or precipice

cudding chewing the cud
cutting penetrating with a sharp-edged instrument

cuddle to hold close for comfort
cuttle to fold finished cloth in pleats; a cuttlefish

cue   to signal to begin action; a hint; a tapered rod used to strike a billiard ball
'que   barbeque (by shortening)
queue   a line of persons or vehicles; a taillike braid of hair

cuff   a part of a glove covering the wrist
koff   a two-masted vessel with spritsails used by the Danes and Dutch

cuir   a light yellowish brown color
queer   strange, curious, or peculiar

cuirie   a hardened leather piece for protecting the breast, worn over mail
query   to question; an inquiry

cuisse   defensive plate armor for the thighs
quis   a European woodcock

culler   (see color)

cully   a companion or mate (slang); to impose on or cheat
Kulli   relating to a prehistoric culture of southern Baluchistan

culpa   actionable negligence or fault
kalpa   a duration of time in Hinduism covering a complete cosmic cycle

cum   (see come)

cumbly   (see comely)

cumenyl   any of three univalent radicals derived from cumene by removal of one hydrogen atom
cuminyl   the univalent radical derived from the para isomer of cymene

cumulous   increasing in size or strength by successive additions
cumulus   a massy cloud form usually occuring at elevations between 2,000 and 15,000 feet; the projecting mass of granulosa cells that bears the developing ovum in a Graafian follicle

cupay   (see coupe)

cupper   a person who draws blood from the surface of the body by forming a partial vacuum over a spot; a device for making cup leathers for use in hydraulic cylinders and pumps
kupper   the saw-scaled viper, a small fierce and aggressive desert-dwelling viper found from North Africa to India

cupula   a rounded vault raised on a circular or other base and forming a roof or ceiling
cupulo   the bony apex of the cochlea

cur   a mongrel or inferior dog; a surly, low, or cowardly person
curr   to make a murmuring sound, as a dove
Ker   a malignant spirit in Greek religion and mythology

curaçao   an orange-flavored liqueur
curassow   an arboreal bird of South and Central America

curd   the part of milk coagulated by souring or being treated with certain enzymes
Kurd   one of a numerous pastoral and agricultural people of the high plateau region of Turkey, Iran, Iraq, and Syria

curdle   to cause to coagulate or congeal, as milk
curtal   a tenor or bass musical instrument of the oboe type
kirtle   a garment resembling a tunic reaching the knees and worn by men until the 16th century

curr   (see cur)

currant   (see courant)

current   (see courant)

currier   (see courier)

curser   a person who utters maledictions
cursor   part of a mathematical instrument that moves back and forth

curses utters malediction, execration, or an oath
cursus a pattern of cadence at the end of a sentence in medieval Latin prose

cursor (see **curser**)

cursus (see **curses**)

curtal (see **curdle**)

curtesy (see **courtesy**)

curve a bending without angles
kirve to undercut coal in a mine

curvet a leap of a horse in which at one point all four legs are in the air simultaneously
curvette a gemstone with a raised cameolike design carved on its hollowed surface

cutler a person that makes, deals in, or repairs cutlery
cuttler a person that folds cloth in pleats after it has been finished

cutting (see **cudding**)

cuttle (see **cuddle**)

cuttler (see **cutler**)

cwm (see **coom**)

cyan any of a group of colors of greenish-blue hue
Cyon a genus of Asiatic wild dogs, including the dhole
(s)cion a detached living portion of a plant prepared for union with a stock in grafting; a descendant
Sion the city of God (also Zion); utopia

cyanin a violet crystalline anthocyanin pigment found in rose petals and the cornflower
cyanine any of several usually unstable dyes that are important in photography

cyanite a mineral consisting of an aluminum silicate
syenite a phanerocrystalline intrusive igneous rock composed of dominant alkaline feldspar

Cyclamen a genus of widely cultivated Eurasian plants; a very dark reddish purple
cyclamin a white amorphous saponin, formerly used as a purgative
cyclamine a cyclic nitrogenous base, as pyrrole

cyclar moving in cycles or at definite periods
cycler a person that rides or travels on a bicycle, tricycle, or motorcycle

cycle to ride a bicycle, tricycle, or motorcycle
Seckel an small American reddish-brown sweet juicy pear
Sicel a member of an ancient people occupying part of Sicily
sickle an agricultural cutting implement consisting of a hook-shaped metal blade with a short handle

cycle an interval of time in which a regularly recurring succession of events is completed; a bi-, tri-, or motorcycle
psychal relating to the mind

cycler (see **cyclar**)

cygnet a young swan
signate having markings like letters; designated
signet an identifying or authenticating mark or stamp

cyke a cyclorama (by shortening)
psych to psycholanalyze; to overcome an opponent as a result of analyzing psychologically
syke in heraldry, a rounded barry-wavy of six argent and azure

cyma a projecting molding whose profile is a double curve
sima basic igneous rock whether solid or molten

cymbal a large concave brass plate producing a brilliant clashing musical tone

symbol   something representing something else

cynicism   disbelief in commonly accepted human values and in man's sincerity of motive
Sinicism   anything peculiar to the Chinese

cynocephalous   having a head or face like that of a dog
Cynocephalus   a genus of mammals including the flying lemurs
cynocephalus   a baboon

Cyon   (see **cyan**)

Cyon   a genus of Asiatic wild dogs, including the dhole
psion   in subatomic physics, a psi particle
(s)cion   a detached living portion of a plant prepared for union with a stock in grafting; a descendent

cyp   (see **cepe**)

cyp   either of two tropical American timber trees called princewood
sip   to drink a small quantity

cypress   a tree of the genus Cupressus
Cypris   a genus of small ostracod crustaceans that live in stagnant fresh water
Cyprus   an island in the Mediterranean sea

cyst   (see **cist**)

cyst(e)in   a crystalline amino acid occurring as a constituent of many proteins
Sistine   a pale blue color
sistine   relating to any of the popes named Sixtus; relating to the Sistine chapel

cyte   (see **cite**)

cytology   the branch of biology concerned with the study of cells
sitology   the science of nutrition and dietetics

czar   an emperor, king, or other person having absolute authority
Saar   a coal-producing and industrial region in southwest Germany

Czech   (see **check**)

Group I

camphene - camphine
chamois - shammy
child - Childe
chrism - chrisom
cirrous - cirrus
citrous - citrus
clairvoyance - clairvoyants
clanger - clangor
coalescence - coalescents
coiffeur - coiffure
competence - competents
compleat - complete
concomitance - concomitants
concurrence - concurrents
condescendence - condescendents
confidants - confidence
confluence - confluents
conical - conicle
constance - constants
consulter - consultor
convalescence - convalescents
correspondence - correspondents
couturier - couturiere
creamery - crémerie
crenelet - crenellate
critic - critique
culture - Kultur
custodee - custody
cysteine - cystine

Group I and II

coaxal   kō'aksəl
coaxial   kō'aksēəl

Group II

cabal   kə'bɑl
cabble   'kabl

cabinet   'kab(ə)nət
cabinette   'kabə.net

cacur   'kā.kər
caker   'kākər

caddy   'kadē
qadi   'kädē

cairn   'karn
kern   'kərn

calander   kə'landər
calendar   'kaləndər

callee   kȯ'lē
collie   'kälē

caloric   kə'lȯrik
choleric   kə'lerik

camper   'kam.pər
quimper   'kam;per

canaster   kə'nastər
canister   'kanəstər

cancellous   'kansələs
cancellus   kan'seləs

candelilla   .kandə'lēyə
kandelia   kan'dēlyə

cangue   'kaŋ
kang   'käŋ

canna   'kanə
kana   'känə

cantal   kän̄tȯl
cantle   'kantəl

canton   'kantən or 'kan.tän
quinton   kan̄tō̄n̄

careen   kə'rēn
carene   'ka.rēn

carrion   'karēən
carry-on   'karē.än

cater   'kādər
heder   'khādər

caudal   'kȯdəl
coddle   'kädəl

caught   'kȯt
kat   'kät

cauloid   'kȯ.lȯid
colloid   'kä.lȯid

cawed   'kȯd
cod   'käd

cerasin   'serɑ.sin
ceresin   'serəsən

cerate   'sir.āt
cirrate   'si.rāt
serrate   'se.rāt

ceratin   'serətən
serotine   'serə.tən

cercle   'serkl
circle   'sərkəl

cere   'sir
sir   'sər

cerin   'sirən
cerine   'sir.ən
serene   sə'rēn
serine   'si.rēn or 'si.rən

cero   'serō
serow   sə'rō

cerotene   'serō.tēn
serotine   'serō.tin

chagrin   shə'grin
shagreen   shə'grēn

chalk   'chȯk
chock   'chäk

chevret   shəv'rā
chevrette   shəv'ret

chlorogenin   'klōrə'jenən
chlorogenine   klō'räjə.nēn

chic   'shēk
chick   'chik

choree   'kōr.ē
Coree   'kōrē

chucker   'chəkər
chukar   chə'kär

cider   'sīdər
siddur   'sidər

cillosis   si'lōsis
psilosis   sī'lōsəs

citrin   'sitrən
citrine   'sitrēn

clawed   'klȯd
clod   'kläd

clysis   'klīsəs
clyssus   'klisəs

coarser   'kȯrs,ər
corsair   'kȯr,ser

coenurus   sē'nyu̇rəs
senoras   sēn'yōrəs

cola   'kōlə
colla   'kōlyə

columbin   kə'ləmbən
columbine   'käləm,bīn

comity   'kämət·ē
committee   :kə'mit|ē

commence   kə'ments
comments   'kä,ments

commissaire   'kämə,sȯr
commissar   'kämə,sär

compare   kəm'pȯr
quimper   kȯm:per

conation   kō'nāshən
connation   kä:nāshən

conceal   kən'sēl
konseal   'kän,sēl

concord   'kän,kȯrd
conquered   'käŋkərd or 'kȯŋkərd

condemn   kən'dem
contemn   kən'tem

cone   'kōn
koan   'kō,än

conger   'käŋgər
conjure   'känjər

Congo   'käŋgō
Kongo   'käŋgō

consol   'kän,sȯl
console   kən'sōl
consul   'känsəl

cooler   'külər
couleur   kü'lər

copies   'käpēz
coppice   'käpəs

cora   'kōrə
corah   'kōrɑ

corespondent   'kō,rə'spändənt
correspondent   ,kȯrə'spändənt

coria   'kōrēə
Korea   kə'rēə

cosset   'käsət
cossette   kä'set

coteau   kō'tō
coto   'kōdō

courant   'ku̇rənt
current   'kərənt

coyne   'kȯinē
Koine   'kȯi,nē

crasis   'krāsəs
krasis   'kräsəs

cribble   'kribəl
crible   krē'blȧ

cuckhold   'kək,hōld
cuckold   'kəkəld

cunette   kyü'net
cunit   'kyünət

Curete   kyə'rēt
curet(te)   kyə'ret

D

da a valuable fiber plant of the East Indies now widespread in cultivation
dah a large Burmese knife; a dash in radio or telegraphic code

dace a small European cyprinoid fish
dais a raised platform

Dacian relating to Dacia or its inhabitants, an ancient Rome province in central Europe
dation the legal act of giving or conferring

Dactylis a genus of two or three perennial chiefly Eurasian grasses
dactylus the part consisting of one or more joints of the tarsus of certain insects

dah (see **da**)

dahl the pigeon pea, a tropical woody herb
doll a small-scale figure of a human being

daim a fallow deer
dam a female parent; a barrier preventing the flow of liquid
damn to comdemn

daim a fallow deer
dame a woman of rank, station, or authority; a female (slang)

dairy a room, building, or establishment where milk is kept and butter or cheese is made
derry a meaningless refrain or chorus in old songs

dais (see **dace**)

dais a raised platform
dice to cut into small pieces; small cubes, each face of which is marked with one to six spots

dak to transport by relays of persons and horses
dhak an East Indian tree

doc a doctor (by shortening)
dock a place for loading and unloading materials; the solid part of an animal's tail; to cut short

dalli a tropical American tree whose wood is used for staves and its seed yields a wax
dally to waste time; to twist a rope around a saddle horn in roping an animal

dalli a tropical American tree whose wood is used for staves and its seed yields a wax
dally to twist a rope around a saddle horn in roping an animal
dolly a small wheeled platform used to move freight, a child's toy

dally (see **dalli**)

dam (see **daim**)

dame (see **daim**)

dammar a resin derived from various evergreen trees
damner a person who condemns

damn (see **daim**)

damner (see **dammar**)

Dan a people of the border region between the Ivory Coast and Liberia
dan the expert level in the Oriental arts of self-defense and games
dawn to begin to grow light; to become apparent
don to put on clothing; a college or university teacher

Dane a native of Denmark
deign condescend to give or offer

daos large Philippine trees; large heavy knives used by the Burmese
dauws Burchell's zebras
dhows Arabian lateen-rigged boats
dowse to plunge into water or immerse; to use a divining rod

taos unitary first principles from which all existence and change spring

dartars a mange affecting the head of sheep and caused by a mite
darters any of numerous small American freshwater fishes closely related to the perches

dasi a female Hindu slave, servant, or of low caste
dassi a hydrax

dation (see **Dacian**)

dauber a worker who seals with clay the doors of kilns in which brick and tile are burned; a plasterer
dobber a dabchick or other small grebe

daughter a female offspring
dodder to tremble or shake; a parasitic seed plant
dotter a person who makes dots or locates optical and focal centers, axes, and terminal points in ground lenses

dauws (see **daos**)

dawn (see **Dan**)

days periods of 24 hours; times between sunrise and sunset
daze to stupefy or make numb
deys ruling officials of the Ottoman Empire in northern Africa

deader more deprived of life
debtor a person indebted or obligated to another

deal to distribute, as cards to a player; a business transaction
diel involving a 24-hour period that usually includes a day and the adjoining night

deanery the office, position, or residence of a dean
denary based on or proceeding by tens

dear regarded fondly; expensive

deer a ruminant animal of the family Cervidae

deasil right-handwise or clockwise
decile any one of nine numbers in a series that divides a distribution of individuals in the series into ten groups of equal frequency
decyl any of numerous radicals derived from the decans by removing one hydrogen atom
desyl a univalent radical derived from desoxybenzoin

deasil right-handwise or clockwise
diesel a vehicle driven by a diesel engine

debtor (see **deader**)

decade a period of ten years
decayed underwent decomposition; declined in strength or vigor

decal decalomania (by shortening), the process of transferring designs from specially prepared paper to china, glass, or marble and permanently affixing them thereto
deckle the detachable wooden frame around the outer edges of a paper maker's hand mold

decan any of the three divisions of ten degrees in each sign of the zodiac
Deccan a breed of coarse-wooled sheep of southern India
dekan one of 36 equal subdivisions of the equatorial belt of the celestial sphere

decayed (see **decade**)

Deccan (see **decan**)

decile (see **deasil**)

deckle (see **decal**)

decks ship platforms extending within the hull from side to side and stem to stern
dex the sulfate of dextroamphetamine

decyl (see **deasil**)

decyl any of numerous radicals derived from the decans by removing one hydrogen atom
diesel a vehicle driven by a diesel engine

deelie a thing whose name is unknown or forgotten; a thingumbob
dele to delete in printing and editing

deem to form an opinion; to believe
deme a local population of closely related organisms

deer (see **dear**)

deference a yielding of judgment or preference out of respect for another
deferents imaginary circles surrounding the earth in whose periphery either one or more celestial bodies or the centers of their epicycle are supposed to move

deign (see **Dane**)

dekan (see **decan**)

del in mathematics, an operator upon a function of three variables
dell a small secluded natural valley

dele (see **deelie**)

Delhi a city in India
deli ready-to-eat food products; a delicatessen (by shortening)

dell (see **del**)

Delphin related to the Delphin classics
delphine related to dolphins

delphinin a violet crystalline anthocyanin pigment
delphinine a poisonous crystalline alkaloid

deluded deceived or tricked
diluted reduced in strength or quality; watered down

demarch a ruler of a commune in modern Greece
demark to determine the boundary of

deme (see **deem**)

demean to lower in status or reputation
demesne land attached to a mansion; a range of interest or activity

demesne land attached to a mansion; a range of interest or activity
domain the possessions of a sovereign, feudal lord, nation, or commonwealth

demoded no longer fashionable
demoted reduced to a lower grade or rank

denary (see **deanery**)

dense crowded very close together; mentally dull
dents depressions made by a blow or pressure

dental relating to teeth
dentil one of a series of small rectangular blocks forming a molding below the cornice

dents (see **dense**)

depravation corruption; perversion
deprivation taking something away from

derma the sensitive vascula inner mesodermic layer of skin
dharma in Hinduism, social custom regarded as one's duty; the body of cosmic principles by which all things exist

derry (see **dairy**)

descension in astrology, the part of the zodiac in which a planet's influence is thought to be least
dissension disagreement; a breach of friendship

descent moving from a higher to a lower level or state
dissent differ in opinion

desert a reward or punishment deserved or earned

dessert a course served at the close of a meal

desman an aquatic insectivorous mammal of Russia resembling a mole
desmine a mineral of the zeolite family consisting of a hydrous silicate of aluminum, calcium, and sodium

dessert (see **desert**)

desyl (see **deasil**)

deter to inhibit or dissuade
detur a specially bound book awarded to a student for meritorious work

deuce the face of a die or playing card bearing two spots or pips; a tie score in tennis
douce in music, soft or smooth

deviser a person who plans or designs
devisor a person who bequeaths property in a will
divisor a number by which the dividend is divided

dew moisture condensed on the surface of a cool body
do to perform
doux champagne containing at least seven percent sugar by volume
due owing or in debt

Dewar a glass or metal container with at least two walls with the space between them evacuated to prevent heat transfer
dewer a textile machine operator who brushes or sprays water on cloth during the finishing process
doer a performer or actor
dour stern, severe, harsh, or forbidding
dur any of several major musical keys

dewed dampened as if with dew
dude an overfastidious person in dress and manner; a tenderfoot or novice

dewer (see **Dewar**)

dex (see **decks**)

deys (see **days**)

dhai a wet nurse or midwife in India
die to expire or perish; a small cube, each face of which is marked with from one to six spots
dye coloring matter

dhak (see **dak**)

dhan property or wealth, particularly the village cattle, in India
done completed a task
dun dark or gloomy; to ask for repeatedly, as an overdue payment

dharma (see **derma**)

dhauri an East Indian red-flowered shrub; an East Indian tree used for timber, tanning, and a source of gum
dory a flat-bottomed boat with high flaring sides

dhikr the ritual formula of a Sufi (an ascetic Muslim) brotherhood recited devotionally in praise of Allah
dicker to haggle or bargain; the number ten, especially of hides or skins

dhobi a member of a low caste of India employed as launderers
dobe a brick or building material of sun-dried earth and straw

dhole a fierce wild dog of India
dol a unit for measuring pain intensity
dole to distribute material, such as food, clothing, or money to the needy

dhoti a long loincloth worn by Hindu men
doty timber infected by incipient or partial decay often with discoloration
dudie a diminutive fop, dandy, or tenderfoot

dhows (see **daos**)

dhuti a long loincloth worn by Hindu men

duty obligator tasks, conduct, service, or functions enjoined by order or custom

dial the graduated face of a timepiece; a disk or knob for operating a machine; to operate a machine by means of a dial

diel involving a 24-hour period that usually includes a day and the adjoining night

diane a triaene sponge with one ray reduced or absent

diene a chemical compound containing two double bonds

diaphane the art of imitating stained glass with translucent paper

diaphony dissonance; part writing or singing in two, three, or four parts

diarist a person who keeps a daily record of events

direst most ominous or sinister

dicast a member of the highest court of law of ancient Athens who performed the functions of both jury and judge

die-cast to make by forcing molten metal into a die

dice (see **dais**)

Diceras a genus of Jurassic mollusks comprising clams, oysters, and mussels

dicerous having two tentacles or antennae

dicker (see **dhikr**)

die (see **dhai**)

die-cast (see **dicast**)

dieing cutting or shaping with a die

dyeing imparting a new and often permanent color to

dying expiring or perishing

diel (see **deal** or **dial**)

diemaker a worker who makes cutting and shaping dies

dyemaker a worker who mixes and brews coloring matter

diene (see **diane**)

diesel (see **deasil** or **decyl**)

diker a person who makes or works on dikes

duiker any of several small African antelopes having short straight horns

dyker a two-branched candlestick used in the Eastern Church

diluted (see **deluded**)

dine to eat a meal

dyne a unit of force in the cgs system

dinghy a small boat propelled by oars, sails, or a motor

dink(e)y small or insignificant; a small locomotive

dipterous having two wings or winglike appendages

Dipterus a genus of Devonian dipnoan fishes of America and Scotland having ganoid scales

dire ominous or sinister

dyer a person who colors articles

direst (see **diarist**)

disburse to distribute; to expend from a fund

disperse to send or drive into different places

discoursive argumentative or expository

discursive passing from one topic to another; reasoning that proceeds from particulars to generalizations

discreet tactful or prudent

discrete constituting a separate entity

discussed investigated a question by reasoning or argument

disgust a marked aversion or repugnance

discursive (see **discoursive**)

disgust (see **discussed**)

dislimb to dismember by cutting off limbs or parts
dislimn to dim or reduce the light

disperse (see **disburse**)

dissension (see **descension**)

dissent (see **descent**)

divertisement a diversion, amusement, or recreation
divertissement an instrumental musical composition having from four to ten movements and written as a chamber work

divisor (see **devisor**)

do (see **dew**)

dobber (see **dauber**)

dobe (see **dhobi**)

doc (see **dak**)

docile tractable
dossal an ornamental cloth hung behind and above the altar
dossil lint or a small roll of pledget for keeping a wound or sore open

dock (see **dak**)

dodder (see **daughter**)

doddle coarse bran obtained from wheat; a tree cut back to the trunk to promote growth of a dense head of foliage
dottle unburnt and partially burnt tobacco caked in a pipe's bowl; to keep apart by thimbles, as in glost firing

dodo a large heavy flightless extinct bird
Doto a genus of nudibranch mollusks with tuberculated cerata

doer (see **Dewar**)

does adult females of various mammals, as deer and rabbits
dos first tones of the diatonic scale
doughs mixtures of flour and other ingredients sufficiently stiff to knead and roll
doze to sleep lightly or intermittently

dol (see **dhole**)

dole (see **dhole**)

doler a person who gives food, money, or clothing to the needy
dolor mental suffering or anguish

doll (see **dahl**)

dolly (see **dalli**)

dolman a woman's wide-sleeved coat or jacket
dolmen a prehistoric monument consisting of upright stones supporting a horizontal base

dolor (see **doler**)

Dom a member of a Hindu cast of untouchables
dom a doom palm, a large African fan palm important as a soil stabilizer in desert regions
dome a vaulted circular roof or ceiling

domain (see **demesne**)

dome (see **Dom**)

domini owners or principals as distinguished from either users or agents
dominie a pastor of the Reformed Dutch Church

don (see **Dan**)

donar a girl, especially a steady girlfriend or fiancée (slang)
donor a person who gives, presents, or donates

done (see **dhan**)

donjon the strongest and most secure part of a medieval castle, often used as a place of residence
dungeon a close dark prison or vault commonly underground

donné a person dedicated to missionary work
donnée the main assumption(s) on which a work of literature or drama is based

donor (see **donar**)

dook an incline at a mine for hauling
douc a variegated colored monkey of China
duke a nobleman

dooley an outdoor toilet (slang); a sweet potato (slang)
dooly a palanquin, a litter borne on the shoulders of people
duly properly, regularly, or sufficiently

doom judgment or decision of condemnation
doum a doom palm

doon a large tree of Sri Lanka
dune a hill or ridge of sand

door an opening in a room or building
dor an insect that flies with a buzzing noise
dorr a glacial trough crossing a ridge

doorman a person that tends the door of a hotel, apartment house, or other building
dormin abscisic acid, a growth-inhibiting plant hormone

dopey feeling and acting in a dazed state; mentally dull
dopie a person who takes drugs (slang)

dor (see **door**)

dormin (see **doorman**)

dorr (see **door**)

dory (see **dhauri**)

dos (see **does**)

dos property settled by the husband on his spouse at the time of marriage
dose a measured portion of additive, medicine, or labor

dossal (see **docile**)

dossil (see **docile**)

Doto (see **dodo**)

dotter (see **daughter**)

dottle (see **doddle**)

doty (see **dhoti**)

douar an Arabian village consisting typically of a group of tents encircling an open space
duar a tract of land in India leading to a mountain pass

douc (see **dook**)

douce (see **deuce**)

doughs (see **does**)

doughty marked by fearless resoluteness and stoutness in a struggle; able or strong
dowdy lacking neatness, charm, or smartness in apparel or appearance

doum (see **doom**)

dour (see **Dewar**)

dour stern, severe, harsh, or forbidding
dower a gift of property by a husband to or for his bride

doux (see **dew**)

dowdy (see **doughty**)

dower (see **dour**)

downie a tranquilizer or barbituate (slang)
downy soft, quiet, or soothing

dowse (see **daos**)

doze (see **does**)

drias a large European herb the root of which is emetic and cathartic; a deadly carrot
Dryas a small genus of arctic and alpine tufted plants
dryas any plant of the genus Dryas

drogh to transport by means of a small drogher, a small coasting vessel used in the West Indies
drogue a sea anchor; a towed aerodynamic drag device

droop to have a slouched or bent posture; to decline in spirit or courage
drupe a one-seeded indehiscent fruit, as a cherry or peach

dropsie a marble game
dropsy an abnormal accumulation of serous fluid in connective tissue; lethargy or laziness

Dryas and **dryas** (see **drias**)

dual consisting of two parts
duel a combat between two persons

dualist an adherent or advocate of dualism
duelist a person who engages in duels

duar (see **douar**)

duchy the territory or dominions of a duke or duchess
Dutchy characteristically Dutch

ducked lowered the head quickly; avoided
duct a pipe, tube, or channel

ducks lowers the head quickly; avoids; swimming birds
ducts pipes, tubes, or channels
dux a theme of a fugue or canon

duct (see **ducked**)

ducts (see **ducks**)

dude (see **dewed**)

dud(h)een a short tobacco pipe made of clay
dudine a female dude or tenderfoot; an ultrafashionable woman

dudie (see **dhoti**)

dudine (see **dud[h]leen**)

due (see **dew**)

duel (see **dual**)

duelist (see **dualist**)

duiker (see **diker**)

duke (see **dook**)

duly (see **dooley**)

dun (see **dhan**)

dunce a dull-witted or stupid person
dunts in ceramics, cracks made while firing, or afterward by too rapid a temperature change

dune (see **doon**)

dungeon (see **donjon**)

dunts (see **dunce**)

dur (see **Dewar**)

dural relating to the dura mater
duryl a univalent radical derived from durene

dustee the offspring of a white and a fustee; a person who is of 1/32 negro ancestry
dusty marked by or covered with fine dry pulverized particles of earth or other matter

Dutchy (see **duchy**)

duty (see **dhuti**)

dux (see **ducks**)

dye (see **dhai**)

dyeing (see **dieing**)

dyemaker (see **diemaker**)

dyer (see **dire**)

dying (see **dieing**)

dyker (see **diker**)

Dynastes a genus of large chiefly tropical lamellicorn beetles, including the rhinocerous beetle

dynasties groups or classes of individuals having power in some sphere of activity and able to select their successors

dyne (see **dine**)

Group I

dactylous - dactylus
decandence - decadents
deformity - difformity
dependence - dependents
descendance - descendants
despondence - despondents
deterrence - deterrents
devest - divest
deviance - deviants
dextran - dextrin(e)
diestrous - diestrus
dime - disme
dipterocarpous - Dipterocarpus
discous - discus
dissentience - dissentients
dissidence - dissidents
dominance - dominants

Group I and II

distale   dǝ'stɑlē
distally   'distǝlē

Group II

daiquiri   'dīkǝrē
dichoree   dīkǝ'rē

dawdle   'dôdᵊl
doddle   'dädᵊl

deacon   'dēkǝn
decan   'dekǝn

debauch   dǝ'bäch
debouch   dǝ'boùch

decease   dǝ'sēs
disease   dǝ'z|ēz

decision   dǝ'sizhǝn

decission dǝ'sishǝn

decouple   'de,kǝpǝl
decuple   'dekǝpǝl

decry   dǝ'krī
descry   dǝ'skrī

defuse   'dēfyüz
diffuse   dǝ'fyüz

delead   de'led
deled   'de,lēd

delusion   dǝ'lüzhǝn
dilution   dǝ'lüshǝn

dental   'dentᵊl
dentelle   den'tel

depose   dē'pōz
depots   'dē,pōz

dessert   dǝ'zǝrt
dissert   dǝ'sǝrt

d(h)houi   'dōnē
donee   dō'nē

diaper   'dīpǝr
diapir   'dīǝ,pir

diareal   'dī,ɑrēǝl
diarrheal 'dīǝ,rēǝl

dictate   'dik,tāt
diktat   dik'tät

diplomat   'diplǝ,mɑt
diplomate 'diplǝ,mōt

discus   'diskǝs
discuss   dǝ'skǝs

dissimilation   dǝ'simǝ,lɑshǝn
dissimulation   dǝ'simyǝ,lɑshǝn

distant   'distǝnt
distent   dǝ'stent

divers   'dīvǝrs
diverse   'dī,vǝrs

dobby   'däbē
doby   'dōbē

doublet   'dǝblǝt
doublette ,dǝ'blet

draftee   drɑf'tē
drafty   'drɑftē

dramas   'drɑmǝz
dromos   'drɑmǝs

—————————————————— E ——————————————————

earn   to receive an equitable return
for work done or service rendered
ern(e)   a white-tailed sea eagle
urn   a footed vase or vessel for
holding liquids, ashes, and ballots

ease   (see aes)

eaten   taken in through the mouth as
food
Eton   resembling clothing or appearance of boys at Eton College

eau   a watery solution, as of perfume
oe   a violent whirlwind off the Faroe
islands
oh   an expression for various emotions; zero
owe   to be indebted

eave   a roof's lower border that over-
hangs a wall
eve   evening (by shortening)

eboe   a Central American tree the
seeds of which yield eboe oil
Ibo   a group of Negro tribes on the
lower Niger river

echappé   a ballet movement in which
the dancer jumps and lands on the
toes or balls of the feet
échappée   a melodic ornamental
musical tone

ectocarpous   having reproductive
organs developed from the ectoderm
Ectocarpus   the type genus of Ecoto-
carpacae containing numerous
more or less branched filamentous
brown algae

eddo   the edible root or stem of the
taro root
Edo   a Negro tribe in southern Nigeria

edition   (see addition)

Edo   (see eddo)

educe   (see adduce)

eek   an expression of surprise or
fright
eke   to supplement; to live from day
to day with difficulty

e'er   (see air)

eerie   (see aerie)

effect   (see affect)

effective   (see affective)

effusion   (see affusion)

ego   the self; self-esteem
Igo   a Japanese game for two persons

eh   (see a)

eight   (see ait)

Eire   (see aerie and Ara)

Eire   of or from the republic of Ireland
era   a period set off or typified by
some prominent figure or characteristic

Eire   of or from the republic of Ireland
eyra   a solid-colored reddish wildcat
regarded by some as a color phase
of the jaguarundi and by others as
a separate species

eke   (see eek)

el   an elevated railway
ell   an extension at a right angle to a
building

Elaps   a genus of venomous snakes
elapse   to slip or glide away

elapse   to slip or glide away
illapse   flowing into, as a river or a
large number of individuals

elation   high spirits
illation   inference

elegit a judicial writ of execution whereby a defendent's goods and lands are delivered to the plaintiff
illegit contrary to or violating a law or regulation (slang)

elicit to draw or bring out
illicit unlawful

elision (see **allision**)

ell (see **el**)

elude (see **allude**)

eluded (see **alluded**)

eluted (see **alluded**)

elusion (see **allusion**)

Elysian (see **allision**)

em (see **am**)

emanant emerging from a source, used especially of mental acts
eminent noteworthy or conspicuous

emend (see **amend**)

emerge to rise from an enveloping fluid; to come out into view
immerge to plunge into

emersed rising above a surface of surrounding leaves, as a water lily
immersed completely imbedded in or sunk below the surface

eminent (see **emanant**)

emission something sent forth; discharged; released
immission placing a small piece of the host into consecrated wine
omission leaving out or failing to include

emit to send out; to express
omit to leave out

emotion (see **amotion**)

emplastic sticky, gluey, or adhesive
implastic not plastic or readily molded

emu a large Australian ratite bird

imu an Hawaiian cooking pit

en (see **an**)

encyst to form or become enclosed in a cyst or capsule
insist to hold firmly to something

end (see **and**)

ends (see **ands**)

endue to put on; to provide
undo to cancel; to unfasten; to destroy someone's reputation
undue inappropriate or improper

enfold to surround with a covering; to embrace
infold to fold inward or toward one another

engrain to color in imitation of a wood's grain
ingrain an innate quality or character

enrapt absorbed in ecstatic contemplation
enwrapped enfolded with material

ens (see **ands**)

enterocele a hernia containing a portion of the intestines
enterocoele a body cavity that originates by outgrowth from the archenteron

entrada an expedition or journey into unexplored territory
intrada a musical introduction or prelude, especially in 16th and 17th century music

enumerable countable even though infinite
innumerable characterized by a vast or countless number

enunciate (see **annunciate**)

envoi a concluding or parting remark
envoy a messenger, agent, or representative of a sovereign government

enwrapped (see **enrapt**)

ephemeris a tabular statement of the assigned places of a celestial body for regular intervals
ephemerous of interest or value for only a short time; transient

epic heroic; a long narrative poem
epoch a memorable event or date; a new beginning

equation (see **aquation**)

era (see **Eire**)

ere (see **air**)

eria (see **area**)

Erica a large genus of low many-branched evergreen shrubs
erika a reddish-brown dye used on cotton, wool, and silk

erics payments imposed on a slayer and his/her kin for homicide in medieval Irish law
Eryx a genus comprising the typical sand snakes

erika (see **Erica**)

ern(e) (see **earn**)

erose (see **aerose**)

erosive (see **arrosive**)

err (see **air**)

errant (see **arrant**)

erred made a mistake; deviated from a standard
urd a spreading hairy annual bean widely cultivated in warm regions

ers a vetch grown in Mediterranean and Asiatic countries
erse characteristic of Gaelic-speaking people of Scotland

erupt to force out or release suddenly and often violently
irrupt to enter forcibly or suddenly; to intrude

erythrin a mineral consisting of a hydrous cobalt arsenate

erythrine a colorless crystalline substance extracted from certain lichens and yielding certain red compounds

Eryx (see **erics**)

es a unit of quantity of electricity in an electrostatic system
ess resembling the shape of the letter S

escaladed climbed up or over
escalated carried, as if on a moving staircase

eschar a scar
esker a long narrow ridge of sand or debris deposited near a glacier

ess (see **es**)

essay (see **assay**)

estray (see **astray**)

Eton (see **eaten**)

euonymous suitably named
Euonymus a genus of evergreen shrubs, small trees, or vines of north temperate regions
euonymus any plant of the genus Euonymus

Eurya a genus of Asiatic evergreen trees and shrubs with foliage resembling holly
urea a highly soluble crystalline nitrogenous compound formed in nature by the decomposition of protein
Uria a genus of guillemots comprising the murres

eve (see **eave**)

evert (see **avert**)

evulsion (see **avulsion**)

ewe a female sheep, goat, or smaller antelope
yew a shrub or tree with rich evergreen foliage
you the second person pronoun; the one(s) being addressed
yu precious jade

ewer a vase-shaped pitcher with handle and spout
your of or belonging to you
you're the contraction of you are

ewes female sheep, goats, or smaller antelopes
use to put into action or service
yews shrubs or trees with rich ever-green foliage
youse the plural of you (substan-dard)

ex formerly
x to cancel or obliterate; a ten-dollar bill (slang)

exceed (see **accede**)

except (see **accept**)

excess (see **access**)

excided cut out or excised
excited aroused or increased the ac-tivity of

exciter a dynamo or battery that supplies the electric current used to produce a magnetic field in another dynamo or motor
excitor an afferent nerve arousing increased action of the part that it supplies

exercise to discharge an official function; something practiced to develop power or skill
exorcise to drive out (an evil spirit) by adjuration

exitus an export duty; the fatal ter-mination of a disease; an excretory outlet
exodus a mass departure; the part of a Greek drama following the last song of the chorus

exorcise (see **exercise**)

exotic not native to the place where found; strange; romantic or glamo-rous
ixodic relating to or caused by ticks of the genus Ixodes

expatriate a person who lives in a foreign country
ex-patriot a person who formerly loved his/her country and defended and promoted its interests

expiree a (Australian) convict whose time of penal servitude has expired
expiry exhalation of breath; death

exponence correlation between an abstract linguistic category and its specific elements
exponents persons who champion or advocate; expounders or explainers

eye (see **ai**)

eyed having eyes; watched carefully
I'd the contraction of I had or I would
ide a European freshwater cyprinid foodfish

eyelet a small usually round hole
islet a small island

eyer a person who watches carefully
ire anger or wrath

eyra (see **Eire**)

eyre (see **air**)

Group I

efference - efferents
effluence - effluents
ellipses - ellipsis
emergence - emergents
enhydros - enhydrous
ensure - insure
entrance - entrants
epigenous - epigynous
epigonos - Epigonus
epigram - epigramme
equipollence - equipollents
equivalence - equivalents
escallop - scallop
estrous - estrus
euryalae - Euryale

exigence - exigents
existence - existents
exodus - exodusts
expectance - expectants
expedience - expedients
experience - experients
eyetie - itie

Group I and II

escallop	ə̇'skäləp
scallop	'skäləp
especial	ə̇'speshəl
special	'speshəl
espy	ə̇'spī
spy	'spī

Group II

earing	'iriŋ
erring	eriŋ
effete	e'fēt
Ephete	'e,fēt
efficient	ə̇'fishənt
officiant	ə'fishēənt
eidolism	'idō,lizəm
idolism	'īd^{ə}l,izəm
elegance	'elēgəns
elegants	ōlōgä^{n}z
elopes	ə̇'lōps
elops	'e,läps

elusion	ə̇'lüzhən
elution	˙ə'lüshən
eluviate	ē'lüvē,āt
illuviate	i'lüvē,āt
embarras	:ä^{n}bə:rä
embarrass	em'barəs
empres	'ēmprəs
impress	ə̇m'pres
empyreal	'em,pirēəl
imperial	'im,pirēəl
enervate	ə̇'nərvȧt
innervate	i'nər,vāt
ensoul	ə̇n'sōl
insole	'in,sōl
enthrone	in'thrōn
inthrown	'in,thrōn
Equidae	'ekwə,dē
equity	'ekwədē
equites	'ekwə,tēz
equities	'ekwətēz
errands	'erəndz
errants	'erəntz
excite	ek'sīt
exite	'ek,sīt
excyst	ek'sist
exist	eg'zist
exert	eg'zərt
exsert	ek'sərt
expos	'ekspōz
expose	ik'spōz or ek'spōz
extorsion	eks'tȯrshən
extortion	ek'stȯrshən

F

---

facet   a plane surface produced on a precious stone

fascet   a carrying tool used in glass manufacturing

facial concerned with improving the appearance of the human face
fascial relating to a flat horizontal member of an order or building having the form of a flat band or broad fillet

facks tells the truth (slang)
facts assertions purporting to have objective reality
fax facsimile (by shortening)

faddish resembling an object or style followed widely but briefly
fattish somewhat overweight or obese

faddy a person's father (slang)
fatty corpulant, greasy, or sticky

fade to lose freshness, vigor, color, or health
fayed fitted closely together

faded lost freshness, vigor, color, or health
fated determined or controlled by fate or destiny
feted entertained or celebrated

fagan a stick for poking holes in the side of a charcoal pit
Fagin an adult who instructs others in crime

faille a semilustrous closely woven fabric with good draping qualities
file a hardened steel smoothing tool; to arrange in a particular order
phial a small container for liquids

fain gladly, willingly, or happily
fane a temple
feign to pretend or sham; to assert as if true

faint to swoon; barely perceptible; lacking courage or spirit
feint a false or deceptive act; a trick

fair attractive in appearance; pleasing to hear; just or equitable; not stormy or foul
fare a transportation charge; the range of food or stock

phare a lighthouse or beacon to guide seamen

fairer in a more equitable, attractive, or agreeable manner
farer a traveller

fairy a tiny mischievous creature of folklore
ferry to convey by ship or airplane over water or to a shipping point

fait a legal deed
fate foreordination, destiny, or lot
fete a festive celebration or entertainment

faker a fraud, swindler, or pretender
fakir an itinerant wonder-worker of other religions; a pale orange yellow color

false untrue or disloyal
faults defects or imperfections; fractures in the earth's crust

fane (see **fain**)

fanner a person who circulates air by fanning
phanar Greek officials of Turkey, as a class

farce a light satirical or humorous dramatic composition; a ridiculous show
farse an interpolation inserted in a liturgical formula

farci a stuffed roast or fowl dish
farcy a chronic ultimately fatal disease of cattle that is caused by an actinomycete
Farsi a native of Fars, Iran

fare (see **fair**)

farer (see **fairer**)

faro a banking game
farrow a litter of pigs
pharaoh a ruler of ancient Egypt

farrier a person in charge of horses and their shoeing
ferrier a person who operates a ferry

farrow   (see **faro**)

farse   (see **farce**)

Farsi   (see **farci**)

fascet   (see **facet**)

fascial   (see **facial**)

fate   (see **fait**)

fated   (see **faded**)

father   a male parent
fother   to cover with oakum to temporarily stop a leak in a ship's hull

fattish   (see **faddish**)

fatty   (see **faddy**)

faults   (see **false**)

faun   a half man half goat rural deity
fawn   a young deer; to court favor by cringing or exuding an overly flattering manner
Fon   a Negro people of Benin in West Africa
phon   a unit of loudness

faux   artificial, imitation, or fake
foe   enemy or adversary

fawned   to give birth to a young deer
fond   loving or affectionate

fax   (see **facks**)

fay   to fit closely together
fey   behaving in an excited irresponsible manner; mad; a visionary

fayed   (see **fade**)

fays   fits closely together; white persons (slang)
faze   to disturb the composure of or disconcert
phase   a stage or interval in development or a cycle

feared   was afraid or frightened of
fyrd   the national militia in England prior to the Norman Conquest

feast   an elaborate meal
feest   untidy, unkempt, or filthy; disgusted with

feat   a specialized act or deed
feet   an arthropod's limbs; units of measure each equal to twelve inches

feeder   a person who gives or provides food; a source of supply
fetor   stench or fetidness

fees   admission charges; compensation for professional services
feeze   to disturb, worry, or beat
phis   the 21st letter (plural) of the Greek alphabet

feest   (see **feast**)

feet   (see **feat**)

feeze   (see **fees**)

feign   (see **fain**)

feint   (see **faint**)

fella   a fellow (informal)
fellah   a peasant or agricultural laborer in several Arabic-speaking countries

fellen   a sprawling Old World poisonous plant, otherwise called bittersweet
felon   a person who has committed a felony; a severe inflammation on a finger or toe

felloe   the rim of a wheel supported by spokes
fellow   a companion, comrade, or associate

felon   (see **fellen**)

felt   cloth or wool and fur fibers; sensed or perceived a stimulus by tactile sensation
veldt   an African grassland

femerell   a small open structure on a roof for ventilation
femoral   relating to or located near the femur or thigh

fence   a barrier to prevent escape or intrusion
fents   cloth remnants

fends protects, repels, or defends
fens low peaty lands covered wholly or partly with water
foehns warm dry winds blowing down a mountain side

fennel a perennial European herb imperfectly naturalized in North America and cultivated for the aromatic flavor of its seeds
phenyl a univalent radical derived from benzene by removal of one hydrogen atom

fens (see **fends**)

fents (see **fence**)

feoff to put in possession of a leasehold
fief a feudal estate; something over which one has rights or exercises control

feral existing in a state of nature or untamed; suggestive of a beast of prey
ferrule a band of metal around the end of an object to strengthen it or prevent splitting
ferule an instrument used to punish students

fern a vascular plant constituting the class Filicineae
foehn a warm dry wind blowing down a mountain side

ferrier (see **farrier**)

ferrule (see **feral**)

ferry (see **fairy**)

ferule (see **feral**)

fess confess (shortened)
fesse a buttock

fessed confessed (shortening)
fest an informal meeting or gathering

fete (see **fait**)

feted (see **faded**)

fetor (see **feeder**)

feudal founded upon or involving the relationship of lord and vassal; constituting a ruling class
futile serving no useful purpose, fruitless

few not many
phew an expression of discomfort or distaste

fey (see **fay**)

fibrin a white insoluble fibrous protein formed from fibrogen by the action of thrombin, especially in the clotting of blood
fibrine consisting of fibers

fiche a sheet of microfilm usually containing several rows of images (microfiche, by shortening)
fish any of numerous cold-blooded strictly aquatic water-breathing craniate vertebrates

fie an expression of disgust or dislike
phi the 21st letter of the Greek alphabet

fief (see **feoff**)

filander a kangaroo native to the Aru islands
philander any of several medium-sized wooly opossums of Central and South America; to make love frivolously

filar possessing threads across the field of view
filer a file clerk; a worker who smooths or shapes with a file
phylar relating to a phylum, a major taxonomic unit comprising organisms sharing a fundamental pattern of organization

file (see **faille**)

filé powdered young sassafras leaves
filet a lace with geometric designs; a piece of boneless fish or meat

filer (see **filar**)

filet (see **filé**)

filiform having the shape of a thread or filament
phylliform having the shape of a leaf

fillipeens nuts with two kernels each; gifts given as a forfeit
Philippines an archipelago of 7,083 islands in the Pacific Ocean southeast of China

filly a young female horse or woman
Philly relating to Philadelphia, Pennsylvania

filter a porous article to separate liquid or gas from matter in suspension
philter a potion credited with magical power

filum a filament or threadlike structure
phylum a major taxonomic unit comprising organisms sharing a fundamental pattern of organization and presumably a common descent

fin a membranous appendage resembling a wing or paddle in fish and certain aquatic mammals
Finn a native or inhabitant of Finland

finally eventually; conclusively; decisively
finely precisely; admirably; in an impressive or elegant manner

find to come upon or locate
fined punished by assessment of a monetary penalty

finds comes upon by searching or effort
fines finely crushed or powdered material; monetary penalties imposed as punishment

fined (see **find**)

finely (see **finally**)

fines (see **finds**)

finick to become excessively dainty or refined in speech or manner
Finnic relating to the Finns

finish to bring to an end or terminate
Finnish relating to Finland or its inhabitants

Finn (see **fin**)

Finnic (see **finick**)

finnie to lay claim to; to latch on to
finny having or characterized by membraneous appendanges resembling a paddle in fish

Finnish (see **finish**)

finny (see **finnie**)

fireboat a boat equipped for fighting fire
firebote a tenant's right to take from land occupied by the tenant sufficient wood to maintain fires in the tenant's house

firry made of or abounding in any of several evergreen trees
furry consisting of or resembling the fine soft thick hairy covering of mammals

firs evergreen trees
furs fine soft thick hairy coverings of mammals; pieces of a dressed animal's pelt
furze a spiny evergreen shrub common throughout Europe

fish (see **fiche**)

fisher a person or animal that fishes; a large dark brown somewhat vulpine arboreal carnivorous mammal
fissure a narrow crack or cleft

fishery a fishing establishment
fissury abounding in fissures or cleavages

fissure (see **fisher**)

fissury (see **fishery**)

fizz to effervesce; a hissing sound
phiz the face (by shortening physiognomy)

Fjäll a Swedish breed of small white polled dairy cattle
fjeld a barren plateau of the Scandanavian plateau

flacks professional publicity workers or press agents (slang); recurrent sounds of striking, as of loose tire chains on pavement
flax a plant whose long silky bast fibers are the source of linen

flagellate to whip, scourge, or flog; having or bearing various elongated filiform appendages of animals
flageolet a small flute resembling a treble recorder

flair a discriminating sense; instinctive discernment
flare to flame up brightly

flask a somewhat narrow-necked container
flasque an heraldic bearing narrower than a flanch

flavan an aromatic heterocycle compound from which all flavonoids are derived
flavin a yellow dye extracted from the bark of the quercitron tree
flavine a yellow crystalline base obtained artificially

flax (see **flacks**)

flea a wingless bloodsucking insect
flee to run from

flèche a slender spire above the intersection of a church's nave and transcept
flesh parts of an animal body composed chiefly of skeletal muscle, fat, and connective tissue

flecks spots, blemishes, or flakes
flex to bend repeatedly

flee (see **flea**)

Flem a member of the Germanic people inhabiting northern Belgium
phlegm viscid mucus secreted in abnormal quantity in respiratory passages

flesh (see **flèche**)

fleuret a light fencing sword
fleurette a small decorative floral motif

fleury having the ends of the arms of a cross broadening out into the heads of fleurs-de-lis; in heraldry, having the heads of fleurs-de-lis projecting out from the edge
flurry a spasmodic agitation or nervous commotion

flew moved through the air
flu influenza (by shortening), an ill-defined transitory disease
flue an enclosed passageway for directing a gas or air current

flews pendulous lateral parts on a dog's upper lip
flues enclosed passageways for directing a gas or air current

flex (see **flecks**)

flicks light sharp strokes, often with something flexible; quick sudden movements; movies (slang)
flics police officers, especially in Paris (slang)
flix flax, a slender erect annual plant

flighting a system of flights, as on a conveyor belt
flyting a dispute or exchange of personal abuse or ridicule in verse form

flix (see **flicks**)

flocks natural assemblages of animals, as sheep or geese
flocs wooly masses formed by aggregation of fine suspended particles
Phlox a large genus of American herbs

floe   a floating ice sheet
flow   to issue or run in a stream

floor   the lower inside surface of any hollow structure
flor   a coating of microorganisms that is allowed to form on the surface of some sherry wines

florescence   being in a state of bloom or flourishing
fluorescence   the emission by a substance of electromagnetic radiation, especially of visible light

florin   an old gold coin first struck in Florence in 1252 weighing about 54 grains
fluorene   a colorless crystalline cyclic hydrocarbon that has a violet fluorescence
fluorine   a nonmetallic univalent element belonging to the halogens

flour   finely ground meal of wheat or other cereal grain
flower   the part of a seed plant that normally bears reproductive organs

flow   (see **floe**)

flower   (see **flour**)

flu   (see **flew**)

flue   (see **flew**)

flues   (see **flews**)

fluorene   (see **florin**)

fluorescence   (see **florescence**)

fluorine   (see **florin**)

flurry   (see **fleury**)

flyting   (see **flighting**)

foaled   brought forth a young horse
fold   to lay one part over another part; a sheep pen

focal   relating to or having a focus or central point
phocal   relating to or resembling seals

foe   (see **faux**)

foehn   (see **fern**)

foehns   (see **fends**)

fold   (see **foaled**)

Fon   (see **faun**)

fond   (see **fawned**)

footie   an action of flirting or becoming friendly or intimate
footy   paltry or insignificant; foolish or simple-minded

for   sent to; in connection with; to the extent that
fore   previous, former, or earlier; situated in front of something else
four   a number between three and five

foram   one of the order of Rhizopoda comprising large chiefly marine protozoas
forum   a public meeting place for open discussion

forced   compelled, coerced, or constrained
Forst   a white wine of the Palatinate region in Bavaria

forcene   in heraldry, a rearing horse
forescene   a preliminary view, sight, or vista
foreseen   anticipated or known beforehand

forcite   a variety of dynamite
forecite   to call to attention preliminarily
foresight   an act or the power of foreseeing; foreknowledge

fore   (see **for**)

forecite   (see **forcite**)

foreheaded   characterized by a brow
four-headed   having extraordinary mental power

forescene   (see **forcene**)

foreseen   (see **forcene**)

foresight   (see **forcite**)

forewarn to caution in advance
foreworn exhausted by effort

foreword a preface
forward situated in advance of or before something; toward the future

foreworn (see **forewarn**)

form the shape and structure of something
forme a low bench on which shoemakers formerly sat when working; a pattern for the upper of a shoe

formal following or according to established form, custom, or rule
formyl the radical HCO- of formic acid that is also characteristic of aldehydes

formally in a prescribed or customary form; explicitly
formerly in a previous time

forme (see **form**)

formerly (see **formally**)

formyl (see **formal**)

Forst (see **forced**)

fort a strong or fortified place
forte a person's strong point

forte in music, loudly
forty a number between 39 and 41

forth onward in time or place
fourth the number four in a countable series

forty (see **forte**)

forum (see **foram**)

forward (see **foreword**)

fother (see **father**)

foul offensive to the senses; wet and stormy, as weather; an infringement of a game's rules
fowl a gallinaceous bird, as a chicken or turkey

fouler one of the several rounds fired before a rifle match to warm the barrel
fowler a person who hunts wild fowl for sport or food

four (see **for**)

four-headed (see **foreheaded**)

fourth (see **forth**)

fowl (see **foul**)

fowler (see **fouler**)

frage the lowest bid in a card game, such as skat

frog any of various smooth-skinned web-footed tailless agile leaping amphibians

fraid afraid (shortened slang); a ghost or spectre
frayed unraveled or worn

fraise a fluted reamer; in heraldry, a strawberry blossom; an obstacle used in fortifications
frays commotions; wears off by rubbing
fraze a small milling cutter used to cut down the ends of canes or rods to receive a ferrule
phrase a mode or form of speech; a group of words or musical notes expressing a thought

franc basic monetary unit of France
Frank a member of one of the West Germanic peoples entering the Roman provinces in A.D. 253
frank candid or open

frap to draw tight
frappe an iced and flavored semi-liquid mixture served in a glass

fraser an heraldic representation of a strawberry blossom
phraser a person that utters fine-sounding but often meaningless and unoriginal phrases

frater a monastery's refectory
freighter a ship or airplane used chiefly to carry goods
phrator a member of a social tribal subdivision or totemic clan

fratry   the residental quarters of a monastery
phratry   a social tribal subdivision or clan

fray   a clerical title in various religious orders in Spanish countries
fry   to cook in a pan or griddle over high heat, often in hot fat

frayed   (see **fraid**)

frays   (see **fraise**)

fraze   (see **fraise**)

frazil   ice crystals or granules formed in turbulent water
frazzle   to reduce to a state of extreme nervous or physical fatigue; to upset

freak   an odd, unexpected, or seemingly capricious action or event; a person with a physical oddity
phreak   to use an electronic device without paying the appropriate charge or toll

freedom   a quality or state of not being coerced or constrained
fretum   an arm of the sea; a strait

frees   liberates; rids of something
freeze   to become congealed by extreme cold, as water at zero degrees Centigrade
frieze   in architecture, a sculptured band between the architrave and cornice; a heavy rough-surfaced durable fabric

freighter   (see **frater**)

frequence   a condition occurring frequently or often
frequents   familiarizes oneself with another's thoughts or writings

fret   to cause to suffer emotional wear and tear; irritation; to decorate with interlaced designs
frett   in ceramics, frit
frette   a hoop of wrought iron or steel shrunk on a cast-iron gun to strengthen it

fretum   (see **freedom**)

friable   easily pulverized or reduced to powder
fryable   capable of being cooked in a pan or griddle over direct heat

friar   a member of a religious order
fryer   something used in frying; a young chicken

frieze   (see **frees**)

frits   materials from which glass is made
Fritz   a German, often used disparagingly

fro   backward, as "to and fro"
froe   a steel wedge for cleaving or splitting logs
frow   a woman or housewife

froes   steel wedges for cleaving or splitting logs
frows   women or housewives
froze   became congealed by extreme cold

frog   (see **frage**)

fronds   leaves of a palm or fern
frons   the upper anterior part of the head capsule of an insect

frow   (see **fro**)

frows   (see **froes**)

froze   (see **froes**)

fry   (see **fray**)

fryable   (see **friable**)

fryer   (see **friar**)

fuge   an early 19th century hymn characterized by polyphony and imitation
fugue   a contrapuntal musical composition in which one or two melodic themes are repeated by successively entering voices

fuhrer   a person in authority or leader

furor an angry fit or rage; hectic activity

Ful a member of a pastoral and nomadic people scattered from Senegal to Cameroon
full completely filled

fulgid in zoology, denoting fiery red with metallic reflections
fulgide the anhydride of fulgenic acid

full (see **Ful**)

fund a quantity of resources maintained as a source of supply; a sum of money set aside for a specific purpose
funned indulged in banter or play

funds money on deposit which is held at a specified place on which checks or drafts can be drawn
funs indulges in banter or play

funned (see **fund**)

funs (see **funds**)

furor (see **fuhrer**)

furred lined, trimmed, or faced with fur
fyrd the national militia in England prior to the Norman Conquest

furry (see **firry**)

furs (see **firs**)

furze (see **firs**)

fusel an acrid oily liquid having an unpleasant odor
fusile a rhomboidal heraldic bearing longer in proportion to its width; a light flintlock musket

fustee an offspring of a white and mustee (or octoroon); a person of 1/16 negro ancestry
fusty moldy, ill-smelling, or without freshness; old-fashioned or rigidly conservative

futile (see **feudal**)

fyrd (see **feared** or **furred**)

Group I

faerie - fairy
faineance - faineants
feme - femme
fermenter - fermentor
fiancé - fiancée
figurant - figurante
flocculence - flocculents
frau - frow

Group II

facundity fɑ·kəndədē
fecundity fē·kəndədē

fagot ·fɑgət
fagott fä·gȯt

fairy ·ferē
Ferae ·fe.rē

fanatic fə·nɑdik
phonetic fə·nedik

farci ·fär.sē
farcy ·färsē

faucet ·fȯsət
fossette fä·set

fili fi·lē
filly ·filē

forced ·fȯrsd
forest ·fȯrəst

forgone fȯr·gȯn
fourgon färgō^n

formulate ·fȯrmyə.lāt
formylate ·fȯrmə.lāt

freezer ·frēzər
friseur frē·zər

frison frē·zō^n
frisson frē·sō^n

furfural ·fərfə.rɑl
furfuryl ·fərfərəl

fusel ·füzəl
fusil ·fyüzə̇l

--------------------------------- G ---------------------------------

gade   a gadoid fish, especially a rockling

gayed   behaved gaily; made bright or cheerful

Gael   a Scottish Highlander

gail   wort in the process of fermentation that is added to a stout or ale

gale   a strong air current with a speed of 32 to 63 mph

Gaelic   characteristic of the Celtic Highlanders of Scotland; the Goidelic speech of the Celts

Gallic   French, especially in quality; relating to Gaul or the Gauls

gaff   an iron hook with a handle used in fishing and logging; an ordeal

gaffe   a social or diplomatic blunder or clumsy mistake

gage   a personal belonging cast on the ground to be taken up by an opponent as an agreement of combat; any of several small cultivated plums of European origin

gauge   a measurement according to some standard or system; an instrument for testing and measuring

gagor   in law, a person that pledges or secures something

gauger   a person that inspects the dimensions of parts in a machine shop

gail   (see **Gael**)

gain   to obtain or increase; a resource or advantage acquired or increased; profit

gaine   a support beneath a sculptured bust or head

gait   a manner of moving on foot

gate   an opening in an enclosing fence, wall, or barrier

gaiter   a leg-covering reaching from the instep to the ankle, mid-calf, or knee

gater   a person that attends to the hole through which liquified metal is poured in the process of casting iron

gator   alligator (by shortening)

gala   a gay and lively celebration

Gal(l)a   any of the several groups of Cushitic-speaking peoples occupying Kenya, Tanzania, and Uganda

galla   any of certain nut galls from oaks that are used in phamacy for their astringent properties

gallow   to put to flight by frightening

galant   relating to or composed of the light and elegant free homophonic style of musical composition in the 18th century

gallant   notably marked by courtesy and attentiveness to women especially in a spirited, dashing, or elaborate way

gale   (see **Gael**)

galena   a mineral consisting of lead sulfide

Gallina   related to an ancient New Mexican culture characterized by painted pottery

galipot   a crude turpentine oleoresin exuded on the bark of the cluster pine tree

gallipot   a small ceramic vessel with a small mouth used to hold medicine

gall   bile; something bitter to endure; brazen boldness with impudent assurance

Gaul   a member of the Celtic people that inhabited ancient Gaul

ghol   a sciaenid fish of the Indian coast

Gal(l)a and **galla**   (see **gala**)

gallant   (see **galant**)

gallein a metallic-green crystalline phthalein dye

galleon a heavily built square-rigged sailing ship of the 15th to early 18th centuries

galley a short crescent-shaped sea-going ship of classical antiquity propelled chiefly by oars; the kitchen of a ship or airplane; an oblong tray to hold set type

gallie any of various large North American woodpeckers

gally to put to flight by frightening

Gallic (see **Gaelic**)

gallie (see **galley**)

Gallina (see **galena**)

gallipot (see **galipot**)

gallop a fast natural three-beat horse's gait; to go at great speed

galop a lively dance in duple measure performed with sliding steps

gallow (see **gala**)

gally (see **galley**)

galop (see **gallop**)

gam a school of whales; a friendly conversation

gamb(e) in heraldry, a leg or shank

gamme an entire range from one extreme to another

gama a tall coarse American grass valuable for forage

gamma the third letter of the Greek alphabet

gamb(e) (see **gam**)

gambet the redshank, a common Old World limicoline bird

gambit a remark, comment, or tactical maneuver designed to launch a conversation or make a telling point

gamble to play games of chance for money or other stakes

gambol playful leaping, frolicking, or cavorting

gamin(e) a roguish impudent boy (or girl); an urchin

gammon a ham or flitch of cured bacon; to fasten to a ship's stem by lashings; to deceive or fool

gamma (see **gama**)

gamme (see **gam**)

gammon (see **gamin[e]**)

gang a group of persons drawn together by a common interest, tastes, or activity

gang(ue) worthless rock or vein matter in which valuable metals or minerals occur (seldom **gang**)

gantlet a stretch where two lines of railroad track overlap

gauntlet a glove designed to protect a hand from injury; a challenge to combat

gap a break in continuity; an intervening distance

gape to open the mouth wide (although usually 'gāp)

garret a room on the top floor of a house; an attic

garrote a Spanish method of execution by strangulation using an iron collar

garrulous loquacious, talkative, or wordy

Garrulus a large genus of Old World jays including the common jay of Britain and Europe

garter a circular elastic band worn to hold up a stocking or shirt sleeve

guarder a person who watches or protects

gatch a plaster used especially in Persian architectural ornamentation

gotch drooping or cropped, as of an animal's ears

gate (see **gait**)

gateau a fancy cake filled with custard and glacéed fruits and nuts
gato an Argentine composition in
lively 3/4 time for singing and
dancing

gater (see **gaiter**)

gato (see **gateau**)

gator (see **gaiter**)

gaud a showy bit of jewelry or finery
God the supreme ultimate reality
god a superhuman person or being

gaufre a very thin crisp wafer baked
with a wafer iron
gofer an employee whose duties include running errands
goffer to crimp, plait, or flute linen
or lace with a hot iron
gopher a burrowing rodent; a burrowing land tortoise

gaufre a very thin crisp wafer baked
with a wafer iron
goffer to crimp, plait, or flute linen
or lace with a hot iron
golfer a person who plays the game
of golf

gauge (see **gage**)

gauger (see **gagor**)

Gaul (see **gall**)

gauntlet (see **gantlet**)

gayed (see **gade**)

gays makes bright and cheerful;
homosexuals
gaze a steady intent look or stare

gean the fruit of a wild or cultivated
sweet cherry
gene a complex protein molecule that
transmits hereditary characteristics
jean a durable twilled cotton cloth

gear personal belongings or equip-
ment; a toothed wheel used in
machinery
Gir a breed of medium-sized dairy
type Indian cattle

gees turns a horse or draft animal
to the right
jeez a mild exclamation of surprise
or wonder (slang)

gel a semisolid substance
jell to take shape; to achieve dis-
tinctness

gelid extremely cold or icy
jellied brought to the consistency of
jelly

gene (see **gean**)

genet a small European carnivorous
mammal related to the civet
jennet a female donkey; a small
Spanish horse

geophilous living or growing in or
on the ground
Geophilus a cosmopolitan genus of
geophilomorph centipedes

ger a circular tent consisting of skin
or felt stretched over a collapsible
lattice framework and used by the
Kirghiz and Mongols
grr an exclamation expressing dislike

germ a small mass of living substance capable of developing into
an animal, plant, organ, or a part
jerm a small Levantine sailing vessel
with one or two masts and lateen
sails

German a native or inhabitant of
Germany; a person who speaks the
German language
german a dance consisting of
capriciously involved figures inter-
mingled with waltzes
germen germ cells and their precursors; a primary sex gland, such as
an ovary or testis

Gerres the type genus comprising
long-bodied compressed marine
fishes with protusible mouths and
large silvery scales
jerries railroad section workers;
Germans (slang)

gest(e) a notable deed or action

jessed attached two short leather straps to a hawk's legs, in falconry

jest a prank or act intended to provoke laughter; a jeering remark

ghat in India, a mountain range, mountain pass, or landing place on a river bank

got gained possession, acquired, or obtained

ghee a semifluid clarified butter made in India and neighboring countries from buffalo milk

Gi a people of the border region between the Ivory Coast and Liberia

gi a lightweight, two-piece garment worn by practitioners of the Oriental martial arts

ghol (see **gall**)

ghol a sciaenid fish of the Indian coast

goal an objective or aim

ghoul a legendary evil being that robbed graves and fed on corpses

gool an ill-mannered offensive introvert (slang); a goal

gul something resembling a rose in form

Gi and gi (see **ghee**)

gib a castrated male cat; a removable machined metal plate that holds other mechanical parts in place

guib a small harnessed antelope of western Africa

gibbous the moon when seen with more than half the apparent disk illuminated

gibbus the hump of the deformed spine in Pott's disease

gil an insecure or phony person (slang)

gill an organ in fish for obtaining oxygen from water

gild to overlay with a thin covering of gold

gilled having an organ for obtaining oxygen from water

guild persons associated in a kindred pursuit

gilder a person whose occupation is to overlay with gold or gilt

guilder a member of a modern guild or association of artisans; a Dutch monetary unit

gilgai one of the shallow holes that honeycomb parts of the soil in interior Australia, attributed to the burrowing of pademelons

gilguy a rope temporarily used as a guy or lanyard

gill (see **gil**)

gill a U.S. liquid measure equal to $\frac{1}{4}$ pint

jill a female ferret

gilled (see **gild**)

gilt false glitter; a young female swine

guilt a state of one who has committed an offense

gimbal a device that permits a body to incline freely in any direction so that it will remain level when its support is tipped

gimble to make a face or grimace

gimel the third letter of the Hebrew alphabet

gimmal joined work whose parts move within each other

gimp a flat narrow braid used as trimming or decorative finish for upholstery and clothing; a limp or bobble

guimpe a wide usually stiffly starched cloth used to cover the neck and shoulders of some nuns

gimpy crippled or limping

gympie an Australian nettle tree having foliage and twigs covered with stinging hairs

gin   any of several machines, as a cotton gin; a strong alcoholic liquor
jinn   a supernatural spirit
Kin   a Tatar people that founded an 11th century dynasty in China

ginney   an Italian (slang), usually used disparagingly
Guinea   a coastal region in West Africa
guinea   an English gold coin circulated from 1663 to 1813, equivalent to 21 shillings in 1717

ginny   affected with a strong alcoholic liquor
jinni   Islamic spirits believed to inhabit the earth
jinny   a block carriage on a crane that sustains pulley blocks

Gir   (see **gear**)

giro   a rotating winged aircraft
gyro   a gyroscope or gyrocompass

girt   bound by a cable; prepared or ready; geared; a heavy timber framed into the second floor corner posts as a footing for roof rafters
girth   a band or strap encircling the body of a horse or other animal to fasten a saddle, pack, or other article on its back

glace   a frozen dessert
glass   an amorphous inorganic usually translucent substance consisting typically of a mixture of silicates

glacier   a large body of ice moving slowly down a slope or valley
glazier   a person who cuts and sets glass, as in windowpanes

glacis   a slope used for defense against attack; a buffer state
glasses   a device used to correct defects of vision; drinking receptacles

glacis   a slope used for defense against attack; a buffer state
glassie   a marble made of glass
glassy   suggestive of glass; having a dull fixedness of expression

glair(e)   a sizing liquid made from egg white and vinegar
glare   a harsh uncomfortably brilliant light

glands   secreting organs of animals or plants
glans   the conical vascular body forming the extremity of the clitoris or penis

glare   (see **glair[e]**)

glass   (see **glace**)

glasses   (see **glacis**)

glassie   (see the second **glacis**)

glassy   (see **glacis**)

glaucous   having a powdery or waxy coating that gives a frosted appearance
Glaucus   a genus of slender elongate pelagic nudibranches

glaze   a smooth slippery coating of thin ice; a fine translucent glassy film
gleys   bluish grey or olive-gray sticky layers of clay formed under the surface of certain water-logged soils

glazier   (see **glacier**)

gleys   (see **glaze**)

Glis   a genus comprising the common Old World dormice
gliss   a rapid series of connective notes played on a stringed instrument by sliding one or more fingers across adjacent strings or keys (slang for glissando)

glögg   a sweetish Swedish hot punch served usually at Christmas
glug   a gurgling sound

gloom   partial or total darkness; a state of melancholy or depression
glume   one of two empty bracts at a spikelet's base in grasses

glows   becomes incandescent; shines with suffused radiance
gloze   to make a false or perverse interpretation

glucide any of a class of carbohydrates comprising both the glycoses and glycosides
gluside saccharin

glug (see glögg)

glume (see gloom)

gluside (see glucide)

glutenin glutelin found in wheat
glutinin a blocking antibody

glutenous characteristic of the tenacious, tough, elastic protein in flour that gives cohesiveness to bread dough
glutinous gluey or sticky

glutinin (see glutenin)

glutinous (see glutenous)

gnarred snarled or growled
knarred knotty or gnarled
nard rhizomes of several pharmaceutically useful plants

gnatty infested with gnats
natty trimly neat and tidy

gnaw to chew on with teeth
naw no (slang)

gnawed chewed on with teeth
nod a quick downward motion of the head

gnawer an animal that gnaws or chews with teeth
knaur a knot or burl on wood

gneiss laminated or foliated metamorphic rock, as granite
nice refined, cultured, pleasant, or satisfying

gnir a ball of dust
near within a short distance or time

gnome an ageless often deformed dwarf of folklore; a dry wizened little old man; a maxim or proverb
Nome an Alaskan seaport city
nome a musical composition of ancient Greece

gnomic expressive of pithy wisdom concerning the human condition
nomic generally valid, as a statement

gnomon an object on a sundial that casts a shadow
nomen a grammatical form with functions of a noun

gnu a large compact blocky African antelope
knew comprehended, understood, or perceived
new recent, fresh, or modern
Nu Tibeto-Burman inhabitants of the upper Salween river region in Yunnan
nu the 13th letter of the Greek alphabet

go to move; a Japanese game
ko a 12th century Chinese porcelain distinguished by dark clay and fine crackle

goad a rod pointed at one end used to urge on an animal
goed past tense of go (slang)

goal (see ghol)

goaled scored a point in a game
gold a malleable, ductile, yellow metallic element

gob a lump or mass of indefinite or variable shape; a large amount
gobbe a tropical leguminous African creeping herb also known as Bambarra groundnut

Gobi an east Asian desert mostly in Mongolia
gobi the lenticular mass of sedimentary deposits that occupies a downwarp basin
goby any of numerous spiny-finned fishes

God and god (see gaud)

goed (see goad)

goer a person or animal that moves
gore to pierce with a pointed instrument or animal horn; thick or

clotted blood; a triangular piece of land or cloth

gofer (see **gaufre**)

goffer (see **gaufre**)

Gola an African people of Liberia and Sierra Leone
gola a warehouse for grain in India
golah the people of one country dispersed into other countries

gold (see **goaled**)

golfer (see **gaufre**)

gon a railroad gondola; a thief (slang)
gone passed from a point; departed or left

goo a viscid or sticky substance; sickly sentimentality
gou a freshwater drum (the gaspergou fish, shortened)
goût artistic or literary good taste

gool (see **ghoul**)

gopher (see **gaufre**)

gorce any obstruction in a river preventing passage of vessels
gorse juniper; furze, a spiny evergreen shrub

gore (see **goer**)

gored pierced with a pointed instrument or animal horn
gourd a hard-rinded inedible fruit of vines
gourde the basic monetary unit of Haiti

gorilla an anthropoid ape
guerrilla a member of an independent group engaged in predatory excursions in wartime

gorse (see **gorce**)

got (see **ghat**)

gotch (see **gatch**)

gou (see **goo**)

gourd (see **gored**)

gourde (see **gored**)

goût (see **goo**)

grace a short prayer before or after a meal; charming or attractive characteristics
graisse a disease of white wines and cider

grade a degree of value or quality; a stage in a process
grayed became dull or cheerless

grader a worker or machine that sorts products according to certain specifications; a person who evaluates students' test papers
grater a device for reducing material to small bits of abrasion
greater larger or more prominent

graff a trench used in fortifications, as a moat
graph a diagram comparing one variable to another

graft the point of insertion of a scion in plant stock; acquisition of money or position by dishonest or questionable means
graphed plotted a curve or line on a graph

graham made wholly or largely of whole wheat flour
gram a metric unit of mass and weight

grain the unhusked or threshed seeds or fruits of various food plants including the cereal grasses
graine the eggs of the silkworm

graisse (see **grace**)

gram (see **graham**)

Granat any of several azo dyes giving red colors
granat a small bridge or culvert; a strong red or reddish orange color
granite a natural igneous rock formation of visibly crystalline texture

grantee   a person to whom a grant or award is made

granthi   a reader of the sacred scriptures of the Sikhs

Granth   the sacred scriptures of the Sikhs

grunt   a deep short sound characteristic of a hog

granthi   (see grantee)

graph   (see graff)

graphed   (see graft)

graser   a device that uses gamma rays to produce a high-energy beam

grazer   an animal that feeds on growing herbage

grassie   the red-backed parrot of Australia

grassy   covered or abounding with grass

grater   (see grader)

grave   an accent mark indicating a vowel is pronounced with a fall in pitch

graves   red or white table wines

gray   to become dull or cheerless

greige   woven fabric as it comes from the loom and before it is submitted to the finishing process

grès   a piece of ceramic stoneware, especially when decorated

griege   a variable color averaging a grayish yellow green

grayed   (see grade)

grays   becomes dull or cheerless

graze   to feed on growing herbage

grèses   pieces of ceramic stoneware, especially when decorated

grazer   (see graser)

grease   an oily substance; to influence with bribes

Greece   a country in southeastern Europe

gr(i)ece   in heraldry, a step in a series

gris(e)   a costly gray fur used decoratively on medieval costumes

greased   smeared with a thick lubricant; smoothed or made easy of passage; affected with a chronic inflammation of the skin of the fetlocks and pasterns, as a horse

grieced   in heraldry, standing on steps

greater   (see grader)

greave   armor for the leg below the knee

grieve   to mourn or sorrow

Greece   (see grease)

greige   (see gray)

grès   (see gray)

grèses   (see grays)

grew   developed or increased

grue   a shiver; gruesome quality

gr(i)ece   (see grease)

grieced   (see greased)

griege   (see gray)

grieve   (see greave)

griff   a white person newly arrived in the Orient (slang)

griffe   in architecture, an ornament at the base of a column projecting from the torus toward a corner of the plinth; a person of mixed black and American Indian ancestry

griffin   a white person newly arrived in the Orient; an untried Chinese racing pony; a fabulous bird typically having the head, forepart, and wings of an eagle and hindparts and tail of a lion

Griffon   a breed of small short-faced compact dogs of Belgian origin; a breed of medium-sized long-headed sporting dogs originating in Holland

Griffon   a breed of small short-faced compact dogs of Belgian origin; a breed of medium-sized long-headed sporting dogs originating in Holland

griffone   a woman of 3/4 negro and 1/4 white ancestry

grills   cooking utensils; broils; distresses with continued questioning

grilse   a young mature Atlantic salmon returning from the sea to spawn for the first time

grim   stern or forbidding in action or appearance

grimme   a small African antelope

grip   to seize tightly; a spasm of pain; a suitcase

grippe   an acute febrile contagious viral disease similar to influenza

gris(e)   (see **grease**)

grisly   dreadful or terrible

gristly   containing tough fibrous matter

grizzly   a large powerful brownish yellow bear

gro   a heavy durable cross-ribbed silk fabric

grow   to spring up and come to maturity

groan   a deep harsh sound indicative of pain or grief

grown   arrived at maturity; cultivated

grocer   a dealer in foodstuffs

grosser   ruder, coarser, or more vulgar

grommet   an eyelet of material set into a perforation to strengthen the inner circumference of material surrounding the perforation

grummet   a cabin boy on a ship (also **gromet**)

groom   a person in charge of tending horses; a bridegroom

grume   a thick viscid fluid, as a blood clot

grosser   (see **grocer**)

grow   (see **gro**)

growan   decomposed granite

grown   arrived at maturity; cultivated

grown   (see **groan**)

grr   (see **ger**)

grue   (see **grew**)

grume   (see **groom**)

grummet   (see **grommet**)

grunt   (see **Granth**)

Grus   the type genus of Gruidae consisting of the typical cranes

gruss   a finely granulated rock that has not decomposed by weathering

guan   any of various large tropical American birds, somewhat resembling turkeys, that are highly regarded for sport and food

Kuan   a type of Chinese porcelain pottery of the Sung period in the 12th century

guarder   (see **garter**)

guddle   to grope for fish in their lurking places

guttle   to eat or drink greedily and noisily

guerilla   (see **gorilla**)

guessed   formed an opinion from insufficient evidence; conjectured

guest   a person to whom hospitality is extended

Guhr   a loose earthy deposit from water occurring in the cavities of rocks

Gur   a branch of the Niger-Congo language family centered in the upper Volta river valley in Ghana and the Upper Volta territory in West Africa

gur   an unrefined brown sugar made especially from jaggery palm sap

guib   (see **gib**)

guide   to lead or steer

guyed   steadied with a rope or chain; ridiculed good-humoredly

guild   (see **gild**)

guilder   (see **gilder**)

guile   crafty or deceitful cunning
gyle   beer produced at one brewing

guilt   (see gilt)

guimpe   (see gimp)

Guinea and guinea   (see ginney)

guise   external appearance, shape, or
   semblance
guys   ropes or chains attached to
   steady or brace something

gul   (see ghoul)

gull(e)y   a small valley or gulch
gullie   a tern (seabird)

gumbee   a small marble
gumby   a drum made of skin stretched
   over a piece of hollowed tree

gumbo   the okra plant or its edible
   pods
gumboe   a small marble
gum-bow   a slingshot

gumby   (see gumbee)

Gur and gur   (see guhr)

Guti   a mountain people ruling
   Sumer and Akkad near Babylon in
   the 24th century B.C.
gutty   in heraldry, an ornamental
   pattern of drops argent

guttae   two or more in a series of ornaments in a Doric entablature;
   gray to brown tough plastic substances obtained from the latex of
   several Malaysian sapotaceous trees
gutty   having courage or fortitude;
   having a significant or challenging
   substance or quality; in heraldry,
   an ornamental pattern of drops
   argent

guttle   (see guddle)

gutty   (see guttae and Guti)

guyed   (see guide)

guys   (see guise)

gyle   (see guile)

gympie   (see gimpy)

gyro   (see giro)

gyve   to bind or restrain with fetters
jive   a special slang jargon

Group I

galaks - Galax
gecko - Gekko
granter - grantor
grievance - grievants

Group I and II

gluten   'glüt^{ə}n
glutin   'glütin

guarantee   :gɑrən:tē
guaranty   :gɑrəntē

Group II

galerie   gɑl'rē
gallery   'gɑlrē

galette   gə'let
gal(l)et   'gɑlət
gullet   'gələt

Galeus   'gōlēəs
galleass   'gɑlēəs

Galium   'gōlēəm
gallium   'gɑlēəm

gally   'gȯlē
golly   'gȧlē

gambet   'gɑmbət
gambette   gɑm'bet

garbill   'gär.bil
garble   'gärbəl

garnet   'gärnət
garnett   gär:nət

garrot   gȧrō
garrot(t)e   gaʹrōt

genae   ʹjē.nē
genie   ʹjēnē

ghouls   ʹgülz
gules   ʹgyülz

Golo   ʹgō.lō
goloe   gōʹlō

goody   ʹgu̇dē

Guti   ʹgüdē

gorgeous   ʹgȯrjəs
gorges   ʹgȯrjəz

Gouda   ʹgüdə
gutta   ʹgu̇də

greisen   ʹgrīzᵊn
grison   ʹgrizᵊn

guttie   ʹgət.tī
gutty   ʹgədē or ʹgüdē

H

haaf deep-sea fishing grounds off the Shetland and Orkney Islands
haff a long shallow lagoon separated from the open sea by a narrow sandbar or barrier beach
half one of two equal parts into which a thing is divisible

hache an axe or hatchet
hash a mixture, jumble, or hodge-podge; a dish usually consisting of leftover meat chopped into small pieces, mixed with potatoes, and browned

hachure a short line used in map-making for shading and denoting surfaces in relief; a contour line
hasher a worker who feeds un-marketable meat into a hashing machine so it may be used for by-products; a waiter or waitress (slang)

hackee a chipmunk
hackie a cab driver
hacky a short and dry manner of coughing

hade an angle made by a rock fault plane or vein with the vertical
hayed cut and cured grass for hay

Hadean characteristic of the abode of the dead or hell
Haitian characteristic of the people or the island of Haiti

haded in geology, deviated from the vertical, as a vein, fault, or lode
hated felt extreme enmity toward

haff (see **haaf**)

haik a voluminous piece of cloth worn as an outer garment in northern Africa
hake a fish related to cod

haik a voluminous piece of cloth worn as an outer garment in northern Africa
hike to march, walk, or tramp
hyke an exclamation used to urge dogs onward in a chase

hail precipitation in the form of small ice balls; to salute or greet
hale healthy or sound; to haul, pull, or draw

hair a threadlike outgrowth on an animal's epidermis
hare a long-eared gnawing animal
herr mister or a gentleman, in German

hairier covered with more hair
harrier a hunting dog; a cross-country runner

hairy covered with hair
harry to assault or ravage

Haitian (see **Hadean**)

hake (see **haik**)

hale (see **hail**)

half (see **haaf**)

hall a large assembly room; a passageway; a large building
haul to pull, drag, or transport

hallo a call used to attract attention
hallow to make holy; to venerate
halo containing halogen (by shortening)
hollo a call of encouragement or jubilation

hallocks rectangular wood veneer berry boxes with straight sides and a raised bottom
hallux the first or preaxial digit of the hind limb; the big toe

hallow (see **hallo**)

hallux (see **hallocks**)

halo (see **hallo**)

halve to divide in two equal parts
have to possess or hold

Hamburg a city in northern Germany
Homburg a man's hat of smooth-finished felt with a stiff curled ribbon-bound brim and a high tapered crown creased lengthwise

hamus in biology, a hook or curved process
jemez a group of Tanoan Amerindian peoples of New Mexico

hance a ship's curved contour
hanse a trading association in foreign countries; an entrance fee into a merchant guild

handmade produced by hand
handmaid a female servant

hands terminal parts of a vertebrate's forelimb when modified for grasping

Hans an Athaspakan people of the Yukon river district in east central Alaska and the Yukon territory of Canada; members of a people now comprising the dominant culture group of China

handsome attractive or having an impressive and pleasing appearance; of considerable value
hansom a two-wheeled covered carriage

hangar an enclosed area for housing and repairing aircraft
hanger a device from which something is hung; a person who hangs articles

Hans (see **hands**)

hanse (see **hance**)

hansom (see **handsome**)

harass to annoy continually or plague; to raid
harras a herd of stud horses

hardy strong or robust; resolute
hearty exhibiting vigorous good health; exuberant

hare (see **hair**)

harras (see **harass**)

harrier (see **hairier**)

harry (see **hairy**)

hart a stag or male deer
heart a muscular organ which acts as a pump to maintain blood circulation

hash (see **hache**)

hasher (see **hachure**)

hatcher a device to which eggs are transferred from the incubator shortly before they are due to hatch
hatchur a short line used in mapmaking for shading and denoting surfaces in relief; a contour line

(see **hachure** for an alternate pronunciation)

hated (see **haded**)

hau an irregularly spreading or shrubby tree widely distributed on tropical shores
how in what manner or way

haul (see **hall**)

haute high-class, high-toned, or fancy
oat a cereal grass cultivated for its edible seed

have (see **halve**)

haws commands to a team of draft animals to turn left; sounds of hesitation in speech; inflamed nictitating membranes of a domesticated mammal
hawse the part of a ship's bow containing holes through which cables pass

hayed (see **hade**)

hays cuts and cures grass for hay
haze dull or cloudy; to subject a person to unnecessary or ridiculous treatment
he(h)s the fifth letter of the Hebrew alphabet (plural)
heighs expressions of cheeriness
heys expressions of interrogation or attention-getting

headward in the direction of the head
headword a word or term often in distinctive type placed at the beginning of a chapter or entry

heal to restore to health or cure
heel the hind part of a foot; to cause a boat to list
he'll the contraction of he will

healer a person or circumstance that cures or heals
heeler a local worker for a political boss; a dog that urges lagging animals onward by nipping at their heels

hear to perceive with the ear
heer an old unit of measure for linen and woolen yarn of about 600 yards
here at this point in space

heard apprehended with the ear
herd several of one kind of animal together; to lead or gather animals into a group

hearse a vehicle for conveying the dead; a usually triangular wooden or metal frame used in the Tenebrae service during Holy Week and normally designed to hold 15 candles
hirse broomcorn millet

hearsed conveyed in a hearse; buried
hurst a grove or wooded knoll; a sandbank in a river

heart (see **hart**)

hearty (see **hardy**)

heated raised the temperature of
heeded had regard for or paid attention to

heater a device that generates or retains heat or warmth
heder an elementary Jewish school in which children are given religious instruction often in Hebrew
heeder a person who pays attention to circumstances, things, or people

heaume a large helmet supported by the shoulders

holm an evergreen oak of southern Europe
home a principal place of residence

hecks wooden gratings set across a stream to obstruct the passage of fish; devices on a vertical frame for controlling warp threads in textile manufacturing
hex to practice witchcraft on; hexagonal in shape

he'd the contraction of he would or he had
heed to have regard for or pay attention to

heder   (see header)

heed   (see he'd)

heeded   (see heated)

heeder   (see heater)

heel   (see heal)

heeler   (see healer)

heer   (see hear)

he(h)s   (see hays)

heigh   an expression of cheeriness
hi   a greeting
hie   to hasten
high   tall or having considerable upward extension

heighs   (see hays)

heinous   hatefully or shockingly evil; abominable
highness   the quality or state of being high; a person of honor

heir   (see air)

heiress   (see arras)

heirless   (see airless)

heirship   (see airship)

helicin   a glucoside obtained by partial oxidation of salicin
helicine   pertaining to the helix of the ear; curled, spiral, or helicoid (in designating certain small arteries of the penis)

he'll   (see heal)

hello   (see hallo)

herb   a plant or plant part valued for its medicinal, savory, or aromatic qualities
urb   an urban area

herd   (see heard)

herds   groups of several people or animals of one kind
hurds   coarse parts of flax or hemp adhering to the fiber after separation

here   (see hear)

herl   a barb of feather used in dressing an artificial fly
hurl   to throw, toss, or cast

heroin   a bitter white crystalline narcotic made from morphine
heroine   a principal female character in a drama, novel, or event

herr   (see hair)

hertz   a unit of frequency equal to one cycle per second
hurts   injuries or damages

heterogenous   not originating with the body
heterogynous   having females of more than one kind

heteronomous   subject to or involving different laws of growth
heteronymous   having different designations

heugh   an exclamation expressing surprise
hoo   an expression of emotional reaction; a call
Hu   an ancient Tatar people of northwest China
who   what person(s)
whoo   the cry of an owl

heumer   a maker of medieval helmets
homer   a home run in baseball

hew   to cut with a heavy cutting instrument; to adhere, conform, or stick to
hue   a color or complexion
whew   an expression of relief, amazement, or discomfort; to make a half-formed whistling sound

hewer   a person who cuts or fells with hard rough blows
hure   the head of a bear, boar, or wolf

hex   (see hecks)

heys   (see hays)

hi (see **heigh**)

hic a sound of a hiccup

hick an awkward unsophisticated person

hickey a pimple; a defect in a negative or printing plate

hicky unsophisticated, awkward, or provincial

hide to conceal, put out of sight, or keep secret; an outer covering of an animal

hied hastened

hie (see **heigh**)

hied (see **hide**)

high (see **heigh**)

highbred coming from superior stock; refined

hybrid a cross breed; an individual produced by a union of gametes from parents of different genotypes

higher taller or having greater upward extension

hire to employ for wages

highly in or at an elevated place, level, or rank

hyle in philosophy, whatever receives form or determination from outside itself

highness (see **heinous**)

hike (see **haik**)

hila scars on a seed marking the point of attachment of the ovule to the funiculus

Hyla a large genus of archiferous amphibians comprising the typical toads

hyla any amphibian of the genus Hyla

hillie a small pinch of dirt on which a marble is sometimes elevated

hilly abounding with natural elevations of land; difficult or obscure

him the objective case of he

hymn a song of praise or joy

hipe in wrestling, a means of throwing an opponent

hype a narcotic addict; to promote or publicize extravagantly

hippie a baby's diaper

hippy having or resembling large haunches or hips

hire (see **higher**)

hirse (see **hearse**)

hissed made the sound by which an animal indicates alarm, fear, irritation, or warning

hist an expression or sound used to attract attention

Ho a people of the northeastern part of the Indian subcontinent south of the Ganges plain

ho an expression of surprise, delight, or derision

hoe an agricultural implement

Hoh an India people of the Olympic Peninsula, Washington

whoa a command to a draft animal to stop or stand still

hoar frost or rime; a grayish coating

hoer a person that works the soil with a hoe

whore a female prostitute

hoard to accumulate something

horde a loosely organized group of individuals, animals, or insects; a swarm

whored acted as a prostitute

hoarse rough sounding, grating, or rasping

horse a large solid-footed herbivorous mammal

hobo a migratory worker; a vagrant

jobo a tropical American tree sometimes cultivated for its edible yellow plum-like fruit

hoc   a card game in which a holder gives certain cards any value
hock   restraint of goods usually as a pledge for a loan; the last card in a faro dealing box
hok   a small enclosure or pen

hockey   a game played on the ice by two six-person teams
hocky   having faulty tarsal joints, as a dog

hocks   tarsal joints or regions in the hind limbs of digitigrade quadrapeds, as a horse
hoks   small pens to contain animals
hox   to pester or annoy by following

hocky   (see hockey)

hoe   (see Ho)

hoer   (see hoar)

hoes   works the soil with a hoe
hose   a cloth leg covering; a flexible tube for conveying fluid or gas

Hoh   (see Ho)

hok   (see hoc)

hokey   characterized by or the product of fakery or false value
hokie   a large marble

hoks   (see hocks)

hold   to maintain possession of; to grasp; a ship's interior below decks
holed   made an opening in something; drove an animal into a hole

hole   an opening
whole   entire or total; free of defect

holed   (see hold)

holey   having a hole or full of holes
Holi   a Hindu spring festival characterized by boisterous and ribald revelry
holy   hallowed, sacred, or venerated
wholly   to the full extent

hollo   (see hallo)

hollo   a call of encouragement or jubilation
hollow   empty; a depression; false or deceitful

holm   (see heaume)

holy   (see holey)

hombre   a man, fellow, or guy
ombre   shaded, especially of fabrics with a dyed or woven design in which the color is graduated from light to dark

Homburg   (see Hamburg)

home   (see heaume)

homer   (see heumer)

homily   a discourse on a religious or moral theme
hommilie   a calf or dehorned cow

hon   sweetheart, dear, or honey
Hun   a member of a nomadic Mongolian people; a German soldier in World Wars I and II

hoo   (see heugh)

hooey   something false or unacceptable; hokum
hui   a partnership, club, syndicate, or community gathering in Hawaii

hookie   a meaningless expression or mild expletive
hooky   truant; full of or covered with metal or tough curved material for holding something

hoop   a strip of wood or metal bent in circular form and united at the ends
whoop   an expression of eagerness, exuberance, or jubilation; to arouse sentiment for

hoos   expressions of emotional reaction; calls
hoose   verminous bronchitis of cattle, sheep, and goats
whos   what persons
who's   the contraction of who is, who was, or who has

whose relating to what person(s)

horde (see **hoard**)

hornie a horn agate marble
horny hard or callous; easily excited sexually

horse (see **hoarse**)

horsed handled roughly; played; provided with a horse
horst part of the earth's crust separated by faults

hose (see **hoes**)

hostel a public house for entertaining or lodging travelers
hostile marked by malevolence, antagonism, or unfriendliness

hosteler a person who lodges or entertains guests or strangers
hostler a person who takes care of horses at an inn or stable; a person who takes charge of a railroad locomotive after a run

hostile (see **hostel**)

hostler (see **hosteler**)

hostler a person who takes care of horses at an inn or stable; a person who takes charge of a railroad locomotive after a run
hustler an active, enterprising, sometimes unscrupulous individual

hour (see **Aor**)

house to provide with living quarters; to store in a secure place
hows ways in which something is or can be done
how's the contraction of how is, how has, or how was

houseboat a yacht, barge, or boat outfitted as a dwelling or for leisurely cruising
housebote wood allowed to a tenant for repairing a house

Hova the dominant native people of central Madagascar

Jova an important division of the Piman peoples of northeastern Sonora, Mexico

how (see **hau**)

howel a plane used by a barrel or cask maker
Howell a game of duplicate bridge in which match-point scoring is used
howl to utter a loud sustained doleful sound characteristic of dogs and wolves

hows (see **house**)

how's (see **house**)

hox (see **hocks**)

hsin the cardinal Confuscian virtue of faithfulness or veracity
shin the front part of a leg below the knee

Hu (see **heugh**)

hue (see **hew**)

hui (see **hooey**)

human characteristic of mankind
humin a dark-colored insoluble amorphous substance formed in many chemical reactions
Yuman a language family of the Hokan stock in Arizona, California, and Mexico; belonging to a culture of western Arizona about A.D. 700–1200

humbles brings down the pride or arrogance of a person
umbels racemose inflorescences characteristic of the family Umbelliferae, which includes anise, carrot, and parsley
umbles entrails of an animal used as food

humeral belonging to the shoulder or situated in the region of the humerus

humoral relating to a bodily humor, now often used of endocrine factors as opposed to neural or somatic

humerus the longest bone of the upper arm or forelimb
humorous jocular or funny

humin (see human)

humoral (see humeral)

humorous (see humerus)

humpie a humpback salmon; a humpback sucker (fish); a mooneye (fish)
humpy covered with protuberances; a California wrasse (fish)

Hun (see hon)

hurdle an obstacle or barrier
hurtle to propel violently, move rapidly, or dash headlong

hurds (see herds)

hure (see hewer)

hurl (see herl)

hurley an Irish game resembling field hockey
hurly confusion or uproar

hurst (see hearsed)

hurtle (see hurdle)

hurts (see hertz)

hustler (see hostler)

hybrid (see highbred)

hydrocele an accumulation of serous fluid in a sacculated cavity, especially the scrotum
hydrocoele the water-vascular system of an echinoderm, or the pouch or cavity in the embryo from which it develops

hydrous containing water
Hydrus a fabulous water serpent; a Southern constellation

hyke (see haik)

Hyla and hyla (see hila)

hyle (see highly)

hymn (see him)

hype (see hipe)

hypogenous growing on a leaf's lower side
hypogynous inserted on the axis below the carpels in a flower

Group I

hippish - hyppish
hoax - hokes
hocker - hougher
humous - humus
hydrocephalous - hydrocephalus

Group II

hairy   'herē
here   'he,re

haje   'häjē
hajji   'hɑjē

haka   'häkä
Hakka   'häk'kä

halling 'hälin
hauling 'hôlin

harpes   'här,pēz
harpies 'härpēz

hawk   'hôk
hoc(k)   'häk

hilum   'hīləm
hylam   'hī,läm

hostal   'hōstᵊl
hostel   'hästᵊl

humas   'hyüməs
hummus   'həməs

Hungary 'hangərē
hungry   'hungrē

I

I (see **ai**)

Ibo (see **eboe**)

icer (see **Aissor**)

I'd (see **eyed**)

ide (see **eyed**)

Idaean characteristic of the ancient Greek goddess Rhea or Cybele with whom Mt. Ida was associated
idaein an anthocyanin pigment obtained in the form of a greenish brown crystalline chloride

idem the previously mentioned or as mentioned above
item a detail or particular

ideogram a symbol used in a system of writing to represent a thing but not a particular word for it
idiogram a diagrammatic representation of a chromosome complement

ideograph a symbol used in a system of writing to represent a thing but not a particular word for it (the identical definition as **ideogram**)
idiograph a mark or signature peculiar to an individual

idle not occupied; unemployed
idol a symbol of a deity, being, or thing used as an object of worship
idyll a descriptive work usually dealing with pastoral or rural life

Igo (see **ego**)

ileum the last division of the small intestine constituting the part between the jejunum and large intestine
ilium the dorsal and upper one of three bones composing either lateral half of the pelvis
illium an alloy containing 60% nickel, 25% chromium, plus some copper, manganese, silicon, and tungsten

I'll (see **aisle**)

illapse (see **elapse**)

illation (see **elation**)

illegit (see **elegit**)

illicit (see **elicit**)

illiterate (see **alliterate**)

illium (see **ileum**)

illuded (see **alluded**)

illumen (see **alumen**)

illusion (see **allusion**)

immanent confined to consciousness or to the mind; indwelling, inherent, or intrinsic
imminent near at hand or impending

immerge (see **emerge**)

immerse (see **amerce**)

immersed (see **emersed**)

imminent (see **immanent**)

immission (see **emission**)

immortal not subject to death; imperishable
immortelle any of various coral trees, especially a large red-flowered tree in tropical America

impartable capable of being communicated or transmitted
impartible not subject to division

impassable incapable of being traveled on or crossed
impassible unfeeling or impassive; incapable of suffering or of experiencing pain

Impatiens a large genus of widely distributed annual plants
impatience restlessness or chafing of spirit

implastic (see emplastic)

impressed aroused strong feeling about; applied with pressure
imprest a loan or advance of money

imu (see emu)

in a preposition indicating a place with respect to time or space
inn a public house for lodging, feeding, and or entertainment of travelers

incite to stir up, spur, or urge on; to instigate
insight discernment or understanding

inciter a person that instigates
insider a person having access to confidential information because of his/her position; a person recognized or accepted as a member of some group

incubous leaves so arranged that the anterior margin of each overlaps the posterior margin of the next younger
incubus an evil spirit believed to lie on sleeping persons; a nightmare

indict to formally accuse
indite to compose a poem or story

indie an organization, such as a motion-picture studio, that is independent (slang); a self-employed person
Indy pertaining to the capital of Indiana or the "Indianapolis-500" car race

indiscreet imprudent, inconsiderate, or untactful
indiscrete not separated into distinct parts

indite (see indict)

Indy (see indie)

infirmation the process of making invalid, as opposed to confirmation
information knowledge of a particular event or situation; news or intelligence

influence an act or power to produce an effect on
influents tributary streams; animals having an important effect on an ecological community's balance

infold (see enfold)

information (see infirmation)

ingrain (see engrain)

inn (see in)

innumerable (see enumerable)

insider (see inciter)

insight (see incite)

insist (see encyst)

insolate to place in sunlight
insulate to separate or shield from conducting bodies to prevent transfer of electricity, heat, or sound

insole a loose thin strip placed inside a shoe for warmth or comfort
insoul to endow or imbue with a soul

insolent haughty, contemptuous, or brutal in behavior or language
insulant a material that retards the passage of temperature, electricity, or sound

insoul (see insole)

installation giving possession of an office, rank, order with the usual ceremonial rites; something that is set up for use or service
instillation gradual introduction a drop at a time

instance a case, illustration, or example
instants points of time

instillation (see installation)

insulant (see insolent)

insulate (see insolate)

intendance the care, control, or management of an administrative department

intendence attendance; presence; attention

intense extremely marked or pronounced; strained or deep
intents proposed ends or objects; meanings

intension connotation; determination or intentness
intention a purpose, aim, or objective

intents (see **intense**)

intercession an interposition between parties at variance with a view to reconciliation; a mediation
intersession a period between two academic terms or conference meetings

interdental situated between the teeth
interdentile in architecture, the space between two dentils under the corona of a cornice

interned confined within prescribed limits; impounded; acted as an intern
inturned turned inward; introverted

interosseous situated between bones
interosseus a muscle arising from the metacarpals (in the hand) and metatarsals (in the foot)

interpellate to question formally a governmental policy or decision
interpolate to insert between other things or parts

intersession (see **intercession**)

interval a space of time between recurrences of similar conditions or states; a space between things
intervale low-lying grassland and fields along a watercourse

intrada (see **entrada**)

inturned (see **interned**)

invade to overrun with a view toward conquest or plunder; to enter in a hostile manner; to permeate
inveighed complained vehemently

inverter a device for converting direct current into alternating current
invertor a muscle that turns a limb or part inward

io a large hawk that is Hawaii's only indigenous raptorial bird
iyo a Philippine woody vine; the stiff coarse bast fiber of an African palm

ion (see **ayin**)

Iran (see **airan**)

ire (see **eyer**)

ironic (see **Aaronic**)

irrupt (see **erupt**)

isle (see **aisle**)

islet (see **eyelet**)

isotac a line on a map connecting points where ice melts at the same time in the spring
isotach a line on a map connecting points of equal wind speed

istle a fiber obtained from various tropical American plants
iztle a type of obsidian used by the Mexican Indians to make knives and arrow points

item (see **idem**)

its of, associated with, or belonging to it
it's the contraction of it is

ius a legal principle, right, or power
use the act of employing something
youse your, or substandard version of **you**

ixodic (see **exotic**)

iyo (see **io**)

iztle (see **istle**)

Group I

ileal - ilial
illuminance - illuminants
impatience - impatients
impenitence - impenitents
impertinence - impertinents
impotence - impotents
incidence - incidents
incompetence - incompetents
independence - independents
indifference - indifferents
indigence - indigents
indolence - indolents
ingredience - ingredients
innocence - innocents
insignificance - insignificants
insistence - insistents
insolence - insolents
insurance - insurants
insurgence - insurgents
intelligence - intelligents
intendance - intendants
intolerance - intolerants
intransigence - intransigents
intrigant - intrigante

invariance - invariants
iridescence - iridescents

Group I and II

indemnitee   ən'demnə.tē
indemnity   ən'demnətē

Group II

idea   'i:dēə
itea   id·ēə

incendive   in'sendiv
incentive   in'sentiv

incision   ən'sizhən
insition   in'sishən

incus   'in.küs
incuse   'in.kyüs

ingenious   ən'jēnyəs
ingenuous   ən'jenyəwəs

J

---

jacinth   a plant of the genus Hyacinthus
jacinthe   a moderate orange color

jack   a portable device for raising or lifting heavy objects
jak   a large East Indian tree

Jacobean   representing an early 17th century style of architecture, furniture, literature, or drama
Jacobian   a determinant in which the elements of the first column are partial derivatives of the first of a set of n functions with respect to each of n independent variables, those of the second column are partial derivatives of the second of a set of n ... etc.

jaeger   a large spirited rapacious bird inhabiting northern seas
yager   a large-bore rifle formerly used in the U.S.

Jain   an adherent of Jainism, a dualistic religion founded in India during the 6th century B.C.
jane   a girl or woman (slang)

jak   (see jack)

jam   to press into a close or tight position; a product made by boiling fruit and sugar into a thick consistency
jamb   an upright piece forming a side of an opening, as a doorway

jambeau a piece of plate armor for the leg between the knee and ankle; a spikefish
jambo a rose apple tree of the tropics

jane (see **Jain**)

Jat an Indo-Aryan people of the Punjab and Uttar Pradesh
jot the smallest amount; to write briefly or hurriedly

jaun a small Calcutta conveyance similar to a sedan chair for transporting a person on the carriers' shoulders
john a fellow, guy, or chap; a toilet

jay a noisy, vivacious bird of the crow family; a simpleton
jeh a female demon in Zoroastrianism

jean (see **gean**)

jeered spoke or cried out with derision or mockery
jird any of several North African gerbils

jeez (see **gees**)

jeh (see **jay**)

jell (see **gel**)

jellied (see **gelid**)

jemez (see **hamus**)

jen the cardinal Confucian virtue of benevolence toward one's fellowman
run to go by moving the legs quickly

jen the cardinal Confucian virtue of benevolence toward one's fellowman
wren a small brown singing bird

jennet (see **genet**)

jerm (see **germ**)

jerries (see **Gerres**)

jes an African insectivorous animal about the size of a stoat but similar in form and habits to an otter
jess a short leather strap used in falconry that is secured to each leg of a hawk

jessed (see **gest[e]**)

jest (see **gest[e]**)

jewel a precious stone; an ornament
jhool trappings for a horse, elephant, or other animal
joule a unit of work or energy equal to .7375 foot-pounds

Jewry part of a population that adheres to Judaism
jury a group of persons sworn to give a verdict on some matter

jhool (see **jewel**)

jigger (see **chigger**)

jill (see **gill**)

jing (see **ching**)

jinks pranks or frolics; moves quickly with sudden turns or changes of direction
jinx something that is felt or believed to bring bad luck
Jynx a genus of woodpeckers

jinn (see **gin**)

jinni (see **ginny**)

jinny (see **ginny**)

jinx (see **jinks**)

jird (see **jeered**)

jive (see **gyve**)

jobo (see **hobo**)

john (see **jaun**)

jook an establishment having a jukebox
juke to make a sound or call like a partridge

jot (see **Jat**)

joule (see **jewel**)

joule a unit of work or energy equal to .7375 foot-pounds
jowl a jaw; a hog's boneless cheek

meat; loose flesh surrounding a lower cheek and jaw

joust a combat on horseback between two persons
just reasonable, equitable, or fair

Jova (see **Hova**)

jowl (see **joule**)

judding vibrating with intensity
jutting projecting or protruding

juggler a person skilled in acts of manual dexterity
jugular relating to the throat, neck, or jugular vein (substandard speech)

juke (see **jook**)

June (see **Chun**)

Jur a member of a tribe on the White Nile
jure jurisprudence; a right; to impanel as a juror

jurel any of several carangid food fishes of warm seas, as the blue runner and crevalle

xurel a saurel which includes several elongated compressed fishes having a series of bony plates extending the full length of the lateral line

jury (see **Jewry**)

just (see **joust**)

jutting (see **judding**)

Juvenal a writer resembling or suggestive of the Roman poet Juvenal in his use of biting satire and pungent realism
juvenile psychologically immature or undeveloped; young

Jinx (see **jinks**)

Group II

Jews ˈjüz
juice ˈjüs

juba ˈjübə
jubba(h) ˈjübə or jəbə

K

kaama (see **comma**)

Kabul (see **cobble**)

Kadir (see **cotter**)

Kaf (see **cough**)

Kafa (see **caffa**)

Kaffa (see **caffa**)

Kai (see **cay**)

kains sarongs
kinds natural groupings without taxonomic connotations

Kaiser a head of an Ancient or medieval empire; the Austrian sovereign from 1804 to 1918; the ruler of Germany from 1871 to 1918

kayser a unit of length equal to the reciprocal of 1 centimeter (in spectroscopy)

kakar (see **cocker**)
kaki (see **cocky**)

kaligenous (see **caliginous**)

kalij (see **college**)

kalpa (see **culpa**)

Kama and **kama** (see **comma**)

kame (see **came**)

kami (see **commie**)

kamiks (see **comics**)

kapelle (see **Capella**)

kaph   (see calf and cough)

kappa   (see capa)

kaput   (see caput)

karat   (see carat)

karate   (see carate)

Karel   (see carol)

karri   (see carry)

karris   (see caries)

kart   (see cart)

karusel   (see car[r]ousel)

Kasha   (see Cassia)

katar   (see catarrh)

kate   (see cate)

katel   (see coddle)

Kaw   (see caw)

kay   (see cay)

kaya   a Japanese tree with light red bark and yellow lustrous close-grained wood
Khaya   a genus of African timber trees with wood closely resembling mahogany
khaya   any tree of the genus Khaya

k(a)yak   a fully decked-in Eskimo skin canoe propelled by a double-bladed paddle
kyack   a packsack swung on either side of a pack saddle

kayser   (see Kaiser)

kecks   retching sounds
kex   a Mayan therapeutic rite in which a sick person pledged to offer food in return for health

keel   the longitudinal timber extending from stem to stern along the center of a ship's or boat's bottom
Kiel   a city in northern Germany

keesh   graphite that separates on a slow cooling of molten cast or pig iron

quiche   a baked custard pie

kelt   (see Celt)

ken   (see can)

keno   a game resembling lotto and bingo
kino   the dried juice obtained from the trunk of an East Indian tree; a motion picture theater in Europe

kepi   (see cape)

Ker   (see cur)

keriah   (see chorea)

Kermes   a genus of scales comprising those that form kermes and various related North American and Australian scales
kermes   dried female bodies of various scaled insects used as red dye
kermis   entertainment usually given to raise money

kernel   (see colonel)

kerrie   (see carry)

kerril   (see carol)

Kerry   (see carry)

keryl   (see carol)

Ket   a people of the middle Yenisei region of Siberia
quête   a collection of money, such as a payment to a street musician or a strolling player

ketch   (see catch)

ketol   a compound that is both a ketone and an alcohol
kitol   a crystalline alcohol obtained from whole-liver oil containing vitamin A

kettle   a metallic vessel in which liquids or semifluid masses are boiled
ketyl   a class of unstable compounds made by treating ketones with a metal

kex   (see kecks)

key   (see cay)

khaki   (see cocky)

khan   (see can and con)

Khaya and khaya   (see kaya)

Khond   (see cond)

khor   (see core)

khud   (see cud)

kiddy   a small child
kitty   a kitten; a fund in a poker game

Kiel   (see keel)

kike   (see caique)

kill   to put to death; to put an end to
kiln   an oven of furnace

Kin   (see gin)

kindal   an Indian tree with hard gray wood resembling walnut
kindle   to start a fire; to awaken or intensify to awareness

kinds   (see kains)

kino   (see keno)

kirtle   (see curdle)

kirve   (see curve)

kissar   a five-stringed lyre of northern Africa
kisser   the face (slang)

kissed   (see cist)

kisser   (see kissar)

kist   (see cist)

kitchen   a place for cooking and preparing meals
Kitchin   a business cycle formed by a 3½-year recession during a prosperity phase

kitol   (see ketol)

kitty   (see kiddy)

Klan   (see clan)

Klang   (see clang)

klatch   (see clatch)

Klepht   (see cleft)

klick   (see click)

Kling   (see cling)

klip(pe)   (see clip)

klister   (see clyster)

klomp   (see clomp)

Klucker   (see clucker)

Klux   (see clucks)

knack   a clever or adroit way of doing something
nak   the stigmatic point of the fruit of the mango

knaggy   covered with gnarled, knotty protuberances
naggy   a little nag, as a pony; characterized by being persistently annoying

knap   a sharp or abrupt blow
nap   to sleep briefly; a soft fuzzy fibrous surface
nape   the back part of the neck
nappe   a sheet of water falling down from the crest of a dam

knarred   (see gnarred)

knaur   (see gnawer)

knave   an unscrupulous person
nave   the main part of a church's interior; a block or hub in a wheel's center into which the axle is fitted

knead   to mix into a blended whole by repeatedly working and pressing the mass, as bread dough
kneed   struck or touched with the knee
need   to want or desire; poverty

knee   the joint in the mid-part of a leg
ne(e)   originally or formerly called

kneed   (see knead)

kneel   to bend the knee

neele any of several grasses of the genus Lolium, including bearded darnel

knell to ring a bell with slow solemnity
nell the second highest trump in various card games

knew (see **gnu**)

knickers loose-fitting knee-length pants gathered at the knee with a band; small balls of baked clay used as marbles
nickers neighs, as a horse; persons who notch objects; fabulous water monsters or water sprites; 18th century night brawlers of London who broke windows with a halfpence

knight a person on whom a sovereign has conferred a dignity or title; a chess piece
night the time from dusk to dawn

knighthood the rank or profession of a person on whom a sovereign has conferred a dignity or title
nighthood a condom (slang)

knit to form fabric by interlocking yarn in a series of connected loops; to consolidate
nit a parasitic insect's egg, as a louse

knitted formed fabric by interlocking yarn in a series of connected loops; consolidated
nited bright, glossy, or lustrous

knitter a person or machine that makes knit goods
nitter an insect that deposits its eggs on horses

knob a small rounded projecting mass
nob to strike in the head; in cribbage, the jack of the same suit as the starter card

knocks strikes or raps
nocks notches in arrows to accommodate the bowstring
nox a unit of low-level illumination measurement equal to 10^{-3} lux; ni-

trogen oxide that is emitted by an energy source into the atmosphere (by shortening)

knorr a single-sail medieval ship of northern Europe
nor or not, used with neither as a negative correlative

knot a fastening made by intertwining pliant rope or tubing; a unit of nautical or air speed; a sandpiper
nat a class of spirits in Burmese folklore
naught nothing
naut a sea mile of 2,029 yards used as a measure for submarine cables
not negative; in no manner

knotting fancywork made by twisting and looping thread into knots to form designs
nodding bending downward or forward

knotty full of difficulties or complications; gnarled or nobby
naughty guilty of misbehavior or disobedience
noddy a stupid person; a card game resembling cribbage

knout a flogging whip with a lash of leather thongs twisted with wire
newt any of various small semi-aquatic salamanders
Nut the goddess of the sky, in Egyptian religion

known comprehended or understood
none the canonical ninth hour

knows comprehends or understands
noes denials; negative votes
nose a prominent part of a mammal's face which bears the nostrils

knubs waste silk usually taken from a cocoon's outside
nubs knobs or lumps; cores or gists of an argument

knut a fop or dandy of the late 19th and early 20th centuries
nut a hard-shelled dry fruit or seed; a perforated block of metal with

an internal screw thread for attachment to a bolt

ko   (see **go**)

kob   (see **cob**)

Koch   (see **coach**)

koel   (see **coil**)

koel   any of several cuckoos of India, the East Indies, and Australia
kohol   a preparation used in Arabia and Egypt to darken the edges of eyelids

koff   (see **cough** and **cuff**)

Ko(h)l   (see **coal**)

kohl   (see **coal**)

kohol   (see **koel**)

koi   (see **coy**)

Koko and **koko**   (see **cocoa**)

kokoon   (see **cocoon**)

Koli   (see **coaly**)

kolm   (see **comb**)

Komi   (see **comby**)

Konyak   (see **Cognac**)

kooky   crazy, offbeat, or eccentric
Kuki   any of numerous hill people in southern Assam, India

kopje   (see **copy**)

koppa   (see **coppa**)

kora   (see **Cora**)

Koran   the book forming the basis of the Islamic world
korin   a gazelle of West Africa

Korea   (see **chorea**)

korin   (see **Koran**)

Kot   (see **cat** and **caught**)

Kota   (see **coda**)

koto   (see **Coto**)

kou   (see **cow**)

KP   (see **cape**)

kraal   (see **crawl**)

kraft   (see **craft**)

kral   (see **crawl**)

krantz   (see **crance**)

kraton   (see **craton**)

kris   (see **criss**)

krises   (see **creases**)

krona   the basic monetary unit of Iceland and Sweden
krone   the basic monetary unit of Denmark, and of Austria from 1892 to 1925

Kruman   (see **crewman**)

Krus   (see **crews**)

Kuan   (see **guan**)

Kuki   (see **kooky**)

kuku   (see **cuckoo**)

Kulaman   (see **coolamon**)

Kulli   (see **cully**)

kupper   (see **cupper**)

Kurd   (see **curd**)

Kwa   a branch of the Niger-Congo language family that is spoken along the coast and a short distance inland from Liberia to Nigeria
qua   in the capacity or character of; a European night heron

kweek   a grass of the genus Cynodon
quake   to shake, vibrate, or tremble

Kweri   a people of the southern British Cameroons
query   a question or inquiry

kyack   (see **k[a]yak**)

Kyloe   (see **Chilo**)

kyphosis   an abnormal backward curvature of the spine
Kyphosus   a genus that includes the Bermuda chub, a gray percoid fish

Group II

kibbutz   ki'bùts
kibitz   'kibəts

L
---

la   the sixth tone of the diatonic scale
law   a role or mode of conduct

laager   a defensive position protected by a ring of armored vehicles
lager   a beer brewed by bottom fermentation and stored in refrigerators
logger   a lumberjack; a device that records data automatically

label   an identification tag or stamp
labile   changeable or unstable; adaptable

Labrus   the type genus of the large and important family of percoid fishes of Labridae, such as the wrasse
labrys   an ancient Cretan sacred double ax

lace   a fine openwork fabric; to thread or intertwine
laisse   an irregular rhythmic system of Old French poetry

laces   beats or lashes; adds a dash of alcoholic liquor to food or beverage
lacis   a square-meshed lace with darned patterns

laches   negligence or carelessness
lashes   whips; binds with rope; moves suddenly or violently

laches   negligence or carelessness
latches   devices that hold something in place, as a door; grasps

lacis   (see **laces**)

lacks   wants or is in need of

lacs   resinous substances secreted by the lac insect and used as shellac
Lak(h)s   members of a division of the Lezghian people in southern Russia on the western shore of the Caspian Sea
laks   performances of the male capercaillie (the largest European grouse) during courtship
lax   not stringent; easygoing

ladder   a structure for climbing up and down; to scale
latter   coming after something else

lade   to put a load or burden on
laid   put or set down

lader   a person that loads
later   tardier; after

lager   (see **laager**)

lagopous   having hairy rhizomes suggestive of a hare's foot
Lagopus   a genus of northern game birds comprising the ptarmigans and red grouse

laid   (see **lade**)

lain   rested or remained in a horizontal position
laine   a woolen cloth
lane   a narrow passageway; an alley

lair   a wild animal's living place; a den
layer   a person that lays something; a hen that lays eggs; a thickness lying over or under another
lehr   a long oven in which glassware is annealed

lais medival short tales or lyric poems in French literature
lase to emit coherent light
lays puts or sets down
laze to pass in idleness or relaxation
leas pastures or grasslands
leis garlands or necklaces of flowers

Lais a Mongoloid people of the Chin Hills in Myanmar
lie to rest in a horizontal position; to convey an untruth
lye a strong alkaline solution

laisse (see **lace**)

laisse an irregular rhythmic system of Old French poetry
less fewer or smaller
loess an unstratified deposit of loam ranging from clay to fine sand

laitance an accumulation of fine particles on freshly placed concrete
latents scarcely visible fingerprints

Lak(h)s (see **lacks**)

Lak(h)s members of a division of the Lezghian people in southern Russia on the western shore of the Caspian Sea
lochs lakes
locks tresses of hair; fastenings for a door or a box
lox liquid oxygen (by shortening); smoked salmon (also 'lax)

lakie a temporary retrograde movement of the tide, especially in the Firth of Forth, Scotland
laky resembling hemoglobin dissolved in plasma

laks (see **lacks**)

laky (see **lakie**)

lali a large drum made of a hollowed log to summon people in Western Polynesia and Fiji
lolly soft ice that is ground down from floes or formed in turbulent seawater

lam to flee hastily
lamb a young sheep

lama a Tibetan Buddhist priest or monk
llama a South American ruminant

lamb (see **lam**)

lance a weapon of war consisting of a long shaft with a sharp steel head
lants any of several small elongate marine teleost fishes of the genus Ammodytes (sometimes **launce**)

lande an infertile moor
lawned made into or like grass-covered ground

lane (see **lain**)

langur any of various Asiatic long-tailed monkeys
lunger a glob of sputum, phlegm, or other expectoration; a person suffering from a lung disease

lants (see **lance**)

Laos a kingdom of Indochina
louse any of various small wingless usually flattened insects that are parasitic on warm-blooded animals

Lapps people of northern Scandinavia and the Kola peninsula of northern Russia
laps folds over or around something; circuits around a racetrack
lapse a trivial fault or oversight; to depart from an accepted standard

lase (see **lais**)

laser a device that uses natural oscillations of atoms to amplify or generate electromagnetic waves
lazar a person afflicted with a repulsive disease

lashes (see **laches**)

lat a separate column or pillar in some Buddhist buildings in India similar to the Greek stela

lot a portion of land; a considerable quantity or number
lotte any large pediculate fish of the family Lophiidae found along the Atlantic coast of America

latches (see **laches**)

latents (see **laitance**)

later (see **lader**)

Latin a language of ancient Latium and Rome
latten an alloy of or resembling brass that is hammered into thin sheets

latter (see **ladder**)

laud to praise or acclaim
lawed mutilated an animal so as to prevent mischief, as cut the claws from the forefeet of a cat or dog

laureate a recipient of an honor for preeminence in one's field
loriot the golden oriole of Europe

laurel a tree or shrub, the leaves of which yield a fragrant oil
lauryl a mixture of alkyl radicals derived from commercial lauryl alcohol
loral related to the space between the eye and bill of a bird, or the corresponding area in a reptile or fish
lorel relating to a body of knowledge

lauter clear or clarified
louder more intense sound; noisier

law (see **la**)

lawed (see **laud**)

lawned (see **lande**)

lax (see **lacks**)

layer (see **lair**)

lays (see **lais**)

lazar (see **laser**)

laze (see **lais**)

lea a pasture or grassland
lee a side sheltered from the wind; dregs or sediment
Li an ethnic group that is culturally a branch of the early Tai people of southern China
li a cardinal virtue in Confucianism consisting of correct behavior as an outward expression of inner harmony; the solmization syllable for the semitone between the 6th and 7th degrees of the diatonic scale

leach to draw out or remove as if by percolation or seepage
leech a carnivorous or blood-sucking annelid worm

leachy permitting liquids to pass by means of percolation
lichi an African antelope somewhat smaller than the related waterbuck
Litchi a genus of Chinese trees cultivated for its edible fruit

lead a heavy metallic element
led guided or marked the way

leader an individual who goes before or guides
lieder German folk songs
liter a metric unit of capacity equal to 1.057 liquid quarts

leads guides or marks the way
Leeds a city in Yorkshire, England

leaf a lateral outgrowth constituting part of a plant's foliage
lief gladly, willingly, or freely

leag a kelp
league a unit of distance varying from 2.4 to 4.6 statute miles; an association of nations or persons united in a common interest

leak an opening that permits escape
leek a biennial herb related to garlic and onion

lean to deviate from a vertical position; free of fat or rawboned
lien a charge on property in satisfaction of a debt

leaner a pitched horseshoe that leans against the stake without ringing it
lienor a person holding a valid lien

leap to project oneself through the air
leep to plaster (as a wall) with cow dung

leas (see **lais**)

lease to rent property from or to another
lis a fleur-de-lis
lisse silk gauze used for dresses and trimmings

leased rented property from or to another
least lowest, smallest, or slightest

leave to withdraw or depart; to abandon; to bequeath
lief gladly or willingly

leaver a person who leaves
lever a rigid device that transmits and modifies motion when a force is applied and it turns about a point, as a crowbar, oar, or canoe paddle
levir the now abolished custom of a husband's brother assuming his place (see **levirate**)
liefer more gladly, willingly, or freely

lechs prehistoric monumental capstones
leks sites where birds regularly resort for purposes of sexual display and courtship
lex the law

Lecythis a genus of very large South American trees
lecythus a cylindrical or round and squat vase used by ancient Greeks for oils and ointments

led (see **lead**)

lee (see **lea**)

leech (see **leach**)

Leeds (see **leads**)

leek (see **leak**)

leep (see **leap**)

leer to give a lascivious, knowing, or malicious look
lehr a long oven in which glassware is annealed

leet a ceremonial English court
lied a German folksong

lehr (see **lair** and **leer**)

leis (see **lais**)

leister a spear with several barbed prongs for catching fish
lister a person who itemizes articles or costs of materials and labor; a double-moldboard plow that throws a ridge of earth both ways

leks (see **lechs**)

lends gives temporarily to another; loans
lens an optical instrument consisting of a transparent substance with two opposing regular surfaces

leopard a large strong cat with black spots
lepered afflicted with leprosy

Lepas a widely distributed genus of goose barnacles
Lepus a genus comprising the typical hares

leper a person afflicted with leprosy
lepper a horse skilled in jumping

lepered (see **leopard**)

lepper (see **leper**)

leptocephalous characterized by or exhibiting abnormal narrowness and tallness of the skull
Leptocephalus a genus of small pelagic fishes

leptodactylous having slender toes
Leptodactylus a genus of toothed toads

Lepus   (see **Lepas**)

less   (see **laisse**)

lessen   to decrease or diminish
lesson   a segment of instruction

lets   services in racket and net games
that do not count and must be re-
played; obstructions; allows or
permits
let's   the contraction of let us
Letts   people closely related to Lith-
uanians mainly inhabiting Latvia

Leucifer   a genus of free-swimming
slender macruran crustaceans
Lucifer   the devil; a person resembling the devil especially in evil or
pride

leucine   a white crystalline amino acid
loosen   release from restraint

leucite   potassium aluminum silicate
occurring in igneous rock
lucite   an acrylic resin or plastic

leucon   a sponge or sponge larva
leukon   a body organ consisting of
white blood cells and their precursors

leud   a feudal tenant in ancient
Frankish kingdoms
lewd   indecent, obscene, or salacious
lood   methaqualone (slang)
looed   obligated to contribute an
amount to a new pool in the game
of loo because of a failure to win a
trick

leukon   (see **leucon**)

levee   an embankment to prevent
flooding; a fashionable party to
honor someone
levy   an imposition of a tax, assessment, or fine; conscription for military service

lever   (see **leaver**)

leveret   a hare in its first year
levirate   the marriage of a widow by
the brother or occasionally the heir

of her deceased husband (see **levir**)

levir   (see **leaver**)

levirate   (see **leveret**)

levy   (see **levee**)

lewd   (see **leud**)

lewder   more indecent, obscene, or
salacious
looter   a person that plunders, sacks,
or robs
loutre   a dark grayish yellowish
brown color, such as otter brown
luter   a person who seals coke oven
doors with cement or a clay mixture

lewdest   most indecent, obscene, or
salacious
lutist   a maker or player of lutes

lex   (see **lechs**)

Li and **li**   (see **lea**)

liable   exposed or subject to an
adverse contingency or action;
likely
libel   a written or oral defamatory
statement or representation

liar   a person who utters a
falsehood; a prevaricator
lier   a person that lies or waits, as in
ambush
lyre   an ancient Greek stringed musical instrument resembling a harp; a
triangular area of the ventral surface of the corpus callosum between the posterior pillors of the
fornix

libel   (see **liable**)

lice   small wingless parasitic insects
lyse   to cause to undergo the gradual
decline of a disease process

lichen   a thallophytic plant composed of alga and fungus
liken   to compare; to represent as
similar

lichi   (see **leachy**)

licker   a person or animal who passes the tongue over
liquor   a distilled alcoholic beverage; a cooking broth

lickerish   fond of good food; desirous
licorice   a dried root of gummy texture with a sweet astringent flavor

licorice   a dried root of gummy texture with a sweet astringent flavor
liquorous   resulting from or resembling an intoxicated condition

lidder   a person who fastens lids on containers
litter   the offspring at one birth of a multiparous animal; a stretcher for carrying a sick or injured person; refuse or rubbish

lie   (see **Lais**)

lied   (see **leet**)

lied   conveyed an untruth
lyed   treated with a strong alkaline solution

lieder   (see **leader**)

lief   (see **leaf** and **leave**)

liefer   (see **leaver**)

lien   (see **lean**)

lienor   (see **leaner**)

liens   spleens
lions   large carnivorous animals of the cat family
Lyons   a city in southeast France

lier   (see **liar**)

lies   rests in a horizontal position; conveys an untruth
lyes   strong alkaline solutions
lyse   to cause to undergo the gradual decline of a disease process

lieu   instead
loo   halloo; an ancient card game; a toilet
Loup   a member of the Skidi tribe of Pawnee Indians that dwelled

from along the Platte river in Nebraska to Arkansas
loup   a half mask usually of silk or satin
Lu   a Tai ethnic and Buddhist group inhabiting the extreme southwest part of Yunnan province in southern China

lieut   a military officer with the rank of lieutenant (slang)
loot   plunder or booty
lute   a stringed musical instrument with a large pear-shaped body; a packing or caulking compound to make joints impervious to gas or liquid

liken   (see **lichen**)

lim   a blue pine
limb   an animal's projecting appendage; a primary tree branch
limn   to draw or paint on a flat surface; to delineate

limbous   with slightly overlapping borders, as of a suture
Limbus   a region on the border of hell where souls abide who are barred from heaven through no fault of their own
limbus   the marginal region of the cornea of the eye by which it is continuous with the sclera

lime   a small globose citrus fruit of the lime tree; to whitewash with a solution of lime and water
lyme   in heraldry, a leash or a bloodhound

limen   the point at which a physiological or psychological effect begins to be produced
limon   a hybrid citrus fruit produced by crossing a lime and a lemon

limey   an English sailor (slang)
limy   smeared with or consisting of lime; viscous

limn   (see **lim**)

limon   (see **limen**)

Limousin a French breed of medium-sized yellow-red cattle bred especially for meat
limousine a large luxurious sedan or small bus, especially one for hire

limy (see **limey**)

lin a female unicorn in Chinese mythology
linn a tree of the genus Tilia, including the European linden
llyn a lake or pool

linde a synthetic gemstone, as a sapphire
lindy a jitterbug dance originating in Harlem

linen a cloth made of flax
linon a fine sheer plainwoven cotton fabric

links a gold course; connecting structures, as in a chain
Lynx the genus of Felidae comprising the lynxes
lynx a wildcat, often with tufted ears and a short stubby tail

linn (see **lin**)

linon (see **linen**)

lions (see **liens**)

liquor (see **licker**)

liquorous (see **licorice**)

lira a ridge on some shells resembling a fine thread or hair
lyra a glockenspiel with a lyre-shaped frame

lis (see **lease**)

lisse (see **lease**)

lister (see **leister**)

Litchi (see **leachy**)

liter (see **leader**)

literal adhering to the primary or exact meaning of a term, phrase, or expression

littoral a coastal region including land and water near the shoreline

litter (see **lidder**)

littoral (see **literal**)

llama (see **lama**)

llyn (see **lin**)

Lo a North American Indian
lo an interjection used to draw attention or to express wonder or surprise
low having relatively little upward extension; a deep sustained sound characteristic of cattle

Loa a genus of African filarial worms infesting the subcutaneous tissues and blood of man
loa any worm of the genus Loa
lowa an Indian quail

loach any of a family of small Old World freshwater fishes closely related to the Cyprinidae but resembling catfishes in appearance and habits
loche a freshwater fish related to the cod, such as the eelpout

load a mass or weight; to pack or fill with something
lode an ore deposit
lowed uttered deep sustained sounds characteristic of cattle

loam a clay mixture
loom a device or interlacing sets of thread or yarn at right angles to form cloth

loan something given temporarily to another, as money at interest
lone solitary

loath reluctant to do something contrary to one's tastes or ways of thinking
loathe to feel strong aversion to, detest, or abhor

locale a place or site
lo(w)-cal low in calories, as a food or drink

loche (see **loach**)

lochs (see **Lakhs**)

locks (see **Lakhs**)

locus a place or locality
locusts migratory grasshoppers that often travel in vast swarms and strip all vegetation from areas through which they pass

lode (see **load**)

loess (see **laisse**)

logger (see **laager**)

logie a piece of imitation jewelry designed for use in theater productions
logy marked by sluggishness and lack of vitality

loir a large European dormouse
Loire the largest river in France

lolly (see **lali**)

lone (see **loan**)

long extending for a considerable distance; to yearn or pine for
longue a large dark North American char that is an important commercial food fish in northern lakes

longe a lake trout; a muskellunge; a long rope used to lead or guide a horse in training
lunge a sudden thrust, pass, or plunge forward

longer having greater length; a row of barrels stored fore and aft
longueur a dull or tedious passage or section, as in a book, play, or musical composition

longue (see **long**)

longueur (see **longer**)

loo (see **lieu**)

lood (see **leud**)

looed (see **leud**)

loom (see **loam**)

loon a fish-eating diving bird; a crazy person
lune a hawk's leash; half-moon shaped

loons fish-eating diving birds; crazy persons
lunes fits of lunacy or frenzy

loop the doubling of a line with an aperture between; a turning area for vehicles
loupe a small magnifying glass

loos halloos; toilets
lose to mislay; to fail to win; to fail to keep in sight

loose not securely attached; lacking precision
luce a full-grown pike (a fish)

loosen (see **leucine**)

loot (see **lieut**)

looter (see **lewder**)

looting plundering or robbing
luting a sealant for packing a joint or coating a porous surface to produce imperviousness to gas or liquid

loral (see **laurel**)

lore a body of knowledge or traditions; something learned
lower situated further below or under; to bring down; to reduce

lorel (see **laurel**)

lori either of two small nocturnal slow-moving lemurs
lory any of numerous parrots of Australia, New Guinea, and adjacent islands

loriot (see **laureate**)

lory (see **lori**)

lose (see **loos**)

loser a person, animal, or thing that fails to win or lags behind
luser an uninformed user of a computer system

lot   (see lat)

lotte   (see lat)

louder   (see lauter)

Loup and loup   (see lieu)

loupe   (see loop)

loure   a dance in slow triple or sex-
tuple time

Lur   a chiefly nomadic Muslim people inhabiting a wild part of the
Zagros mountains in Iran

lur   a large bronze S-shaped Scandinavian trumpet of the Bronze Age

lure   a bait, decoy, enticement, or
incentive; to attract or entice

louse   (see Laos)

loutre   (see lewder)

low   (see Lo)

Iowa   (see Loa)

lo(w)-cal   (see locale)

lowed   (see load)

lower   (see lore)

lox   (see Lakhs)

Lu   (see lieu)

luce   (see loose)

Lucifer   (see Leucifer)

lucite   (see leucite)

lucks   prospers or succeeds through
good fortune or change, as "lucks
out"

lux   a unit of illumination

luxe   a quality or state of being
sumptuous

luggar   a large dull-brown Asiatic
falcon

lugger   a person who carries materials

lumbar   related to the abdominal
areas on either side of the umbilicus
and above the inguinal regions; related to the vertebrae between the
thoracic vertebrae and the sacrum

lumber   timber or logs; to move
heavily or clumsily

lumen   a cavity or passageway in a
tubular organ; the bore of a tube

lumine   to illuminate; to give physical
light to

lune   (see loon)

lunes   (see loons)

lunge   (see longe)

lunger   (see langur)

Lur and lur   (see loure)

lure   (see loure)

luser   (see loser)

lute   (see lieut)

luter   (see lewder)

Lutheran   a follower or adherent of
Martin Luther or of doctrines and
practices of the Lutheran Church

luthern   a dormer window

luting   (see looting)

lutist   (see lewdest)

lux   (see lucks)

luxe   (see lucks)

lyddite   a high explosive composed
chiefly of picric acid

lydite   basanite, a basaltic extensive
rock closely allied to the chert, jas-
per, and flint; a test or criterion to
determine the quality or genuine-
ness of a thing, such as using a
touchstone

lye   (see Lais)

lyed   (see lied)

lyes   (see lies)

lyme   (see lime)

Lynx and lynx   (see links)

Lyons   (see liens)

lyra   (see lira)

lyre   (see liar)

lyse   (see lice and lies)

lysin   a substance capable of dissolving bacteria and blood corpuscles
lysine   a biologically important basic amino acid

Group I

laggar - luggar
lapan - lapin
lapses - lapsus
legumen - legumin
light - lite
lupous - lupus
lupulin - lupuline

Group I and II

liqueur   li'kər
liquor   'likər

Group II

larigo   'lärə̇,gō
larigot   'larə̇,gō

larin   'lärən
larine   'la,rə̇n

lauds   'lȯdz
Lodz   'lädz

laws   'lȯz
Laz   'läz

leaven   'levən
levan   'le,van

lesser   'lesər
lessor   'le,sȯr

leucon   'lü,kän
Lucan   'lükən

liard   lē'är
lierre   lē'er

lightening   'līt^əniŋ
lightning   'lītniŋ

likeness   'līknə̇s
lychnis   'liknə̇s

likin   'lē'kēn
leaking   'lē,kiŋ

lineament   'linēəmənt
liniment   'linəmənt

lisa   'lēsə
lyssa   'lisə

longer   'lȯŋgər
longueur   lōŋ'gər

loose   'lüs
lose   'lüz

loots   'lütz
lutz   'lu̇tz

lorry   'lȯrē
lory   'lōrē

lunare   lu'narē
lunary   'lünərē

luscious   'ləshəs
lushes   'ləshəz

M

---

ma   mother
maa   a sheep's bleat
maw   a receptacle (as a stomach) into which food is taken by swallowing

ma'am   madam
malm   a soft friable chalky limestone
Mam   an Indian people of southwestern Guatemala

mom　mother

ma'am　madam
mom　mother
mum　silent; to go about merrymaking in disguise; a chrysanthemum

maar　a volcanic crater in a low relief area
mar　to injure, deface, or damage

mach　the ratio of the speed of a body to the speed of sound; a mach number
moc　a moccasin (by shortening)
mock　to deride, treat with scorn, or ridicule; to make a sham of

mackintosh　a lightweight waterproof fabric originally of rubberized cotton
McIntosh　a late-ripening variety of brilliant-red apple

McIntosh　(see mackintosh)

mackle　a blur on a printed sheet
macle　chiastolite, a mineral consisting of andalusite; a twinned crystal

macks　pimps (slang)
Macs　fellow, used informally to address men whose names are unknown
macs　mackinaw coats or jackets
max　a weevil that feeds on henequen buds; the maximum (by shortening)

macle　(see mackle)

maco　Egyptian cotton, especially in its natural undyed state
mako　a large vigorous shark of the Atlantic

macrocephalous　having an exceptionally large head; having the cotyledons of a dicotyledonous embryo consolidated
Macrocephalus　a genus of mammals comprising the warthogs

macrurous　having a long tail; relating to the Macrura, a suborder of crustaceans comprising shrimps, lobsters, and prawns

Macrurus　the type genus of Macroridae, a family of fishes comprising the grenadiers

Macs and macs　(see macks)

madam　a female head of a house of prostitution
madame　a female member of a French royal family

madder　angrier; an herb whose root was formerly used in dyeing
matter　the substance of something; a topic under consideration

made　manufactured or produced
maid　an unmarried girl or woman; a female employed to do domestic work

Madi　a negro people of the upper Nile region north of Lake Albert
Mahdi　a Muslim leader who assumes a messianic role

madid　wet or moist
matted　having parts adhering closely together

maggot　a soft-bodied legless grub that is the larva of various dipterous insects
magot　a Barbary ape; a small grotesque figure of Chinese or Japanese style

magnate　a person of influence, distinction, or prominence
magnet　something that attracts, especially a body that attracts iron

magot　(see maggot)

Mahdi　(see Madi)

Mahri　a native or inhabitant of the Mahra region of the Arabian peninsula
Maori　a native Polynesian population of New Zealand
Mari　a Baluchi people of Baluchistan; a Finnish people of eastern Russia that are forest dwellers and farmers

marri   a very large Australian red gum tree

mai   a slow Japanese folk or theater dance featuring hand gestures
my   belonging to me

Maia   a nearly cosmopolitan genus of spider crabs
Maya   a people of Yucatan, Belize, and northern Guatemala
maya   an illusion-creating power of a god or demon

maid   (see made)

mail   postal matter; armor made of metal links or plates
male   the sex that usually performs the fertilizing function in generation

mailer   a container in which to mail something
malar   relating to a cheek or side of the head

main   the first in any respect; the principal item
Maine   the northeasternmost state in the U.S.
mane   neck hair
mein   Chinese wheat-flour noodles

Mainer   a native or resident of the state of Maine
mainour   in Old English law, something stolen that is found in the thief's possession

mais   slow Japanese folk or theater dances featuring hand gestures
mise   the issue in a legal proceeding upon a writ of right

Maithili   an Indic dialect of north Bihar, India
mightily   earnestly, vigorously, or powerfully

maize   Indian corn; a light yellow color
Mayes   a variety of dewberry important in northern Texas and the Middle West
Mays   the fifth month of the Gregorian calendar (plural)

maze   intricate passages that ramify and interconnect in confusing ways

maizer   a redwing blackbird
maser   a device that utilizes the natural oscillations of an atomic or molecular system to amplify or produce electromagnetic waves
mazer   a large drinking bowl originally of hard wood that is often footed and silver mounted

mako   (see maco)

mal   a disease or sickness
mall   a public area for shopping or leisurely strolling
maul   a heavy hammer; to injure by beating
moll   a gangster's girlfriend; composed in a minor mode

malacia   abnormal softening or loss of consistency of an organ or tissue
Malaysia   a constitutional monarchy in southeast Asia

malaise   a sense of physical, mental, or moral ill-being or uneasiness
Malays   members of people of the Malay peninsula, eastern Sumatra, and part of Borneo

malar   (see mailer)

Malay   a member of the people of the Malay peninsula, eastern Sumatra, and parts of Borneo
mele   an Hawaiian poem adapted to vocal music
melee   a confused struggle; a diamond, usually less than 1/8-carat, cut from a fragment of a larger stone

Malays   (see malaise)

Malaysia   (see malacia)

male   (see mail)

Mali   a republic in west Africa
mal(l)ie   a person belonging to a caste in India whose usual occupation is gardening

molle in music, lower by a half step; flat

molly a pampered darling (slang); a spineless weakling; a gangster's girl friend

moly molybdenum, a fusible polyvalent metallic element

mall (see **mal**)

mal(l)ie (see **Mali**)

malm (see **ma'am**)

Mam (see **ma'am**)

manakin a small bird of Central and South America

mannequin a representation of a human figure for displaying or fitting clothes

mannikin a small weaver bird of Africa, Asia, and Australia

mandrel an axle inserted in a piece of work to support it during machining

mandrill a large fierce gregarious baboon of western Africa

mane (see **main**)

Mangar a people of Nepal

monger a person engaged in the sale of a commodity; a person engaged in petty or discreditable dealings

mangel a large coarse yellow to reddish orange beet extensively grown for cattle food

mangle to cut, bruise, or hack with repeated blows or strokes; to maim

mangle (see **mangel**)

manism the worship of the spirits of deceased humans

monism the metaphysical view that only one kind of substance or ultimate reality exists

mannequin (see **manakin**)

manner a mode of procedure or way of acting; normal behavior

manor a mansion; a lord's house; a large estate

mannikin (see **manakin**)

Mano a Negro people inhabiting the northern tip of the central province of Liberia and adjacent Ivory Coast

mano a handstone used as the upper millstone for grinding grains

mono monotype, a typesetting machine; a bullring attendant; containing one atom, radical, or group of a particular kind

manor (see **manner**)

mantel a supporting beam, stone, or arch for masonry above a fireplace

mantle a loose sleeveless garment worn over clothing; a part of the earth's interior

many consisting of or amounting to a large but indefinite number (although usually 'menē)

money something generally accepted as a medium of exchange, as a measure of value, or a means of payment

mao a peacock

mow a stack of hay or straw

Maori (see **Mahri**)

maqui a Chilean shrub from whose berries wine is made

maquis a thick scrubby underbrush along Mediterranean shores; a member of an underground organization

mar (see **maar**)

marabou a large stork, as an African stork or adjutant bird

Marabout a Muslim monk, hermit, or saint

marabout a tomb or shrine erected to a Marabout

marc a residue remaining after fruit (as grapes) has been pressed

mark something that records position; the basic monetary unit of Germany

marque a brand or make of a product; a governmental license granted to a private person to use an armed vessel at sea to plunder the enemy

mare a female horse
Mayer a person who celebrates May Day
mayor the chief magistrate of a municipality

Mari (see **Mahri**)

maria any of several shrubs and trees of tropical America
Moraea a genus of southern African or Australian bulbous or tuberus plants

marine relating to the sea
moreen a strong cross-ribbed uphol-stery fabric of wool or wool and cotton

marischal an earl marshal of Scot-land from the 15th century to 1716
Marshall the Austronesian language of the Marshall Islands
marshal(l) to arrange or assemble according to some scheme; a mili-tary commander
martial warlike; falling under the astrological influence of Mars

mark (see **marc**)

marli an ornamented raised border on a dining plate
marly resembling clay

marlin a large oceanic gamefish
marline a small tarred two-strand line used to cover wire rope

marly (see **marli**)

marque (see **marc**)

marquees permanent canopies over entranceways; large field tents for-merly used by high-ranking officers
Marquis an important variety of wheat in the U.S.
marquis a nobleman of hereditary rank
marquise an elliptical gem, ring mounting, or bezel with pointed ends

marri (see **Mahri**)

marry to unite in wedlock
mere a Maori war club
merry cheerful or joyous

Marshall and **marshal(l)** (see **marischal**)

marten a slender-bodied carnivorous mammal
martin a swallow or flycatcher

martial (see **marischal**)

martin (see **marten**)

martineta an Argentine tinamou, a gallinaceous bird with a long slender crest
martinete a Cuban heron that forms a variety of the green heron

maser (see **maizer**)

Mason a member of a widespread secret society called Free and Ac-cepted Masons
mason a skilled worker who builds with stone or similar material
meson an unstable nuclear particle first observed in cosmic rays

massed gathered into a large quantity
mast a long vertical spar rising from a ship's deck

mat a flat relatively thin article placed on a horizontal surface
matte a mixture of sulfides formed in smelting sulfide ores of metals

mater a worker who packs shoes or hosiery in pairs
Mehter a member of an harijan caste of sweepers and scavengers in India
mehter a groom or stable boy in Iran

matte (see **mat**)

matted (see **madid**)

matter (see **madder**)

mat(t)rass a rounded long-necked glass flask

mattress   a pad used as a resting place

maud   a gray and black plaid cloth
mod   modern (by shortening)

maul   (see **mal**)

maw   (see **ma**)

max   (see **macks**)

Maya and **maya**   (see **Maia**)

Mayer   (see **mare**)

Mayes   (see **maize**)

mayor   (see **mare**)

Mays   (see **maize**)

maze   (see **maize**)

mazer   (see **maizer**)

me   the objective case of I, a personal pronoun
mi   the third note of the diatonic scale

mead   a fermented drink of water, honey, malt, and yeast
Mede   a native or inhabitant of ancient Media, a kingdom in what is now northwestern Iran
meed   a fitting return or just dessert

mealie   an ear of Indian corn
mealy   soft, dry, and friable

mean   displaying petty selfishness; lacking dignity; to have in mind; to signify; an average or measure of central tendency
mesne   intermediate in time of occurrence or performance
mien   a person's bearing

meat   animal tissue used for food
meet   to come into contact with or encounter
mete   to allot or apportion

meatier   more full of meat; furnishing more solid food for thought

meteor   a streak of light in the night sky produced by passage through the earth's atmosphere of solid matter in the solar system

medal   an inscribed medal commemorating a person or event, or awarded for a deed
meddle   to interfere without right or propriety
metal   any of a large group of substances that typically are opaque, lustrous, temperature and electrical conductors, and can be fused
mettle   qualities and abilities relative to a given situation

meddler   a busybody
medlar   a small Eurasian tree; a small deciduous tree of southern Africa
metal(l)er   a person who places metal sheets on sized work

meddlesome   officiously intruding
mettlesome   spirited

Mede   (see **mead**)

medic   a plant of the genus Medicago, which includes the typical clovers; a person engaged in medical work
metic   an alien resident of an ancient Greek city who had some civil privileges upon payment of a tax

medlar   (see **meddler**)

meed   (see **mead**)

meet   (see **meat**)

meeter   a person who encounters or comes in contact with
meter   a unit of length equal to 39.37 inches; an instrument for measuring; a systematically measured rhythm

Mehter and **mehter**   (see **mater**)

mein   (see **main**)

mele   (see **Malay**)

melee   (see **Malay**)

mellow relaxed and at ease; pleasantly convivial; fully matured or aged
Melo a genus of marine shells, usually designated as Cymbium, comprising the melon shells
melo a melodrama (by shortening)

mends repairs or improves
men's the possessive form of human males

menology an ecclesiastical calendar of festivals celebrated in honor of particular saints and martyrs
monology the habit of soliloquizing

men's (see **mends**)

meow a cat's cry; a spiteful or malicious remark
Miao an aboriginal people of China inhabiting southwestern China into northern parts of Vietnam, Laos, and Thailand

mer a monomeric unit of polymer
murre a narrow-billed auk-like bird, as the razorbill
myrrh an aromatic bitter gum resin used as an ingredient of incense and perfume

merc a mercenary soldier (by shortening)
murk darkness, gloom, or thick heavy air

mere (see **marry**)

mere exclusive of anything else
Mir a chief or leader, used especially in India for descendents of Mohammed
mir a Russian village community
mire a fixed mark due north or south of a meridian

merle a bluish grey color of the coats of some dogs
merl(e) a common English black thrush with an orange bill and eye trim
murral a common freshwater snakehead food fish of southeast Asia

and the Philippines

merlin a small European falcon
merlon the solid interval between embrasures of a battlemented parapet

merry (see **marry**)

mesne (see **mean**)

meso a molecule or compound that is optically inactive because it is internally compensated
miso a paste made of grinding steamed rice, cooked soybeans, and salt that is used in preparing soups and other foods

meson (see **Mason**)

metal (see **medal**)

metal(l)er (see **meddler**)

metanym a generic name rejected because it is based on a type of species congeneric with the type of a previously published genus
metonym a word used for another that it may be expected to suggest

mete (see **meat**)

meteor (see **meatier**)

meter (see **meeter**)

methene a bivalent hydrocarbon radical derived from methane
methine a trivalent hydrocarbon radical derived from methane

metic (see **medic**)

metonym (see **metanym**)

mettle (see **medal**)

mettlesome (see **meddlesome**)

meuse a gap through which a wild animal customarily passes
mews utters a cry characteristic of a cat or gull; sheds the horns
mus bridging groups that join central atoms or ions; the twelfth letter of the Greek alphabet (plural)

Muse one's creative spirit (from the Muses of Greek mythology)
muse to fall into a state of deep thought or dreamy abstraction

meute a cage for molting hawks
mute debatable; deprived of practical significance

mewl a whine or cry
mule a hybrid between a horse and an ass; a very stubborn person

mews (see **meuse**)

mho a unit of electrical conductance equal to the reciprocal of the ohm
mo a moment (slang); a book or volume (by shortening duodecimo)
mot a pithy or witty saying
mow to cut down or off

mi (see **me**)

Miao (see **meow**)

micks persons of Irish descent, often used offensively
mix to blend or stir

micropterous having small or rudimentary fins or wings
Micropterus a genus of sunfishes that includes the American freshwater black basses

Midas a genus of South American marmosets comprising the tamarins
mitis tending to be less than average virulent, such as strains of diphtheria bacilli

middy a student naval officer or midshipman
midi a skirt or coat of mid-calf length

mien (see **mean**)

might possible or probably; power or authority
mite a small to minute arachnid; a very little bit

mightily (see **Maithili**)

mighty powerful, notable, or extraordinary; extremely

mity infested with mites

mignon a moderate purple color; a filet mignon (by shortening)
mignonne daintily small or petite

mikado an emperor of Japan; a strong to vivid reddish orange
mockado a woolen fabric made chiefly in the 16th and 17th centuries in imitation of velvet

mil a unit of measurement equal to 1/1000 inch; a monetary unit of property tax assessment
mill a factory for manufacturing activity, as grinding grain

milch a domestic animal bred for or suitable for milk production
milk to shuffle cards by drawing one from the top and one from the bottom and simultaneously allowing them to fall face down on the table; to exploit, bleed, or elicit

miliary accompanied or marked by an eruption or formation of lesions the size of millet seeds
milliary marking the distance of a mile

milk (see **milch**)

mill (see **mil**)

millenary a group of a thousand things
millinary women's headwear

milliary (see **miliary**)

millinary (see **millenary**)

mince to cut or chop into small bits
mints places where coins are made; confections flavored with peppermint or spearmint

mind the intellect or brain; to obey; to take care of
mined dug or extracted from the earth

miner a person or machine that extracts ore and coal from the earth

minor of lesser or inferior importance; a person younger than majority age

mini something that is small of its kind

Minni a primitive Mongol people inhabiting the foothill region of the southern Caucasus during pre–Babylonian times

minnie a hand barely strong enough for an opening bid in bridge

minion a servile dependent; a piece of light artillery; a person that is highly esteemed and favored

Minyan having characteristics of a prehistoric Greek civilization noted for its pottery

minyan the required number (ten) of males at least thirteen years old to conduct public Jewish worship

minks slender-bodied semi-aquatic carnivorous mammals

minx a pert or flirtatious girl

Minni (see **mini**)

minnie (see **mini**)

minor (see **miner**)

mintie a homosexual (slang)

minty having the flavor of an aromatic plant of the family Labiatae

mints (see **mince**)

minty (see **mintie**)

minx (see **minks**)

Minyan and **minyan** (see **minion**)

Mir and **mir** (see **mere**)

mire (see **mere**)

misbilled erroneously charged a customer for merchandise or service

misbuild to construct something in error or by mistake

miscreance an opinion or doctrine thought to be false

miscreants those who behave criminally or viciously

mise (see **mais**)

Miskito a people of the Atlantic coast of Nicaraqua and Honduras

mosquito any of numerous two-winged flies

miso (see **meso**)

missal a book containing what is said and sung at Roman Catholic mass during the year

missel a large European thrush which feeds on mistletoe berries

missile a weapon or object thrown or projected

missed failed to hit, reach, or make contact with

mist moisture in the form of minute particles suspended in the atmosphere; a haze or film

myst an intiate in a mystery

missel (see **missal**)

misses fails to hit, reach, or make contact with; girls or unmarried women

missus a wife; the mistress of a household

missile (see **missal**)

missus (see **misses**)

mist (see **missed**)

misti intraspecific hybrid plants

misty dim or obscure

mistic a small lateen-rigged sailing ship used in the Mediterranean

mystic constituting or belonging to something occult or esoteric

misty (see **misti**)

mite (see **might**)

mitis (see **Midas**)

mity (see **mighty**)

mix (see **micks**)

mnemonic assisting or intended to assist memory
pneumonic relating to the lungs or pneumonia

mo (see **mho**)

moa any of various extinct flightless ratite birds of New Zealand
mohwa any of several East Indian trees of the genus Madhuca

moan a low prolonged sound of pain or grief
Mon the dominant native people of Pgu in Myanmar
mown cut or cropped close to the ground

moat a deep wide trench around a fortified place, often filled with water
mote a small particle or speck

moc (see **mach**)

mock (see **mach**)

mockado (see **mikado**)

mod (see **maud**)

Mod a meeting to study and perform Gaelic arts
mode a form or manner of expression
mowed cut grass close to the ground

model an example, pattern, or standard
mottle an appearance resembling a surface having colored spots, blotchings, or cloudings

Moho a genus of Hawaiian honey eaters; a depth ranging from 3–25 miles beneath the ocean floor
moho any of several Hawaiian honey eaters having pectoral tufts of yellow feathers
Mojo an Arawakan people of northern Bolivia
mojo an irregularly spreading or shrubby tree widely distributed along tropical shores; an erect forest tree of the West Indian uplands

mohr a gazelle of northern Africa
Moor a member of a dark-skinned people of mixed Arab and Berber ancestry inhabiting ancient Mauretania in northern Africa
moor an extensive area of open rolling land often covered with heather, moss, and grass; to make fast with cables and lines
mor forest humus consisting of a layer of largely organic matter distinct from the mineral soil beneath
more larger in size, quantity, or extent
mower an implement to cut grass or grain

mohwa (see **moa**)

moiles metallic oxide adhering to glass knocked from the end of the blowpipe
moils works with grueling persistence; is in continuous agitation

moirés irregular wavy finishes produced on fabric
morays savage voracious often brightly colored eels
mores customs and folkways of a particular group

Mojo and **mojo** (see **Moho**)

mol a molecule (by shortening)
mole a congenital mark or discoloration on the skin; a burrowing mammal

moll (see **mal**)

molle (see **Mali**)

molly (see **Mali**)

moly (see **Mali**)

mom (see both **ma'am** entries)

Mon (see **moan**)

money   (see many)

monger   (see Mangar)

monism   (see manism)

mono   (see Mano)

monogeneous   developing without cyclic change of form; the presumed origin of all life from one original entity or cell
monogynous   having but one wife or mate

monology   (see menology)

months   measures of time corresponding to the period of the moon's revolution around Earth
Muntz   an alloy of copper and zinc

moo   a cow's natural throat noise
moue   a little grimace or pout
mu   a bridging group joining central atoms and ions; the twelfth letter of the Greek alphabet

mood   a feeling, temper, or atmosphere
mooed   made a cow's natural throat noise

Moonie   a member or follower of the Unification Church founded by Sun Myung Moon
moony   shaped like the moon; abstracted or dreamy
muni   a Hindu hermit sage; a bond issued by a governmental unit (by shortening municipal)

Moor and moor   (see mohr)

Moorish   relating to or in the style characteristic of the Moors
moreish   causing a desire for more; palatable

moose   a large ruminant mammal of northern North America
mousse   a frothy dessert; a food prepared with whipped cream

moot   debatable; deprived of practical significance

mute   silent or characterized by an absence of speech; a device to soften or dampen a musical instrument's sound

mor   (see mohr)

Moraea   (see maria)

moral   ethical or principled; a lesson taught by a story or fable
morel   an edible fungus

morale   a state of individual psychological well-being and buoyancy; a sense of common purpose or degree of dedication to a common task; esprit de corps
morral   a fiber bag usually used as a food bag for horses

morays   (see moirés)

mordant   a biting and caustic thought or style; a chemical that fixes dye
mordent   a melodic musical ornament

more   (see mohr)

moreen   (see marine)

moreish   (see Moorish)

morel   (see moral)

mores   (see moirés)

morn   the beginning of a day
morne   gloomy or dismal
mourn   to feel or express deep regret; to grieve

Mornay   a white sauce containing cheese, especially Parmesan or Gruyère
morné   in heraldry, a lion without teeth, tongue, or claws

morne   (see morn)

Moro   any of several Muslim peoples of the southern Philippines chiefly of the Sulu archipelago
morro   a round hill or point of land
Moro   any of several Muslim peoples

of the southern Philippines chiefly of the Sulu archipelago

morrow   the next following day

Morone   a genus of carnivorous fresh and saltwater percoid fishes, including white perch

Moroni   the angel who appeared on September 21, 1823, in a vision telling Joseph Smith that a record engraved on golden plates contained the history of the ancient inhabitants of America

morral   (see **morale**)

morris   a vigorous dance done by men; an ancient game for two persons

Morus   a widely distributed genus of trees comprising the mulberries

morro   (see **Moro**)

morrow   (see **Moro**)

morsal   relating to the grinding or biting surface of a tooth or occlusion of the teeth

morsel   a small piece or quantity of food

Morus   (see **morris**)

Moso   a people closely related to the northern Lolo and found mainly in the high plateaus and mountains of southwest China

mozo   a male servant or domestic; a handyman

mosquito   (see **Miskito**)

Mossi   a people of the west central Sudan

mossie   a mosquito, in Australia

mossy   overgrown or covered with moss or something like moss; antiquated

mot   (see **mho**)

mote   (see **moat**)

moter   a person or device that removes small underdeveloped seeds or fragments from cotton

motor   a device that imparts motion or is a source of mechanical power

mottle   (see **model**)

moue   (see **moo**)

mourn   (see **morn**)

mousse   (see **moose**)

moutan   a shrubby Chinese peony

mouton   processed sheepskin that has been sheared and dyed to resemble seal or beaver; a spy planted in a prison cell to obtain incriminating evidence

mow   (see **mao** and **mho**)

mowed   (see **Mod**)

mower   (see **mohr**)

mown   (see **moan**)

mozo   (see **Moso**)

mu   (see **moo**)

mucks   covers with manure or other fertilizing material; clears of manure or filth

mux   to make a mess of

mudder   a race horse that runs well on a wet or muddy track

mutter   to talk indistinctly or with a low voice

muhly   a grass

muley   hornless or polled, as an animal; stubborn or obstinate

mule   (see **mewl**)

muleta   a small cloth attached to a short tapered stick and used by a matador during the faena

muletta   a Portuguese coasting ship with a lateen sail and pointed bow painted with a human eye

muley   (see **muhly**)

mullar   a die cut in intaglio for stamping an ornament in relief

muller   a hard relatively flat-based

implement for grinding or mixing materials; a pestle

multichord two or more chords sounded together
multicored having more than a single axial portion or core, as a boil

mum (see **ma'am**)

mumu filariasis caused by a slender white filaria transmitted in larval form by mosquitoes
muumuu a loose gaily colored and patterned dress worn chiefly in Hawaii

Muncie a city in north central Indiana
Munsee a Delaware Indian people of northern New Jersey and neighboring parts of New York

munds states of peace or security imposed or guaranteed in Anglo-Saxon and early medieval England
muns classes of London street roisterers of the mid-17th century

muni (see **Moonie**)

muns (see **munds**)

Munsee (see **Muncie**)

Muntz (see **months**)

murk (see **merc**)

murra a material thought to be of semiprecious stone or porcelain used to make costly vessels in ancient Rome
Murrah an Indian breed of dairy type buffaloes with distinctive coiled horns

murrain a pestilence of plague affecting domestic animals or plants
murrhine made of semiprecious stone or porcelain

murral (see **merle**)

murre (see **mer**)

murrhine (see **murrain**)

mus (see **meuse**)

Mus a genus of rodents including the common house mouse
muss a state of confusion or disorder

muscadin a young French fop, especially one with royalist sympathies during the French Revolution
muscadine a tall-growing grape of the southern U.S.

Muscat the capital city of (the Sultanate of) Oman
muscat a cultivated vinifera grape used in making wines and raisins
musket a heavy smoothbore large caliber shoulder firearm; a male sparrow hawk

muscle a tissue of modified elongated cells that produces motion when contracted; strength or brawn
mussel a marine bivalve mollusk (seldom **muscle**)

muscleman a person hired to enforce compliance by strong-arm methods; a goon
Mus(s)ulman a Muslim

Muse and **muse** (see **meuse**)

musket (see **Muscat**)

muss (see **Mus**)

mussed untidy or wrinkled
must is required, compelled, or obliged to
musth a murderous frenzy of a bull elephant usually occurring during rut

mussel (see **muscle**)

Mus(s)ulman (see **muscleman**)

must (see **mussed**)

mustard a plant from whose seeds a pungent yellow condiment is made
mustered convened, assembled, or accumulated; enlisted

mustee the offspring of a white and a quadroon; a person of 1/8 negro ancestry; an octoroon

musty impaired by damp or mildew; moldy

mustered (see **mustard**)

musth (see **mussed**)

musty (see **mustee**)

mute (see **meute** or **moot**)

mutter (see **mudder**)

mutual shared in common

mutuel the pari-mutuel, a system of betting on a (horse) race whereby those who bet on the winner share the total stakes, less a small percentage for the management

muumuu (see **mumu**)

mux (see **mucks**)

my (see **mai**)

myatonia lack of muscle tone or muscular flabbiness

myotonia a tonic spasm of one or more muscles

myrrh (see **mer**)

myst (see **missed**)

mystic (see **mistic**)

Group I

magnificence - magnificents
malevolence - malevolents
malfeasance - malfeasants
marasmous - marasmus
marcescence - marcescents
metis - metisse
militance - militants
milk-toast - milquetoast
modern - moderne
monoculous - monoculus
mucous - mucus

multivalence - multivalents

Group I and II

massif mɑ:sēf
massive ˈmɑsiv

material məˈtirēəl
materiel mə:tirēˈel

Mousquetaire :müskə:ter
musketeer :məskə:tir

mystic ˈmistēk
mystique miˈstēk

Group II

Macá məˈkä
macaw məˈkȯ

macabi :mäkə:bē
Maccabee ˈmakə,bē

madge ˈmɑj
mage ˈmōj

Mahri ˈmärē
Maori ˈmau̇rē

maidou mīˈdü
maidu ˈmidü

majorat ˌmɑzhōˈrɑ
majorate ˈmōjərōt

malign məˈlīn
meline ˈme,līn

mammee mɑˈmē
mammy ˈmamē

mana ˈmänə
manna ˈmɑnə

marquessate ˈmärkwə,zət
marquisette ˈmärkwə,zet

maser ˈmōzər
mazar məˈzär

megameter   .me'gamēdər
megohmmeter   'me.gōm.mēdər

meridian   mə'ridēən
meridienne   mə:ride:en
Meridion   mə'ride.än

microhmmeter   'mī.krōm.mēdər
micrometer   'mīkrō.medər

migraines   'mī.grānz
migrans   'mī.granz

milieu   mēl'yü
mi-lu   'mē·lü

mistaken   mə'stākən
Mixtecan   mē'stākən

mistakes   mə'tāks
mystax   'mi.staks

Mohawk   'mō.hôk

Mohock   'mō.häk

motif   mō'tēf
motive   'mōtəv

mootable   'müd·əbəl
mutable   'myütəbəl

moral   'mórəl
morale   mó'ral
morral   mə'ral or mə'räl

morceau   mór'sō
moreso   'mórsō

mucic   'myüsik
music   'myüzik

mudar   mə'där
mudder   'mədər

murein   'myùr.ēn
murine   myü'rēn

N

nacre   an irridescent inner layer of various mollusk shells; mother-of-pearl
naker   a kettledrum

naggy   (see knaggy)

naiad   the distinctive aquatic young of mayflies and dragonflies that differ markedly from the adult counterparts
naid   any of numerous small freshwater annelids constituting Nais

naissant   in heraldry, rising from the middle of an heraldic field, as an animal with only its upper part visible
nascent   beginning to exist

nak   (see knack)

naker   (see nacre)

nal   the giant reed, a tall European grass with woody stems used in making organ reeds

nul   in law, not any
null   invalid, void, or of no consequence

nance   an effeminate male (slang)
Nantes   a city in west central France

nap   (see knap)

nape   (see knap)

nappe   (see knap)

Nara   relating to the 9th century Buddhistic renaissance in Japan
narra   any of several timber trees of the genus Pterocarpus

nard   (see gnarred)

narra   (see Nara)

nascent   (see naissant)

nat   (see knot)

natty   (see gnatty)

naught   (see knot)

naughty (see **knotty**)

naut (see **knot**)

naval relating to ships or a navy
navel the mid-abdomen depression marking the point of attachment of the umbilical cord

nave (see **knave**)

navel (see **naval**)

naw (see **gnaw**)

nay a negative reply or vote
ne(e) originally or formally called
neigh a horse's typical loud prolonged cry

nays negative replies or votes
naze a headland or promontory
neighs typical loud prolonged cries of a horse

near (see **gnir**)

necklace a string of beads or other small objects worn about the neck as an ornament
neckless having no neck

ne(e) (see **knee** or **nay**)

need (see **knead**)

neele (see **kneel**)

neigh (see **nay**)

neighs (see **nays**)

nell (see **knell**)

nester an animal that builds or occupies a nest; a homesteader or squatter who takes up rangeland for farming
Nestor a wise elder counselor; a grand old patriarch of a particular field; a genus of large parrots in New Zealand

neumatic characterized by symbols in the musical notation of the middle ages, or square symbols in the plainsong notation of the Roman Catholic Church
pneumatic relating to or using air, wind, or other gas; having cavities filled with air

neuter belonging to neither of two usually opposed classes; sexless
nuder more devoid of clothing

new (see **gnu**)

Newcomb a game resembling volleyball
newcome recently come or arrived

newer more recent or fresher
Nuer a Nilotic people in the Sudan

newsy given to gossip; filled with news items
Nuzi a dialect of Akkadian used in Iraq

newt (see **knout**)

nibble a small bite or morsel of food
nybble a group of binary digits (in computing) consisting of four bits or one-half byte

nice (see **gneiss**)

Nice a city on the southeast coast of France; a grayish-blue color (also called Quimper)
niece a daughter of one's sister, brother, sister-in-law, or brother-in-law

Nichol a clear calcite prism for producing and analyzing polarized light
nickel a nearly silver-white hard malleable ductile ferromagnetic metallic element; a five-cent U.S. coin

nickers (see **knickers**)

nicks notches
nix not or nothing; to cancel or reject; a supernatural creature in Germanic folklore
Nyx an ancient Greek goddess personifying night
Pnyx the place where regular meetings of the Athenian ecclesia or public assembly of voters were held

nide a group of pheasants
nighed approached

nidor a strong smell, especially of cooking or burning meat or fat
niter potassium nitrate, especially occurring naturally in northern Chile

niece (see **Nice**)

niepa an East Indian tree whose bark contains a bitter principle similar to quassia
Nipa a monotypic genus of creeping semiaquatic palms
nipa an alcoholic beverage made from fermented sap of an Australian palm; any palm of the genus Nipa

niggard a miser
niggered divided a log by burning

nigger a steam-operated capstan for warping river steamboats over snags and shallows; any of several dark-colored insect larvae; a negro, usually taken to be offensive
nigre a dark-colored water solution of soap and impurities formed during soap manufacture

niggered (see **niggard**)

nighed (see **nide**)

night (see **knight**)

nighthood (see **knighthood**)

nigre (see **nigger**)

nimbed having a halo around the head
nimmed stolen or filched

Nipa and **nipa** (see **niepa**)

nisse a friendly goblin or brownie of Scandanavian folklore that frequents farm buildings
nyssa a small genus of American and Asiatic trees, including the black gum and tupelo

nit (see **knit**)

nited (see **knitted**)

niter (see **nidor**)

nitrile characterized by the presence of the cynanogen group, CN
nitryl the nitro group, radical, or cation, especially in names of inorganic compounds
nytril a synthetic fiber composed chiefly of a long-chain polymer of vinyl-idene

nitter (see **knitter**)

nix (see **nicks**)

nob (see **knob**)

nocks (see **knocks**)

nocturn one of three principal divisions of the office of matins in Roman Catholicism
nocturne a musical or artistic night piece

nod (see **gnawed**)

nodal relating to or located near a node or nodes
notal belonging to the back; dorsal

nodding (see **knotting**)

noddy (see **knotty**)

noded having or divided into thickened or swollen enlargements; nobbed
noted well-known by reputation; provided with musical notation or score

nodous knotty
nodus a center or central point; a complication of difficulty; a hinge on the front margin of the wings of insects of the order Odonata
notice an announcement
Notus the ancient Greek personification of the south wind

noes (see **knows**)

nog a beverage made with beaten eggs, usually with alcoholic liquor; to fill in with brickwork
nogg in carpentry, a shave for shaping dowels and handles

Nome and nome   (see gnome)

nomen   (see gnomon)

nomic   (see gnomic)

none   (see known)

none   not any
nun   a woman belonging to a religious order, especially under vows
of poverty, chastity, and obedience

nonfeudal   not founded upon or involving a lord-vassal relationship
nonfutile   serving a useful purpose;
fruitful

nontidal   not tidal or involving the
tides, as a waterway
nontitle   a nondescriptive name, title, or designation; a pseudo-legal
document that does not substan-
tiate a legal claim to ownership

noon   the middle of the day when
the sun is on the meridian
nun   the 14th letter of the Hebrew
alphabet

noose   a loop with a running knot
that binds closer the more it is
drawn; to execute by hanging
nous   the highest intellect

nor   (see knorr)

nose   (see knows)

nosy   of a prying or inquisitive
disposition; intrusive
Nozi   an extinct Indian people of the
Pitt river valley of northern California

not   (see knot)

notal   (see nodal)

noted   (see noded)

notice   (see nodous)

Notus   (see nodous)

nous   (see noose)

nox   (see knocks)

Nozi   (see nosy)

Nu and nu   (see gnu)

nubs   (see knubs)

nuder   (see neuter)

Nuer   (see newer)

nuke   to destroy with nuclear bombs;
a nuclear-powered electric generating station
nuque   the back of the neck

nul   (see nal)

null   (see nal)

nulla   a hardwood club used by Australian aborigines
nullah   a watercourse that is often
dry

nun   (see none or noon)

nuque   (see nuke)

Nut   (see knout)

nut   (see knut)

Nuzi   (see newsy)

nybble   (see nibble)

nyssa   (see nisse)

nytril   (see nitrile)

Nyx   (see nicks)

Group I

nebulose - nebulous
negligence - negligents
nervous - nervus
nonadherence - nonadherents
nonassonance - nonassonants
nonresidence - nonresidents

Group II

nautch   ˈnȯch
notch   ˈnäch

nectarous 'nektərəs
Necturus nek'tyůrəs

Nobelist nō'belə̇st
noblest 'nōb(ə)lə̇st

noel nō'el
nowel 'nōəl

nonpros 'nän:präs
nonprose 'nän:prōz

O

oar a long wooden pole with a broad flat blade at one end for propelling a boat
o'er the contraction of over
or a conjunction indicating an alternative or choice; either
ore a natural usually unrefined mineral that can often be mined

oat (see huate)

oater a horse opera, a movie or show about the frontier days in the U.S. west
Oder a major river of central Europe
odor a scent, fragrance, or aroma

obdurate to make stubbornly persistent in ill-doing
obturate to obstruct or close, especially to stop a gun breech so as to prevent the escape of gas in firing

obe (see aube)

obeyance (see abeyance)

obturate (see obdurate)

Occident related to or situated in the West, as opposed to the Orient
oxidant an oxidizing agent

ocellate having minute simple eyes or eyespots
oscillate to move to and fro like a pendulum, to vibrate

ocelot a medium-sized American wildcat
osselet a bony outgrowth on the leg of a horse

octroi a tax on commodities brought into a city, especially in certain European countries; a municipal customs duty
octroy to grant or concede as a privilege

od a natural power underlying hypnotism and magnetism and held by some to reside in certain persons and things
odd unusual or peculiar

od a natural power underlying hypnotism and magnetism and held by some to reside in certain persons and things
ode a lyric poem
owed was obligated to pay; was indebted to

odd (see od)

odder (see attar)

ode (see od)

Oder (see oater)

odeum a contemporary theater or music hall
odium hatred and condemnation often marked by loathing or contempt

odor (see oater)

oe (see eau)

o'er (see oar)

offal (see awful)

oh (see eau)

oleo oleomargarine, a butter substitute (by shortening)
olio a miscellaneous mixture of hodgepodge

ombre (see **hombre**)

omission (see **emission**)

omit (see **emit**)

on (see **awn**)

once one time and no more
wants desires or wishes; suffers from a lack of
wonts customs or habits; has the habit or custom of doing something

one a single unit; the first whole number between zero and two
won gained victory, achieved, prevailed, or succeeded

oner a heavy blow with a fist (slang)
owner a person who has legal or rightful title to something

oppressed (see **appressed**)

or (see **oar**)

oracle (see **auricle**)

oral (see **aural**)

ordinance an authoritative decree or directive; a public enactment
ordnance military supples

ordinance an authoritative decree or directive; a public enactment
ordonnance an arrangement of a composition's parts with respect to one another and the whole

ordnance (see **ordinance**)

ordonnance (see **ordinance**)

ore (see **oar**)

Oregon a state in northwestern continental U.S.
origan any of various aromatic mints, as wild marjoram

oriel a large bay window

oriole a colorful American bird

origan (see **Oregon**)

oriole (see **aureole**)

orion (see **Arion**)

orle (see **aural**)

orris (see **aurous**)

oscillate (see **ocellate**)

osselet (see **ocelot**)

Ossetic (see **acetic**)

Ostrea (see **Austria**)

ostria (see **Austria**)

Ostrya (see **Austria**)

Otis a genus of typical bustards, including the great bustard
Otus a genus of rather small-eared owls

otter (see **attar**)

Otus (see **Otis**)

ouf an expression of discomfort, aversion, or impatience
ouph an elf

ought (see **aught**)

oui yes, in French
we a group including me
wee very small
whee an expression of delight or general exuberance

ouph (see **ouf**)

our (see **Aor** and **are**)

outcast regarded with contempt or despised; exiled from one's domicile or country
outcaste a person who has been ejected from his/her caste for violating its customs or rules

outlimb an extremity of the body
outlimn to represent or delineate in sharpness of detail above some

norm or another person's performance

outpraise to exceed or surpass in commending or applauding
outprays surpasses in entreating, imploring or praying

outright completely; instantaneously
outwrite to surpass in ability to write

outsea an open part of a sea or ocean
outsee to surpass in power of vision or insight

outside in the open air; situated outside a particular place
outsighed exceeded another person's grieving or lamenting

outsighs exceeds another person's grieving or sorrowing
outsize a size larger than standard

outsole the exterior or outside sole of a boot or shoe
outsoul a spirit or intelligence exterior to man

outwrite (see **outright**)

overate consumed food excessively
overrate to value too highly

overbilled charged more than the full amount
overbuild to build beyond actual requirements; to supply with buildings in excess of demand

overchute an overhead flume
overshoot to pass swiftly beyond or ahead of; to overstate a case or point

overdo to do too much or in excess
overdue delayed; unpaid; more than ripe

overflour to sprinkle with excess flour
overflower to cover over with flowers; to put forth flowers beyond strength or well-being

overlade to load with too great a burden
overlaid superimposed; covered

overmeddled interferred excessively without right or propriety
overmettled exhibited qualities of courage or ardor exceeding those required by a given situation

overpaid compensated, rewarded, or paid beyond what was due
overpayed allowed an excessive amount of rope or line to run out

overrate (see **overate**)

overseas beyond or across oceans or seas
oversees supervises; looks down on

oversew to sew books by a machine that simulates hand overcasting; to top-sew
oversow to plant or scatter too much seed

overshoot (see **overchute**)

oversow (see **oversew**)

overstaid overly sober, sedate, or serious
overstayed remained beyond the time or limits of

overtaught instructed beyond the point of proficiency
overtaut tightened or stretched excessively

owe (see **eau**)

owed (see **od**)

owl (see **aoul**)

owner (see **oner**)

ox (see **Akhs**)

oxen adult castrated males of domestic bovine usually used as draft animals
oxyn a solid product (as linoxyn) formed when a drying oil is oxidized

ox-eyed   having oxlike eyes
oxhide   the outer skin of an ox
oxide   a binary compound of oxygen with an element

oxidant   (see **Occident**)

oxide   (see **ox-eyed**)

oxyn   (see **oxen**)

Group I

obedience - obedients
obsequence - obsequents
occurrence - occurrents
omniscience - omniscients

Group II

obliger   ə'blījər
obligor   'äblə,gȯr

ohm   'ōm
om   'ȯm

OK   ō:kā
oke   'okā

orchestral   ȯr'kestrəl
orchestrelle   ȯrkə'strel

origin   'ȯrəjən
orogen   'ōrəjən

ostracean   ä'strāshən
ostracion   ä'strashē,än

oxine   'ak,sən
oxyn   'aksən

P

pa   father
pah   an expression of disdain, contempt, or disgust
pas   dance step(s) forming a pattern or figure
paw   a quadruped's foot; to touch clumsily or rudely

paar   a depression produced by crustal blocks moving apart
par   a common level or value
parr   a young salmon

pace   proceed with a slow or measured step; to regulate the speed of
pes   a part resembling a foot

paced   went with a slow or measured step; regulated the speed of
paste   a glue or cement; a dough used for pastry crust

packed   stowed in a container; carried
pact   a treaty or agreement

packs   bundles of goods; stows in a container; carries

PACS   political action committees, corporations, or unions that distribute money to political candidates (an acronym)
pacs   laced heelless sheepskin or felt shoes worn inside boots or over shoes in cold weather
pacts   treaties or agreements
Paks   individuals from Pakistan (sometimes regarded as offensive)
Pax   a period characterized by the absence of major wars
pax   a tablet or board decorated with a figure of Christ or a religious person

pact   (see **packed**)

pacts   (see **packs**)

padder   a person or machine that makes sheets of paper into pads, or places ordered tobacco leaves in boxes
patter   to repeat in a rapid manner; a quick succession of slight sounds; a relatively meaningless chatter

paddle a rather short light wooden, metal, or plastic pole with a broad fairly flat blade at one end that is used to propel and stop a canoe or other watercraft

padle a soft thick clumsy marine fish of both coasts of the northern North Atlantic ocean, also called lump fish

paddy a heavily irrigated piece of land for growing rice

patty a small pie or pasty

paty in heraldry, a cross with the ends splayed or spread out

padle (see **paddle**)

paean a joyously exultant song or hymn

paion a metrical foot of four syllables with one long or stressed, and three short or unstressed syllables

peon a person in a position of subordination or servility

pah (see **pa**)

paid received compensation; discharged an obligation

pate the top of the head

payed allowed a rope or line to run out

pail a bucket

pale deficient in color or intensity; pallid or wan

pain physical or mental discomfort or agony

pane a window or door section

paion (see **paean**)

pair a set of two items

pare to trim off or peel

pear a fleshy oblong pome fruit

pairle an heraldic ordinary in the form of a Y extending to the upper corners and base of the field

parrel a rope loop or sliding collar by which a yard or spar is held to a mast

peril exposure to the risk of being injured, destroyed, or lost

pais in law, the country

pay to discharge an obligation

pe the 17th letter of the Hebrew alphabet

Paks (see **packs**)

palar resembling a stake

paler more deficient in color or intensity

palate the roof of the mouth

palette a thin oval board with a thumbhole on which a painter lays and mixes pigments

pallet a straw-filled mattress; a portable platform for storing materials

pallette a usually rounded plate at the armpit of a suit of armor

Palau the Austronesian language of the Palau islands

pilaf rice cooked in stock and usually combined with meat and vegetables

pale (see **pail**)

palely with an effect of dimness or pallor

paly in heraldry, divided into four or more equal parts by perpendicular lines

paler (see **palar**)

palette (see **palate**)

Pali an Indic language found in the Buddhist canon

pali an Indian timber tree; a steep slope in Hawaii

palli a member of a Sudra caste of field laborers

pall to lose strength, vigor, or effectiveness

pawl a small double-poled tent with steep sloping sides

pol a politician (slang)

poll a college or university degree without honors

pallae loose outer garments worn by women in ancient Rome

pally informally intimate

pallar a member of a depressed caste in India

pallor a wan or blanched appearance

pallet (see **palate**)

pallette (see **palate**)

palli (see **Pali**)

pall-mall a 17th century European game resembling croquet
pell-mell mingled confusion or disorder; indiscriminately

pallor (see **pallar**)

pally (see **pallae**)

palmar involving the palm of the hand
palmer a person wearing two crossed palm leaves to denote having made a pilgrimage to the Holy Land

paly (see **palely**)

pament a tile or brick used to pave malthouse floors
payment something given or received to discharge a debt or obligation

pamper to treat with excessive care and attention
pampre an ornament of vine leaves and grapes

Pan a genus of anthropoid apes including the chimpanzee
pan a shallow container; to rotate a camera in any direction; to wash earth deposits in search of precious metal
panne a finish for velvet or satin

pan a betel palm leaf; a card game resembling rummy
paon a greenish blue color called peacock blue
pawn to deposit something with another as collateral for a loan; the least powerful chess piece

pane (see **pain**)

panel a group of persons selected for some service or activity; a distinct

part of a surface, as a fender or door
pannel a saddle blanket

panne (see **pan**)

pannel (see **panel**)

paon (see **pan**)

papagallo a large brightly colored food fish related to the amberfishes and found from northern California to Peru
papagayo a violet often tornadic northerly wind occurring along the Pacific coast of Central America

par (see **paar**)

parade (in rapid speech) a ceremonial formation of troops; to march ceremoniously; a formal display
prayed entreated or implored; made application to
preyed made raids for the sake of booty

paragnathous having both mandibles of equal length with the tips meeting, especially of a bird
paragnatus one of the paired lobes of the hypopharynx in various insects

paragon a model of excellence or perfection
perigon an angle obtained by rotating a half line in the same plane once around the point from which it extends

paragraph a distinct section of a written composition consisting of one or more sentences
perigraph a marking around something; a small tracing instrument used in drawing outlines of bones

paraphrase a restatement of a work or section giving the meaning in another form, usually for clearer and fuller exposition
periphrase the use of a negative, passive, or inverted construction in

place of a positive, active, or normal construction

parasite an organism living in or on another organism; a sycophant or toady
parisite a mineral consisting of a carbonate and flouride of calcium, cerium, and lanthanum
pericyte an adventitious cell of connective tissue about capillaries

pard a partner or chum (slang)
parred placed on an equal footing or par; made a golf score equal to par

pardoner a person who forgives or excuses
partner an associate or colleague

pare (see **pair**)

Paridae a large family of passerine birds that includes the titmice
parity close equivalence or likeness
parody a literary style characterized by reproducing stylistic peculiarities of a work for comic effect or ridicule

Paris a small genus of Eurasian herbs; the capital of France
parous having produced offspring
Parus a type genus comprising common titmice

parish an ecclesiastical area committed to one pastor
perish to die; to pass away completely; to become destroyed or ruined

parisite (see **parasite**)

parity (see **Paridae**)

parlay to transform into something of greater value
parley a discussion or discourse; a conference held to discuss points in dispute

parodic having the character of parody or caricature

parotic adjacent to the ear

parody (see **Paridae**)

parol an oral declaration or statement
parole a conditional and revocable release of a prisoner serving an unexpired sentence
pyrrole a colorless toxic liquid heterocyclic compound

parolee a prisoner serving an unexpired sentence who is conditionally and revocably released
paroli a betting system in which a bettor leaves staked money and its winnings as a further stake

parotic (see **parodic**)

parous (see **Paris**)

parr (see **paar**)

parred (see **pard**)

parrel (see **pairle**)

parrot a zygodactyl (two toes in front and two behind) bird
perit a unit of weight equal to 1/20 droit, formerly used by coiners of money

parrs young salmon
pars makes a golf score equal to par
parse to divide speech into component parts and describe them grammatically; to analyze critically

parry to turn aside or otherwise avert; to dodge
perry a fermented liquor made from pears

pars (see **parrs**)

parse (see **parrs**)

parshall a device for measuring flow in conduits
partial favorably disposed toward someone or something

parti   the basic concept of an architectural design; a person eligible to enter into marriage and viewed with regard to his/her advantages or disadvantages as a marriage partner for a prospective mate
party   persons forming a constituency; a social gathering for entertainment or pleasure

partial   (see **parshall**)

partner   (see **pardoner**)

party   (see **parti**)

Parus   (see **Paris**)

pas   (see **pa**)

pase   a maneuver by a bullfighter with the cape to gain the bull's attention
passé   a ballet movement in which one leg passes behind or in front of the other; past one's prime; no longer fashionable

passable   able to be crossed, traveled, or passed on; able to pass inspection
passible   capable of feeling or suffering

passé   (see **pase**)

passed   proceeded; went by
past   belonging to a former time; gone by

passible   (see **passable**)

past   (see **passed**)

paste   (see **paced**)

pastiche   a musical composition or piece of writing made up of selections from different works
postiche   false hair or a toupee

pasties   small round coverings for a woman's nipples
pastys   a meat pie or turnover

pat   to stroke or tap gently with the hand
patte   a decorative band, strap, or belt to fasten garments

pate   (see **paid**)

pâte   a plastic material for pottery
pot   a deep rounded container; a common resource or fund; marijuana (slang)
pott   a size of paper about 13″ × 16″ used in printing

patens   metal plates used for bread in the eucharistic service; thin metal disks
patents   government grants of a monopoly right to inventors or discoverers of new processes or devices
pattens   shoes, often with devices to elevate the foot
Pattons   a type of tanks named after General George S. Patton

patience   a capacity to endure pain, adversity, or evil with fortitude; forbearance
patients   sick persons awaiting treatment

patte   (see **pat**)

pattens   (see **patens**)

patter   (see **padder**)

Pattons   (see **patens**)

patty   (see **paddy**)

paty   (see **paddy**)

pau   in Hawaii, completed, consumed, or finished
pow   a sound of a blow or explosion

pauper   a very poor person
popper   a device for popping corn

pause   a temporary stop, hesitation, or respite
paws   a quadruped's feet; touches clumsily or rudely

paw   (see **pa**)

pawl   (see **pall**)

pawn   (see **pan**)

pawned   deposited something with another as collateral for a loan
pond   a small body of water

paws (see **pause**)

Pax and **pax** (see **packs**)

Pax a period characterized by the absence of major wars
pax a tablet or board decorated with a figure of Christ or a religious person
pocks holes or pits
pox a virus disease characterized by pustules or eruptions; a disease of sweet potatoes

pay (see **pais**)

Paya an Indian people of northern Honduras
pia the delicate and highly vascular membrane of connective tissue investing the brain and spinal cord
pyre a combustible heap usually of wood for burning a dead body as a funeral rite

payed (see **paid**)

payment (see **pament**)

pe (see **pais**)

peace freedom from civil clamor, confusion, and war; serenity of spirit
piece a fragment or part of a whole

peaceable tranquil, quiet, or undisturbed
pieceable capable of being repaired or extended

peaced became quiet or still
pieced repaired, renewed, or completed by adding component parts or pieces
piste a beaten track or trail made by an animal; a hard packed ski trail

peachy unusually fine; resembling a peach
pichi a small armadillo of southern South America

peak a sharp or pointed end; the top of a hill or mountain; to grow thin or look sickly

peek to look slyly or furtively; to peep
peke a pekingese dog
pique to stimluate by wounding pride, or inciting jealousy or rivalry

peaky pointed or sharp; having peaks; sickly
piki maize bread baked in thin sheets by Indians of the southwestern U.S.

peal to ring a bell or chime
peel to strip off an outer layer; to pare

pean an heraldic fur of gold ermine spots on a black field
peen the formed head of a hammer opposite the face

pear (see **pair**)

pearl a dense concretion of calcium carbonate formed around a small foreign particle in various mollusks
perle a soft gelatin capsule enclosing volatile or unpleasant tasting liquids
purl a type of knitting stitch

pearlite a lamellar mixture of ferrite and cementite occurring in steel and iron
perlite volcanic glass with a concentric shelly structure

peas(e) small round edible vegetables produced by a variable annual leguminous vine
pees urinates
pes a part resembling a foot; the ground bass of a canon

peat partially carbonized vegetable matter
pete a metal box sometimes built into a wall or vault to protect valuables against fire or theft (slang)

peavey a stout lever equipped with a sharp spike that is used in lumbering
peavie a newly enlisted person in the Civilian Conservation Corps (slang)

pecks U.S. units of dry capacity equal to 537.605 cubic inches; makes holes in a material with quick movements of the beak
pecs pectoral muscles (slang)

pecten an animal's body part resembling a comb
pectin a colorless amorphous methylated pectic substance used as an ingredient of fruit jellies

pectous resembling the consistency of jelly
pectus a bird's breast

pedal a foot-activated lever
peddle to travel about with wares for sale
petal a leaf-shaped part of a flower

peek (see **peak**)

peel (see **peal**)

Peelite one of a group of 19th century British Tories supporting Peel in the repeal of the Corn Laws
pelite a rock composed of fine particles of clay or mud

peen (see **pean**)

peened drew, bent, or flattened by hammering with the hammer head opposite the face
piend a sharp edge formed by the meeting of two surfaces, as in moldings

peepee to urinate
pipi a bivalve mollusk

peer a person of equal standing; to look intently or curiously
pier a structure built on piles into water as a landing place or pleasure resort
Pierre the capital of South Dakota
pir a Muslim saint or spiritual guide
pirr a gust of wind or a flurry
pyr a unit light intensity equal to .954 candles

peery inquisitive or suspicious

peri a supernatural being, as a fairy or elf

pees (see **peas[e]**)

peke (see **peak**)

pekoe a tea made from the first three leaves on the spray
picot one of the small ornamental loops forming the edging on ribbon or lace

pelisse a long cloak or coat made of, or trimmed or lined with fur
police a government unit concerned with maintaining public order and safety

pelite (see **Peelite**)

pell-mell (see **pall-mall**)

penal prescribing, enacting, or threatening punishment
penile relating to the penis

penance sorry or contrition for sin; repentance
pennants nautical flags usually tapering to a point

pence a former British coin representing one penny
pents penthouses or smaller structures joined to a building

pencil an implement for writing, drawing, or marking
pensile suspended from above

pend to be undecided or unsettled
penned placed in an enclosure to prevent straying; recorded in writing

penetrance the ability of a gene to express its specific effect in the organism of which it is a part
penetrants things that pass into or through, or are capable of doing so

penile (see **penal**)

pennants (see **penance**)

penned (see **pend**)

pensile (see pencil)

pentamerous divided into or consisting or five parts
Pentamerus a genus comprising Paleozoic brachiopods

pents (see pence)

peon (see paean)

people human beings
pipal a fig tree of India remarkable for its great size and longevity

Peplis a genus of chiefly aquatic herbs
peplos a garment worn by women of ancient Greece

per by means of; through
pirr to blow with a whiz; to speed along
purr a cat's low vibrating murmur

perches bird roosts; small freshwater spiny-finned American fish
purchase to buy merchandise by payment of money or its equivalent; a position from which to exert power or leverage

peri (see peery)

pericyte (see parasite)

perigon (see paragon)

perigraph (see paragraph)

peril (see pairle)

periodic occurring at regular intervals
periotic situated around the ear

periphrase (see paraphrase)

perish (see parish)

perit (see parrot)

perjury a deliberate giving of false testimony
purgery the part of a sugarhouse where molasses is drained from sugar

perle (see pearl)

perlite (see pearlite)

permeance the reciprocal of magnetic reluctance
permeants animal influents ranging widely within an ecological community of which they are a part

pern a honey buzzard
pirn bobbins on which filling yarn for weaving is wound before insertion into the shuttle

perpetuance perpetuation or perpetuity
perpetuants in mathematics, a semivariant which cannot be expressed rationally in terms of other semivariants

perry (see parry)

perse a dark grayish blue color
purse a receptacle used to carry money and small objects

pertinence relevance
purtenance the heart, liver, and lungs of an animal

pervade to spread throughout
purveyed obtained or supplied for use; provided

pes (see pace and peas[e])

petal (see pedal)

pete (see peat)

petrel a sea bird
petrol gasoline; petroleum

petti a woman's underskirt that is full and often trimmed and ruffled and of decorative fabric; a half slip
petty minor or subordinate

Peul a member of a Sudanese people of African Negroid stock and Mediterranean Caucasoid admixture
pool a small body of water
poule a prostitute; the third figure of a quadrille

pew a seating compartment in church for several persons

phew   an expression of discomfort or distaste

piu   in music, more of something

phanar   (see **fanner**)

pharaoh   (see **faro**)

phare   (see **fair**)

phase   (see **fays**)

phaser   a person who introduces or carries out an activity in stages
phasor   a vector whose angle from the polar axis to the radius vector represents a phase or phase difference

phenetic   relating to classificatory systems and procedures that are based on overall similarity without regard to the evolutionary history of the organisms involved
phonetic   representing the sounds and other phenomena, as stress and pitch of speech

phenology   a branch of science concerned with relationships between climate and periodic biological phenomena
phonology   the science of speech sounds

phenyl   (see **fennel**)

phew   (see **few** and **pew**)

phi   (see **fie**)

phial   (see **faille**)

philander   (see **filander**)

Philippines   (see **fillipeens**)

Philly   (see **filly**)

philter   (see **filter**)

phis   (see **fees**)

phiz   (see **fizz**)

phlegm   (see **Flem**)

Phlox   (see **flocks**)

phocal   (see **focal**)

phon   (see **faun**)

phonetic   (see **phenetic**)

phonology   (see **phenology**)

phosphene   a luminous impression due to excitation of the retina of the eye by some cause other than the impingement of light rays
phosphine   a colorless very poisonous gaseous compound that may ignite spontaneously when mixed with air or oxygen

photogen   a light oil obtained by distilling bituminous shale, coal, or peat
photogene   an afterimage or retinal impression

phrase   (see **fraise**)

phraser   (see **fraser**)

phrator   (see **frater**)

phratry   (see **fratry**)

phreak   (see **freak**)

phylar   (see **filar**)

phylliform   (see **filiform**)

phyllin   a complex magnesium derivative of a porphyrin or phorbin
phylline   leaflike

phylum   (see **filum**)

physic   to treat with or administer medicine
physique   physical form or construction, especially of the human body

phthalic   derived from phthalic acid
thallic   relating to or containing thallium

phthalin   any of a group of colorless compounds obtained by reduction of the phthaleins
thalline   a crystalline base derived from quinoline; consisting of or constituting a plant body that is characteristic of the thallophytes

phthiocol   a yellow crystalline qui-
none with vitamin K activity
thiokol   any of a series of commer-
cially produced polysulfide rubbers,
closely related liquid polymers, or
water-dispersed lattices

physocarpous   having bladdery fruit
Physocarpus   a genus of chiefly
North American shrubs

pi   the ratio of a circle's circumference to its diameter (3.1416);
spilled or mixed type; the 16th letter of the Greek alphabet
pie   meat or fruit baked in, on, or
under dough

pia   (see Paya)

pial   related to the membranous connective tissues investing the brain
and spinal cord
pile   things heaped together; a cylinder or slender rod driven into the
ground to support a vertical load

Pica   a genus containing magpies
pica   a typesetting unit equal to 1/6
inch
pika   a small lagomorph mammal inhabiting rocky parts of high mountains; a cony

pich   a West Indian shrub or small
tree
pitch   any of various black or dark-
colored viscous semisolid to solid
substances or residues in the
distillation of tars; to throw or cast

pichi   (see peachy)

picked   selected as being the best ob-
tainable or best for the purpose
Pict   one of a possibly non–Celtic
people once occupying Great
Britain

pickel   an ice ax
pickle   a brine or vinegar for preserving or corning fish, meat, or other
foodstuffs

pickerel   any of several fishes of the

genus Esox
picryl   the univalent radical derived
from picric acid by removing the
hydroxyl group

pickle   (see pickel)

picks   chooses or selects; heavy
curved metal tools with both ends
pointed
pics   photographs or motion pictures
Picts   members of a possibly non–
Celtic people who once occupied
Great Britain
pyx   an ecclesiastical container
holding the reserved sacrament on
the altar

picnic   an outing with food eaten in
the open
pyknic   characterized by short
stature, broad girth, and powerful
muscles

picot   (see pekoe)

picryl   (see pickerel)

pics   (see picks)

Pict   (see picked)

Picts   (see picks)

pie   (see pi)

piece   (see peace)

pieceable   (see peaceable)

pieced   (see peaced)

piend   (see peened)

pier   (see peer)

Pierre   (see peer)

pierrot   a standard comic character
of old French pantomime, usually
with whitened face and loose white
clothes
Piro   a Tanoan people of Pueblo Indians in central New Mexico and
the state of Chihuahua, Mexico

pika   (see Pica)

piki (see peaky)

Pila the type genus of the family Pilidae comprising the apple and dextral snails
pila heavy javelins of a Roman foot solider
pyla the opening from the third ventricle into the aqueduct of Sylvius in higher vertebrates

pilaf (see Palau)

pilaf rice cooked in stock and usually combined with meat and vegetables
pillow a head support while resting or sleeping

pilar hairy
piler a person that heaps things up

pile (see pial)

pileous hairy
pileus an umbrella-shaped upper cap of many fungi; a cloud resembling a cap that sometimes appears above and partially obscures the bulging top of a cumulus cloud

piler (see pilar)

pileus (see pileous)

pillary resembling or formed into a pillar
pillory a means by which to expose or hold up a person to public ridicule

pillow (see pilaf)

pimento the wood of the allspice tree; a vivid red color
pimiento a thick-fleshed sweet pepper used as a stuffing for olives and as a source of paprika

pinion the distal part of a bird's wing; to disable or restrain by binding the arms; a gear
piñon any of various low-growing nut pines

pinkie a rabbit bandicoot
pinky tinged with pink color

piñon (see pinion)

pipal (see people)

pipi (see peepee)

pique (see peak)

piqué a durable ribbed cotton, rayon, or silk clothing fabric; inlaid, as a knife handle; a ballet movement; a glove seam
piquet a two-handed card game

pir (see peer)

pirn (see pern)

Piro (see pierrot)

pirr (see peer and per)

pishpash an India rice broth containing bits of meat
pishposh nonsense

piste (see peaced)

pistil a seed plant's ovule-bearing organ
pistol a short firearm fired with one hand, as a revolver

pitch (see pich)

pitchi a large shallow elongated wooden receptacle much used by Australian aborigines as a container for food and drink
pitchy coated, smeared, or sticky with pitch

pitiless without mercy or compassion
Pitylus a genus of Central and South American grosbeak birds

piu (see pew)

place a space or area; a specific portion of a surface; to put into, set, or position
plaice a European flounder fish

plain unadorned or simple; an extensive area of level or rolling countryside
plane to make smooth or even; a tree of the genus Platanus; to soar on wings or skim across water

plainer more unadorned or simpler
planar having a flat two-dimensional quality
planer a power tool for surfacing wood

Plains of or belonging to North American Indians of the Great Plains or to their culture
plains extensive areas of level or rolling countryside
planes makes smooth or even; soars on wings or skims across water; trees of the genus Platanus

plait to interweave strands of yarn, fabric, or locks of hair
plat a detailed map of an area; a small tract of land
Platt a colloquial language of northern Germany comprising several Low German dialects
Platte a major river flowing through central Nebraska
platte a resistant knob of rock in a glacial valley or rising in the midst of a glacier

plait to interweave strands of yarn, fabric, or locks of hair
plate a piece of domestic hollowware, as a dish; a flat sheet or metal
Platt a colloquial language of northern Germany comprising several Low German dialects
played engaged in recreational activity or frolicked

plaiter a person or machine that interweaves strands of yarn, fabric, or locks of hair
plater a worker that plates metal objects with gold or silver; an inferior race horse

plaiter a person or machine that interweaves strands of yarn, fabric, or locks of hair
platter a large shallow plate; a phonograph record

planar (see **plainer**)

plane (see **plain**)

planer (see **plainer**)

planes (see **Plains**)

plantar related to the sole of the foot
planter a person who cultivates plants; a container in which plants are grown; a farmer

plastic pliable, pliant, or adaptable
plastique a technique of statuesque posing in dancing

plat (see **plait**)

platan a treen of the genus Platanus
platen a flat plate usually designed to press against something, as in a printing press
platten to flatten and make into sheets or plates of glass

plate (see **plait**)

platen (see **platan**)

plater (see **plaiter**)

Platt (see both **plaits**)

Platte and **platte** (see **plait**)

platten (see **platan**)

platter (see **plaiter**)

played (see **plait**)

pleader an intercessor; a person who conducts pleas, especially in court
pleater a person that makes pleats in cloth, paper, or other material

pleas appeals or petitions
please a word to express politeness in a request; to give delight, satisfaction, or pleasure

pleater (see **pleader**)

pleural related to sides of the thorax
plural more than one
plurel the aggregate resulting from categorizing or statistical analysis

pliers a small pincers with roughened jaws for holding objects or cutting wire

plyers a balance or timbers used in operating a drawbridge; persons working diligently or steadily

plodder a person who proceeds or works slowly, steadily, or unimaginatively

plotter a person or device that marks on a map or display board the positions of airplanes or ships in transit; a schemer

plots conspiracies or intrigues; small areas of ground

plotz to collapse or faint from surprise, excitement, or exhaustion (slang)

plotter (see **plodder**)

plotz (see **plots**)

plum a tree and shrub that bear globular smooth-skinned fruit

plumb a small weight attached to a line to indicate vertical direction

plumber a person who installs and maintains piping and fixtures

plummer a block of material serving as a bearing plate

plural (see **pleural**)

plurel (see **pleural**)

pluripotence in heraldry, having several flat bars across the ends of the arms in a cross

pluripotents in heraldry, having several rows of interlocking upright and inverted short-stemmed T-shaped panes

plyers (see **pliers**)

pneumatic (see **neumatic**)

pneumatics spiritual beings held by Gnostics as belonging to the highest of the three classes into which mankind is divided; a branch of mechanics that deals with the mechanical properties of gases

pneumatiques letters or messages transmitted by compressed-air dispatch

pneumatophorous having the characteristics of a submerged or exposed root that often functions as a respiratory organ of a swamp or marsh plant

Pneumatophorus a genus of small warm-water mackerels

pneumonic (see **mnemonic**)

Pnyx (see **nicks**)

Po the longest and largest river in Italy

poh an expression of contempt

pocks (see **Pax**)

poem a composition in verse form

pome a fleshy fruit (as an apple) with a central core of usually five seeds

pomme in heraldry, a rounded vert

poh (see **Po**)

pois Hawaiian food made of taro roots

poise easy composure of manner marked especially by assurance and gracious dignity

pol (see **pall**)

polar related to one of the Earth's poles; diametrically opposite in nature or action

poler a person who propels a boat with a long staff or rod

poller a person who lops or trims trees; a person who asks questions in a poll or canvass

Pole a native or inhabitant of Poland

pole a long slender cylindrical piece of wood or metal

poll a voting at an election; to cut off the head, horns, or treetops

poler (see **polar**)

police (see **pelisse**)

poling a process used in refining some metals such as copper

polling casting ballots at an election

politic expedient or judicious; sagacious in devising or promoting a policy
politik to engage in political discussion or activity

poll (see **pall** and **Pole**)

pollan a whitefish of the Irish lakes
pollen microscopes in a seed plant

poller (see **polar**)

polling (see **poling**)

pollster a person who conducts or asks questions in a poll or canvas
polster a cushion plant

polly a poll parrot
poly a polymorphonuclear leukocyte (by shortening)

polster (see **pollster**)

poly (see **polly**)

polydactylous having more than the normal number of toes or fingers
Polydactylus a genus of fishes found in warm seas

polypous relating to or characteristic of a polyp
Polypus a genus of octopuses

pom a pomeranian dog; an ornamental ball or tuft on clothing; the characteristic noise of a small caliber cannon
pomme in heraldry, a rounded green area

pomace a substance resulting from crushing by grinding
pumice a porous powdered volcanic stone used for smoothing and polishing
pummice the head and entrails of a sheep or other animal

pome (see **poem**)

pomme (see **poem** or **pom**)

pommée a cross having the end of each arm terminating in a ball or disk
pommy an English immigrant recently arrived in Australia

pommel an ornamental terminal knob, as a saddle horn; a removable handle on a gymnastic horse
pummel to thump or pound

pommy (see **pommée**)

pond (see **pawned**)

ponds small bodies of water
pons a broad mass of transverse nerve fibers

pone a player on the dealer's right who cuts the cards
pony a small horse; a translation used as an aid in learning a language

pons (see **ponds**)

pontil a solid metal rod used for fashioning hot glass
pontile appropriate for a bridge

pony (see **pone**)

poof an expression of disdain, disapproval, or contempt
pouf something inflated or insubstantial, as clothing or furniture accessories

pooka a mischievous or malignant goblin specter in Irish folklore
puka a hole or tunnel, in Hawaii; either of two New Zealand trees that are sometimes epiphytic

pool (see **Peul**)

pooli a tropical African timber tree
pooly swampy; having many pools

poo-poo excrement or feces
pupu any hot or cold usually bite-size Polynesian-Hawaiian appetizer

poor lacking material possessions, destitute, or needy
pore to look searchingly; a minute opening on an animal or vegetable

pour   to diffuse, discharge, or decant

poort   a pass between or across mountains

port   a place where ships may ride secure from storms; a harbor or haven

Porte   formerly the Ottoman court; the government of the Turkish Empire

popery   Roman Catholicism, especially its government and forms of worship

potpourri   a general mixture of often disparate or unrelated materials on subject matter

popper   (see **pauper**)

populace   the total number of people; the common people

populous   numerous; filled to capacity; popular

Populus   a genus of trees native to the Northern Hemisphere

pore   (see **poor**)

porous   full of holes; capable of absorbing moisture or permeable to liquids

porus   a pit on an insect's body connected with its sense organs

porphyrin   any of a group of reddish brown to purplish black metal-free usually octa-substituted derivatives of porphin

porphyrine   an alkaloid obtained as a bitter amorphous powder from Australian fever bark

port   (see **poort**)

Porte   (see **poort**)

porus   (see **porous**)

posit   to postulate, often in the absence of supporting evidence

posset   to pamper with delicacies; a hot drink consisting of sweetened and spiced milk curdled with ale or wine

positivest   most positive

positivist   an adherrent of the philosophy of positivism

posset   (see **posit**)

postiche   (see **pastiche**)

pot   (see **pâte**)

potence   a supporting watchwork bracket; the integrated dominance effect of a group of polygenes

potents   in heraldry, rows of interlocking upright and inverted short-stemmed T-shaped panes

potpourri   (see **popery**)

pott   (see **pâte**)

pouf   (see **poof**)

poule   (see **Peul**)

pour   (see **poor**)

pow   (see **pau**)

pox   (see **Pax**)

praise   to commend, applaud, glorify, or laud

prase   greenish chalcedony

prays   entreats or implores

preys   makes raids for booty or food

praiss   a fluid extract of tobacco

press   to squeeze or crowd

pram   a small lightweight nearly flat-bottomed boat usually with a squared-off bow

prom   a formal dance given by a high school or college class

prase   (see **praise**)

prau   one of several usually undecked Indonesian boats propelled by sails, oars, or paddles

prow   the bow of a ship

prayed   (see **parade**)

prayer   a person who prays; a supplicant

preyer   a person, animal, organism that hunts and preys on others

prays (see **praise**)

preaccept to take or suggest taking without protest prior to the actual occurrence
preexcept to omit something prior to another event

preaffect to influence or make an impression on beforehand or in preparation of another event
preeffect to cause to come into being or accomplish prior to another occurrence

precedential having the force or character of a precedent
presidential related to a president

precession a comparatively slow gyration of the rotation axis of a spinning body about another line intersecting it so as to describe a cone
presession occurring before a session of a legislative body, committee, or group

precipitance headlong haste
precipitants agents that cause the formation of a precipitate

preeffect (see **preaffect**)

preexcept (see **preaccept**)

premier a prime minister; the first in importance or rank; a bluish-white diamond
premiere a first performance or exhibition

presence a state of being in one place and not elsewhere
presents donations or gifts

presession (see **precession**)

presidential (see **precendential**)

press (see **praiss**)

pressed crowded, forced, or squeezed
prest a duty formerly paid by a sheriff on his/her account into the exchequer

presser a person or device that shapes, molds, or irons items
pressor involving or producing an increase in blood pressure

prest (see **pressed**)

preyed (see **parade**)

preyer (see **prayer**)

preys (see **praise**)

pride a sense of one's worth or self-esteem; a group of lions
pried peered curiously; moved or opened with a lever

prier a person who peers curiously; an inquisitive person
prior earlier in time or order; the rank below an abbot in a monastery

pries moves or opens with a lever
prize something offered or striven for in a contest or competition

primer an elementary instruction book
primmer more formal in manner or appearance; neater or trimmer

prince a male member of a royal family
prints makes an impression or mark on; copies of paintings or photographs

principal the most important or salient; main; a person who has a leading position, as in a school
principle a general or fundamental truth, law, doctrine, or assumption

prints (see **prince**)

prior (see **prier**)

prize (see **pries**)

procellas a glass manufacturing tool for imparting a characteristic shape to an object as it is rotated by the punty
procellous stormy

profit the excess of returns over expenditures; net income (revenues and gains less expenses and losses)

Prophet   the accredited leader of a religious group, as the Mormons or Muhammud, the founder of Islam

prophet   a person gifted with extraordinary spiritual and moral insight; a spiritual seer

projicience   reference of a perceived quality or modification of consciousness to an external reality

projicients   persons who project or thrust forward

prom   (see **pram**)

prominence   the quality of being notable or eminent

prominents   moths of the family Notodontidae

proper   appropriate; in accord with established traditions and feelings of rightness

propper   a person or device that prevents something from falling or collapsing; a supporter

Prophet and **prophet**   (see **profit**)

propper   (see **proper**)

pros   arguments favoring a position or argument; affirmative sides of a question or position; professionals (by shortening)

prose   a literary medium distinguished from poetry; a language intended primarily to give information or communicate ideas

prosar   a service book in the Roman Catholic church of sequences, hymns, or rhythms

proser   a person who talks or writes tediously; a writer of prose

prose   (see **pros**)

proser   (see **prosar**)

protean   exceedingly variable; capable of change

protein   a natural complex combination of amino acids

Provençal   relating to Provence, a region of southeastern France

provençale   cooked with garlic, olive oil, onion, mushrooms, and herbs

prow   (see **prau**)

psalter   a translation or version of the Psalms

salter   a person that manufactures or deals in sodium chloride; a person or device that applies salt

psaltery   an ancient and medieval stringed musical instrument that is played by plucking its stretched strings

saltery   an establishment in which fish are salted for market

psammite   sandstone

samite   a rich medieval fabric of silk interwoven sometimes with gold or silver threads

psephite   a coarse fragmental rock composed of rounded pebbles

psephyte   a lake bottom deposit consisting mainly of coarse, fibrous plant remains

pshaw   an expression of disapproval or disbelief

sha   the urial, a wild sheep of the uplands of southern and central Asia

shah   a sovereign of Iran

psicose   a syrupy ketohexose sugar in the unfermentable residue of cane molasses

psychos   persons with emotional disorders

psion   (see **Cyon**)

psis   (see **cees**)

psis   plural of the 23rd letter of the Greek alphabet

scyes   armhold shapes or outlines

sighs   expresses weariness, relief, or grief

size   the area, magnitude, or volume of something

psittaceous   like a parrot

setaceous   consisting of or resembling bristles

psora a chronic skin disease characterized by circumscribed red patches covered with white scales
sora a small short-billed North American rail

psorosis (see **cirrhosis**)

psorous pertaining to or affected by the itching disease (psora) of the skin
sorous a cluster of reproductive bodies or spores on a lower plant, such as ferns

psych (see **cyke**)

psychal (see **cycle**)

psychos (see **psicose**)

psychosis a profound disorganization of the mind, personality, or behavior
sycosis a chronic inflammatory disease of hair follicles, especially of the bearded part of the face

Psylla a genus of jumping plant lice
psylla any insect of the family Psyllidae
Scilla a large genus of Old World bulbous herbs comprising the squills
scilla any plant, bulb, or flower of the genus Scilla
Scylla a destructive peril

Psyllia (see **cilia**)

psyllium (see **cilium**)

Ptelea a small genus of North American shrubs or small trees including the hop tree
telea aggregations of teliospores, often stalked

Pteris a genus of coarse ferns
teras a grossly abnormal organism
terrace a raised embankment with a leveled top; a gallery or portico

pterocarpous having winged fruit
Pterocarpus a genus of tropical flowers

pteron a side (as of a temple) in classical architecture
Teh(e)ran the capital of Iran

pudding boiled or baked soft food with the consistency of custard or thick cream
putting placing in a specified position

puer a dog dung mixture used in tanning hides and skins
pure free from admixture; containing no added substance

puisne in law, of a subsequent date or later; junior or subordinate
puny weak, insignificant, or sickly

puka (see **pooka**)

puli an Hungarian breed of intelligent vigorous medium-sized farm dog
pulley a mechanical device for lifting a heavy weight

pumice (see **pomace**)

pummel (see **pommel**)

pummice (see **pomace**)

puny (see **puisne**)

pupal related to the pupa stage in an insect's life cycle
pupil a student; the contractile aperture in the eye's iris

pupu (see **poo-poo**)

purchase (see **perches**)

pure (see **puer**)

purgery (see **perjury**)

puri a light fried wheatcake of India
purree an Indian yellow color

purl (see **pearl**)

purr (see **per**)

purree (see **puri**)

purse (see **perse**)

purtenance (see **pertinence**)

purveyed (see **pervade**)

put a blockhead or dolt

putt   a golf stroke made on or near a putting green

puts   sets, lays, or places in a specific position

putz   a decoration built around a representation of the Nativity scene; a crèche

putt   (see **put**)

puttee   a leg covering from the ankle to the knee

putty   a pliable cement for fastening glass in sashes

putting   (see **pudding**)

putty   (see **puttee**)

putz   (see **puts**)

pyknic   (see **picnic**)

pyla   (see **Pila**)

pyr   (see **peer**)

pyr   a unit of light intensity equal to .954 candles

pyre   a combustible heap usually of wood for burning a dead body as a funeral rite

pyre   (see **Paya**)

pyric   resulting from or associated with burning

Pyrrhic   relating to or resembling that of Pyrrhus, king of Epirus

pyrrhic   an ancient Greek martial dance; a foot in prosody consisting of two short or unaccented syllables

pyrrole   (see **parol**)

pyx   (see **picks**)

pentine - pentyne
percipience - percipients
perivitellin - perivitelline
permanence - permanents
petulance - petulants
phaser - phasor
phosphorescence - phosphorescents
phosphorous - phosphorus
phylostomous - phylostomus
pilous - pilus
planar - planer
policlinic - polyclinic
polyvalence - polyvalents
porcelainous - porcelanous
preadolescence - preadolescents
precedence - precedents
precisian - precision
predominance - predominants
presidence - presidents
prevalence - prevalents
princes - princess
prodromous - prodromus
proestrous - proestrus
profluence - profluents
protégé - protégée
ptisan - tisane
pungence - pungents
pursuance - pursuants

Group I and II

pignon	ˈpēnˌyän
pinon	ˈpēnˌyōn
poser	ˈpōzər
poseur	pōˈzər
promiser	ˈpräməsər
promisor	ˈpräməˌsȯr

Group I

palmar - palmer
pediculous - Pediculus
pedipalous - pedipalpus
penitence - penitents

Group II

palea	ˈpālēə
pallia	ˈpalēə
parotid	pəˈrätəd
parroted	ˈparətəd

pase 'på,så
passe pɑ'så or 'pås

pastoral 'pɑstərəl
pastorale ,pɑstə'räl

pastourelle ,pɑstə'rel
pastural 'pɑschərəl

pavilion pə'vilyən
pavillon 'påvē,yōⁿ

pawed 'pȯd
pod 'påd

pearlish 'pərlēsh
perlèche 'per,lesh

peeking 'pēkiŋ
Peking 'pē,kiŋ

penal 'pēnᵊl
pinal pē'näl

perilless 'perəlȧs
perilous 'perələs

periodic :pirē:ädik
periotic :perē:ädik

phenol 'fē,nōl
phenyl 'fēnᵊl

picarel ,pikə'rel
pickerel 'pikərəl

picker 'pikər
piqueur pē'kər

picture 'pikchər
pitcher 'pichər

pillory 'pilərē
pilori pȧ'lōrē

pincher 'pinchər
pinscher 'pinshər

pinnae 'pi,nē
pinny 'pinē

Piro 'pirō
pyro 'pīrō

placate 'plā,kāt
placket 'plakȧt
plakat plə'kɑt
plaquette 'plɑ,ket

plaintiff 'plāntȧf
plaintive 'plāntiv

plastic 'plɑstik or 'plɑstēk
plastique plɑ'stēk

pooch 'püch
putsch 'pu̇ch

poulette 'pü:let
pullet 'pu̇lȧt

precent prē'sent
present prē'zent

Precis 'prēsȧs
precise prē'sīs

precisian prē'sizən
precision prē'sizhən

promoter prə'mōdər
promotor prō'mōdər

psammon 'sɑ,män
salmon 'samən

pulley 'pu̇lē
pulli 'pə,lī

puree pyu̇'rē
purey 'pyu̇rē
puri 'pu̇rē

pyrite 'pī,rīt
pyrrhite 'pi,rīt

Q

qre (see Cree)

qua (see Kwa)

quack (see couac)

quad a block of type metal; a quadrangle on a college campus

quod a prison (slang)

quadrat a game in which printer's quads are thrown like dice; a small usually rectangular plot laid off for the study of vegetation or animals

quadrate relating to a bony or cartilaginous element of each side of the skull

quaff (see **coif**)

quai (see **cay**)

quaily an upland plover

quale a feeling having its own particular quality without meaning or external reference

quake (see **kweek**)

quale (see **quaily**)

qualmish affected by scruples, compunction, or conscience

quamish a plant of the genus Camassia of the western U.S.

quarl(e) a large brick or tile

quarrel a dispute, conflict, or altercation; to argue

quartan recurring at approximately 72-hour intervals, as chills and fever of malaria

quartern a fourth part of various units of measure

quart(e) (see **cart**)

quarten (see **quartan**)

quartre (see **cotter**)

quarts U.S. liquid measures equal to two pints or ¼ gallon

quartz a mineral consisting of silicon dioxide

quay (see both **cays**)

'que (see **cue**)

quean a prostitute

queen a female monarch; a king's wife; the most privileged chess piece

queer (see **cuir**)

queerest strangest, most curious, most eccentric, or most unconventional

querist a person who inquires or asks questions

query (see **cuirie** or **Kweri**)

quester a person that makes a search or goes in pursuit of something or someone

questor an agent of a pope or bishop charged with collecting alms

quetch to break silence or utter a sound

quetsch a dry white Alsatian brandy distilled from fermented plum juice

quête (see **Ket**)

queue (see **cue**)

quiche (see **keesh**)

quidder a horse that drops chewed food from the mouth due to an inability to swallow

quitter a person who gives up, admits defeat, or stops trying; a coward

quittor a pus-filled inflammation of the feet of horses

quince a fruit of a widely cultivated central Asiastic tree

quints sequences of five playing cards of the same suit; quintuplets (by shortening)

quintain an object to be tilted in a sport during the middle ages

quintan occurring as the fifth after four others

quintal a metric unit equal to 100 kilograms

quintile any of the four values that divides the items of a frequency distribution into five classes each containing one-fifth of the total number of items

quintan (see **quintain**)

quinte (see **cant**)

quintile (see **quintal**)

quints (see **quince**)

quire (see **choir**)

quis (see **cuisse**)

quitter (see **quidder**)

quittor (see **quidder**)

quod (see **quad**)

quoin (see **coign**)

Group I

quiescence - quiescents

Group II

quadrans ˈkwä.dranz
quadrants ˈkwädrənz

R

Ra the great sun god and principal deity of historical Egypt

rah to cheer or express joy, approbation, or encouragement

rath a circular earthwork serving as a stronghold for an ancient Irish chief

raad an electric catfish; a legislative assembly in a South African Boer republic prior to British administration

rod a slender pole for fishing, measuring, hanging, or lightning protection

rodd a crossbow for shooting stones

rabat a polishing material made from potter's clay

rabbet a channel or groove cut from the edge of material

rabbit a small grayish brown mammal related to hares

rabot a hardwood block used for rubbing marble before polishing

rabi relating to India's spring and major crops

ruby a precious stone that is a red corundum

rabot (see **rabat**)

race a speed contest; descendants of a common ancestor

res in law, a particular thing

rack a frame on which articles are placed; a pair of antlers; a device for inflcting pain by pulling or straining

wrack to wreck beyond repair; a piece of wreckage

racket a confusing clattering noise; a light bat used in tennis and badminton

rackett a bass instrument of the oboe family

racquet a grayish brown to grayish yellowish brown color

raddle to interweave; a red ocher; to color with rouge

rattle a rapid succession of sharp clattering sounds; a noisemaker

radiance a deep pink color; vivid brightness; splendor

radiants organisms that have reached their present geographical location as a result of dispersal from a primary place of origin

radical the considerable departure from the usual or traditional; a fundamental constituent of chemical compounds

radicle the lower portion of the axis of a plant embryo or seedling

radish the pungent fleshy root of a plant

rattish resembling or having characteristics of a rat

raff a coarse disputable person; riff-raff

raffe a usually triangular topsail set above a square lower sail

raggee an East Indian cereal grass from whose seeds is ground a somewhat bitter flour that is an Oriental staple food

raggy rough or ragged

rah (see **Ra**)

raid a hostile or predatory incursion

rayed having lines that appear to radiate from a bright object

raider a person involved in hostile incursions; a fast unarmored lightly armed ship for capturing or destroying merchant ships

rater a person who scores (examination papers) or estimates (premiums on property insurance)

rail a long piece of wood, metal, or other material used as a structural member or support; a wading bird related to the crane; to rant or utter abusive language

rayl a unit of specific acoustical impedance equal to the sound pressure of one dyne per square centimeter divided by the sound particle velocity of one centimeter per second

rain water falling in drops from the atmosphere

reign a monarch's power or rule

rein a line fastened to the bit through which a rider or driver directs a horse or other animal

rainy wet or showery

ranny a poor quality calf of mongrel breeding

Rais a Mongoloid people of Nepal who speak Kiranti

rais a Muslim chief, ruler, or ship captain; a person in charge in Muslim countries

rice an annual cereal grass widely cultivated in warm climates for its seeds

raise to lift or set upright; to grow plants or animals

rase to erase; to incise by carving or engraving

rays lines that appear to radiate from a bright object

raze to level to the ground; to destroy

rehs mixtures of soluble sodium salts appearing as an efflorescence on the ground in arid or semiarid regions in India

res second notes of the diatonic scale

reys kings or male monarchs that reign over major territorial units

rigs ancient Irish kings

raiser a person who lifts, sets upright, or grows plants or animals

raser a person who erases; a person that forms by carving or engraving

razer a person who demolishes structures

razor a keen-edged cutting instrument

raki a Turkish liqueur distilled usually from fermented raisins

rocky abounding in or consisting of extremely hard dense stones; unstable; hard

ram a male sheep; a device for exerting considerable pressure or driving force on another subject

rhamn a buckthorn tree or shrub

ramie a tall perennial herb of eastern Asia or its strong lustrous bast fiber

rammy resembling a ram

ramous relating to or resembling branches

ramus the posterior vertical part of each lower jaw which articulates with the skull

ranch an establishment where live-stock is raised
ranche a pin pool stroke that leaves only the center pin standing

rancor vehement hatred or ill will
ranker a person who draws up in line or serves in military ranks

randem three horses harnessed to a vehicle, one behind the other
random lacking a regular plan or order; haphazard

rangle bits of gravel fed to hawks
wrangle an angry, bitter, noisy, or prolonged dispute or quarrel

ranker (see **rancor**)

ranny (see **rainy**)

rapee the victim of a rape
rappee a moist pungent snuff made from dark rank tobacco leaves

rapped struck with a quick sharp blow
rapt lifted and carried up or away; enraptured
wrapped enclosed in a covering

rappee (see **rapee**)

rappel to descend a cliff by means of a double-rope arrangement
repel to drive back, repulse, or turn away

rapport a relationship characterized by harmony and accord
report a record or something that provides information

rapt (see **rapped**)

ras a cape or headland; a ruler of an Ethiopian province; a local Italian Fascist boss
ross the rough often scaly exterior of tree bark

rase (see **raise**)

raser (see **raiser**)

rasse a grizzled black-marked semi-arboreal civet
wrasse a brilliantly colored marine fish related to parrot fish

ratal an amount by which a person is rated with reference to assessment
ratel any of several powerful noc-turnal carnivorous mammals re-sembling the badger

rater (see **raider**)

rath (see **Ra**)

rath a circular earthwork serving as a stronghold for an ancient Irish chief
wrath an enraged feeling expressed vehemently and accompanied by bitterness; righteous indignation and condemnation
wroth moved to intense anger; highly incensed; turbulent

rattish (see **radish**)

rattle (see **raddle**)

rayed (see **raid**)

rayl (see **rail**)

rays (see **raise**)

raze (see **raise**)

razer (see **raiser**)

razor (see **raiser**)

re regarding or concerning
Ree a Caddo people west of the Missouri river in the Dakotas
ree a female ruff, a European sand-piper
rhe the unit of fluidity equal to the reciprocal of one dyne-second per square centimeter
rig an ancient Irish king

rea a person required to provide an answer in an action or suit in law, equity, or a criminal action
Rhea a genus of large tall flightless South American birds resembling but smaller than the African ostrich

rhea any bird of the genus Rhea; the ramie plant or fibre

ria a long narrow inlet that gradually gets shallower inward

rya a Scandinavian handwoven rug with a deep resilient comparatively flat pile

reactance impedance of an AC circuit that is due to capacitance and or inductance

reactants chemically reactive substances

read mentally formulated words or sentences

red a color

redd the spawn of fish

read to mentally formulate words or sentences as represented by letters or symbols

reed a tall grass with a slender stem; a device on a loom resembling a comb

reader a person who reads; a book for instruction in reading; a textile worker who records a design that is read from a card

reeder a person who thatches with reeds; a textile worker who tapes a reed or wire on sweatband leathers

rhetor a master or teacher of rhetoric; a person concerned with rhetoric

Reading a city in southeast Pennsylvania

redding material which is, or is used to make red color; a compound used to redden the hearth and sides of a fireplace; the action of arranging, tidying, or clearing up

retting soaking or exposing (as flax) to moisture in order to promote the loosening of fiber from woody tissue by bacterial action

ready prepared for something about to be done or experienced

Reddi a Munda-speaking migratory agricultural people of southeast Hyderabad, India

reddy reddish in color

real actual, true, or objective

reel a device to wind yarn, thread, string, or line

reamer a rotating finishing tool with straight or spiral cutting edges used to enlarge or shape a hole

rimur a complex form of versified saga or treatment of episodes from the sagas popular in Iceland from the 15th century

reams bundles of 500 sheets of book paper or newsprint; widens a hole opening

reems horned wild animals, probably wild oxen

rhemes semantic units or elements of speech

R(h)eims a city in northern France famous for its Gothic cathedral

riems pliable strips of rawhide; thongs

rear the back part of something; to rise up to an erect position

rier in whaling, a small oil cask of about ten gallons stowed at the end of tiers

reason a horizontal timber over a row of posts supporting a beam

resin any of various hard brittle solid to soft semisolid amorphous fusible flammable substances

rebait to place another lure in a trap or on a fishing line

rebate to diminish or lessen; a repayment

rebilled reissued notice to a customer for payment

rebuild to restore to a previous condition

reboard to reenter a ship, plane, bus, or train

rebored pierced or drilled a hole again

rebuild (see **rebilled**)

rec recreation (by shortening)
reck to take heed or thought
wreck a thing that is disabled, shattered, or ruined

recede to depart, withdraw, or retreat; to grant or yield again to a former possessor
reseed to replant or resow

receipt a written acknowledgment of goods or money delivered
reseat to sit again; to fit with a new seat, as a chair

reciting repeating from memory or reading aloud, especially before an audience
re-siding placing new siding on a structure
resighting looking carefully again in a certain direction
resiting placing on a new site

reck (see **rec**)

recks is apprehensive or fearful; considers, deems, or regards
rex a genetic variation of a domestic rabbit and various rodents
wrecks things that are disabled, shattered, or ruined

rect an element analogous to a right line in a geometrical system
wrecked ruined or damaged

red (see **read**)

redd (see **read**)

redder having a deeper or more red color
retter a person who soaks flax to loosen fiber from the woody tissue

Reddi (see **ready**)

redding (see **Reading**)

reddy (see **ready**)

redo to execute again or do over
redue something that is again owed or due

reducts to reduce

redux brought back; resurgent

redue (see **redo**)

redux (see **reducts**)

Ree and **ree** (see **re**)

reed (see **read**)

reeder (see **reader**)

reedy abounding in or covered with reeds; having the tone quality of a reed instrument
rete a circular plate with many holes on the astrolabe to indicate positions of the principal fixed stars; a network of blood vessels or nerves

reek to emit a strong or disagreeable fume or odor
wreak to bring about, cause, or inflict

reel (see **real**)

reemerge to appear again after concealment, retirement, or suppression
reimmerge to plunge into or sink again

reems (see **reams**)

refind to recover or rediscover
refined reduced to a fine, unmixed, or pure state; free of impurities

reflects turns, throws, or bends back at an angle; thinks about or considers
reflex a reaction to a stimulus, often unconscious

regal of notable excellence or magnificence; stately; splendid
regle a groove or channel for guiding a sliding door
riegel a low transverse rock ridge on the floor of a glaciated valley

regence related to a furniture style prevalent between about 1680 to 1725
regents persons who govern in the absence, disability, or minority of a sovereign

regle　(see **regal**)

rehs　(see **raise**)

reign　(see **rain**)

reimmerge　(see **reemerge**)

rein　(see **rain**)

reiter　a German cavalry soldier of the 16th and 17th centuries

rider　a person who rides a vehicle or form of transportation; an addition to a legislative bill

righter　a person who does justice or redresses wrongs

writer　a person who produces symbols or words on paper

rejecter　a person that refuses or rejects

rejector　a circuit that combines inductance and capacitance in parallel

relaid　put to set down again

relayed　passed along by successive reliefs or relays

relaps　folds over or around something anew or again

relapse　to slip or fall back into a former state of illness; to backslide

relater　a narrator or storyteller

relator　a private person in whose behalf a mandamus is filed

relayed　(see **relaid**)

releaser　a stimulus in lower organisms serving as an intiator of complex reflex behavior

releasor　a person giving a release

remand　to return a case from one court to a lower court or an administrative agency

remanned　supplied with people or a crew again or anew

remark　an expression in speech or writing

remarque　a sketch done on the margin of a plate and removed before regular printing

remittance　money sent to another person or place

remittents　fevers the symptoms of which temporarily abate and moderate at regular intervals

remitter　a person who sends a remittance; a legal principle concerning a person who obtains possession of property under a defective title

remittor　a sending back of a case or some portion of a verdict from an appelate or superior court to a trial or inferior court for further proceedings or reconsideration

rends　pulls violently from a person or thing; wrenches

reyns　an abstract number characteristic of the flow of a fluid in a pipe or past an obstruction, used especially in testing airplane models in a wind tunnel; a unit of dynamic viscosity of a fluid equal to 14.8816 poise; Reynolds numbers (by shortening)

wrens　small brown singing birds

repand　a plant leaf having a slightly undulating margin

repanned　rewashed earth deposits in search of precious metals

repassed　crossed or traveled again

repast　something taken as food; a meal

repel　(see **rappel**)

report　(see **rapport**)

reroot　to reattach or replant a tree or shrub

reroute　to replan an itinerary

res　(see **race** and **raise**)

resail　to sail again

resale　selling again or as second hand

reseat　(see **receipt**)

reseed　(see **recede**)

resew   to stitch again
resow   to replant with seed

re-siding   (see reciting)

resighting   (see reciting)

resin   (see reason)

resister   a person that strives or reacts against
resistor   a device used in an electrical circuit for protection or control

resiting   (see reciting)

resold   sold again or as second hand
resoled   put a new sole on a shoe

resow   (see resew)

rest   relaxation, repose, or leisure for body or mind
wrest   to move by violent wringing or twisting movements

resteal   to again take another's property illegally
resteel   to equip with new steel

resultance   something that results as a consequence, effect, or conclusion, as a resolution of a legislative body
resultants   mathematical vector sums

retard   to delay or impede progress
retarred   recovered with tar
ritard   a gradually slackening musical tempo

retch   to strain to vomit
wretch   a miserable person

rete   (see reedy)

retracked   traced or tracked again
retract   to draw or pull back; to remove; to withdraw

retter   (see redder)

retting   (see Reading)

revere   to regard with profound respect and affection
revers   a lapel on women's garments

review   to inspect or examine
revue   a light theatrical entertainment

reviver   a stimulant; a person who restores, reestablishes, or reintroduces something
revivor   revival under law of a suit that is abated

revue   (see review)

rex   (see recks)

reyns   (see rends)

reys   (see raise)

rhamn   (see ram)

rhe   (see re)

Rhea and rhea   (see rea)

R(h)eims   (see reams)

rhemes   (see reams)

rhetor   (see reader)

rheum   a watery discharge from the mucous membranes of the eye or nose
room   space; part of a building's interior
Rum   a term originally applied by Moslems in medieval times to peoples of the Byzantine empire
rum   a blue dye resembling indigo obtained from an East Indian shrub

Rhine   a major river in western Germany
rine   Russian hemp

RHM   a unit of gamma-ray source intensity
rhumb   a line on the earth's surface making equal oblique angles with all meridians; a point on a mariner's compass
rum   an alcoholic liquor prepared from fermented molasses

rhodeose   an aldose sugar
roadeos   a contest featuring events that test driving skills of professional truck drivers

rodeos public performances featuring such contests as bareback bronco riding, calf roping, and steer wrestling

rhoding the journal bearing of a pump brake
roading highway construction and maintenance

rhodite a native alloy of gold and rhodium
roadite a person addicted to driving (slang)

Rhoeo a monotypic genus of herbs, including the oyster plant
Rio Rio de Janeiro, a city on the southeast coast of Brazil

Rhône a major river flowing through southeastern France into the Mediterranean sea
roan a moderate reddish-brown; a roan-colored animal
rohun an East Indian tree having hard durable wood and tonic bark
rowan a Eurasian tree; an American mountain ash

rhos the 17th letter (plural) of the Greek alphabet
roes small European and Asiatic deer
Ros artificial languages intended to be international, such as esperanto
rose a flower; a perfume; a moderate purplish red color
rows propels a boat with oars; continuous lines or stripes

rhumb (see **RHM**)

Rhus a genus of shrubs and trees native to temperate and warm regions
ruse a stratagem or trick intended to deceive

rhyme identical or similar sounding words or lines of verse
rime granular ice tufts on the windward side of an exposed object
ryme the surface of water

ria (see **rea**)

riband a decorative ribbon
ribband a long narrow strip or bar used in shipbuilding; a single bendlet that surrounds outer heraldic bearings
ribboned adorned, trimmed, or marked with a narrow band of material

rice (see **Rais**)

rick a pile of cordwood, stave bolts, or other material split from short logs
rikk a small tambourine used in Egypt
wrick a strain or sprain of muscles

ridder a person that removes, clears off, or takes away
ritter a member of one of the lowest orders of German or Austrian nobility

ride to sit or be carried on the back of an animal or in a vehicle
wried twisted around

rider (see **reiter**)

riegel (see **regal**)

riems (see **reams**)

rier (see **rear**)

riffed discharged from government service for reasons of economy
rift a fissure or split

rig (see **re**)

rigger a person who manipulates or fits ship riggings, or works on oil and gas well rigs
rigor severity, sternness, or exactness

right good or just; a privilege or prerogative; the position opposite to left
Rite the liturgy, especially an historical form of eucharistic service
rite a ceremonial act
wright a carpenter

write   to produce symbols or words on paper

righter   (see **reiter**)

rigor   (see **rigger**)

rigs   (see **raise**)

rikk   (see **rick**)

rime   (see **rhyme**)

rimur   (see **reamer**)

rine   (see **Rhine**)

ring   a circular or curved band
wring   to compress by squeezing or twisting

Rio   (see **Rhoeo**)

riot   a noise, uproar, or disturbance; persons acting in a turbulent and disorderly manner
ryot   a peasant, in India

ripe   ready for harvesting
rype   the ptarmigan, a grouse of northern regions having completely feathered feet

rise   to assume an upright or standing position; to get up from resting or sleeping
ryes   hardy annual cereal grasses; whiskies distilled from rye; gypsy gentlemen
wrys   twists around or wrings

ritard   (see **retard**)

Rite and **rite**   (see **right**)

ritter   (see **ridder**)

ritz   to snub or behave superciliously toward
writs   written documents; legal instruments or mandatory processes

rival   one of two or more persons striving for what only one can possess
rivel   to wrinkle or shrivel

road   a passageway or highway for vehicles
rode   traveled by vehicle or animal
roed   filled with fish eggs
rowed   propelled a boat with oars

roadeos   (see **rhodeose**)

roading   (see **rhoding**)

roadite   (see **rhodite**)

roam   to wander or rove
rom   a male gypsy
Rome   the capital of Italy; Roman Catholicism

roan   (see **Rhône**)

roar   a full loud heavy prolonged sound; to utter such a sound
rower   a person who uses oars to propel a boat

roband   a small piece of spun yarn or marline used to fasten the head of a sail to a spar (also **robbin**)
robin   a large North American thrush; a small European thrush

rober   a person who covers or invests with a robe
robur   an English oak

robin   (see **roband**)

robur   (see **rober**)

roc   a legendary bird of great size and strength
rock   a large fixed stone; to move a child back and forth, as in a cradle
ROK   a member of the armed forces of the Republic of South Korea

roccellin   a red monoazo dye
roccelline   resembling plants of the genus Roccella

rock   (see **roc**)

rocky   (see **raki**)

rod   (see **raad**)

rodd   (see **raad**)

rodder   a textile worker who folds double-width goods

rotter an unprincipled, lazy, or weak person

rode (see **road**)

rodeos (see **rhodeose**)

roed (see **road**)

roer a heavy long-barreled gun formerly used for hunting big game in southern Africa
Ruhr a mining and industrial region centered in western Germany

roes (see **rhos**)

rohun (see **Rhône**)

roil to make turbid by stirring up sediment or dregs
royal magnificent or regal; of kingly ancestry

ROK (see **roc**)

roke a seam or scratch filled with scale or slag on the surface of an ingot or bar
roque croquet played on a hard-surfaced court having a raised border to cushion bank shots

role a character assumed by a person
roll a list of names or items; to revolve by turning over and over

rom (see **roam**)

Rome (see **roam**)

rondeau a fixed form of verse
rondo a dance composition with a recurring movement theme

Rong a Mongolian people of Sikkim, India
wrong a principle, practice, or conduct contrary to justice, goodness, equity, or accepted law

rood a crucifix symbolizing the cross on which Christ died
rude lacking craftsmanship or artistic finish; raw, unpolished, coarse, or uncouth

rued regretted; repented

rookie a novice or beginner
rooky full of common Old World gregarious birds similar to the American crow

room (see **rheum**)

roomer a lodger
rumor a belief having no discernible foundation; heresay

roomy spacious
roumi a non–Muslim, often used disparagingly

roos kangaroos
roux mixtures of flour and fat or butter used as thickening agents
rues regrets or repents
ruse a strategem or trick designed to deceive

root a portion of a plant growing underground; to dig in search of something; to fix or firmly attach
route a pathway, road, or highway

rooter a heavy plowing device for tearing up the ground surface, especially for a roadbed; an enthusiastic supporter
ruder more ill-mannered, discourteous, impolite, or uncivil

roque (see **roke**)

Ros (see **rhos**)

rose (see **rhos**)

roset a dark reddish-orange color, often called brazil red
rosette an ornament or structure resembling a rose

ross (see **ras**)

rosy characterized by or tending to promote optimism; having a rose-colored complexion
Rozi a Bantu-speaking people in Zambia known for their woodworking

rot to decompose, decay, or deteriorate

wrought fashioned, formed, or created

rote the noise of the surf crashing on the shore
rut a track made by the continual passage of anything; sexual excitement in a mammal, especially a male deer

rote a thing learned by memorizing; the mechanical repetition of a pattern
wrote produced symbols or words on paper

roter a person who repeats by rote
rotor a part that rotates in a stationary part

rotter (see **rodder**)

rough coarse, shaggy, or harsh
ruff a fringe of long hair or feathers about a bird's or animal's neck

roumi (see **roomy**)

rouse to awaken or stir
rows noisy disturbances; heated arguments

rout to expel by force or eject
route a road, highway, or pathway

route (see **root**)

roux (see **roos**)

rowan (see **Rhône**)

rowan a Eurasian tree; an American mountain ash
rowen a stubble field left unplowed until late autumn

rowed (see **road**)

rowen (see **rowan**)

rower (see **roar**)

rows (see **rhos** and **rouse**)

royal (see **roil**)

Rozi (see **rosy**)

rubiconed to defeat, as in bezique

or piquet, with a score so low that it is added to the winner's
rubicund inclining to redress

ruby (see **rabi**)

rucks draws or works into wrinkles or creases; large quantities indistinguishable from the aggregate
rux to worry; to play or sport (slang)

rud to redden
rudd a European freshwater cyprinid fish

rudder a ship's or airplane's steering mechanism
rutter a plow for cutting ruts in a logging road for sled runners; a person or animal that ruts; a set of sailing instructions used by ship captains and pilots

ruddy having a reddish color associated with the glow of good health or a suffusion of blood
rutty full of tracks worn by a wheel or the habitual passage of something

rude (see **rood**)

ruder (see **rooter**)

rue (see **roo**)

rued (see **rood**)

rues (see **roos**)

ruff (see **rough**)

Ruhr (see **roer**)

Rum (see **rheum**)

rum (see **rheum** and **RHM**)

Ruman a native or inhabitant of Romania or Wallachia
rumen the large first compartment of a ruminant's stomach from which food is regurgitated

rumor (see **roomer**)

run (see **jen**)

rung a ladder crosspiece; a stage in an ascent; sounded clearly as a bell
wrung compressed by squeezing or twisting

ruse (see **Rhus** and **roos**)

rusot an extract from the wood or roots of various shrubs of the genus Berberis that is mixed with opium and applied to infected eyelids
russet a reddish or yellowish brown or reddish gray color

russel a strong twilled woolen cloth
rustle to steal cattle; a quick succession of small clear sounds, like leaves in a breeze

russet (see **rusot**)

rustle (see **russel**)

rut (see **rote**)

rutter (see **rudder**)

rutty (see **ruddy**)

rux (see **rucks**)

rya (see **rea**)

ryes (see **rise**)

ryme (see **rhyme**)

ryot (see **riot**)

rype (see **ripe**)

Group I

reactance - reactants
recalcitrance - recalcitrants
recipience - recipients
recision - rescission
recreance - recreants
recumbence - recumbents
recusance - recusants
reentrance - reentrants
reference - referents
remanence - remanents

reminiscence - reminiscents
remontrance - remonstrants
repellence - repellents
residence - residents
resonance - resonants
respondence - respondents
responser - responsor
resurgence - resurgents

Group I and II

ramose ˈrā.mōs
ramous ˈrāməs

relic ˈrelik
relict ˈrelikt

Renaissance :renəˈsäns
renascent rəˈnasᵊns

resin ˈrezᵊn
rosin ˈräzᵊn or ˈrózᵊn

Group II

racy ˈrāsē
recit räˈsē

rail ˈrāl
rale ˈral

raki rəˈkē or ˈrakē or ˈräkē
Reki ˈräkē

raucous ˈrókəs
Roccus ˈräkəs

rawed ˈród
rod ˈräd

recent rēsᵊnt
resent rēˈzent

reclaim reˈklām
réclame rāˈklàm

recognizer ˈrekə̀g.nīzər
recognizor rə̀:kägnə:zór

recoverer   rə'kəvərər
recoveror   rə:kəvə:rȯr

registrar   'rejə,strȧr
registrer   'rejəstrər

rhesis   'rēsis
rhesus   'rēsəs

rhyton   'rī,tän
righten   'rīt^ən

rillet   'rilət

rillett(e)   rə'let

roer   'rüər
ruer   'rüər

roily   'rȯilē
royally   'rȯiəlē

rupia   'rüpēə
Ruppia   'rəpēə

rushee   rə'shē
rushy   'rəshē

S

Saar (see **czar**)

sabbat a midnight assembly of witches and sorcerers held in medieval and Renaissance times to renew allegiance to the devil
sabot a strap or wide band fitting across the instep in a shoe of the sandal type

sabra a reddish prickly edible fruit of cacti growing on the coastal plains of Palestine; a prickly pear; a native-born Israeli
zabra a 16th and 17th century Spanish sailing vessel resembling a small frigate

Sacae an ancient people settled in eastern Iran
Sakai a forest people of Malaya
sockeye a small but very important Pacific salmon

saccharin a crystalline cyclic imide, remarkable for its sweetness and no food value
saccharine overly or affectedly pleasant; syrupy

sachet a small bag or packet
sashay to strut about in a conspicuous manner

Sacs members of an Indian people of the Fox river valley and shores of Green Bay, Wisconsin
sacs pouches within an animal or plant
sacks plunders; large rectangular bags of coarse strong material
sacques baby jackets
sax a saxophone (by shortening)
Saxe a grayish blue color

sadder more unhappy or mournful
satyr a lecherous man; a hairy desert demon

saddest most unhappy or mournful
sadist a person who delights in physical or mental cruelty

saeter a pasture high in the Norwegian or Swedish mountains
setter a large bird dog; a person that sets, as traps

saeter a pasture high in the Norwegian or Swedish mountains
satyr a lecherous man; a hairy desert demon
Seder a Jewish ceremonial dinner held on the first evening of Passover

safe secure from threat of danger; a receptacle to keep articles secure
seif a long narrow sand dune or chain of dunes

Sagai a group composed of the Beltir, Koibal, and other peoples

on the Abakan river in south central Russia that speak a Turkic dialect

sagaie   a Paleolithic bone javelin
point

sail   an expanse of fabric using wind
to propel boats and ships
sale   a transfer of property title for a
consideration

sailer   a sailing ship
sailor   a member of a ship's crew

Sakai   (see **Sacae**)

sake   a Japanese alcoholic beverage
made from fermented rice
saki   any of several South American
monkeys having a bushy non-pre-
hensile tail

sal   an East Indian timber tree
Sol   the sun
sol   the sunny side or section of a
bullfight arena; a fluid colloidal
system; gold, as used in alchemy

salah   a Muslim ritual prayer made
five times daily
selah   an exclamation used in the
Psalms, possibly as a direction to
temple musicians to play music or
sing

sale   (see **sail**)

salon   (see **Ceylon**)

saloop   a hot drink made from sassafras, milk, and sugar or from dried
tubers of various East Indian or
European orchids
salop   a widely distributed English
breed of dark-faced hornless
mutton-type sheep

salter   (see **psalter**)

saltery   (see **psaltery**)

salver   a tray for serving food or
beverages
salvor   a person who engages in
salvage

salvy   resembling salve in texture or
oiliness
savvy   expertness in a particular field
based on experience or native ability

samara   a dry indehiscent usually
one-seeded winged fruit
samarra   a Spanish Inquisition garment resembling a scapular

samba   a Brazilian dance in duple
time of African origin; a variation
of canasta using three decks of
cards and six jokers
tsamba   flour made from parched
ground barley or wheat

sambar   a large Asiatic deer
somber   gloomy, sullen, or melancholy in appearance or mood

same   something identical with or
similar to another
Sejm   Poland's lower house of parliament

samite   (see **psammite**)

sandhi   modification of the sound of
a morpheme conditioned by the
context in which it is uttered, as in
"dontcha" for "don't you"
sandy   full of or resembling sand; an
Australian swimming crab

sandhi   modification of the sound of
a morpheme conditioned by the
context in which it is uttered, as in
"dontcha" for "don't you"
sundae   ice cream served with a topping of fruit, nuts, or syrup
Sunday   the Christian sabbath; the
first day of the week

sands   small loose grain resulting
from a rock's disintegration
sans   without; deprived of

sandy   (see **sandhi**)

sane   mentally sound
Seine   a major river in France that
flows through Paris
seine   a large net

sang produced musical tones with the voice
sangh an association whose goal is to unify different groups in Hinduism

sang a Persian harp of the middle ages
sangh an association whose goal is to unify different groups in Hinduism
sung produced musical tones with the voice

sangh (see both **sangs**)

sank (see **cinque**)

sann an East Indian plant the fiber of which closely resembles true hemp
son a male offspring
sun a star around which Earth revolves
sunn an East Indian plant, the fiber of which is used for rope and bags

sans (see **sands**)

Saracen (see **ceresin**)

sara(h) the painted trillium plant, a perennial herb of northeastern North America
sera the watery portion of animal fluids remaining after coagulation

saran a tough flexible thermoplastic made of copolymerized vinylidene chloride
serein a mist or fine rain falling from an apparently clear sky
serin a small European finch related to the canary

sarcel a pinion feather of a hawk's wing
sarcelle any of the short-necked river ducks of America and Europe, such as the teal

sarcophagous carnivorous
sarcophagus a coffin made of stone

sarcophilous fond of flesh

Sarcophilus a genus of marsupials consisting of the Tasmanian devil

sardonics disdainful or skeptically humorous remarks
sardonyx onyx marked by parallel layers of sard and another colored mineral

sari a lightweight cloth garment worn by Hindu women
saury a slender long-beaked fish related to needle fish
sorry feeling regret, penitence, or sorrow

sarsen a large loose residual mass of stone left after the erosion of a once continuous bed or layer
sarson an Indian cole resembling rape

sashay (see **sachet**)

sassy given to back talk; impertinent
saucy smart or trim, as a ship or automobile

sate to cloy with overabundance
sett a banker or rich merchant in India

satem constituting a part of the Indo-European language family in which palatal stops became palatal or alveolar fricatives
Sodom a place notorious for vice and corruption

satinay the wood of an Australian tree of the family Myrtaceae
satiné a timber tree of Brazil and the Guianas

satiric fond of or skilled at ironic or ridiculing comment
satyric related to a lecherous man or hairy desert demon

satyr (see **sadder** or **saeter**)

satyric (see **satiric**)

saucy (see **sassy**)

sault a fall or rapid in a river

sew to become grounded, as a ship
Sioux a language stock of central and eastern North America; a group of peoples speaking Siouan languages
sou the smallest piece of money
sous of subordinate rank
sue to bring action against or prosecute judicially
suite a set of matched furniture for a room

saurel a horse mackerel (fish)
sorel a male fallow deer in its third year
sorrel a light bright chestnut horse

saury (see **sari**)

saver a person who economizes or hoards
savor to taste or smell with pleasure

savvy (see **salvy**)

sawder to flatter or praise excessively
sodder a person or machine that lays sod
solder a metallic alloy which, when melted, joins metallic surfaces; to unite with solder

sawer a person who cuts with a saw
soar to fly aloft; to rise
sore painful or tender; angered or vexed

sax (see **Sacs**)

Saxe (see **Sacs**)

say to express in words
sei a widely distributed small white-spotted whalebone whale

sayyid an Islamic leader
side a direction or place with respect to the center; a surface that encloses or bounds space
sighed made a sound expressing weariness, relief, or grief

scag heroin (slang)
skag a vessel's keel near the sternpost; a cigarette (slang)

scalar having an uninterrupted series of steps; a quantity in vector analysis having no direction, as time or mass
scaler a climber; a person who removes scale from metal or fish scales

scald to burn with steam or hot liquid
skald an ancient Scandinavian poet

scaler (see **scalar**)

scallop a marine bivalve mollusk whose shell is characteristically radially ribbed and the edge undulated
scolop the thickened distal tip of a vibration-sensitive organ in insects

scary frightening or alarming
skerry a rocky isle

scat a three-handed game played with 32 cards
Scot a native or inhabitant of Scotland; one of a Gaelic people of northern Ireland settling in Scotland about A.D. 500
scot to assess for tax

scends heaves upward under the influence of a natural force
sends dispatches to a destination
sens Japanese monetary units each equal to 1/100 yen

scene a subdivision of a dramatic presentation; a display of passion or temper
seen perceived or verified by sight
sin the 21st letter of the Hebrew alphabet

scenery a picturesque view or landscape
senary consisting of six parts of things

scent (see **cent**)

scenter (see **center**)

scents (see **cense**)

(s)chappes (see **chaps**)

schapping a European method of fermenting and removing gum from silk wastes
shopping searching for, inspecting, or buying goods or services

schih dry grasslands of northern Africa
she a female person or animal
shea a rough-barked tropical African tree
sidhe an underground fort in which Gaelic fairies live

schiz a schizophrenic or schizoid person
skits satirical or humorous stories or sketches often outwardly serious; parodies

schout a Dutch sheriff
scout to explore an area to obtain information

schouw a light-draft open pleasure boat of the Netherlands
scow a large flat-bottomed boat for transporting materials; to fasten an anchor by its crown to the end of a cable

schuyt a bluff-bowed Dutch boat fitted with leeboards
skate a device worn on foot to glide on ice or roll over smooth ground; a ray (fish)

schwa an unstressed mid-central vowel that is the usual sound of the first and last vowels of "America"
Tswa a southeastern African people chiefly of northern Transvaal province and southern Mozambique

Scilla and **scilla** (see **Psylla**)

(s)cion (see **cyan** and **Cyon**)

scirrhus (see **cerous**)

scissel metal clippings remaining after various mechanical operations

scissile able to be smoothly or easily split
Sicel a member of an ancient people occupying part of Sicily
sisal a strong durable white fiber used for cordage and twine
sisel a large short-tailed ground squirrel
syssel an Icelandic administrative district

scissel metal clippings remaining after various mechanical operations
scissile able to be smoothly or easily split
sizzle to burn up or sear with scorching heat or heated language

scissile (see both **scissels**)

scold to utter a harsh reprimand or rebuke
skoaled drank an alcoholic beverage as a toast

scolop (see **scallop**)

scoot to go suddenly and swiftly
scute an external bony or horny plate

scop an Old English poet
scope a general range of cognizance, activity, or influence

Scot and **scot** (see **scat**)

scout (see **schout**)

scow (see **schouw**)

scrapie a virus disease of sheep
scrapy sounding like harsh grating

scrips paper currencies or tokens issued for special or temporary use in an emergency
scripts written texts of a stage play, screen play, or radio or television broadcast

scudder a leather worker who scrapes skins by hand or machine
scutter to move with a brisk rapidly alternating step; to damage severely or destroy completely

scuff to walk with a scraping movement without lifting the feet
squff to eat heavily (slang)

scull an oar used to propel a boat; a long narrow very light racing shell
skull the skeleton of a vetebrate's head

scur a small rounded portion of horn tissue attached to the skin of the horn pit of a polled animal
skirr a whirring, rasping, or roaring sound

scute (see **scoot**)

scutter (see **scudder**)

scyes (see **psis**)

Scylla (see **Psylla**)

sea-born originating in or rising from the sea
seaborne transported by ship

seal (see **ceil**)

sealer (see **coeler**)

seam a line of junction
seem to appear

seaman a person whose occupation is association with ships and the sea; a sailor
semen a viscid whitish fluid containing spermatozoa produced in a male's reproductive tract

seamer a person who fastens by stitches of thread or filament
seemer a pretender

sear (see **cere**)

seas (see **cees**)

season a period of time characterized by a particular feature or event
seisin a possession of land or chattels

seat (see **cete**)

seated situated or located

seeded sown; an area planted with seed

seater (see **cedar**)

seau a pottery pail used in typical 18th-century dinner service
sew to fasten with stitches of thread or filament
so in the manner indicated; conforming with actual fact(s); the fifth tone of the diatonic scale
sow to plant or scatter seed

Seckel (see **cycle**)

second to remove a person temporarily from one position for employment
seconde a parry or guard fencing position defending the lower outside right target

sects groups holding similar political, religious, or socio-economic views
sex one of two divisions of organisms designated as male or female; gender

Seder (see **saeter**)

seeded (see **seated**)

seeder (see **cedar**)

seedy abounding in seeds; shabby in dress or appearance
sidi an African Muslim holding a high position under a King of the Deccan

seek to search, look for, or hunt
sic intentionally so written
sikh an adherent of the religion of Sikhism

seel (see **ceil**)

seem (see **seam**)

seemer (see **seamer**)

seen (see **scene**)

seep (see **cepe**)

seer (see **cere**)

seeress   (see **cirrhus**)

sees   (see **cees**)

sei   (see **say**)

seidel   a large beer glass or mug
sidle   to move sideways

seif   (see **safe**)

seignior   a feudal lord of a manor
(or **seigneur**)
senior   an older person in age or
service

Seine and seine   (see **sane**)

seisin   (see **season**)

seize   (see **cees**)

seizer   (see **Caesar**)

Sejm   (see **same**)

sela   rice that is heated before milling
selah   an exclamation used in the
Psalms, possibly as a direction to
temple musicians to play or sing

selah   (see **salah**)

sell   (see **cell**)

sella   (see **cella**)

sellar   (see **cellar**)

seller   (see **cellar**)

sematic   serving as a warning of
danger
somatic   relating to or affecting the
body of an organism

semen   (see **seaman**)

semi   a trucking rig composed of a
tractor and a semitrailer; a second-
year student at some Scottish universities
semy   in heraldry, having a pattern
of small charges

senary   (see **scenery**)

senate   an assembly with legislative
functions

senit   a game of ancient Egyptian
origin resembling backgammon
sen(n)et   any of several barracuda
fish
sinnet   a signal call on a trumpet or
cornet for entrance or exit on a
stage

sends   (see **scends**)

senior   (see **seignior**)

senit   (see **senate**)

sen(n)et   (see **senate**)

sens   (see **scends**)

sense   (see **cense**)

senser   (see **censer**)

senses   (see **census**)

senso   (see **censo**)

sensor   (see **censer**)

sensorial   (see **censorial**)

sensual   (see **censual**)

sent   (see **cent**)

Seoul   the capital of South Korea
sol   the fifth tone of the diatonic scale
sole   the undersurface of a foot or
shoe; a flatfish
soul   the immortal part of a person

seps   a lizard of an Old World genus
of the family Scincidae
septs   branches of a family, members
of which are believed to have descended from a single ancestor;
partitions in a screen or railing that
mark off an enclosed area set aside
for a special purpose

septime   a parry or guard position in
fencing
septum   a dividing wall or membrane

septs   (see **seps**)

septum   (see **septime**)

sequence   a continuous or connected
series

sequents conclusions resulting from reason or argument

sera (see **sara[h]**)

seral (see **cirral**)

seraph a fiery six-winged angel guarding God's throne
serif a short line stemming from and at an angle to strokes of a letter

sere (see **cere**)

serein (see **saran**)

Seres (see **ceres**)

serf a person belonging to the lower class in various feudal systems
surf a sea swell that breaks on shore

serge a durable twilled fabric with a smooth clear face
surge to swell, roll, or sweep forward

serial (see **cereal**)

sericin (see **ceresin**)

series (see **ceres**)

serif (see **seraph**)

serin (see **saran**)

serious (see **Cereus**)

serous (see **cerous**)

serval a common African wildcat
servile related to or befitting a slave

service (see **cervus**)

servile (see **serval**)

session (see **cession**)

sessionary (see **cessionary**)

set to place with care or deliberate purpose
sett a Scottish tartan pattern; a small rectangular paving stone

setaceous (see **cetaceous** and **psittaceous**)

setal (see **cetyl**)

seton (see **cetin**)

sett (see **sate** and **set**)

setter (see **saeter**)

settler a colonist; a person who establishes a residence or community
settlor a person who creates a trust of property

sew (see **sault** and **seau**)

sewer a person who fastens by stitches of thread or filament
soar to fly aloft; to rise
sore painful or tender; angered or vexed
sower a planter of seed

sewer a conduit to carry off waste material
soor a mycotic disease of the upper digestive tract in infants and young children; a purulent degenerative inflammation of the frog in a horse
suer a person who seeks justice from another by legal process

sewn fastened with stitches
son a folk song of Cuba, Mexico, and Central America; a Latin American ballroom dance
sone a subjective measure of loudness
sown planted or scattered seed

sex (see **sects**)

sexed having sexual instincts or sex appeal
sext the fourth of the seven canonical hours

sextan a fever characterized by paroxysms that occur every six days
sexton a church custodian

sferics atmospherics; an electronic detector of storms using devices for plotting electrical discharges
spherics spherical geometry or spherical trigonometry

sha (see **pshaw**)

shah (see pshaw)

shake to undergo vibration; to
quiver or tremble
sheik(h) a head of an Arab family,
tribe, or village

shames the candle used to light the
other candles in a Hanakkah
menorah; the sexton of a synagogue
shamus a detective or police officer
(slang)

shanker (see chancre)

shant a large stein or pot
shan't a contraction of shall not

shanty (see chant[e]y)

sharki a southeasterly wind of the
Persian gulf
shirky disposed to avoid a task
because of laziness, lack of courage, or distaste

sharky (see charque)

sharpie (see charpie)

shaup a shell, pod, or husk
shop to search for, inspect, or buy
goods or services

shay (see chez)

shays (see chaise)

she (see schih)

shea (see chez and schih)

shear to cut, clip, or sever something
sheer of very thin or transparent
texture; absolute or pure

sheas rough-barked tropical African
trees
she's the contraction of she is, she
has, or she was

sheave a pulley block's grooved
wheel
shiv a knife
shive a small fragment of plant
matter

sheen a bright or shining condition
Shin a major Japanese Buddhist
sect growing out of Jodo
shin the 22nd letter of the Hebrew
alphabet

sheer (see shear)

sheik(h) (see chic or shake)

sherd a brittle piece or fragment
shirred gathered cloth together
along two or more parallel lines;
baked until set, as of eggs

she's (see sheas)

shier more timid, bashful, or
modest; a horse given to starting
aside suddenly
shire an administrative subdivision
of land, as in colonial America

shiever a double-crosser (slang)
shiver to tremble, quake, or vibrate,
especially from an abnormally cold
temperature

Shik (see chic)

shin (see hsin)

Shin and shin (see sheen)

shine to emit rays of light
sinh the hyperbolic sine

shire (see shier)

shirky (see sharki)

shirr to gather cloth together along
two or more parallel lines; to bake
until set, as of eggs
sure certain, positive, or reliable

shirred (see sherd)

shiv (see sheave)

shive (see sheave)

shiver (see shiever)

shoal a sandbank or sandbar; a
shallow place in a body of water
shole a plate placed beneath an
object

shoddy inferior, vulgar, shabby, or disreputable
shotty hard and round, like a pellet of shot

shoe (see **choux**)

shoed put on or furnished with a shoe
shood rice husks used in adulterating linseed cake
shooed drove or sent away; dispelled

shoer a horseshoer
sure certain, positive, or reliable

shoes (see **choux**)

shofars (see **chauffeurs**)

shole (see **shoal**)

shone emitted light rays; gleamed
shown displayed or exhibited

shoo (see **choux**)

shood (see **shoed**)

shooed (see **shoed**)

shoos (see **choux**)

shoot (see **chute**)

shop (see **shaup**)

shopping (see **schapping**)

shor a salt lake, marsh, or pond
shore land bordering a large body of water

shore land bordering a large body of water
shower a person that exhibits or demonstrates

shot (see **chott**)

shott (see **chott**)

shotty (see **shoddy**)

shous (see **chose**)

shower (see **shore**)

shown (see **shone**)

shows (see **chose**)

shrewd marked by cleverness, discernment, or sagacity
shrewed treated with ill-tempered and intractable abuse

shu (see **choux**)

shudder to tremble or shake convulsively
shutter a movable cover or screen for a window or door

sibyl (see **cibol**)

sic (see **seek**)

sic intentionally so written
sick diseased or unwell

Sicel (see **cycle** and **scissel**)

Sicilian (see **Caecilian**)

Sicily (see **cicely**)

sick (see **sic**)

sickle (see **cycle**)

sics incites or urges to attack, as a dog
sicks vomits
six the whole number between five and seven

siddur a Jewish prayer book containing both Hebrew and Aramaic prayers
sitter a broody hen; a person who sits for a portrait or a bust

side (see **sayyid**)

sided (see **cited**)

sider (see **cider**)

siderous (see **Cidaris**)

sidhe (see **schih**)

sidi (see **seedy**)

sidle (see **seidel**)

Siena a strong reddish brown color; a city in central Italy

sienna any of various earthy substances that are brownish yellow when raw

sig (see **cig**)

sighed (see **sayyid**)

sigher a person who makes a sound expressing weariness, relief, or grief
sire a male parent

sighs (see **psis**)

sight (see **cite**)

sighted (see **cited**)

sighter (see **cider**)

sign a signal, mark, or gesture
sine a trigonometric function
tsine a wild ox of the Malay peninsula sometimes used for draft

signate (see **cygnet**)

signet (see **cygnet**)

sikh (see **seek**)

sil yellow ocher, a mixture of limonite usually with clay and silica used as a pigment
sild young herring canned as sardine
sill a horizontal member at the base of a door or window opening

Silicea (see **Cilicia**)

siliceous (see **cilicious**)

sill (see **sil**)

sima (see **cyma**)

sin (see **scene**)

sin a transgression of religious law; a serious offense
syn characterized by certain atoms or groups on the same side of the molecule

sine (see **sign**)

single-seated a vehicle with one seat only, or seats suitable for one person to a seat

single-seeded a plant bearing fruit that contains one seed

singular (see **cingular**)

sinh (see **cinch** and **shine**)

Sinicism (see **cynicism**)

sink (see **cinque**)

sinnet (see **senate**)

Sion (see **cyan**)

Sioux (see **sault**)

sip (see **cyp**)

sipe (see **cepe**)

sir a respectful form of address
sur in law, on or upon

sire (see **sigher**)

Sirian resembling or relating to the star Sirius, a star in the constellation Canis Major and the brightest star in our sky
Syrian a native or inhabitant of Syria

siris (see **cerise**)

Sirius (see **Cereus**)

sirred addressed as sir
surd lacking reason or rationale; in mathematics, an irrational radical with rational radicands

sis (see **cees** and **cis**)

sisal (see **scissel**)

sisel (see **scissel**)

siss (see **cis**)

sissed (see **cist**)

Sistine and **sistine** (see **cyst[e]in**)

sit (see **cit**)

site (see **cite**)

sitology (see **cytology**)

sitter (see **siddur**)

six   (see sics)

sixte   a parry or guard position in fencing

sixth   the number six in a countable series

sixteen   the whole number between fifteen and seventeen

Sixtine   relating to any of the popes named Sixtus; relating to the Sistine chapel in the Vatican

sixth   (see sixte)

Sixtine   (see sixteen)

size   (see psis)

sizzle   (see scissel)

skag   (see scag)

skald   (see scald)

skate   (see schuyt)

skating   gliding along on skates propelled by alternate action of the legs

skeyting   a Scandinavian tribal ceremony used in making conveyances of land

skee   whiskey (slang)

ski   one of a pair of narrow strips of wood, metal, or plastic that are used to glide over snow

skeet   trapshooting in which clay targets are thrown to simulate bird flight

skete   a settlement of Eastern Orthodox monks inhabiting a group of small cottages around a church

skerry   (see scary)

skete   (see skeet)

skeyting   (see skating)

ski   (see skee)

skidder   a person or machine that skids or uses a skid, as with logs

skitter   to pass or glide lightly or hurriedly

skiddles   a game in which sticks are thrown at pins

skittles   enjoyment or play

skil   a large elongated scorpaenid food fish of the Pacific coast from Alaska to southern California

skill   a developed or acquired aptitude or ability

skirr   (see scur)

skits   (see schiz)

skitter   (see skidder)

skittles   (see skiddles)

skoaled   (see scold)

skull   (see scull)

sky   an expanse of space surrounding Earth

Skye   a Skye terrier dog

slack   not tight, tense, or taut; lacking in firmness

slake   to bring thirst to an end with refreshing drink

slade   the sole of a plow

slayed   killed or slaughtered

sleyed   separated and arranged the warp threads in a loom's reed

slake   (see slack)

slay   to kill or slaughter

sleigh   a vehicle on runners for transportation over snow or ice

sley   to separate and arrange warp threads in the reed of a loom

slayed   (see slade)

sleave   to separate into filaments

sleeve   a part of a garment covering an arm

sleigh   (see slay)

sleight   cunning, trickery, or deftness

slight   having a slim or delicate build; scanty or meager

slew   a large number or quantity; killed or slaughtered

slough   a marshy place

sley   (see slay)

sleyed   (see slade)

slight   (see sleight)

slipe   pulled wool removed from skins by a lime process
slype   a narrow passage

sloe   a small dark-colored plum with astringent green flesh
slow   mentally dull; lacking speed

slough   (see slew)

slough   something shed or cast off
sluff   to discard a playing card; to eat (slang)

slow   (see sloe)

sluff   (see slough)

slype   (see slipe)

smellie   a motion picture having odors synchronized with the action
smelly   malodorous

snees   cuts
sneeze   a sudden violent audible spasmodic expiration through the nose and mouth

snide   slyly disparaging or subtly derisive
snyed   bent upward, especially the edge of a plank near a ship's bow or stern

snoose   snuff
snooze   to take a nap or doze

snubbee   a person that is checked or stopped with a cutting retort or remark
snubby   having a snub-nose; blunt, stubby, or stumpy

snyed   (see snide)

so   (see seau)

soak   to saturate
soke   the specific territory or group

of men included in a specific jurisdiction, in Anglo-Saxon law

soaper   a serial drama performed usually on daytime radio or television (slang); a person that makes or deals in a cleansing agent made from fats and oils
sopor   a profound or lethargic sleep

soar   (see sawer and sewer)

soared   flew aloft; rose
sward   a grassy surface of land
sword   a long-bladed weapon for cutting, slashing, and thrusting

soccer   a game whose object is to manipulate a ball into a goal without using hands or arms
socker   a hard puncher

sockeye   (see Sacae)

socks   hits or strikes forcefully
sox   cloth foot coverings

sodder   (see sawder)

Sodom   (see satem)

soke   (see soak)

Sol and sol   (see sal)

sol   (see Seoul)

solace   alleviation of grief or anxiety
solus   without companions; in solitude

solan   a large white gannet with black wing tips
Solen   a genus of razor clams
solen   a razor clam
solon   a member of a legislative body

solar   relating to the sun
soler   a person who soles footwear

sold   exchanged goods or services for money or the equivalent
soled   put soles on footwear; having so-many soles, as "double-soled"
souled   having a soul

solder   (see sawder)

sole   (see Seoul)

soled   (see sold)

Solen and solen   (see solan)

soler   (see solar)

solon   (see solan)

solus   (see solace)

somatic   (see sematic)

somber   (see sambar)

some   part of a number of things
sum   a total or aggregate

son   (see sann)

son   (see sewn)

sone   (see sewn)

sonny   a young boy
sunny   full of sunshine; optimistic

soor   (see sewer)

soot   a black substance (chiefly carbon) formed by combustion
suit   a set of garments; cards in a
   pack of playing cards bearing the
   same symbol, as diamonds

sooter   a person who removes soot,
   as from a boiler
suitor   a person who courts a
   woman; a pleader

sopor   (see soaper)

sora   (see psora)

sordid   covered with filth; dirty; vile
sorted   arranged according to some
   characteristics; classified
sworded   armed, wounded, or killed
   with a sword

sordor   refuse or dregs
sorter   a person or machine that
   classifies or arranges things

sore   (see sawer and sewer)

sorel   (see saurel)

sorosis   (see cirrhosis)

sorrel   (see saurel)

sorry   (see sari)

sorted   (see sordid)

sorter   (see sordor)

sorus   (see psorous)

sou   (see sault)

sough   a moaning or sighing sound
sow   an adult female swine

soul   (see Seoul)

souled   (see sold)

souma   a disease of animals caused
   by insect vectors such as the tsetse
   and stable flies
Suma   a people or group of people
   of the state of Chihuahua, Mexico
summa   one or more treatises encom-
   passing an entire field of learning

soup   a liquid food having meat,
   fish, or vegetables as a base
sup   in mathematics, a least upper
   bound
supe   a supernumerary; a superintendent

souple   partially degummed silk
supple   limber or lithe

sous   (see sault)

sous   the space outside the white ring
   of an archery target
souse   to steep in a preservative; to
   pickle; to soak or submerge

sow   (see seau or sough)

sower   (see sewer)

sown   (see sewn)

sox   (see socks)

spade   a tool for digging or turning
   soil; a card of one of the four suits
   in a deck of playing cards
spayed   removed ovaries of a female
   animal

spawn to produce or deposit eggs of an aquatic animal
spon money (slang)

spay to remove ovaries of a female animal
spet a small barracuda fish

spayed (see **spade**)

spear a long-shafted sharp-pointed throwing or thrusting weapon
spier a fixed and often architecturally treated screen

specks spots or stains; tiny bits
specs spectacles; specifications (or **spex**)

speel to climb
spiel to play music; to talk in a voluble often extravagant manner

speiss a mixture of impure metallic arsenides
spice any of various aromatic vegetable products used in cookery to season and flavor foods

spet (see **spay**)

spherics (see **sferics**)

spice (see **speiss**)

spiel (see **speel**)

spier (see **spear**)

spier a person that watches in a furtive or stealthy manner
spire a steeply tapering roof surmounting a tower; a steeple

spinner a person or machine that spins fibers
spinor in mathematics, a quantity that resembles a vector with complex components in a two- or four-dimensional space

spinous having spines, thorns, or prickles
Spinus a genus of small active often brightly colored finches

spire (see **spier**)

spiritous impregnated with alcohol obtained by distillation; containing the nature of spirit
spiritus either of two marks used in writing Greek, the one to indicate aspiration, the other to indicate absence of aspiration

spits slender pointed metal rods for holding meat or other food while cooking; expectorates
spitz a dog native to northern areas, as a chow or pomeranian

spon (see **spawn**)

spoor a sign or mark left by an animal that has passed
spore a minute unicellular reproductive body

sprits spars that cross a fore-and-aft sail diagonally from the mast
spritz a quick brief spray of liquid or rain

spudder a person that sets up and operates well-drilling machinery
sputter confused or excited speech; to expel particles from the mouth with mildly explosive sounds

squadder a member of a police squad
squatter a person that settles on land without right or title

squaller a baby that cries excessively
squalor corruption; crassness; degradation

squatter (see **squadder**)

squff (see **scuff**)

squirl a curlicue or flourish
squirrel an arboreal rodent with a bushy tail

stade a stadium; a period of time represented by a glacial deposit
staid sober, sedate, or serious
stayed paused or remained; brought a ship about to the other tack

staff a long stick carried for support; personnel responsible for operating an organization

staph a staphylococcus bacteria (by shortening)

staggard a male red deer in its fourth year

staggered reeled from side to side; tottered; placed alternately on either side of a midline

staid (see **stade**)

stain a discoloration or blemish; a dye or pigment used to alter color or shade

steen a line with solid material to prevent soil caving in or washing away

stair a series of steps for moving from one level to another

stare to look fixedly

stere a metric measure of volume equal to one cubic meter

stake a pointed rod designed to be driven into the ground; a wager

steak a slice of meat cut from a fleshy part of a carcass

staph (see **staff**)

stare (see **stair**)

starlet a young movie actress who is being coached and publicized for starring roles; a little star

starlit lighted by the stars

starlight the light emitted by stars

starlite a blue zircon mineral

starlit (see **starlet**)

starlite (see **starlight**)

stater an ancient gold or silver coin of the Greek city-states

stator a stationary part in a machine in or about which a rotor revolves

Statice a genus of low-growing usually coastal herbs

status a comparative position of rank or condition

stationary immobile, stable, or static

stationery materials for writing or typing

stator (see **stater**)

status (see **Statice**)

stayed (see **stade**)

steaded assisted or supported

stetted annotated with the word "stet" to nullify a previous direction to delete or amend

steak (see **stake**)

steal to take property of another illegally; to pilfer

steel commercial iron containing carbon; an instrument for sharpening knives

stele an arrow's shaft; the cylindrical central portion of a vascular plant

stealer a person that robs or steals

steeler a smith who steels edged tools; a person that inserts steels

stelar located in or resembling a stele

steel (see **steal**)

steeler (see **stealer**)

steelie the steelhead, a silvery rainbow trout that migrates to the sea before returning to spawn in fresh water

steely resembling or containing steel

stelae slabs or pillars of stone, usually carved or inscribed and used for commemorative purposes

stele the cylindrical central portion of the axis of a vascular plant

steen (see **stain**)

steer a bull castrated before sexual maturity; to guide or control

stere a metric measure of volume equal to one cubic meter

stelae (see **steelie**)

stelar (see **stealer**)

stele (see **steal** or **steelie**)

step a degree in a scale or range; a movement made by raising the foot and bringing it down in a different position

steppe arid land characterized by xerophilic vegetation

stere (see **stair** and **steer**)

stetted (see **steaded**)

stichs measured parts of something written in verse; tricks in various card games

sticks wood parts of a tree or shrub; twigs; pierces with something pointed; adheres to

Styx a river in Hades

Stieng a people related to the Cambodians and inhabiting Thudaumot province, Vietnam

sting something that causes a keen pain or stimulation of the mind

stile a set of steps over a fence

style a manner, method, or mode

stilo in the style of, with reference to the calendar

stylo a stylographic pen (shortened)

sting (see **Stieng**)

stirrup a ring or bent piece of metal made horizontal at the bottom for receiving the foot of a rider and attached by a strap to a saddle

stir-up agitation or turmoil

stolen obtained by theft

stollen a repeated section in a meistergesang

stolon a horizontal branch from a plant's base that produces new plants, as a runner

stoop to bend the body forward and downward; to lean or bow; a basin at the entrance of a Roman Catholic church containing holy water

stupe a cloth with hot water wrung out for external application

stooper a person who bends the body forward, or one who is bent forward

stupor numbness or stupefaction

store to accumulate; a business establishment where goods are kept for retail sale

stower a person who stores, especially a stevedore

straight free from curves, bends, or angles; direct and uninterrupted; upright

strait a comparatively narrow passageway connecting two bodies of water; difficulty

straighten to alter from being crooked or bent to a straight form; to make correct

straiten to afflict physically or mentally; to continue in a narrow space

strait (see **straight**)

straiten (see **straighten**)

streak an irregular strip or line of contrasting color or texture; a narrow band of light

streek to stretch out

stricks bunches of hackled flax, jute, or hemp

Strix the type genus of the family Strigidae comprising owls that lack ear tufts

strix a fluting of a column

strider a person or animal that moves with long steps

stridor a harsh, shrill, or creaking noise

Strix and **strix** (see **stricks**)

studder a person who inserts hairsprings into watches

stutter to speak with involuntary disruption or blocking of speech

stupe (see **stoop**)

stupor (see **stooper**)

stutter (see **studder**)

stylar leading to a seed plant's ovary; related to an elongated process

styler   a person who designs, develops, or advises on fashions or styles

style   (see **stile**)

styler   (see **stylar**)

stylo   (see **stilo**)

Styx   (see **stichs**)

subaural   situated beneath the ear
suboral   situated beneath the mouth

subbase   another foundation below that which ordinarily forms the base
subbass   a 16- or 32-foot pipe organ stop used in a pedal organ

subcast   a secondary swarm of bees
subcaste   a subdivision of an hereditary class in Hinduism

subhyalin   beneath or under the opalescent substance resembling chiton which is the chief constituent of the wall of a hydatidcyst
subhyaline   being somewhat less transparent than glass

suboral   (see **subaural**)

subsequence   a later or following event
subsequents   streams that developed along a belt or belts of underlying weak rock

subsistence   an irreducible minimum necessary to support life
subsistents   abstract entities; things having existence

subtle   delicate, refined, or skillful
suttle   the weight remaining after the weight of a vehicle or container is deducted; net weight

subtler   more delicate, refined, or skillful
sutler   a provisioner to an army

succor   help or assistance
sucker   a person or device that draws something into itself by producing a partial vacuum; a shoot originat-

ing from roots or a lower part of a plant's stem

succubous   leaves arranged so that the posterior margin of each overlaps the anterior margin of the next older
succubus   a demon assuming female form

sucker   (see **succor**)

sudds   floating vegetable matter composed of papyrus stems and aquatic grasses
suds   froth or bubbles formed on a soapy water or beer

sue   (see **sault**)

suede   leather finished by buffing the flesh side with an emery wheel
swayed   moved in rhythmic back and forth oscillations; influenced a course of action or viewpoint

suer   (see **sewer**)

suit   (see **soot**)

suit   a set of garments; cards in a pack of playing cards bearing the same symbol, as spades
suite   a retinue or set; an instrumental musical form
sute   a flock of mallards
tzut   a brightly patterned square of cotton used as a head cover

suite   (see **sault**)

suite   a retinue or set; an instrumental musical form
sweet   charming or nice; pleasing to the taste, as opposed to sour or bitter; sugary

suitor   (see **sooter**)

sulfinyl   the bivalent group or radical SO occurring in sulfoxides, sulfinic acids, and derivatives of the acids
sulfonyl   the bivalent group or radical SO_2 occurring in sulfones, sulfonic acids, and derivatives of the acids

sum   (see some)

Suma   (see souma)

sumac   a shrub or tree of the genus Rhus
Sumak   a smooth-faced pileless carpet from eastern Transcaucasia, woven in a peculiar form of tapestry weave with a herringbone effect

summa   (see souma)

summary   a short restatement of the main points
summery   relating to the season between spring and autumn

sun   (see sann)

sundae   (see sandhi)

Sunday   (see sandhi)

sundri   an East Indian tree with tannin-rich bark
sundry   an indeterminate number

sung   (see sang)

sunn   (see sann)

sunny   (see sonny)

sup   (see soup)

supe   (see soup)

superepic   extraordinarily heroic
superepoch   an extraordinary memorable event or date

supple   (see souple)

sur   (see sir)

sura(h)   a section or chapter of the Koran
surah   a soft light lustrous fabric usually made of silk or rayon

sura   the fermented juice of various East Indian palms
surra(h)   a severe Old World febrile and hemorrhagic disease of animals transmitted by biting insects

surah   (see sura)

surculus   (see circulus)

surd   (see sirred)

sure   (see shirr and shoer)

surf   (see serf)

surface   one of the faces of a three dimensional object
syrphus   any of numerous active day-flying flies that feed on nectar; the hoverfly

surge   (see serge)

surgency   a personality factor characterized by quickness and cleverness
surgeoncy   the office or position of a medical specialist who performs surgery

surplice   a loose white ecclesiastical vestment
surplus   the excess of receipts over disbursements; more than sufficient

surra(h)   (see sura)

sute   (see suit)

sutler   (see subtler)

suttle   (see subtle)

swallo   a large holothurian, a worm-like aquatic animal
swallow   to take through the esophagus into the stomach; to devour; to engulf; a small long-winged bird

sward   (see soared)

swath   a stroke of a scythe
swathe   to wrap or cover tightly in enveloping material

swatter   a device to kill insects
swotter   a student who studies hard and constantly, especially for examinations in Great Britain and New Zealand

swayed   (see suede)

Swedish   related to Sweden

sweetish pleasing to the taste, as opposed to sour or bitter; sugary

sweet (see **suite**)

sweetish (see **swedish**)

sword (see **soared**)

sworded (see **sordid**)

swotter (see **swatter**)

sycosis (see **psychosis**)

syenite (see **cyanite**)

syke (see **cyke**)

symbol (see **cymbal**)

syn (see **sin**)

sync(h) (see **cinque**)

synechological pertaining to a continuum

synecological involving a branch of ecology that deals with the structure, development, and distribution of ecological communities in relation to the environment

sypher (see **cipher**)

Syria (see **ceria**)

Syrian (see **Sirian**)

syrphus (see **surface**)

syssel (see **scissel**)

Szis (see **cees**)

Group I

salience - salients
scalenous - scalenus
schedular - scheduler
scirrhous - scirrhus
semblance - semblants
senhor - senor - signor
senhora - senora - signora
senhorita - senorita
sentience - sentients

septal - septil
sibilance - sibilants
significance - significants
silence - silents
somnolence - somnolents
sonance - sonants
sorceress - sorcerous
sphacelous - sphacelus
stabile - stable
steroptican - steropticon
stimulance - stimulants
stratous - stratus
strepsipteran - strepsipteron
subdominance - subdominants
subservience - subservients
subtile - subtle
subtiler - subtler
succulence - succulents
superintendence - superintendents
suppliance - suppliants
surculous - surculus
surveillance - surveillants
susurrous - susurrus
syngnathous - Syngnathus

Group I and II

salon sɑ:lōⁿ
saloon sə'lün

sclerose 'sklɪ.rōs
sclerus 'sklɪrəs

Group II

Sa'an 'sän
sawn 'sȯn

sabaean sə'bēən
sabian 'sābēən

sabal 'sā.bɑl
sable 'sābəl

salleeman 'sālemən
sallyman 'salimən

sapience	'sapēəns
sapiens	'sapē,enz
sappare	'sa,per
sapper	'sapər
sasin	'sāsᵊn
sasine	'sāsən
sauce	'sȯs
soss	'säs
Sauk	'sȯk
sock	'säk
sawed	'sȯd
sod	'säd
scissel	'sisəl
scissile	sisəl or sizəl
sessile	'sesəl
sistle	'sisl
second	'sekənd
secund	'se,kənd
secret	'sēkrət
secrete	sə'krēt
seesee	'sē,sē
tsetse	'sēsē
serene	sə'rēn
serine	'si,rēn
servant	'sərvənt
sirvente	sər'vent
shaikh	'shā,kē
shaky	'shākē
shall	'shȯl
shell	'shel
sharki	'shərkē
sharky	'shörkē
shivaree	'shivə,rē
shivery	'shivərē
silicon	'siləkən
silicone	'silə,kōn

simbil	'simbil
symbol	'simbəl
Sinapsis	sə'nāpsəs
synapsis	'sə,napsəs
sing	'siŋ
singh	'siŋg
skeletin	'skelətin
skeleton	'skelətᵊn
slaughter	'slȯdər
slotter	'slädər
solan	'sōlən
so-lun	'sō,lən
solely	'sōlē
soli	'sō,lē
sot	'sät
sought	'sȯt
spiritual	'spirəchəwəl
spirituel	:spirəl|chə:wel
stadic	'stātik
static	'statik
stalk	'stȯk
stock	'stäk
stamen	'stāmən
stamin	'stamən
stoop	'stüp
stupp	'stəp
succus	'səkəs
succuss	,sə'kəs
sunglo	'səŋ'lō
sunglow	'sən,glō
suni	'sünē
Sunni	'sunē
sunny	'sənē
superaffluence	,süpər'aflüəns
supereffluence	,süpər'eflüəns

T

tabaret   a stout upholstery silk with satin stripes
taboret   a cylindrical seat or stool without arms or back

tachs   tachometers, devices indicating speed of rotation (by shortening)
tacks   attaches or joins; nail-like fastening devices; changes direction of a sailing vessel
tax   a pecuniary charge imposed by a public authority

tacit   unspoken or implicit
tasset   one of a series of overlapping plates in a suit of armor that forms a short skirt

tacked   attached or joined; changed direction of a sailing vessel
tact   diplomacy; considerateness; poise

tacks   (see **tachs**)

Tacoma   a city in west central Washington
Tecoma   a genus of tropical American shrubs and trees having large showy flowers

tact   (see **tacked**)

tahr   a Himalayan beardless wild goat
tar   a dark brown or black bituminous odorous viscid liquid obtained by the destructive distillation of organic materials

tailer   a person or animal that follows another
tailor   a person who makes or alters wearing apparel
talar   an ankle-length robe

tailles   royal taxes in 15th century France; middle or tenor voices in early choral music
tails   (plural) the part of a vertebrate's body that is posterior to the portion containing the body cavity

tales   narratives of events

tailles   middle or tenor voices in early choral music; royal taxes in 15th century France
Tais   members of a widespread group of people in south China and southeast Asia associated ethnically with valley paddy-rice culture
tais   Pacific porgy fish
Thais   natives or inhabitants of Thailand

ties   fastens, attaches, or brings together; equal scores in a contest
tyes   chains or ropes, one end of each of which passes through the mast
Tyighs   a Shahaptian people of west central Oregon

tailor   (see **tailer**)

tails   (see **tailles**)

taint   to corrupt, defile, or stain
'taint   the contraction of it ain't (substandard)

Tais and tais   (see **tailles**)

tait   a honey possum, a small chestnut-brown long-muzzled phalanger of western Australia
tête   a high elaborately ornamented style of woman's hairdress or wig worn in the latter half of the 18th century
tet(h)   the ninth letter of the Hebrew alphabet

takt   a beat or pulse in music
tocked   made a sound similar to a tick, but slightly lower and therefore more resonant, especially in a clock

talar   (see **tailer**)

tales   (see **tailles**)

talkee-talkee a broken or corrupted speech
talky-talky abounding in or containing too much talk

talkie a sound motion picture
talky talkative
tawkee an arrow arum; an American aquatic plant with a spadix of minute yellow flowers

talky-talky (see **talkee-talkee**)

Tallin(n) the capital of Estonia
talon the claw of an animal, especially that of a bird of prey

tamar relating to the last of four recognized ripening stages of the date
tammar a dama pademelon, a dark stocky thick-coated wallaby of southern and western Australia

Tampan a native or resident of Tampa, Florida
tampon a plug of cotton or other material introduced into a body cavity to arrest hemorrhage, absorb secretions, or fill a defect

tang a sharp distinctive flavor; the extension of a knife blade that connects with the handle
tangue any of numerous small often spiny insectivorous mammals of the family Tenrecidae of Madagascar

tangi a lamentation or dirge that accompanies a Maori funeral rite
tangy suggestive of a sharp distinctive flavor that lingers on the tongue

tangue (see **tang**)

tangy (see **tangi**)

tanto much
Tonto one of various subgroups of the Apache people

tao the unitary first principle in Taoism from which all existence and change spring; in Confucianism, the right way of life

tau the 19th letter of the Greek alphabet; a T-shaped mark or object

taos (see **daos**)

taper a slender wax candle; gradually narrowing to a point; a person or device that applies tape
tapir a large perissodactyl ungulate of tropical America and southern Asia

tapet worked or figured cloth such as carpet, wall hanging, or tapestry
tappet a lever or projection moved by another device to cause a particular action, as in some forms of an internal-combustion engine

tapir (see **taper**)

tappet (see **tapet**)

tar (see **tahr**)

tare a seed of vetch; the weight of a container or vehicle deducted from its gross weight to obtain the net weight of the cargo
tear to divide or separate forcibly

tariff a system of duties imposed by a government on imported or exported goods
teraph an image representing a primitive household god among ancient Jews and other Semitic peoples

taro an aroid of the Pacific islands grown for its edible starchy tuberous rootstalks
tarot any of 22 pictoral playing cards used for fortune-telling

tarrier a person who lags behind, delays, or dawdles
terrier any of various usually small and rather low-built dogs kept chiefly as pets

tarry to linger, dawdle, or procrastinate
terry a loop forming the pile in uncut pile fabrics

Tartar   a native or inhabitant of Tatary of Mongolic or Turkic origin; a person of irritable, violent, or intractable temper
tartar   a reddish acidic compound found in the juice of grapes; an incrustation on teeth
tarter   more acid, sharp, or piquant to the taste

tartarous   containing or resembling cream of tartar
Tartarus   the infernal regions of ancient mythology; hell

tarter   (see **Tartar**)

Tass   a Russian news-gathering agency
tasse   one of a series of overlapping metal plates in a suit of armor that forms a short skirt covering just below the waist

Tass   a Russian news-gathering agency
toss   to throw around, heave, or tumble

tasse   (see **Tass**)

tassel   a pendent ornament used on clothing, curtains, and other articles
tosyl   the para isomer of toluene sulfonyl

tasset   (see **tacit**)

Tatar   a member of one of the numerous chiefly Turkic peoples probably originating in Manchuria and Mongolia
totter   to oscillate or lean dizzily; to move unsteadily

tatou   an armadillo
tattoo   a native-bred pony of India

tau   (see **tao**)

tau   the 19th letter of the Greek alphabet; a T-shaped mark or object
taw   a shooter used in the game of marbles; to convert skin into white leather; the 23rd letter of the Hebrew alphabet

taught   instructed
taut   tightly drawn

taupe   a brownish gray color
tope   a small shark; to drink intoxicating liquor to excess

Taurus   the second sign of the zodiac
torus   a large architectural molding of convex profile often occurring at the lowest molding in the base of a column

taut   (see **taught**)

taw   (see **tau**)

tawkee   (see **talkie**)

tax   (see **tachs**)

taxer   a person or authority that levies a tax
taxor   a former officer at older British universities empowered to regulate the prices of student room and board

taxes   manual restorations of displaced body parts, as reductions of a hernia; reflex movements by a freely motile and usually simple organism
taxi(e)s   taxicabs, vehicles for hire (by shortening)

taxes   pecuniary charges imposed by a public authority
taxis   a manual restoration of displaced body parts, as the reduction of a hernia; a reflex movement by a freely motile and usually simple organism
Taxus   a genus of trees and shrubs comprising yews

taxi(e)s   (see **taxes**)

taxis   (see **taxes**)

taxor   (see **taxer**)

Taxus   (see **taxes**)

tchus (see chews)

tea an aromatic beverage prepared from cured leaves of the shrub Camellia sinensis
tee a small artificial elevation from which a golf ball is struck; a short piece of T-shaped pipe
Ti an early Tatar people related to the Hsiung-Nu
ti the seventh tone of the diatonic scale; an Asiatic and Pacific tree

teal a small short-necked river duck
teil a large European linden tree
til sesame, an East Indian annual erect herb

team a group of persons or animals associated in an activity
teem to abound or swarm; present in large quantity

tear (see tare)

tear a drop of fluid secreted by the lacrimal gland near the eye
tier a row, rank, or layer of articles
Tyr the Norse god of war and son of Odin

tearer a person who separates cloth from bolts
terrar a bursar of a religious house
terror intense fright or stark fear

teas aromatic beverages prepared from the cured leaves of the shrub Camellia sinensis
tease to disturb or annoy by persistent irritating action; to tantalize
tees small artificial elevations from which a golf ball is struck

teat a protuberance through which milk is drawn from a mammal's breast
tit a titmouse; a small or inferior horse

tec a detective (by shortening)
tech technician or technology (by shortening)

technology the science of the application of knowledge to practical problems
tecnology the science and study of the life and development of children; soil science

Tecoma (see Tacoma)

tedder a machine for stirring and spreading hay to hasten drying and curing
tetter any of various vesicular skin diseases

tee (see tea)

teem (see team)

teen (see ctene)

tees (see teas)

teeter to move unsteadily or waver precariously; to seesaw
titar a partridge of southern Asia
titer a point of temperature at which fatty acid that is liberated from fat solidifies

Teh(e)ran (see pteron)

teil (see teal)

telea (see Ptelea)

telestic mystical
telestich a poem in which consecutive final letters of lines spell a name

Tempe a city in central Arizona
tempi rates of motion or activity, especially in musical passages

temps temporary employees (by shortening); temperatures (by shortening)
tempts entices to do wrong; seduces

tenace a combination of two high cards in a bridge hand separated in rank by the intervening card held by an opponent
tennis a game played with rackets and an elastic ball

tenant a person who rents or leases property from a landlord
tenent a projecting member of a piece of wood or other material for

insertion into a mortise to make a joint; a tenon

tendance looking after someone or something
tendence tendency

tends cares for the wants of; directs toward a particular direction
TENS a self-operated portable device used to treat chronic pain by generating electrical impulses (*trans*cutaneous *e*lectrical *n*erve *s*timulator)
tens ten-dollar bills

tenent (see **tenant**)

tenner a ten-dollar bill
tenor an intent or substance; the highest natural adult male voice

tennis (see **tenace**)

tenor (see **tenner**)

TENS and **tens** (see **tends**)

tense distinction in a verb form; taut or rigid; jittery
tenths musical intervals embracing an octave and a third; two or more of ten equal parts into which something is divisible
tents collapsible shelters of canvas or other material

tenser more rigid or jittery
tensor a generalized vector with more than three components

tenths (see **tense**)

tents (see **tense**)

tenuis an unaspirated voiceless stop
tenuous having little substance or strength; weak; vague

teraph (see **tariff**)

teras (see **Pteris**)

terce the third of the canonical hours
terse brief, concise, or devoid of superfluity

termen the outer margin of a triangularly shaped insect wing
termine determine (by shortening)
termon church land exempt from secular taxation

termer a person serving a specific term, such as a prisoner
termor a person who has an estate for a specified period of years or life

termon (see **termen**)

termor (see **termer**)

tern a sea bird; something consisting of three items
terne sheet iron or steel coated with a lead-tin alloy
turn to move in a curved path; to change position

ternar a university student assigned to the third and lowest social rank and required to pay the lowest fees
turner a person that turns, or a device that is used in turning

ternary having three elements
ternery a place where flocks of terns breed
turnery fashioning material with a lathe

terne (see **tern**)

terneplate sheet iron or steel coated with a lead-tin alloy
turnplate a turntable; a flat steel plate used for turning railway cars from one line to another

ternery (see **ternary**)

terp a large artificial mound in the Netherlands providing a site for a prehistoric settlement in a seasonally flooded area
turp turpentine (by shortening)

terrace (see **Pteris**)

terrain ground or a geographical area
terrane a rock formation or formations

terrar   (see tearer)

terrene   relating to this world or life; mundane
terrine   an earthenware jar containing a table delicacy and sold with its contents
tureen   a deep-footed serving dish

terrier   (see tarrier)

terrine   (see terrene)

terror   (see tearer)

terry   (see tarry)

terse   (see terce)

testae   the hard external coatings or integuments of a seed
teste   the witnessing or concluding clause of a writ
testee   a person who takes an examination

testar   a West Indian clingfish
tester   the frame on which the canopy of a bed rests; a person who checks the quality and conformance to predetermined specifications

teste   (see testae)

testee   (see testae)

testees   persons who take an examination
testes   male reproductive glands; witnessing or concluding clauses of a writ

tester   (see testar)

testes   (see testees)

tête   (see tait)

tet(h)   (see tait)

tetrastichous   arranged in four vertical rows
Tetrastichus   a genus of minute chalcid flies comprising numerous hyperparasites

tetravalence   in chemistry, having a valence of four

tetravalents   quadruples, groups of four homologous chromosomes each of which is associate in synapsis

tetrazene   either of two hypothetical isomeric hydrides of nitrogen
tetrazine   an isomeric parent compound resembling benzene with four methylidyne groups replaced by nitrogen atoms

tetter   (see tedder)

Thais   (see tailles)

thallic   (see phthalic)

thalline   (see phthalin)

thallous   relating to or containing the metallic element thallium
thallus   a plant body that is characteristic of the thallophytes

than   a conjunction used with comparative adjectives and adverbs
then   at that time

the   a definite article preceding a noun
thee   a form of address; thou

their   belonging to them
there   in or at that place
there're   the contraction of there are
they're   the contraction of they are

theirs   what belongs to them
there's   the contraction of there is or there was

then   (see than)

theocracy   government by God's direction
theocrasy   a fusion of different deities in the minds of worshipers

there   (see their)

therefor   in return for that
therefore   because of that

there're   (see their)

there's   (see theirs)

therm any of several units of quantity of heat

thurm to work a piece of wood with saw and chisel across the grain so as to produce patterns resembling those produced by turning

thermos a vacuum bottle or flask

Thermus a genus of gram-negative aerobic bacteria

they're (see **their**)

thiokol (see **phthiocol**)

threw propelled through the air by the hand

through denoting penetration or passage

throes a condition of struggle, anguish, or disorder

throws propels through the air by the hand

thrombin a proteolytic enzyme that is formed from prothrombin

thrombon the entire body of blood platelets and their precursors that constitute a distinct organ of the body

throne a ceremonial seat

thrown propelled through the air by the hand

through (see **threw**)

thrown (see **throne**)

throws (see **throes**)

thruster a person who intrudes or pushes him or herself forward; a pusher

thrustor a combination oil pump and piston cylinder

Thule belonging to the Eskimo culture extending over arctic lands from Alaska to Greenland about A.D. 500–1400; a settlement in northwest Greenland

tule either of two large bulrushes growing abundantly on overflowed land in the southwestern U.S. and adjacent Mexico

thurm (see **therm**)

thyme a common garden herb

time a measured duration, period, or interval

thymene a liquid used for perfuming soap

thymine a crystalline compound obtained from fish spermatozoa

Ti and ti (see **tea**)

tiaras decorative bands or ornaments for the head

tiaris a tropical American finch

tical the basic monetary unit of Thailand

tickle to excite amusement or merriment in

ticker something that ticks or produces a ticking sound, as a watch or the heart; a telegraphic instrument that prints stock quotations or news on a paper ribbon

tikor a starch or arrowroot made from the tubers of an East Indian herb

tickle (see **tical**)

ticks bloodsucking arachnids; light rhythmic tapping sounds

tics convulsive motions of muscles, especially facial

tix tickets (slang)

tidal related to the alternate rise and fall of oceans

title a descriptive or general heading; the distinguishing name of a book or production

tiddle to occupy oneself aimlessly; to putter about

tittle an extremely small or least possible amount; a point or small mark used in writing or printing

tide the alternate rise and fall of an ocean

tied fastened or attached; made an equal score in a contest tier   (see tear)

tier   a person who fastens, closes
   openings, or binds articles
tire   to become weary or exhausted;
   a continuous pneumatic rubber
   cushion encircling a wheel

ties   (see tailles)

tig   the game of tag
tyg   a large usually slip-decorated
   ceramic drinking cup with two or
   more handles

tighten   to become tense or taut
titan   a person gigantic in size or
   power

tighter   more taught, tense, or dense
titer   a point or temperature at
   which fatty acid that is liberated
   from fat solidifies

tigress   a female tiger
Tigris   a major river in Turkey and
   Iraq that joins the Euphrates

tikor   (see ticker)

til   (see teal)

til   sesame, an East Indian annual
   erect herb
'til   until
till   up to a specified time; to work
   the soil

tilley   seeds of the croton-oil plant
tilly   composed of or having the
   character of clay

timbal   a kettledrum; a vibrating
   membrane in a cicada's shrilling
   organ
timbale   a creamy mixture of food
   cooked in a mold or cup

timber   trees or their wood
timbre   the quality of sound depending chiefly on various overtones;
   the crest on a coat of arms

time   (see thyme)

timpani   a set of usually two or
   three kettledrums played by one
person in a musical group
tympany   a distention of the abdo-
   men caused by accumulation of air
   or gas in the intestinal tract

tincal   a mineral consisting of native
   borax
tinkle   a series of short high ringing
   or clinking sounds

Tinne   an Athapaskan people occupying most of the interior of
   Alaska and northern Canada
tinny   resembling, containing, or
   suggestive of tin

tip   an end or extremity; a gratuity
typp   a unit of yarn size

tipit   the game of "up Jenkins"
tippet   a shoulder cape, often with
   hanging ends

tippee   a person receiving a gratuity
   or a tip
tippy   unsteady

tippet   (see tipit)

tippy   (see tippet)

tire   (see tier)

tit   (see teat)

titan   (see tighten)

titar   (see teeter)

titer   (see teeter or tighter)

title   (see tidal)

tittle   (see tiddle)

titty   a teat or nipple on the beast of
   a female animal
tydie   a small bird variously identified as a wren or the blue titmouse

tix   (see ticks)

to   a preposition indicating a spatial
   relationship or a relationship suggesting motion
too   also or moreover
two   the whole number between one
   and three

toa a tall usually spreading tree of northern Australia and the Pacific islands
Towa the language of the Jemez group of Pueblo Indians

toad a tailless leaping amphibian
tode a rude sled for hauling logs
toed reached with a foot's forepart
towed hauled or pulled

toady a person engaging in excessive deference through self-interest
tody a tiny non-passerine insectivorous West Indian bird

toat the handle of a joiner's plane
tote to transport from one place to another

tocked (see **takt**)

tocsin an alarm bell
toxin a poisonous substance produced by a living organism

tode (see **toad**)

tody (see **toady**)

toed (see **toad**)

toi any of several Asiatic and Pacific trees or shrubs
toy something designed for play, amusement, or diversion

toke a puff on a marijuana cigarette (slang); a tip given by a gambler to a dealer in a casino
toque a soft hat with a very narrow brim and a full crown pleated into a snug headband worn in the 16th century

tol a Sanskrit school or college
tole decorative japanned or painted metal
toll a tax or fee paid for some liberty or privilege; to sound a bell as a signal or announcement

told narrated or recounted
tolled taxed; sounded, as a bell

tole (see **tol**)

toll (see **tol**)

tolled (see **told**)

ton the prevailing fashion or mode
tone a vocal or musical sound; a color quality or value

ton a unit of U.S. weight equal to 2000 pounds
tonne a unit of mass equal to 1000 kilograms, or 2204.62 pounds
tun a large cask

tonal the force that acts on the mass of a ton to accelerate it equal to one foot per second squared
tunnel a covered passageway

tone (see **ton**)

tongue a fleshy process in most vertebrates' mouths
tung a Chinese tree grown for its seeds which yield tung oil

tonne (see **ton**)

Tonto (see **tanto**)

too (see **to**)

toodle to make a continuous low sound, as in cooing or playing a small pipe
tootle to sound a short blast continuously or repeatedly on a wind instrument

tool an implement used in work
tulle sheer and often stiffened machine-made netting

toon an East Indian and Australian tree
tune a musical composition

Toona a small genus of Old World trees closely related to a genus that includes the Spanish cedar
toona a Mexican tree that is a minor source of rubber
tuna any of numerous large vigorous scombroid fish; any of various flat-jointed prickly pears

tooter a person who sounds a short blast on a wind instrument
Tudor relating to the English royal family reigning from 1485 to 1603; marked by Tudor arches
tutor a person who instructs and guides

tootle (see **toodle**)

too-too to an affectedly or unpleasantly excessive degree; to produce a flat monotonous tootling sound
tutu a very short projecting skirt worn by a ballet dancer; an Hawaiian grandma or grandpa; any of several New Zealand shrubs or small trees

tope (see **taupe**)

topee a lightweight helmetlike hat often made of sola pith
topi a central African antelope

topography the art or practice of detailed graphic delineation on maps or charts of the physical features of a place or region
typography the art of letterpress printing

topology a branch of mathematics that investigates the properties of a geometric configuration; the history of a region as indicated by its topography
typology a doctrine that things in the Christian dispensation are symbolized or prefigured by things in the Old Testament; a study based on types

toque (see **toke**)

tor a high craggy hill
torr a measure of pressure equal to 1333.2 bars

tora a large reddish hartebeest
Torah a scroll of the Pentateuch used in synagogues

torcel the larva of a South American botfly that lives beneath human skin

torsel a piece of stone, iron, or wood supporting the end of a beam or joist

tore divided or separated forcibly; a torus, a doughnut-shaped surface
tower a person that smooths ceramic ware; a person or animal that pulls a barge or boat

tori large architectural moldings of convex profile commonly occurring as the lowest molding in the base of a column
Tory an American upholding the cause of the British Crown against supporters of the American Revolution
tory a person who emphasizes order, tradition, stability, or accepted canons of conduct

torr (see **tor**)

torsel (see **torcel**)

tort a wrongful act
torte a cake or pastry of ground nuts or bread crumbs

torta a flat heap of moist crushed silver ore
torte a cake or pastry of ground nuts or bread crumbs

torte (see **tort**)

torulous somewhat knobbed
torulus the socket in which an insect's antenna articulates

torus (see **Taurus**)

Tory and **tory** (see **tori**)

toss (see **Tass**)

tosyl (see **tassel**)

tote (see **toat**)

totter (see **Tatar**)

tough strong, firm, or forceful
tuff rock composed of finer kinds of volcanic detritus

toughed endured
tuft a clump or cluster

tour a journey; a circular trip
tur a Caucasian wild goat

tournay a printed worsted upholstery fabric
tournee a game of skat

Towa (see **toa**)

towed (see **toad**)

tower (see **tore**)

towhee any of numerous American finches
towie contract bridge for three or more players

toxin (see **tocsin**)

toy (see **toi**)

trac a tractor (by shortening)
track a trail or pathway

trachycarpous rough-fruited
Trachycarpus a small genus of low East Asiatic fan palms, including the hemp palm

track (see **trac**)

tracked pursued; traveled
tract a pamphlet or leaflet of exhortation or appeal; a land area

trade to barter or buy and sell; a means of livelihood
trayed arranged on trays, as for drying fruit

trader a person who barters, buys, or sells
traitor a person who commits treason against his/her country, betrays another's trust, or is false to an obligation

trail to track game; to plod or trudge
treille in heraldry, a trellis or lattice

traitor (see **trader**)

tramp the succession of sounds made by the beating of the animal feet on a surface
tromp(e) an apparatus in which air is sucked through sloping holes in

the upper end of a large vertical wooden tube and led to a furnace by a stream of falling water, as for a Catalan forge

trance a daze, stupor, or state of suspended animation
trans characterized by atoms on opposite sides of a molecule

transladed transferred cargo, as in transshipping
translated converted into another language

travail physical or mental exertion, especially of a painful or laborious nature (although usually trə'vāl)
travel to proceed on a trip or tour

trave a frame; to control an unruly horse or ox for shoeing
tref a homestead or hamlet acting as a single community

travel (see **travail**)

tray a flat-bottomed low-rimmed open receptacle
trey a card or side of a die containing three spots or pips

trayed (see **trade**)

treatee a person who is entertained or treated to something
treaty a written agreement or convention between two or more political authorities

tref (see **trave**)

treille (see **trail**)

trews close-cut tartan short drawers worn under a Scottish kilt
trues brings to a desired mechanical accuracy

trey (see **tray**)

tri a dog having a coat of black, tan, and white
try to attempt or endeavor; to examine in a court of law

trichi a cigar made in India

tricky   deceptively safe, easy, manageable, or orderly; intricate

trigon   an ancient triangular harp; the cutting region of an upper molar's crown
trygon   a stingray

triker   a tricycle rider
trikir   a three-branched candlestick used by bishops in the Eastern Orthodox Church

triol   a chemical compound containing three hydroxyl groups
triole   a group of three musical notes or tones performed in the time of two of the same value

trip   to dance or skip with light quick steps; a journey
tryp   a member of the genus Trypanosoma which comprises parasitic flagellate protozoans that as adults are elongated and somewhat spindle-shaped

triple   a multiple of three; threefold
tripple   a horse's gait resembling an amble

triptik   a series of road maps
triptych   a picture in three compartments side by side
tryptic   relating to trypsin, a proteolytic enzyme present in the pancreatic juice, or to its action

triptych   a picture in three compartments side by side
triptyque   a customs pass for temporary importation of an automobile

triter   more hackneyed, threadbare, or shopworn
tritor   a grinding surface developed on the tooth

troche   a medicinal lozenge or tablet
trochee   a prosadic foot of two syllables, the first long and the second short

trollop   an unkempt slovenly woman; a straggly mass
trollope   a cry of protest against bad manners or boorish behavior, especially in a theater

tromp(e)   (see tramp)

troolie   one of the immense leaves of the bussu used for thatching
truli   round stone buildings made with conical roofs and without mortar
truly   truthfully; sincerely; realistically; accurately

troop   a group or body of soliders; to move in an orderly manner
troupe   a group of stage performers

trottie   a small child; a toddler
trotty   lively or brisk

troupe   (see troop)

trues   (see trews)

truli   (see troolie)

truly   (see troolie)

trussed   secured closely; tied
trust   confidence, reliance, or faith

truster   a person who relies or believes
trustor   a person creating a trust by transferral of property to a trustee

try   (see tri)

trygon   (see trigon)

tryp   (see trip)

tryptic   (see triptik)

tsamba   (see samba)

tsine   (see sign)

Tswa   (see schwa)

tucks   gathers in a fold; puts in a snug place
tux   a tuxedo, a man's formal attire (by shortening)

Tudor   (see tooter)

tuff   (see **tough**)

tuft   (see **toughed**)

tuille   a hinged plate for the thigh in plate armor
tweel   a closure of a glass furnace

tule   (see **Thule**)

tulle   (see **tool**)

tun   (see **ton**)

tuna   (see **Toona**)

tune   (see **toon**)

tung   (see **tongue**)

tunnel   (see **tonal**)

tur   (see **tour**)

turban   a headdress
turbine   a rotary engine

Turbit   a breed of fancy pigeons
turbot   a large European flatfish that is highly esteemed as a food fish

tureen   (see **terrene**)

Turkey   a country of southeast Europe and southwest Asia
turkey   a large American bird
Turki   relating to the peoples of Turkic speech; one of the Turki peoples

turn   (see **tern**)

turner   (see **ternar**)

turnery   (see **ternary**)

turnip   a biennial herb whose thick edible root is a vegetable
turnup   a turned-up part of an article, as a pant cuff; a card turned face up

turnplate   (see **terneplate**)

turnup   (see **turnip**)

turp   (see **terp**)

tusch   a flourish or fanfare of brass wind musical instruments and drums

Tush   a member of a Georgian people north of Tiflis
tush   buttocks (slang)

tussal   relating to a cough
tussle   a struggle or scuffle

tussic   relating to a cough
tussock   a small hummock of more solid ground in a marsh or bog

tussle   (see **tussal**)

tussock   (see **tussic**)

tutor   (see **tooter**)

tutu   (see **too-too**)

tux   (see **tucks**)

Twaddell   according to a specific gravity reading of a Twaddell hydrometer
twaddle   idle chatter; to babble

twee   a thin or shrill piping note
Twi   a dialect spoken by the Akwapim people of Ghana

tweel   (see **tuille**)

Twi   (see **twee**)

twice-sold   goods or services that are sold two times
twice-soled   footwear that has been soled two times

twill   a textile weave
'twill   the contraction of it will or it shall

twister   a person who wrings, wrenches, or wrests so as to dislocate or distort; a tornado
twistor   a non-volatile computer memory element

two   (see **to**)

two-seated   a vehicle or machine equipped with two seats
two-seeded   an area that is planted with two varieties of seeds

tydie   (see **titty**)

tyes   (see **tailles**)

tyg   (see **tig**)

Tyighs   (see **tailles**)

tympany   (see **timpani**)

typography   (see **topography**)

typology   (see **topology**)

typp   (see **tip**)

Tyr   (see **tear**)

tyrannis   absolute rule, as by a dictator
Tyrannus   the type genus of Tyrannidae comprising the kingbird

tzut   (see **suit**)

Group I

tamis - tamise - tammy
technic - technique
termer - termor
thrash - thresh
transcendence - transcendents
transhumance - transhumants
transience - transients
travois - travoy
trivalence - trivalents
tubulous - tubulus
tumulous - tumulus
Turkman - Turkmen
typhous - typhus
tyrannis - tryannous

Group I and II

thromboses   thräm'bō.sēz
thrombosis   thräm'bōsə̇s

tickling   'tikliŋ
tikling   tə̇'kliŋ

toilet   'toi̇lə̇t
toilette   'toi.let

trustee   :trə:stē
trusty   'trə̇stē

Group II

talesman   'tōlzmə̇n
talisman   'tōlə̇smə̇n

tambor   'tam.bȯr
tambour   'tam.bu̇r

tambourin   'tambə̇rə̇n
tombourine   'tambə.rēn

tarpan   tär:pan
tarpon   'tärpə̇n

tempera   'tempə̇rə̇
tempura   .tempə̇'rä

tendence   'tendə̇nts
tendenz   ten'dents

terete   tə̇'rēt
terret   'terə̇t

testee   'te:stē
testy   'testē

tetanic   te'tanik
titanic   tī:tanik

tetragenous   tə̇'trȧjə̇nə̇s
tetragynous   'tetrə̇.jīnə̇s

tetramine   'tetrə̇.mə̇n
tetrammine   te'tramə̇n

tetrapterous   te'traptə̇rə̇s
tetrapturus   .te.trap'tu̇rə̇s

thermal   'thərmə̇l
thermel   'thər.mel

thigh   'thī
thy   '<u>thī</u>

tippee   ti'pē
tippy   'tipē

toastee   tō'stē
toasty   'tōstē

tootsie   'tu̇tsē
Tutsi   'tütsē

torchere	tȯr'sher
torture	'tȯrchər
torchon	'tȯr.shän
torsion	'tȯrshən
torose	'tōr.ōs
torus	'tōrəs
tour	'tu̇r
turr	'tər
toured	'tu̇rd
turd	'tərd

tourneur	tu̇r'nər
turner	'tu̇rnər
traiteur	'trā.tər
traitor	'trātər
treaties	'trēd·|ēz
treatise	'trēd·ə̇s
trotter	'trätər
trotteur	trä'tər
Tyranni	tə̇'rɑ.nī
tyranny	'tirənē

U

uang a rhinoceros beetle
wang a member of the Chinese ruling class before and after the 3rd century B.C.

Uca a genus consisting of fiddler crabs
Yucca a genus of American sometimes arborescent plants
yucca any plant of the genus Yucca

udder a large pendulous organ consisting of two or more mammary glands
utter to speak; remote; complete

ugli a hybrid between a tangerine or mandarin orange and either a grapefruit or a shaddock
ugly unpleasing, disagreeable, or loathsome in appearance

umbels (see **humbles**)

umber a grayling fish
umbre a dusky brown African wading bird

umbles (see **humbles**)

umbre (see **umber**)

unaffected free from affectation; genuine, sincere, or unpretentious; not acted upon or influenced
uneffected not accomplished, exe-

cuted, or enforced

unaired without air or circulation
unheired having no inheritor(s)

unallowed not permitted; prohibited
unaloud not audible

unamendable not capable of reforming oneself
unemendable a literary work that is not subject to correction or editing

unassayed not analyzed or tested, as a mineral deposit
unessayed not made an effort to accomplish or perform

unbailed a boat that is not clear of water
unbaled an unbundled group of goods

unbilled not charged to a customer
unbuild to demolish

unborn not yet brought into life
unborne not endured or tolerated; not carried

unbreached not in violation of a standard or law
unbreeched not wearing short pants

unbuild (see **unbilled**)

uncal   relating to a hook or claw; the anterior end of the hippocampal convolution

uncle   the brother of either of one's parents

unceded   not surrendered or relinquished

unseated   having been removed or deposed from a political position; having been dislodged as a (horse) rider; not sitting

unseeded   unsown, as a field; not selectively placed in the draw for a tournament

unchased   not following or being followed rapidly and intently

unchaste   not free from lewdness, obscenity, or indecency

uncited   not brought to mind or called to attention

unsided   without surfaces that enclose space

unsighted   unable to see; unperceived; not aimed by means of a sighting device

uncle   (see **uncal**)

uncomplementary   not supplementing; mutually independent

uncomplimentary   derogatory or unflattering

uncord   to loosen or release from cords

uncored   something from which the axial portion has not been removed, as an apple

undammed   an unobstructed flow of water

undamned   not condemned

underbilled   charged less than the full amount

underbuild   to build a supporting structure underneath; to build below standard

underhold   an encircling grip secured advantageously by a wrestler under an opponent's arm

underholed   cut away the lower portion of or cut under a coal seam

undermade   manufactured or prepared short of a required standard quality; incompletely made or finished

undermaid   a domestic worker whose status is below a maidservant

undersold   exchanged goods or services beneath the usual or competitive price

undersoled   put a covering beneath the sole of the foot or shoe

underway   no longer at rest, in port, or at anchor; moving

underweigh   to fall short of a required or standard weight

undo   (see **endue**)

undue   (see **endue**)

uneffected   (see **unaffected**)

unemendable   (see **unamendable**)

unerupted   not yet emerged through the gum, as a tooth not having emerged

unirrupted   without sudden or violent invasion

unessayed   (see **unassayed**)

unexercised   untried or unpracticed

unexorcised   not driven off or expelled

unfaded   without loss of freshness, vigor, color, or health

unfated   not controlled by destiny or fate

unfeted   not celebrated or entertained

unfloured   not sprinkled or coated with flour

unflowered   not covered or decorated with flowers; without flowers

unfoaled   a mare which has not produced an offspring; an unborn colt or filly

unfold   to spread out or lay open to view

unfrees places in bondage; separates from freedom; coerces
unfreeze to thaw

ungild to remove gold or gilding from
ungilled not provided with gills; removed fish from a gill net

ungraded not classified according to ranks or grades; not assigned to a specific grade in school; not reduced to a gradual slope
ungrated not reduced to small bits by abrasion

unhealed not cured or restored to health
unheeled without the hind part of the foot or rear part of a shoe

unheard not perceived by the ear
unherd to disperse or separate from a herd of animals

unheated not warmed
unheeded disregarded or ignored

unheeled (see **unhealed**)

unheired (see **unaired**)

unherd (see **unheard**)

uniparous producing one egg or off-spring at a time
uniporous having one spore

unirrupted (see **unerupted**)

unkeyed not provided with a key
unquayed not provided with a landing place or wharf beside water

unkilled not dead; alive
unkilned not cured, fired, or dried in a kiln

unkneaded unmixed or unblended, as bread
unneeded unnecessary; not needed

unknocked not struck or rapped
unnocked unnotched, as an arrow

unlade to unload
unlaid not placed or fixed

unlead to remove lead from, as between lines of type
unled lacking leadership or guidance

unlessened marked by constancy; not diminished
unlessoned lacking instruction

unlimbed dismembered
unlimned undelineated

unmassed not gathered or formed into a mass
unmast to remove or not furnish a mast

unmedaled not honored or rewarded with one or more medals
unmeddled not interferred with

unmissed not discovered or noticed the absence of
unmist to clear away haze, film, or mist

unneeded (see **unkneaded**)

unpadded not furnished with padding
unpatted not stroked or tapped with the hand

unpaired not matched or mated
unpared untrimmed or unpealed

unpatted (see **unpadded**)

unpealed unrung, as bells or chimes
unpeeled the outer layer not removed or stripped off

unpearled not set or adorned with pearls
unpurled not embroidered or edged with gold or silver thread

unpeddled not peddled, as a bicycle
unpetaled not covered with petals

unpeeled (see **unpealed**)

unpetaled (see **unpeddled**)

unplaited not woven into strands of yarn, fabric, or locks of hair; unbraided
unplated not overlaid with metal or other material

unplaited not woven into strands of yarn, fabric, or locks of hair; unbraided
unplatted not mapped

unplated (see **unplaited**)

unplatted (see **unplaited**)

unpoled not furnished with a pole or poles
unpolled not registered, cast, or counted at the voting polls

unpraying not addressing or seeking through prayer
unpreying not seizing and devouring

unpurled (see **unpearled**)

unquayed (see **unkeyed**)

unraided not victimized by hostile or predatory incursion
unrated not rated, scored, or evaluated

unraised not raised or elevated
unrazed not destroyed, or leveled to the ground; left standing

unrated (see **unraided**)

unrazed (see **unraised**)

unreal artificial or false
unreel to unwind

unreave to unravel
unreeve to withdraw rope from a ship's block or other opening

unrecked to be unconcerned; was of no interest
unwrecked not disabled or ruined

unreel (see **unreal**)

unreeve (see **unreave**)

unrested tired or exhausted
unwrested not forced or moved by violent wringing or twisting movements

unrhymed without identical sounding words or lines of verse
unrimed not covered with granular ice tufts

unright unjust or wrong; an injustice
unwrite to obliterate from writing; to expunge, erase, or rescind

unrimed (see **unrhymed**)

unrooted torn up or out by the roots
unrouted not routed or provided with an itinerary

unrung not having or wearing a ring; not pealed, as a bell or chime
unwrung not painfully affected; unmoved

unscent to deprive of scent or odor
unsent not dispatched or transmitted

unseated (see **unceded**)

unseeded (see **unceded**)

unsent (see **unscent**)

unsewn not stitched together
unsown not planted with seed

unsided (see **uncited**)

unsighted (see **uncited**)

unsold something that has not been exchanged for money or its equivalent
unsoled wearing apparel without soles
unsouled deprived of a soul or spirit

unsonned dispossessed of the character of a son
unsunned not exposed to sunlight

unsouled (see **unsoled**)

unsown (see **unsewn**)

unstaid not demure, reserved, or well-ordered in behavior
unstayed not hindered, checked, supported, or upheld; not fastened with stays

unsunned (see **unsonned**)

untacks unfastens, loosens, or detaches by removing a tack or tacks

untax to remove from taxation; to take a tax from

unthrone to remove from a throne or ceremonial seat; to dethrone

unthrown not propelled through the air by hand

untold not related or revealed; not numbered or enumerated

untolled not having paid a toll or tax

unwaived not relinquished voluntarily

unwaved straight or not waved, as hair

unwanted not needed or desired; superfluous or unnecessary

unwonted unusual or unaccustomed; not made familiar by practice

unwaved (see **unwaived**)

unweaned not accustomed to the loss of a mother's milk; dependent on the mother for nourishment

unweened unbelieved; unimagined

unwonted (see **unwanted**)

unwrecked (see **unrecked**)

unwrested (see **unrested**)

unwrite (see **unright**)

unwrung (see **unrung**)

uranous relating to or containing trivalent uranium

Uranus the plant seventh in order from the sun

urinous having the qualities or odor of urine

urb (see **herb**)

urd (see **erred**)

urea (see **Eurya**)

Uria (see **Eurya**)

urinous (see **uranous**)

urn (see **earn**)

use (see **ewes**)

use (see **ius**)

utter (see **udder**)

Group I

---

unctious - unctuous
unrepentance - unrepentants

Group I and II

---

umbellate ˌəm'belət
umbellet 'əmbelət

--------------------------- V ---------------------------

vagus either of the tenth pair of cranial nerves supplying chiefly the viscera

'Vegas Las Vegas, the largest city in Nevada and a gambling mecca (by shortening)

Vai a Negro people of Liberia

vie to strive for superiority; to contend

vail to let fall; to lower, as a sign of respect or submission

vale a low-lying area usually containing a stream

veil to obscure; a curtain

vain   fruitless or unsuccessful
vane   a movable device to indicate wind direction
vein   a blood vessel; a streak or stripe

vairé   an heraldic vair consisting of tinctures other than argent and azure
vary   to differ or diversify
very   extremely

valance   a pleated drapery or canopy often used for decoration or concealment
valence   the degree of combining power of a chemical element or radical

vale   (see vail)

valence   (see valance)

valet   a servant who performs personal services
valley   an elongated depression of earth commonly situated between hills or mountains

vallar   a gold crown with palisades
valor   bravey or courage

valley   (see valet)

valor   (see vallar)

valse   a concert waltz
vaults   burial chambers; arched masonry structures forming a ceiling; leaps or bounds

vane   (see vain)

varicose   abnormally swollen or dilated
verrucose   covered with wartlike elevations

vary   (see vairé)

vasal   relating to an anatomical vessel
vassel   a dependent, servant, or slave

vau   a letter of the original Greek alphabet approximating the sound of the English w

vow   a solemn promise, pledge, or oath

vault   a burial chamber; an arched masonry structure forming a ceiling; to bound or leap
volte   a gait in which a horse moves sideways and turns around a center

vaults   (see valse)

vealer   a calf suitable for veal, especially one less than three months old
velar   relating to the soft palate

veer   to change direction
vire   an arrow used in a crossbow and feathered so as to acquire a rotary motion

'Vegas   (see vagus)

veil   (see vail)

vein   (see vain)

vela   membranes or membranous parts likened to a veil or curtain
vila   a supernatural being or fairy of Slavonic lands

velar   (see vealer)

veldt   (see felt)

vena   a blood vessel; a streak or stripe
vina   a four-stringed musical instrument of India

venous   characterized by veins
Venus   a genus of marine bivalve mollusk; a beautiful and charming woman; the second planet from the sun

ventil   a valve in various wind musical instruments
ventile   in textiles, designed to exclude water while permitting free circulation of air

Venus   (see venous)

veracious   truthful or accurate
voracious   greedy or ravenous

veracity conformity with truth or face; accuracy

voracity a state of being greedy or ravenous

verdure greenness and freshness of growing vegetation

verger a church official who serves as usher

verrucose (see **varicose**)

verser a person who creates lines of metrical writing

versor in geometry, the turning factor of a quaternion

verses lines of metrical writing

versus in contrast to; against

versor (see **verser**)

versus (see **verses**)

very (see **vairé**)

vesical of or relating to a bladder

vesicle a blister or cyst; a small cavity in a mineral or rock

vial a small bottle

vile morally despicable, contemptible, or base

viol a bowed stringed musical instrument of the 16th and 17th centuries

vice evil conduct

vise a tow-jawed tool for holding work

vie (see **Vai**)

vila (see **vela**)

vile (see **vial**)

villain a scoundrel or knave

villein a free commoner or peasant of a feudal class lower than a thane

villous having soft long hair

villus a small slender vascular process giving a velvety appearance to the surface of the small intestine's mucous membrane

vina (see **vena**)

vinal from wine

vinyl a univalent radical derived from ethylene

viol (see **vial**)

violin a bowed four-stringed musical instrument

violine a moderate to strong violet color

vire (see **veer**)

viscous having a glutinous consistency and stickiness

viscus an internal body organ

vise (see **vice**)

viviparous producing living young (instead of eggs) from within the body

Viviparus a genus of freshwater snails

vocal uttered orally or aloud; fluent

vocule the off-glide of certain consonants, as m and g

voder an electronic device capable of producing a recogizable approximation of speech

voter a person who expresses an opinion or casts a ballot in an election

volé a ballet step that is executed with the greatest possible elevation

volet either folding side compartment or wing of a triptych

volt a unit of electrical potential and electromotive force

volte a gait in which a horse moves sideways and turns around a center

volte (see **vault**)

voracious (see **veracious**)

voracity (see **veracity**)

voter (see **voder**)

vow (see **vau**)

voyager   a traveller
voyageur   a person who transports
   people and material to and from
   remote stations in the Northwest of
   America principally by boat

Group I

valiance - valiants
variance - variants
violet - violette
virous - virus

vitellin - vitelline
vomitous - vomitus

Group II

Veda   'vādə
Vedda   'vedə

vervel   'vərvəl
vervelle   'vər'vəl

virtu   ,vər'tü
virtue   'vərchü

W

Wa   a people in the northeastern
   states of Myanmar and adjoining
   parts of Yunnan province, China
wah   an expression of anger, disgust,
   or grief; a long-tailed Himalayan
   carnivore related to and closely
   resembling the American raccoon

WAACS   members of the Women's
   Army Auxiliary Corps
wacks   crackpots
WACS   members of the Women's
   Army Corps
wax   to increase in size; a natural or
   synthetic substance resembling
   beeswax
whacks   strikes with a smart or resounding blow; chops

wabble   a botfly larva that destroys
   squirrel testes
wobble   to move with an irregular
   rocking or staggering motion

wacks   (see WAACS)

WACS   (see WAACS)

waddle   to walk with short steps
   swinging the forepart of the body
   from side to side, as a duck
wattle   a fleshy process about the
head or neck of an animal; a fabrication of interwoven rods, poles,
   or branches used in building construction

waddy   a straight tapered throwing-
   stick used in hunting and war,
   especially by Australian aborigines
wadi   a bed or valley of a stream in
   arid regions of southwestern Asia
   and northern Africa

wade   to proceed slowly among
   things that hinder, as through water
wayed   broke or trained a horse to
   the road
weighed   determined the heaviness of
   an object; tested or balanced

waded   proceeded slowly among
   hindrances
waited   delayed or postponed until
   proper conditions occur
weighted   made heavy; relatively
   adjusted

wader   a person who steps in or
   through mediums that offer some
   resistance; a waterproof garment
   for wading
waiter   a person who attends, serves,

or waits on another; a tray on which something is carried

weighter a textile worker who increases the weight of yarns or fabrics by adding substances

wah (see **Wa**)

wailer a person who laments or cries
waler a rather large rugged saddle horse of mixed ancestry exported from Australia to India
whaler a person or ship employed in whaling

wails laments, weeps, or cries
Wales the peninsula on the western part of Great Britain
wales streaks or ridges made on the skin; extra thick strong planks in the side of a wooden ship
whales the largest (aquatic) mammals

wain a wagon or cart
wane to decrease in size or extent

waist a small part of the body between the ribs and hips
waste wilderness; useless consumption or expenditure

waister a usually green or broken-down seaman stationed in the waist of the ship
waster a spendthrift or squanderer

waited (see **waded**)

waiter (see **wader**)

waive to relinquish voluntarily
WAVE a woman serving in the U.S. Navy, especially during World War II
wave to flutter in a breeze; to flap; an arm gesture

waler (see **wailer**)

Wales and **wales** (see **wails**)

walk to move on foot
waulk to shrink and thicken woolen fabric by applying moisture, heat, friction, and pressure until the

fibers become felt

wallah a person who holds an important position in an organization or particular situation
wallow to roll or move oneself about in an indolent ungainly manner

wands slender metal or wood rods or staffs
wans causes to appear pale or sickly
wons basic monetary units of South Korea since 1962

wane (see **wain**)

wang (see **uang**)

wans (see **wands**)

want to lack; to desire
wont accustomed to doing something

wants (see **once**)

war an armed hostile conflict
wore attached to the body or clothing

ward a large hospital room; an administrative division of a municipality; a person under protection
warred engaged in armed hostile conflict

ware a manufactured or crafted article or articles
wear to attach to the body or clothing
weir an enclosure placed in a stream or inlet, often for capturing fish
wer the value set in Anglo-Saxon and Germanic law on the life of a person according to a fixed scale and paid as compensation to the kin of that person if slain
where at or in what place
where're the contraction of where are

wared took heed of or bewared of
where'd the contraction of where had or where did

wares merchandise
where's the contraction of where is, where does, or where has

wari any of various two-person games widely played in Africa and southern Asia with pebbles or stones

warree a white-lipped peccary

Warli a people of India inhabiting the region north of Bombay
whorly arranged or formed in coiled or spiral shapes

warn to put on guard or give notice
worn attached to the body or clothing; deteriorated by use

warred (see **ward**)

warree (see **wari**)

warren a place abounding in rabbits
warrin an Australian lorikeet

wart a horny projection on the skin
wort an infusion of malt fermented to form beer; a sweet edible European blueberry

wary keenly cautious or watchfully prudent
wherry a long light rowboat pointed at both ends

waste (see **waist**)

waster (see **waister**)

water an odorless tasteless liquid oxide of hydrogen (H_2O)
watter a light bulb or radio station having a specified wattage

waterie any of numerous chiefly Old World birds related to the pipits, especially the water wagtail
watery consisting of or filled with water

wats Buddhist temples in Thailand
watts measurements of electrical power equal to one absolute joule per second
whats things meant or referred to
what's the contraction of what is, what has, or what does

watter (see **water**)

wattle (see **waddle**)

watts (see **wats**)

waulk (see **walk**)

WAVE and **wave** (see **waive**)

wax (see **WAACS**)

way a path or road; a manner or style
Wei a Tatar dynasty in China during the 4th-6th centuries A.D.
weigh to determine heaviness; to test or balance
whey the watery part of milk separated from curd in making cheese

wayed (see **wade**)

we (see **oui**)

weak deficient in strength
week a sequence of seven days

weal a sound, healthy, or prosperous state
weel a wickerwork or slotted trap for eels
we'll the contraction of we will or we shall
wheal a steep-sided elevation characteristic of urticaria's lesions; a welt
wheel a circular frame attached to an axle on which it revolves

weald a heavily wooded area
w(h)ealed raised lines on the skin with a whip
wheeled revolved, rotated, or turned
wield to use an instrument with full power; to employ

wean to cause to cease to depend on the mother for nourishment
ween to believe, conceive, or imagine

weaner a device to prevent an animal from suckling
wiener a frankfurter

wear (see **ware**)

wearer a person who wears or carries something as a body covering
where're the contraction of where are

weaser   the American merganser

wheezer   a person who breathes with difficulty and with an audible sibilant or whistling sound

weather   an atmospheric state at a specific time and place

wether   a male sheep or goat castrated before sexual maturity

whether   a conjunction indicating a choice between alternatives

weave   to form by interlacing strands, as cloth with yarn or thread

we've   the contraction of we have

weaver   a person who interlaces strands of yarn or thread to make textiles

weever   an edible marine fish with upward-looking eyes

we'd   the contraction of we would or we had

weed   a noxious plant

wedder   a person who joins in marriage

wetter   a worker who wets the work in various manufacturing processes; more damp, moist, or humid

wedding   a marriage ceremony

wetting   moistening or soaking with water or other liquid

whetting   sharpening, as a tool or the appetite

wee   (see **oui**)

weed   (see **we'd**)

week   (see **weak**)

weel   (see **weal**)

ween   (see **wean**)

weeny   exceptionally tiny

wienie   a frankfurter (slang)

weep   to express deep sorrow by shedding tears

wheep   the drawn-out shrill cry or whistle of certain birds, as the

curlew or plover

weever   (see **weaver**)

Wei   (see **way**)

weigh   (see **way**)

weighed   (see **wade**)

weighted   (see **waded**)

weighter   (see **wader**)

weir   (see **ware**)

weir   an enclosure placed in a stream or inlet, often for capturing fish

we're   the contraction of we are

weird   eerie, uncanny, unearthly, or mysterious

weired   placed an enclosure or dam in a stream or inlet, often to capture fish

weld   to join closely or inseparably, as in uniting metallic parts by heating their edges to a fluid state

welled   rose to the surface in a copious stream; constructed with a well

we'll   (see **weal**)

welled   (see **weld**)

wells   holes sunk in the earth to a depth sufficient to reach water supplies

wels   very large elongated catfish of central and eastern European rivers

wen   a sebaceous cyst

when   at which or what time

wend   to proceed or travel

when'd   the contraction of when did

wends   proceeds or travels

wens   sebaceous cysts

when's   the contraction of when is, when does, or when has

wer   (see **ware**)

were   existed

whir(r)   a continuous fluttering sound made by something in rapid motion we're   (see weir)

wet   to soak or moisten with liquid
whet   to hone, sharpen, or make
   keen

wether   (see weather)

wetter   (see wedder)

wetting   (see wedding)

we've   (see weave)

whacks   (see WAACS)

whaler   (see waler)

whales   (see wails)

whats   (see wats)

what's   (see wats)

wheal   (see weal)

w(h)ealed   (see weald)

whee   (see oui)

wheel   (see weal)

wheeled   (see weald)

wheep   (see weep)

whees   expresses delight or exuberance
wheeze   a sibilant whistling sound
   caused by difficult or obstructed
   respiration

wheezer   (see weaser)

when   (see wen)

when'd   (see wend)

when's   (see wends)

where   (see ware)

where'd   (see wared)

wherefor   for which
wherefore   for what reason; an
   answer or statement that provides
   an explanation

where're   (see ware and wearer)

where's   (see wares)

wherry   (see wary)

whet   (see wet)

whether   (see weather)

whetting   (see wedding)

whew   (see hew)

whew   to make a half-formed whistling sound; an expression of
   amazement, relief, or discomfort
whoo   an expression of sudden excitement, relief, or astonishment
woo   to seek to gain or bring about;
   to solicit in love
Wu   a group of Chinese dialects
   spoken in the lower Yangtze valley

whey   (see way)

which   a word introducing a relative
   clause; what one(s) out of a group
witch   a woman practicing the black
   arts

whicker   to neigh or whinny
wicker   a rod for plaiting basketwork

whiff   a quick puff or slight gust of
   air
wiff   a wife (slang)

Whig   an American favoring independence from Great Britain during the Revolution
wig   artificial head hair; a toupee

Whiggery   the principles, policies,
   and practices associated with Whigs
wiggery   a business that deals in wigs

Whigling   a petty Whig
wiggling   tending to jiggle or oscillate; wriggly

whiled   passed time without boredom
   or in a pleasant manner
wild   not tamed or domesticated
wiled   enticed; lured by a magic spell

whines   utters a high-pitched plaintive or distressed cry
winds   twists, coils, or curls

wines   provides with fermented juice of grapes

whing   a sharp high-pitched ringing sound

wing   an organ or manufactured structure that enables aerial flight

whinny   to neigh, especially in a low or gentle fashion

Winnie   any of several bronze statuettes awarded annually by a professional group for fashion design

whins   particularly hards rocks; devices for raising ore or water from mines

winds   natural air movements

wins   gains victory in a contest

winze   a steeply inclined opening connecting one mine with another at a lower level

wynns   timber trucks or carriages

whiny   whining, querulous, or habitually complaining

winy   having the taste or qualities of wine

whirled   moved quickly around an axis; became giddy or dizzy

whorled   arranged in coiled or spiral shapes

world   the earthly state of human existence; the planet Earth; a planet, especially one inhabited

whirley   a crane free to rotate 360 degrees in picking up and depositing its load

whirly   exhibiting a rotary or whirling motion; a small whirlwind

wurley   the nest of the house-building rat of Australia; a native Australian hut

whir(r)   (see were)

whirred   moved rapidly with a vibrating sound

word   a written character or characters representing a spoken sound

whirtle   a perforated steel die

through which steel wires or tubes are drawn

whortle   a sweet edible European blueberry

whish   a rushing sound

wish   an unfulfilled desire or want

whist   a card game

wist   a unit of land area equal to about 16–18 acres

whit   the smallest of particles

wit   intellectual brilliance or astuteness of perception; humor; irony

white   colorless; free from spot or blemish

wight   a living creature

wite   a penal fine for serious crimes

whiter   more free from color; lighter or more palid in color

wider   more extensive or broader

whither   to what place; where

wither   to shrivel up

whitish   approaching being white or colorless

widdish   tending to be wide or broad

whittle   to cut or shape wood with a knife

wittol   a half-witted person

whittling   cutting chips from wood with as knife

witling   a person of little wit or understanding

whiz   to fly or move swiftly with a hissing or buzzing sound

wiz   one endowed with exceptional skill or able to achieve something held to be impossible

who   (see heugh)

whoa   (see Ho)

whoa   a command to a draft animal to stop or stand still

wo   a falconer's summons to a hawk or falcon

woe   a miserable or sorrowful state

whoaed commanded a draft animal to stop

woad a European perennial herb formerly grown for the blue coloring matter yielded by its leaves

whole (see **hole**)

whole-sail being a breeze or wind that permits the use of full or nearly full sail

wholesale relating to the sale of goods in quantity for resale; extensive or massive

wholly (see **holey**)

whomp a loud slap, crash, or crunch

womp an abrupt increase in the illumination of a television screen resulting from an abrupt increase in signal strength

whoo (see **heugh** and **whew**)

whoof a deep full snorting sound

woof threads that cross the warp in woven fabric; the weft

whoop (see **hoop**)

whore (see **hoar**)

whored (see **hoard**)

whorled (see **whirled**)

whorly (see **Warli**)

whortle (see **whirtle**)

whos (see **hoos**)

who's (see **hoos**)

whose (see **hoos**)

whump a bang or thump

wump(h) a heavy sound caused especially by a falling object

whys reasons or causes of something

wise sagacious or prudent

wyes things resembling the letter Y in shape; track arrangements with three switches and three legs for reversing the direction of an entire train

wicked evil, vicious, or vile

wicket a small gate or door; a grilled gate or window; a wire hoop used in croquet

wicker (see **whicker**)

wicket (see **wicked**)

widdish (see **whitish**)

wider (see **whiter**)

wield (see **weald**)

wiener (see **weaner**)

wienie (see **weeny**)

wiff (see **whiff**)

wig (see **Whig**)

wiggery (see **Whiggery**)

wiggling (see **Whigling**)

wight (see **white**)

wild (see **whiled**)

wiled (see **whiled**)

wilkeite a mineral consisting of an hydroxylapatite

Willkieite an adherent of Wendall Lewis Willkie, 1940 Republican candidate for the U.S. presidency

willeys textile machines with a revolving spike drum that opens and cleans cotton or wool

willies waybills for a loaded railroad car; a fit of nervousness or acute mental discomfort

Willkieite (see **wilkeite**)

windlass any of various machines for hoisting or hauling

windless marked by the absence of wind

windroad a pass for a current of air, often underground as in a mine

windrode a moored vessel riding with the force of the wind

windrowed raked hay into rows for drying before being rolled or baled

winds (see **whines** and **whins**)

wines (see **whines**)

wing (see **whing**)

Winnie (see **whinny**)

wins (see **whins**)

winy (see **whiny**)

winze (see **whins**)

wise (see **whys**)

wish (see **whish**)

wist (see **whist**)

wistaria a pale purple or light violet color
Wisteria a genus of chiefly Asiatic mostly woody vines

wit (see **whit**)

witch (see **which**)

wite (see **white**)

with a word to indicate connection, association, or relationship
withe a band consisting of a twisted twig

wither (see **whither**)

witling (see **whittling**)

wittol (see **whittle**)

wiz (see **whiz**)

wo (see **whoa**)

woad (see **whoaed**)

wobble (see **wabble**)

woe (see **whoa**)

womp (see **whomp**)

won (see **one**)

wons (see **wands**)

wont (see **want**)

wont accustomed to doing something

won't the contraction of will not

wonts (see **once**)

woo (see **whew**)

wood a hard fibrous substance making up the greater part of trees and shrubs
would used to express a wish, desire, or intent

woof (see **whoof**)

woold to wind a rope or chain around an item for strengthening
wooled bearing wool

word (see **whirred**)

wore (see **war**)

world (see **whirled**)

worm any of numerous relatively small, elongated, usually naked and soft-bodied animals resembling an earthworm
Würm the fourth and last stage of glaciation in Europe

worn (see **warn**)

worst most unfavorable, unpleasant, or reprehensible
wurst a sausage

wort (see **wart**)

would (see **wood**)

wrack (see **rack**)

wraith an apparition of a living person in his/her exact likeness seen usually just prior to the person's death
wraithe an expansible reed or comb for beaming and warping, in weaving

wrangle (see **rangle**)

wrapped (see **rapped**)

wrasse (see **rasse**)

wrath   (see rath)

wreak   (see reek)

wreck   (see rec)

wrecked   (see rect)

wrecks   (see recks)

wren   (see jen)

wrens   (see rends)

wrest   (see rest)

wretch   (see retch)

wrick   (see rick)

wried   (see ride)

wright   (see right)

wring   (see ring)

write   (see right)

writer   (see reiter)

writs   (see ritz)

wrote   (see rote)

wroth   (see rath)

wrought   (see rot)

wrung   (see rung)

wrys   (see rise)

Wu   (see whew)

wump(h)   (see whump)

wurley   (see whirley)

Würm   (see worm)

wurst   (see worst)

wyes   (see whys)

wynns   (see whins)

Group I

wedgie - wedgy
whirtle - wordle
wreathes - wreaths

Group I and II

warrantee   'wärən:tē
warranty   'wärəntē

Group II

wakan   wä'kän
walk-on   'wȯk‚än

walk   'wȯk
wok   'wäk

wallet   'wȯlət
wallette   wȯ'let

warehous   'wärə:haüz
warehouse   'wȯr‚haüs

warren   'wȯrən
warrin   'wȯrin

weakened   'wēkənd
weekend   'wē:kend

wolffish   'wu̇lf‚fish
wolfish   'wu̇lfish

--- X ---

x   (see ex)

xanthene   an isomeric compound that is the parent of the colored forms

of xanthene dyes

xanthine   a feebly basic crystalline nitrogenous compound that is found in animal tissue and plants

xanthin   a carotenoid pigment that is
soluble in alcohol
xanthine   a feebly basic crystalline
nitrogenous compound that is
found in animal tissue and plants

xanthine   (see xanthene)

xanthous   yellowish
Xanthus   an ancient city of Lycia
near the mouth of the Xanthus
river in southwestern Asia

xat   (see cat)

xenia   the effect of genes introduced
by a male nucleus on structures
other than the embryo; presents
given by ancient Greeks and
Romans to a guest or stranger
zinnia   a tropical American herb
having showy flower heads

Xiphias   a genus of large scombroid
fishes comprising the common
swordfish
Ziphius   a genus of nearly cosmopolitan beaked whales

xiphioid   resembling or related to the
genus Xiphias, a genus of large
scombroid fishes comprising the
common swordfish
ziphioid   relating to the Ziphiidae, a
family of toothed whales

xurel   (see jurel)

Group I and II

---

xenodocheum   ˌzenədəˈkēəm
xenodochium   ˌzenədəˈkīəm

---------------- Y ----------------

yabbi   a Tasmanian wolf
yabby   a small burrowing crayfish

yahoo   an uncouth or rowdy person
yahu   a scholarly transliteration of
the Hebrew tetragrammaton that
constitues a divine proper name,
such as Jehovah

yak   a laugh, joke, or gag; a large
ox of Tibet and central Asia
yock   to laugh in a boisterous or
unrestrained manner
yogh   a letter used in Middle English
to represent a palatal fricative

y'all   you-all, a direct address indicating two or more persons
yawl   a fore-and-aft rigged sailboat

Yap   one of the Caroline Islands in
the west Pacific Ocean
yap   to bark snappishly; to scold; to
chatter
yapp   a bookbinding style often used
for Bibles and hymnbooks

yar   characterized by speed and agil-
ity; nimble
yarr   corn spurrey, a small European
weed

yawl   (see y'all)

yawn   a deep intake of breath
through a wide open mouth usually
as an involuntary reaction to
fatigue or boredom
yon   yonder; an Indian tree yielding
very strong wood

ye   a second person pronoun still
used in selected religious faiths
yi   in Chinese ethical philosophy, the
faithful performance of one's
specified duties to society

yew   (see ewe)

yews   (see ewes)

yi   (see ye)

yock   (see yak)

yock   to laugh in a boisterous or unrestrained manner
yuck   an expression of rejection or disgust

yod   the voiced glide or spirant sound that is the first sound of the English word yes
yodh   the tenth letter of the Hebrew alphabet

yogh   (see yak)

yogh   a letter used in Middle English to represent a palatal fricative
yoke   a framework joining two draft animals at their necks for working together
yolk   a yellow sperhoidal mass of the egg of a bird or reptile (seldom yoke)

yon   (see yawn)

yore   a time long since past
your   belonging to you

you   (see ewe)

you'll   the contraction of you will or you shall
yule   Christmas

your   (see ewer and yore)

you're   (see ewer)

youse   (see ewes and ius)

yu   (see ewe)

Yucca and yucca   (see Uca)

yuck   (see yock)

yule   (see you'll)

Yuman   (see human)

Group II

Yankee   ˈyaŋkē
Yanqui   ˈyäŋkē

Z

zabra   (see sabra)

zacs   Caucasian ibexes
zax   a tool used for trimming and puncturing roofing slates

zax   (see zacs)

zayin   the seventh letter of the Hebrew alphabet
Zion   the Jewish homeland that is symbolic of Jewish national aspiration

Zea   the genus of large grasses having broad ribbon-shaped leaves
zea   the fresh styles and stigmas of Indian corn formerly used as a diuretic
Zia   a Keres people occupying a pueblo in northwestern New Mexico

Zilla   a genus of thorny plants of northern Africa
zillah   a district or administrative division in India

zinc   a bluish white crystalline bivalent metallic element
zink   a Renaissance woodwind instrument used especially with church chorale music

zinnia   (see xenia)

Zion   (see zayin)

ziphioid   (see xiphioid)

Ziphius   (see Xiphias)

zoo   a collection of animals
Zu   an evil storm-god, represented as a black bird

Homographs

A

aba ɑ'bä a loose sleeveless Arabian outer garment
aba 'ɑbə a telescopic instrument

abaisse ə'bāsā a thin undercrust of pastry
abaissé ə'bās in heraldry, turned downward, as a bird's wingtips

abate ə'bāt to diminish
abate 'äbä.tä a title of respect for any ecclesiastic without other distinguishing title

acedia ‚ɑsə'dēə an Atlantic ocean flatfish
acedia ə'sēdēə sloth or apathy

acerous 'ɑsərəs needle-shaped, as pine leaves
acerous ‚ā'sērəs having no antennae or horns

actus 'ɑktəs the right to drive a beast or a vehicle over another's land
actus 'äk.tús a mental or spiritual act done

adage 'ɑdij a saying usually embodying a common experience
adage ɑdääzh an easy graceful manner; in music, adagio

Aedes ā'ēdēz a large cosmopolitan genus of mosquitoes
aedes 'ēdēz a building for worship in Roman antiquity not formally consecrated by the Augurs

Afar 'ä.fär an Hamitic people of northeast Ethiopia
afar ə'fär from or at a great distance

Agama ə'gāmə a genus of Old World terrestrial lizards
agama ə'gāmə a lizard of the genus Agama
agama 'ögəmə a class of tantric treatises accepted as scripture in Hinduism and Buddhism

agape ə'gāp wide open
agape ä'gä.pä spontaneous self-giving love

agnostic ɑg'nästik a person who doubts the existence of a god
agnostic ɑg:nöstik an inability to recognize familiar objects by eye, ear, or touch

ala 'ālə a winglike process
ala 'älä a large Sumerian drum

Alans 'ālɑnz a Scythian people in pre–Slavic Russia and the Black Sea regions
alans 'ɑlɑnz in heraldry, short-eared dogs

Alas 'ä.läs an Indonesian people of northern Sumatra
alas ə'lɑs an expression of sorrow, pity, or concern

alba 'älbə a Provençal lyric dealing with lovers parting at dawn
alba 'ɑlbə the white matter of the brain and spinal cord

alem 'ä.lem a shrub yielding medicinal fruit
alem 'ɑl.em the imperial standard of the Ottoman empire

allege ə'lej to assert without proof
allège ɑ'lezh a thinned part of a wall

allongé :ɑ.lō^n:zhā a ballet movement with both arms and one leg extended to form a long line
allonge ɑ'lō^{n}zh paper attached to a bill of exchange for additional endorsements

allure ə'lúr to lure, sway, or entice with some tempting appeal
allure 'ɑl.úr a passagewalk, as the walk along one side of a cloister

ally 'ɑ.lī someone or something associated with another, as a helper or supporter

ally ˈȯlē a superior playing marble

Aloe ˈȯlə.wē a genus of succulent chiefly southern African plants

aloe ˈȯlō a pale green color

alum ˈȯləm a double sulfate of aluminum having a sweet-sour astringent taste

alum əˈləm a graduate or former student of an educational institution (by shortening **alumna** or **alumnus**)

alvar ˈȯl.vär southern Indian Vaishnara saints of the 7th and 9th centuries

alvar ˈȯl.vär mosses growing on overlying Scandinavian limestone

ambos ˈȯm.bōz large pulpits or reading desks in early churches and in contemporary Greek and Balkan churches

ambos ˈȯm.bäs the middle of a chain of three small bones (the anvil) in the ear of mammals

amental ˈȯmənt⁽ᵊ⁾l resembling an indeterminate spicate inflorescence bearing scaly bracts and apetalous unisexual flowers

amental ˈȯ.ment⁽ᵊ⁾l devoid of mind

anay äˈnī a white ant or termite

anay ȯˈnī a Guatemalan fruit resembling the avocado

ani äˈnē any of several black cuckoos with arched laterally compressed bills found from tropical America to the southern U.S.

ani ˈȯnī the posterior openings of alimentary canals

anon əˈnän at another time

anon äˈnōn the sweet pulpy fruit of the sweetsop

Anti ˈäntē an Arawakan people of the upper valley of the Ucayali river in eastern Peru

anti ˈȯn.tē one who is opposed

Apache əˈpächē an Athapaskan people of Arizona, New Mexico, and northern Mexico

Apache əˈpȯsh a member of a gang of criminals, especially in Paris, noted for their violent crimes

ape ˈāp a monkey; to imitate

ape ˈäpā an herbaceous ornamental plant of Hawaii

aper ˈāpər a person that imitates or mimics

aper ˈäpər a European wild boar

apolysis äˈpȯlē.sēs a concluding prayer in the Eastern Church

apolysis əˈpäləsəs the shedding of segments in the neck area of a tapeworm

appropriate əˈprōprē.āt to take possession of; to take without permission or consent

appropriate əˈprōprēət suitable of fitting for a particular purpose

arête əˈrāt a sharp crested mountain ridge

arete .arəˈtā good qualities that make character

Arkansas ˈärkən.sȯ a state in south central U.S.

Arkansas .ärˈkanzəs a river flowing through east and southeast Kansas, Oklahoma, Arkansas, and into the Mississippi River

arras ˈarəs a wall hanging or hanging screen of tapestry

arras ˈä.räs a gift made by a husband to his wife upon marriage in Spanish cultures

arrive :arēːvā a person who has risen rapidly to success, power, or fame

arrive əˈrīv to reach a destination

As ˈäs in music, A-flat

as ˈäs a Persian card game resembling poker

As ˈas a chief god of pagan Scandinavia

as az like

asana ˈäsənə a manner of sitting in the practice of yoga

asana ˌäsəˈnä any of several timber trees of the genus Pterocarpus

ascon ȯskōⁿ an Haitian voodoo fetish

ascon ˈɑˌskän a sponge

aspirate ˈɑspəˌrāt to draw or withdraw by suction; to pronounce with an h-sound as the initial element

aspirate ˈɑspərət silent but not preceded by liaison or elision

aspire əˈspīər to seek to attain or accomplish something

aspiré ˌɑspəˈrā initial in the orthography of a word before which elision and liaison do not occur (without respect to **h** in French)

assai äˈsī in music, very

assai ːäsäːē a slender pinnate-leaved palm

assemblé ȯsäⁿblā a ballet movement

assemble əˈsembəl to bring together

ate ˈāt consumed food

ate ˈäd·ē a blind impulse or reckless ambition

Atis ˈädēz members of the predominantly pagan Negritoid people of Panay, Philippines

atis əˈtēs a monkshood found in the Himalayas; any of several trees including the sweetsop

Atta ˈɑdə a New World genus of leaf-cutting chiefly tropical ants often very destructive to crops

atta ˈäˌtä unsorted wheat flour or meal, in India

attribute ˈɑtrəˌbyüt a quality or characteristic belonging to a thing or person

attribute əˈtribyüt to explain as caused or brought about by

August ˈȯgəst the eighth month of the Gregorian calendar

august ȯːgəst marked by majestic dignity

august ˈȯu̇ˌgu̇st a clown, typically one suggesting in appearance or action an awkward waiter

aval ɑˈvɑl a written engagement by one not a drawer, acceptor, or endorser of a note or bill of exchange that it will be paid at maturity

aval ˈāvɑl pertaining to a grandparent or grandparents

Aves ˈävāz Ave Marias or salutations to the Virgin Mary

aves ˈävāz salutations of greeting or leave-taking

Aves ˈävēz a class of Vertebrata including all fossil and recent birds

awa ˈäwä a large active silvery herbivorous food fish widely distributed in the warm parts of the Pacific and Indian oceans

awa ˈävə an Australasian shrubby pepper from whose crushed roots an intoxicating beverage is made

awing ˈȯiŋ frightening or terrifying

awing əˈwiŋ flying

axes ˈɑksəs cutting tools

axes ˈɑkˌsēz straight lines around which things rotate

aye ˈī an affirmative vote

aye ˈā for an indefinite time

Group I

absent
abstract
abuse
acerbate
affectionate
aged
agglomerate
agglutinate
alternate
approximate
arithmetic
arsenic

B

bakkie ˈbä.ki excrement
bakkie ˈbäki anything filthy or distasteful, as spoiled soup or rancid butter

balance bəˈläⁿ:sā a ballet movement
balance ˈbaləns a measuring device; equilibrium; to maintain a state of equipoise

ballet ˈbalət a part-song often in stanzas with a refrain
ballet ˈba.lā artistic dancing

ban ˈban to prohibit
ban ˈbän a provincial-military governor of former times in Hungary, Croatia, or Slavonia

banal ˈbänᵊl lacking originality or freshness
banal ˈbänᵊl relating to a provincial governor in Hungary with military powers during war

banged ˈband struck against or bumped
banged ˈbanjd lounged about or loafed

BAR ˈbē.āˈär a Browning automatic rifle
bar ˈbär a straight piece of metal or wood; to confine or shut out

Baré ˈbä.rā an Arawkan people in northern Brazil and Venezuela
bare ˈbar exposed to view

Baris ˈbärēz members of a Nilotic Negro people in the Sudan
baris ˈbärəs a Balinese spear or warrior's dance

barrage bəˈräⁱzh a massive concentrated and continuous discharge or shower of weaponry, speech, or writing
barrage ˈbärij an artificial dam to increase water depth or direct it into a channel

barre ˈbär a handrail for ballet dancers during exercises
barré bäˈrā a striped pattern in fabrics; all strings on an instrument stopped by the forefinger laid across them

bases ˈbā.sēz foundations or principal components; the actual yields on bonds; original costs of property used in computing capital gains or losses for income tax purposes
bases ˈbāsəz compounds capable of reacting with an acid to form salts; the corner bags, including homeplate, in baseball

basis ˈbāsəs a fundamental ingredient or essence
basis ˈbä.sēz fermented Philippine beverages

bass ˈbās a person or instrument able to create the lowest pitched sounds
bass ˈbas an edible spiny-finned fish

Baule .bäüˈlā a people of the Ivory Coast region of West Africa renowned for their carved wooden statuary
baule ˈból or ˈbōl the theoretical amount of nitrogren or a mineral necessary to produce one-half the maximum possible crop yield

begum ˈbōgəm a high-ranking Muslim woman, especially a widow
begum bəˈgəm to smear, soil, or clog with a gummy substance

bend ˈbend to turn from a straight line
bend ˈbē:end the end of a railway car on which the handbrake is located

bene ˈbēnē well
bene ˈbene a wild hog of New Guinea

benet ˈbēnet to ensnare or capture with a net

benet ˈbenet the third of the four minor orders in the Roman Catholic Church; an exorcist who ranks just below an acolyte

Beni ˈbenē a Negro people of southern Nigeria

beni ˈbeni sesame oil used primarily for making soap

berg ˈbərg an iceberg

berg ˈberk a mountain

Bern(e) ˈbərn the capital of Switzerland

berne ˈbernə a botfly that attacks mammals in warm parts of the Americas

Beta ˈbētā a small genus of glabrous succulent herbs, including chard and the beet

beta ˈbetā the second letter of the Greek alphabet

beurre ˈbər buttered, as "peas au buerre"

beurré ˈbü.ri any of many varieties of pear having soft and melting flesh

bin ˈbēn a four-stringed musical instrument of India with a long bamboo fingerboard

bin ˈbin a box or crib used for storage

binocle ˈbinə.kəl binoculars

binocle ˈbīnək.əl a card game of the bezique family

birling ˈbərliŋ the sport of logrolling

birling ˈbirliŋ a chieftain's barge used in the Hebrides

blither ˈblīthər more light-minded, casual, or heedless

blither ˈblithər to talk foolishly or nonsensically

blond ˈbländ flaxen, golden, light auburn, or pale yellow hair; pale white or rosy white skin

blond ˈblȯn a concentrated meat juice or stock added to a sauce to strengthen or color it

bola ˈbōlə a weapon consisting of two or more heavy balls or stones attached to the ends of a cord that is hurled at an animal and entangling it

bola ˈbōlȯ either of two malvaceous tropical trees

bole ˈbōl any cylindrically shaped object or mass

bole ˈbō.lē a unit of momentum equal to one gram moving at one centimeter per second

Bologna bəˈlōnyə a city in north central Italy

bologna bəˈlōnē a large moist sausage; pretentious nonsense (often baloney, but seldom bəˈlonyə)

bombé bämːbā having an outward swelling curve in furniture

bombe ˈbäm a frozen molded dessert

Bon ˈbȯn a pre–Buddhist animist religion of Tibet; a popular Japanese festival

bon ˈbän the broad or kidney bean; the stiff dried hand-cleaned but not completely degummed fiber of ramie

bore ˈbȯr to pierce or drill a hole

bore ˈbȯ.rē a lively old French dance tune in duple meter

borne ˈbȯrn endured or tolerated

borné bȯrːnā lacking scope or variety

bouché büːshā stopped with the hand, as in French horn playing

bouche ˈbüsh a slit in the edge of a medieval shield; a bushing made of metal or other material

boule ˈbül a game similar to roulette; a pear-shaped mass of some substance formed synthetically in a Verneuil furnace

boule ˈbülē a legislative council of ancient Greece

bourgeois ˈbůrzh.wȧ a middle-class person

bourgeois bərˈjȯis an old size of approximately 9-point type

bow ˈbaú to bend down; the forward part of a ship or boat
bow ˈbō a weapon used to propel an arrow; an implement used to play a stringed musical instrument

bower ˈbaúər a covered place in a garden made with tree boughs or intertwined vines
bower ˈbōər a musician who performs with a bow on a stringed instrument

Brava ˈbrävə a descendant of immigrants from the Cape Verde islands, resident especially on Cape Cod and around New Bedford, Massachusetts
brava ˈbrävä a shout of approval or approbation in applauding a woman

broché brō:shō woven with a raised figure
broche ˈbrōsh a shuttle used in hand-weaving tapestry

Brut ˈbrüt a medieval chronicle of Britain
brut ˈbrǖt very dry, as of champagne

buffet ˈbəfət a blow; the vibration of an airplane
buffet :bə:fā a counter for refreshments and food

bund ˈbənd an embanked thoroughfare along a river or the sea used for business or as an esplanade
bund ˈbůnt a grouping for some evil purpose (slang)

Bunter ˈbůntər relating to the lowest division of the European Triassic
bunter ˈbəntər a gripping device for a planing machine; a baseball player who bats or taps the ball lightly into the infield

bure ˈbürō a large house in the Fiji Islands
bure ˈbyůr a moderate yellowish brown color

buro ˈbyürō the policy-forming committee of the Communist party of the former U.S.S.R.
buro ˈbürō a Philippine dish of fish prepared with boiled rice and spicy seasonings

Group I

bacchanal
baton
beloved
blessed

C

Cajun ˈkājən one of a people of mixed white, Indian, and Negro ancestry in Alabama and adjoining sections of Mississippi
cajun kəˈhün a West Indian fiber plant

cala ˈkälə a picnic ham, a shoulder of pork with much of the butt removed commonly smoked and often boned
cala kəˈlä a Creole fried cake made mainly of rice

Caliana kälˈyänə an Indian people of Venezuela

calianá :kälyə:nä a Tupi-Guaranian people of northeastern Brazil

Canada ˈkänədə a country in North America
canada kənˈyädə a small canyon or creek

canal kəˈnäl an artificial waterway designed for navigation, irrigation, or drainage
canal kəˈnäl a waterspout or eaves trough

canard kə'närd a fabricated report
canard kånår the flesh of a duck used as food

Canarian kə'nerēən a native or inhabitant of the Canary Islands
Canarian ,kä'nyäriən pertaining to a minor linguistic family of South American Indians, comprising the extinct Canaris

canon 'kanən an ecclesiastical law or rule of doctrine or discipline enacted by a council
canon kä'nōn the zither, a musical instrument consisting of a shallow soundboard overlaid with 30 to 40 strings

Canton 'kantᵊn a city in Ohio
Canton 'kan,tän a Chinese city
canton 'kantᵊn to divide into parts

cape 'kā,pē a judicial writ, now abolished, relative to a plea of lands or tenements
cape 'kāp an extension of land jutting out into the water; a sleeveless outer garment

capo 'kāpō a bar or movable nut attached to the fingerboard of a guitar or other fretted instrument to uniformly raise the pitch of all the strings
capo 'kap,ō or 'kä,pō the chief of a branch of the Mafia

Cara 'kärə an ancient Indian people of northern Ecuador
cará kə'rä a tropical American yam with small yellow-skinned edible tubers

carbon 'kär,bən a nonmetallic chiefly tetravalent element
carbon kär'bōn a Guatemalan timber tree with reddish wood

Cassia 'kasēə a genus of herbs, shrubs, and trees native to warm regions
cassia 'kashə any of the coarser varieties of cinnamon bark

Cassis 'kasəs a genus of mollusks comprising forms with a very large body whorl
cassis ka'sēs a syrupy liquor of low alcoholic strength made from black currants

cat 'kät a shrub cultivated by the Arabs for its leaves which act as a stimulant narcotic when chewed or used in tea
cat 'kat a member of the family Felidae

cave 'kav the sum which each player puts on the table at the beginning of play in such card games as brelan and bouillote
cave 'kāv a hollowed-out chamber in the earth

cay 'kē a small low island or emergent reef
cay 'kī a monkey of the genus Cebus

cello 'chelō a stringed instrument
cello 'selō made of cellophane

cénacle sānåkl a philosophical, literary, or artistic group
cenacle 'senəkəl a retreat house

centum 'sentəm a hundred
centum 'kentəm belonging to the Indo-European language family

Cete 'sē,tē an order of aquatic mammals, including whales
cete 'sēt a group of badgers

Cha-Cha 'shä,shä one of a group of poor whites of French ancestry in the Virgin Islands
cha-cha 'chä,chä a fast rhythmic ballroom dance of Latin-American origin

Cham 'chäm a people in central coastal Annam linguistically related to the Cambodians
cham 'kam a local chieftan, especially in Afghanistan, Iran, and some areas of central Asia

Chama ˈkāmə a genus of eulamellibranchiate bivalve mollusks of warm and tropical seas
Chama ˈchämə a Panoan people of northeastern Peru

Chamar chəˈmär a member of a low Indian caste whose occupation is leatherworking
chamar ˈchəmər a fan typically made of a yak's tail or peacock feathers

chap ˈchap a fellow; sore roughening of the skin
chap ˈchäp a jaw or the fleshy covering of a jaw

chargé shär:zhō a chargé d'affaires
charge ˈchärj an instruction; an accusation; an expenditure

chassé shɑ:sō a dance or figure skating step
chasse ˈshäs a saint's shrine

chay ˈchī the root of an East Indian herb that yields a red dye
chay ˈshō a light carraige or pleasure cart

chebac chēˈbek a xebec, a Mediterranean sailing ship with a long overhanging bow and stern
chebac shəˈbek the least flycatcher

chela ˈkēlə a claw, as on a crab or lobster
chela ˈchōlä a disciple

chi ˈkī the 22nd letter of the Greek alphabet
chi ˈchē the vital life force in the body supposedly regulated by acupuncture

chil ˈchil an Indian kite (a bird)
chil ˈchēl the cheer pine

chimere shəˈmir a loose sleeveless robe
chimere kīˈmir a fabrication of the mind

China ˈkēnə a large genus of trees native to the Andean region of northwestern South America

China ˈchīnə a country in Asia
china ˈchīnə vitreous porcelain wares

chiné shəˈnā having a mottled pattern of supposed Chinese fashion
chine ˈchīn cut through the backbone

Choco chəˈkō a people of northwestern Colombia and Panama
choco ˈchäkō an Australian conscript in World War II

Chol ˈchōl an Indian people of northern Chiapas, Mexico
chol ˈchäl a desolate plain, in central Asia

chose ˈshōz a piece of personal property
chose ˈchōz selected

Chosen :chō.sen the former official name of Korea
chosen ˈchōzᵊn marked to receive special favor

choux ˈshüz soft cabbage-shaped ornaments or rosettes of fabric used in women's wear
choux ˈshü darlings, used as a term of endearment

civet ˈsivət a substance found in a pouch of a true civet cat
civet sēvō a highly seasoned game stew

classes ˈklɑsəs social ranks; denominations
classes ˈklɑ.sēz ecclesiastical governing bodies of a district

close ˈklōz to shut or terminate
close ˈklōs near; compact

closer ˈklōsər nearer; more compact
closer ˈklōzər a sewing-machine operator who sews the final seams; the last stone completing a horizontal course

Coalite ˈkō.līt a smokeless fuel made by heating bituminous coal in a retort
coalite ˈkōə.līt to unite or associate

coax ˈkōks to persuade or influence

coax kō:ɑks a coaxial transmission line in which one conductor is centered inside and insulated from an outer metal tube that serves as a second conductor

coif ˈkwäf a manner of arranging the hair

coif ˈkȯif a cap covering the sides of the head like a small hood

colla ˈkd̶lə necks or necklike parts or processes

colla ˈkōlyə a period of rainy windy weather from the southwest in the Philippines

collect kəˈlekt to bring together

collect ˈkäl ikt a short prayer during church service

colleter kəˈlēdər one of the mucilage-secreting hairs that clothes many plant surfaces

colleter ˈkälədər a worker who attaches the inner coil of a watch hairspring to a collet for assembly to the balance wheel

colon kəˈlōn a colonial farmer, planter, or plantation owner

colon ˈkōlən part of the large intestine that extends from the cecum to the rectum; the punctuation mark ":"

comal ˈkōməl in botany, having or being an assemblage of branches forming a leafy crown

comal kōˈmäl a griddle of earthenware, metal, or a flat slab of sandstone

combine kəmˈbīn to unite

combine ˈkäm.bīn a harvesting machine

come ˈkōm or ˈkúm the dried rootlets produced in malting grain

come ˈkəm to move toward something or advance

comes ˈkəmz moves toward something

comes ˈkō.mēz a Roman Catholic service book; the answer in a fugue

comes ˈkōmz dried rootlets produced in malting grain

commit ˈkämət a card game

commit kəˈmit to obligate to take some action

commune kəˈmyün to receive Communion by partaking of the Eucharist

commune ˈkä.myün a small group of people living together

comport kəmˈpōrt conduct or behavior

comport ˈkäm.pōrt a bowl-shaped dish

compose kəmˈpōz to calm, settle, or tranquilize; to create by mental or artistic labor

composé ˈkȯn.pōzā combining harmonious colors or tones

compress kəmˈpres to reduce the size, duration, or degree of concentration by pressure

compress ˈkäm.pres a covering of folded cloth applied and held firmly by a bandage over a wound

concha ˈkäŋkə the plain semidome of an apse

concha ˈkänchə a metal disk, usually shell-shaped and silver, used as decoration on clothing and harness

Concord ˈkäŋkərd the capital of New Hampshire

concord ˈkän.kȯrd or ˈkäŋ.kȯrd a state of agreement

concord ˈkənˈkȯrd to act together

conduct ˈkändəkt a standard of personal behavior

conduct kənˈdəkt to manage, control, or direct

confect kənˈfekt to put together; to prepare

confect ˈkän.fekt a confection consisting of a solid center that is coated with layers of sugar

conglomerate kənˈglämərət in zoology, irregularly grouped in spots, such as eyes

conglomerate kənˈglämə.rāt to form into a mass or coherent whole

conjure ˈkänjər to call forth or send away by magic arts
conjure kənˈju̇r to entreat earnestly or solemnly; to beseech

conjuror ˈkänjərər a person who practices magic arts, legerdemain, and illusion
conjuror ˌkänˈjərər a person bound by a common oath with others; a coswearer

connex ˈkäniks constituting one syntactical unit
connex ˈkäneks the infinity of points and lines in mathematics

conserve kənˈsərv to keep in a sound or safe state
conserve ˈkän.sərv a candied fruit preserve

console kənˈsōl to comfort
console ˈkän.sōl a cabinet or panel

consummate känsəmət extremely skilled and accomplished
consummate ˈkänsə.māt to complete marital union by the first act of sexual intercourse after marriage

conte ˈkōnt a short tale, especially of adventure
conté ˈkōn:tā a hard crayon made of graphite and clay

content kənˈtent pleased or gratified
content ˈkän.tent substance or subject matter

contract ˈkän.trakt to enter into with mutual obligations; an agreement or covenant
contract kənˈtrakt to shorten or draw together

converse kənˈvers to engage in conversation
converse ˈkän.vərs a thing or idea that is opposite another

convert kənˈvərt to exchange property or money for a specified equivalent
convert ˈkän.vərt a person that is per-

suaded or converted to a religious faith or to a particular belief, attitude of mind, or principle

convict kənˈvikt to find or declare guilty of an offense or crime
convict ˈkän.vikt any of various striped or barred fishes

coop ˈku̇p a small enclosure for small animals
coop ˈkō.äp a group working for mutual benefit; a cooperative

corselet ˈkȯrslət the hard prothorax of a beetle
corselet ˌkȯrsə:let a foundation garment combining girdle and brassiere

couch ˈkau̇ch an article of furniture for sitting or reclining
couch ˈküch a board covered with flannel on which sheets of handmade paper are pressed

coupe ˈkü p a dessert; a closed two-door automobile with one seating compartment
coupe küˈpā a ballet step

couped ˈkü pt in heraldry, cut off short at the ends so as not to extend to the edges of the field
couped ˈküd executed a bridge coup in playing a hand

cover ˈkəvər something that protects, shelters, or guards
cover ˈkōvər a person who lives in a small sheltered inlet or bay

crabbed ˈkrabd moved sideways or in a diagonal manner
crabbed krabəd difficult to understand or read

crochet krōˈshā needlework consisting of interlocked looped stitches
crochet ˈkrächet one of three secondary folds of the crests of lophodont molar teeth

crooked ˈkru̇kt turned or bent from a straight line, as a crooked neck
crooked ˈkru̇kəd fraudulent or dishonest

crotal ˈkrōdᵊl a small spherical rattle on a harness

crotal ˈkrädᵊl a reddish brown color

crus ˈkrüz French vineyards that produce wine grapes

crus ˈkrüs the part of the hind limb between the thigh and ankle

cube ˈkyüb a regular solid having six equal square sides

cube ˈkyü.bä any of several tropical American shrubs or climbers used as fish poisons

Cuclus ˈkükələs the type genus of Cuculidae comprising the typical cuckoos

cuculus kyüˈkələs the anterior dorsal shield of the cephalothorax in pseudoscorpions

curate ˈkyu̇rət a person who has the care of souls

curate kyu̇ˈrāt to act as curator of

curé kyəˈrā a parish priest

cure ˈkyu̇r to heal; to age or ripen

cussed ˈkəst cursed

cussed ˈkəsəd obstinate or cantankerous

cutin ˈkət.in something inserted

cutin ˈkyütᵊn the insoluble water-impermeable complex aggregate of waxes, soaps, and higher alcohols

Group I

canal
certificate
cleanly
combat
comex
commune
compassionate
concatenate
concinnate
concrete
confederate
confine
congress
conscript
consort
construct
convict
corporate
curate

D

Dago ˈdägō a member of a Negro tribe formerly the most powerful in Darfur

dago ˈdāgō a person of Italian or Spanish birth or descent, usually considered offensive

dah ˈdä a large Burmese knife; a dash in radio and telegraphic code

dah ˈda a Negro nurse

dancetté dan:sed·ā in heraldry, having usually three large indentations

dancette danˈset a zigzag patterned architectural molding

dauphiné :do̅fə:nā mashed potatoes shaped into balls and fried

dauphine do̅ˈfēn a dauphin's wife

decanal dəˈkanᵊl relating to a dean

decanal ˈdekə.nol a high-boiling liquid aldehyde

denier dəˈnīər a person who disavows or contradicts

denier ˈdenyər a unit of fineness for silk, rayon, or nylon yarn

desert dəˈzərǀt a reward or punishment deserved or earned
desert ˈdezert a relatively barren tract

devise dəˈvīz to develop a plan
devise dōˈvēzə foreign exchange in readily available form

diffuse dəˈfyüz to spread out
diffuse dəˈfyüs wordy; unconcentrated or scattered

Diné dəˈnā an Athapaskan people of northern New Mexico and Arizona (also called Navaho)
dine ˈdīn to eat a meal

dit ˈdit a dot in telegraphic code
dit ˈdē a short usually didactic poem in French literature

dive ˈdīv to plunge into water headfirst; to fall precipitously
dive ˈdē.vā prima donnas

Dives ˈdī.vēz a rich man
dives ˈdīvz plunges into water headfirst; falls precipitously; nightspots, often disreputable

do ˈdü to perform
do ˈdō the first tone of the diatonic scale

does ˈdōz adult females of various mammals, as deer and rabbits
does ˈdəz performs or acts

Dom ˈdōm a member of a Hindu caste of untouchables
dom ˈdōm the doom palm, a large African fan palm important as a soil stabilizer in desert regions
dom ˈdäm an address of a dignitary of certain monastic orders

dos ˈdōz the first tones of the diatonic scale
dos ˈdōs property settled by a husband on his spouse at the time of marriage

doublé dü:blō a bookbinding made with ornamental lining
double ˈdəbəl having a twofold character or relation

dove ˈdōv plunged into water headfirst; fell precipitously
dove ˈdəv a bird

drawer ˈdrōr a sliding box or receptacle
drawer ˈdrȯər a person that draws, as a draftsman or wire-former

dulce ˈdülsā a sweet Spanish wine; sweetmeat or candy
dulce ˈdəls any of several coarse red seaweeds found principally in northern latitudes and used as a food condiment

dun ˈdən dark or gloomy; to ask repeatedly for an overdue payment
dun ˈdün a fortified residence in Scotland and Ireland

Durban ˈdürbən a Mongol people in the western part of the Mongolian plateau
Durban ˈdərbən a city in the Union of South Africa

Group I

degenerate
deliberate
desolate
determinate
devote
differentiate
digest
dimidiate
disconcert
discriminate
divaricate
divorce
dona

E

effacé :efə:sā a ballet movement
efface ə'fōs to cause to disappear

effuse e'fyüz to flow out
effuse e:fyüs lips of certain shells being separated by a gap

elaborate əlŏbərə̇t marked by complexity or ornateness; intricate
elaborate əlŏbə.rāt to alter the chemical makeup of a foodstuff to that which is more suited to bodily needs

Elater 'elədər the type genus of Elateridae, comprising the beetles
elater 'elədər any beetle of the family Elateridae
elater ē'lādər a person who raises the spirits of or inspires

elegant 'eləgənt in pharmacy, pleasant in taste, attractive in appearance, and free from objectionable order
elegant ōlōgää^n a fashionable man; a dandy

Empire 'äm.piər the color cadmium green; furniture characterized by classic and oriental motives; clothing characteristic of the French Directoire style
empire 'em.piər extended territory usually comprising a group of nations, states, or people under the domination of a single sovereign power

engage ən'gōj to come in contact with or interlock
engagé 'äŋgä'zhä committed to or supportive of a cause

entrance 'en·trəns a place or passage for admission or penetration
entrance ən·'trɑns to put in a trance; to carry away with emotion

epicrisis :epē:krīsə̇s a secondary crisis
epicrisis ə'pikrəsə̇s an analytical summary of a medical case history

erg 'ərg an absolute unit of work in the centimeter-gram-second system (seldom 'erg)
erg 'erg a desert region of shifting sand

ergotism 'ergə.tizəm logical or sophisticated reasoning
ergotism 'ergəd.izəm a toxic condition produced by eating grain products or grasses infected with ergot fungus

Eta 'ā.tä an outcast class formerly segregated in Japan
eta 'ādə the seventh letter of the Greek alphabet

eve 'ēv evening (by shortening)
Eve 'ā.vä a Negro people of Ghana, Togo, and border regions of Dahomey

Even 'ā.wən a member of a Siberian people living in northeast Russia
even 'ēvən flat or level; truly or indeed
even 'ēv^{ə}m in knitting, without change by increasing or decreasing

evening 'ēvniŋ the latter part and close of the day, and the early part of darkness and night
evening 'ēvəniŋ making a surface smooth or uniform

Ewe 'ā.wä a Negro people of Ghana, Togo, and Dahomey
ewe 'yü a female sheep, goat, or smaller antelope

Group I

effeminate
elegant
essay
excuse
exenterate
expose

F

file 'fīl a hardened steel smoothing
tool; to arrange in a particular
order
filé fə'lā powdered young sassafras
leaves

fine 'fīn a monetary penalty; superior
in character; minute
fine 'fēnā the finish or end
fine fēn an ordinary French brandy

flageolet :flɑjə:let or :flɑjə:lāt a
small flute resembling a treble
recorder
flageolet flɑzhôlā a green kidney
bean of France

fleer 'flēər a person who runs away
fleer 'fliər to laugh at contemptu-
ously

flower 'flaůər the part of a seed plant
that normally bears reproductive
organs
flower 'flōər a river, stream, or other
flowing body of liquid

formal 'fôrməl following or in accord
with established custom, rule, or
form
formal fôr'mɑl any acetal derived
from formaldehyde and an alcohol

forme 'fôrm a pattern for the upper
part of a shoe; a low bench on
which shoemakers formerly sat
when working
formé 'fōr,mā arms of a cross being
narrow at the center and expanding
toward the ends, as a maltese cross

forte 'fôrt a person's strong point
forte 'fôr|d·ā in music, loudly

fourchette 'fůr,shet a small fold of
membrane connecting the labia
minora in the posterior part of the
vulva
fourchette 'fôr,shet the shaped piece
used for the sides of the fingers of
a glove

fourchette :fůrshə:tā in heraldry,
having the end of each arm divided
so as to terminate in a V

frappe 'frɑp an iced and flavored
semiliquid mixture served in glasses
frappe frɑ'pā a ballet movement in
which the free foot beats against
the ankle of the supporting foot

frater 'frādər a monastery's refectory
frater 'frädər a fraternity brother; a
member of certain religious orders
who is studying for the priesthood

fray 'frī a clerical title in various
religious orders in Spanish countries
fray 'frā commotion; to wear off by
rubbing

frette 'fret a hoop of wrought iron
or steel shrunk on a cast-iron gun
to strengthen it
frette 'fre.tā in heraldry, covered
with narrow interlacing bands

fronton ,frə^n·'tō^n a pediment over a
door or window
fronton 'frän·,tän a court or building for the game of jai alai

Fur 'fůr a Nilotic-Negro people in
Darfur province, western Sudan
fur 'fər the fine soft thick hairy
covering of mammals

fusee 'fyü,zē a conical spirally grooved
pulley in a timepiece; a wooden
match with a bulbous head not
easily blown out when ignited; a
red signal flare
fusee ,fü'zā in music, an arbitrary
ornament for the performer

Group I

fade
federate

ferment
fimbriate

fragment
frequent

G

gab ˈgab to talk in an idle, rapid, or thoughtless manner

gab ˈgȯb an East Indian persimmon tree

galet ˈgālət the fossa, a slender lithe mammal that is the largest carnivore of Madagascar

galet ˈgalət a chip of stone

gallant gəˈlant notably marked by courtesy and attentiveness to women especially in a spirited, dashing, or elaborate way

gallant ˈgalənt splendid or stately

gally ˈgalē to put to flight by frightening

gally ˈgȯlē marked by bare spots

gaufre ˈgōfər or ˈgȯfər a very thin wafer baked with a wafer iron

gaufre gȯ.frā crimped, plaited, or fluted linen or lace by means of a heated iron

gene ˈjēn a complex protein molecule that transmits hereditary characteristics

gene ˈzhen embarrassment or uneasiness

genet ˈjenət a small European carnivorous mammal related to the civet

genet zhəˈnā woodwaxen, a yellow-flowered Eurasian shrub

genial ˈjēnyəl diffusing good cheer and warmth

genial jəˈnīl relating to the chin

ger ˈgər a circular domed tent consisting of skins or felt stretched over a collapsible lattice framework and used by the Kirghiz and Mongols

ger ˈger an alien resident in Hebrew territory protected from oppression by a native patron in accordance

with early Hebrew law

gib ˈgib a castrated male cat; a removable machined plate of metal or other material that holds other mechanical parts in place

gib ˈjib a prison (slang)

gibber ˈjibər a rapid, inarticulate, and often foolish utterance

gibber ˈgibər a desert stone polished or sculptured by sandblast

gill ˈjil a U.S. liquid measure equal to ¼ pint

gill ˈgil an organ in fish for obtaining oxygen from water

gimel ˈgiməl the third letter of the Hebrew alphabet

gimel ˈjiməl vocal part writing in medieval music in which the voices usually progress in parallel thirds

glacé glaːsā having a lustrous surface

glace ˈglas a frozen dessert

glower ˈglaůər to stare with sullen brooding annoyance or anger

glower ˈglōər the luminous element in a Nernst lamp

Glycine ˈglisᵊn.ē a widely distributed genus of trailing or climbing herbs having tuberous roots, as the groundnut

glycine ˈglī.sēn a poisonous compound used in photography as a fine-grain developer; a sweet crystalline amino acid usually made by the reaction of chloroacetic acid with ammonia

gone ˈgȯn past

gone ˈgōn a germ cell

goût ˈgü artistic or literary good taste

gout ˈgau̇t a painful inflammatory disease of the joints

granite ˈgranət a natural igneous rock formation of visible crystalline texture

granite grä.niˈtā a frozen dessert of coarse-grained sherbet

grave ˈgräv an accent mark indicating a vowel is pronounced with a fall in pitch

grave ˈgrōv a burial place; a dignified appearance; to practice engraving

grave ˈgrävā in music, slowly and solemnly

graves ˈgräv red or white table wine(s)

graves ˈgravz burial places

grille ˈgril a grating or openwork barrier usually with a decorative metal design

grille ˈgrē.yā having an ornamental bar or grate pattern across open areas of a lace motif

grouser ˈgrau̇sər an habitual complainer

grouser ˈgrau̇zər a set of cleats on a tractor wheel

Guaná gwəˈnä an Arawakan people of Mato Grosso, Brazil and the Chaco region of Paraguay

guana ˈgwänə either of two malvaceous tropical trees, the balibago and the blue mahoe

Guara ˈgwarə a genus of ibises containing the New World white and scarlet ibises

guara gwəˈrä any of several South American wild dogs; a South American crab-eating raccoon

guara ˈgwärə a tropical American tree of the genus Cupania

gyro ˈjī.rō a gyroscope or gyrocompass

gyro ˈzhērˈō or jēr.ō a sandwich of lamb, tomato, and onion on pita bread

Group I

graduate
granulate
guesstimate

H

hache ˈhash a hatchet or axe
hache häˈshā minced or hashed

Hades ˈhā.dēz the abode or state of the dead; hell
hades ˈhādz deviates from the vertical, as a vein, fault, or lode

hakim həˈkēm a Muslim physician
hakim ˈhä.kēm a Muslim ruler

hale ˈhāl sound or healthy; to haul, pull, or draw
hale ˈhälā an Hawaiian house

halo ˈhalō containing halogen (by shortening)
halo ˈhālō a circle of light surrounding a luminous body

halter ˈhȯltər a rope or strap for leading or tying a horse or other animal
halter ˈhaltər one of the modified second pair of insect wings that serve to maintain balance in flight

Hamburg ˈham.bu̇rg a city in northern Germany
Hamburg ˈham.bərg a European breed of rather small domestic fowls
hamburg ˈham.bərg a hamburger (by shortening)

Hamites ˈha.mītz a group of African peoples including the Berbers, Tuaregs, and Tibbu
Hamites həˈmīdez a genus of extinct Cretaceous ammonoids

hartal här'täl concerted cessation of work and business as a protest against a political situation or an act of government
hartal här'tȯl an orange to yellow mineral consisting of arsenic trisulfide

headward ˈhedwərd in the direction of the head
headward ˈhed,wȯrd a feudal service consisting of acting as a guard to the lord

heavy ˈhevē having great weight
heavy ˈhēvē affected with heaves, as a horse

Hebe ˈhēb an offensive term for a Jew
Hebe ˈhēbē a genus comprising the shrubby evergreen venonicas of the southern hemisphere
hebe ˈhēbē any veronica of the genus Hebe

here ˈhe,re an invading army in Anglo-Saxon times
here ˈhir at this point in space

hermitage ˈhərmȧd·ij a hermit's residence
hermitage :hermē:täzh a red Rhône Valley wine

hinder ˈhindər to interfere with activity
hinder ˈhīndər situated behind

his ˈhiz something that belongs to him
his ˈhīz expressions of greetings or to attract attention

housewife ˈhaú,swif a married woman in charge of a household
housewife ˈhəzəf a pocket-sized container for carrying small articles

hum ˈhəm to make a low prolonged sound like that of an insect
hum ˈhüm an isolated residual hill or mass of limestone

Huron ˈhyúrən an Iroquoian people of the St. Lawrence valley, Ontario, and midwestern U.S.; the second largest of the five Great Lakes in North America in water surface area
huron ü'rȯn the weasellike South American grison

Group I

heretic
house

--- I ---

incense ˈin,sens material used to produce a fragrant odor when burned
incense in:sens to arouse the wrath or indignation of

incept in'sept to take in or ingest; to receive as a member
incept ˈin,sept the first accumulation of cells in an embryo recognizable as the start of a developing part or organ

ingenerate in'jenə,rāt to cause
ingenerate in'jenərȧt inborn or innate; not generated

instar in'stär to adorn with stars
instar ˈinz,tär an insect between two successive molts

intimate ˈintə,māt to give notice of
intimate ˈintə,mȧt very close contact

intricate ˈin·trəkət showing complex involvement of detailed considerations requiring precise analysis; difficult to analyze or solve
intricate ˈin·trə,kāt to intermesh or interlock

invalid in:valȧd without foundation
invalid ˈinvəlȧd sickly or disabled

inward ˈinwərd toward the inside
inward ˈin.wȯrd a king's bodyguard

irony ˈīərnē made or consisting of iron
irony ˈīrənē humor, ridicule, or light sarcasm that adopts a mode of speech the intended implication of which is opposite the literal sense of the words (seldom ˈīərnē)

Group I

impersonate

impound
imprint
impropriate
inarch
incipit
incorporate
indurate
infatuate
infuriate
insert
insult
insurge
intermediate
invert
inwall

--- J ---

jacana ˈjɑkənə a coastal freshwater wading bird
jacana ˈhȯkənə a West Indian timber tree

jaeger ˈyōgər a large spirited rapacious bird that inhabits northern seas
jaeger ˈyōgər a high quality diamond of bluish white grade

jam ˈjɑm to press into a tight or close position; a product made by boiling fruit and sugar to a thick consistency
jam ˈjȯm the ruler in some northwest Indian states

Job ˈjōb a person who sustains patiently a life of poverty and affliction
job ˈjäb a piece of work or performance

jog ˈjäg to go at a low leisurely pace; to push or shake by prodding
jog ˈjōg yoga

jube ˈyü.bō a gallery above a screen that separates the church chancel from the nave, or the screen itself
jube ˈjüb a lozenge like a jujube

Jubilate ˌyübəˈlätō the third Sunday after Easter
jubilate ˈjübə.lāt to utter sounds or make demonstrations of joy and exultation

Junker ˈyünkər a member of the Prussian landed aristocracy
junker ˈjəŋkər an automobile ready for scrapping

junkman ˈjəŋkmən a crew-member of a junk
junkman ˈjəŋk.mɑn a person dealing in resalable junk

Jura ˈjùrə the Jurassic geological period, or the rocks belonging to it
jura ˈyùrə legal principles, rights, or powers

jus ˈyüs or ˈjəs a legal principle, right, or power
jus ˈjüs or ˈzhüs juice or gravy

K

Kachin kə'chin a Tibeto-Burman ethnic group inhabiting upper Myanmar
kachin 'kɑchən pyrocatechol used as a photographic developer

kaki 'käkē a Japanese persimmon
kaki kü'kē a blackish stilt of New Zealand

Kasha 'kɑshə a soft napped twilled fabric of fine wool and hair
kasha 'käshə a mush made from coarse cracked buckwheat or other grains

Kate 'kätə a people of the Huon peninsula in New Guinea
kate 'kāt a pileated woodpecker

Kin 'jin a Tatar people that founded an 11th century dynasty in China
kin 'kin one's immediate family or related group

kiri 'kērē a paulownia tree
kiri 'kē.ri a short wooden club with a heavy round knob at one end that may be thrown or used in close combat

kiyi kī:yī an expression of exultation; a bark or yelp of a dog; a small brush used in the U.S. Navy for scrubbing clothing or canvas
kiyi 'kē.yē a small lake herring abundant in deep water in the Great Lakes

Kora 'kōrä the almost extinct Hottentot dialect of the Korana in South Africa
kora 'kōrə a large gallinule of southeastern Asia and the East Indies

Kuba 'kübə a Bantu-speaking people of the central Congo
kuba kü'bä an eastern Caucasian carpet of coarse but firm weave

L

labor 'lābər to work or toil
labor lə'bōr an old Texas unit of land measure equal to about 177 acres

Lais 'līz a Mongoloid people of the Chin Hills in Myanmar
lais 'lāz medieval short tales of lyric poems in French literature

Lak(h)s 'läks members of a division of the Lezghian people in southern Russia on the western shore of the Caspian Sea
laks 'lɑks performances of the male capercaillie (the largest European grouse) during courtship

lamé lɑ:mā a brocaded clothing fabric
lame 'lām physically disabled

lances 'lɑn.səs weapons of war consisting of long shafts with sharp steel heads
lances 'lɑn.sēz or 'läŋ.kās an ancient Roman platter, usually of metal

land 'lɑnd ground or soil; to catch and bring to shore
land 'länt a governmental unit in Germany

landsman 'lɑnzmən an inexperienced sailor below an ordinary seaman
landsman 'läntsmən a fellow Jew, especially from eastern Europe

Lari 'lä.rī a suborder of the Charadriiformes that includes gulls, terns, jaegers, and skimmers

lari ˈlä.rī money consisting of silver wire doubled, either twisted to form a fishhook or straight

laser ˈlā.zər a device that uses natural oscillations of atoms to amplify or generate electromagnetic waves
laser ˈlā.sər a drastic purgative gum resin obtained from laserwort

lat ˈlät a separate column or pillar in some Buddhist buildings in India, similar to the Greek stela
lat ˈlat a broad flat superficial muscle on each side of the lower back (latissimus dorsi, shortened)

lather ˈlathər foam or froth
lather ˈlathər a person who puts up or makes lathing
lather ˈlāthər a person who works with a lathe

laud ˈlȯd to praise; public acclaim
laud lä·üd a lute or cittern

lax ˈlax not stringent; easygoing
lax ˈläx salmon

Laze ˈläzə a Muslim Kartvelian Sunnite people of Caucasia found along both sides of the Turkish-Soviet frontier
laze ˈlāz to pass in idleness or relaxation

lead ˈled a heavy metallic element
lead ˈlēd to guide or precede

legate ˈlegət an emissary or deputy
legate lə·ˈgāt to bequeath

lied ˈlīd conveyed an untruth
lied ˈlēt a German folksong

Liege lē·ˈäzh a city in Belgium
liege ˈlēj bound by obligations resembling those existing between a feudal lord and his vassals

lien ˈlēn a charge on real property in satisfaction of a debt
lien ˈlīən a spleen

Lima ˈlēmə the capital of Peru
lima ˈlīmə a bean; a bivalve mollusk

limbers ˈlimərz loggers who trim limbs from felled trees
limbers ˈlimbərz conduits on each side of ship keels that provide passages for water to the pump well; horse-drawn two-wheel vehicles to which guns may be attached; makes flexible or pliant

limes ˈlīmz small globose citrus fruit of the lime tree; whitewashes with a solution of lime and water
limes ˈlī.mēz a fortified frontier of the ancient Roman Empire

limon lē·ˈmōn an unstratified deposit of loam ranging from clay to fine sand (loess)
limon ˈlīmən a hybrid fruit from crossing a lemon and lime

lineage ˈlīnij the number of lines of printed or written matter
lineage ˈlinēij descent in a line from a common ancestor

lira ˈlīrə a ridge on some shells resembling a fine thread or hair
lira ˈlērə a bowed stringed musical instrument; the basic monetary unit of Italy

lis ˈlēs a fleur-de-lis
lis ˈlis an ancient Irish fortification or storage place enclosed by a circular mound and or trench

litre ˈlētər a metric unit of capacity equal to 1.057 liquid parts
litre ˈlētra a poisonous Chilean shrub whose hardwood is used in cabinetry

liver ˈlivər a large vascular glandular organ of vertebrates
liver ˈlīvər more alive

loa ˈlōə an African filarial worm
loa lə·ˈwä a Haitian voodoo cult deity

lower ˈlōər situated further below or under; to bring down; to reduce
lower ˈlaůər to look sullen; a dark, gloomy, or sullen look

Luger ˈlügər a 9 mm German pistol
luger ˈlüzhər a person who rides on
a small sled (a luge)

lunger ˈlənjər a person who moves
forward forcefully
lunger ˈləŋər a person suffering from
a lung disease; a glob of sputum,
phlegm, or other expectorant

lupine ˈlü.pīn wolfish; ravenous
lupine ˈlüpən a plant of the genus
Lupinus

lure ˈlur to entice, tempt, or seduce
lure ˈlü.rə a long curved trumpet for
calling cattle

lyrist ˈlīrəst a player of the lyre
lyrist ˈlirəst a writer of lyrics

Group I

landward
laureate
learned
leeward
legitimate
live

M

Macon mā·kən a city in central Georgia
Macon mä·kōⁿ a still Burgundy
French wine in both red and white
varieties

Madrilene ˈmadrə.lēn of or from
Madrid, Spain
madrilene :madrə:len a consommé
flavored with tomato and served
hot or cold

maja ˈmäjä a lower class Spanish belle
maja ˈmäjə a crab

mala ˈmälə offenses against right or
the law
mala ˈmälə the grinding surface of an
insect's mandible

Male ˈmälā a member of a Dravidian
animistic people of Bengal; the
capital of the Maldive Islands
male ˈmāl the sex that usually performs the fertilizing function in
generation

Mam ˈmäm an Indian people of southwestern Guatemala
mam ˈmam madam

mamma ˈmämə mother

mamma ˈmamə a mammary gland or
teat

mane ˈmān neck hair
mane ˈmänā in pharmacy, in the
morning

manes ˈmānz neck hairs
manes ˈmä.näs ancestral spirits worshipped as gods

Mangue ˈmäŋgā a Chorotegan people
of southwestern Nicaragua
mangue ˈmaŋ a small dark brown burrowing carnivorous mammal related
to the mongoose

Manil(l)a mə·nilə the capital city of
the Philippines; made from Manilla
hemp
manilla mə·nēlyə a piece of metal
shaped like a horseshoe used by
some peoples of western Africa for
ornamental purposes and as a
medium of exchange

Manis ˈmānəs the type genus comprising the pangolins
manis ˈmänēs peanuts

Mano ˈmänō a Negro people inhabiting the northern tip of the central

province of Liberia and adjacent
Ivory Coast

mano ˈmänō a handstone used as the
upper millstone for grinding grains

mano məˈnō any of several large
sharks

manqué ˈmäⁿˌkā short of fulfilling
one's aspirations

manque ˈmäⁿk in roulette, numbers
1-18 when a bet is placed on them

Manus ˈmäˌnüs a people inhabiting
Manus Island, north of New Guinea

manus ˈmānəs the distal segment of a
vertebrate's forelimb including the
carpus and forefoot or hand

Mara ˈmɑrə of or from Maracaibo,
Venezuela

mara məˈrä a long-legged long-eared
rodent closely related to the cavies

mare ˈmɑər a female horse

mare ˈmä|rä a dark expanse on the
moon or Mars

maria məˈrēə any of several shrubs
and trees of tropical America

maria ˈmärēə dark areas of considerable extent on the surface of
the moon or Mars

Marseilles ˈmärˌsā of or from the city
of Marseilles in southeast France
on the Mediterranean sea

Marseilles märˈsālz a firm reversible
cotton fabric that usually has small
fancy designs and is used for vests
or trimmings

mate ˈmāt one customarily associated
with another; to checkmate in
chess; a deck officer

mate ˈmätä an aromatic South American beverage

math ˈmath the relationship and sym-
bolism of numbers and magnitudes
(by shortening **mathematics)**

math ˈməth a Hindu monastery

matie ˈmäd·ē a young fat herring with
roe

matie ˈmäd·ē a shipmate or comrade
(slang)

matte ˈmɑt a mixture of sulfides
formed in smelting sulfide ores of
metals

matte ˈmätä an aromatic South American beverage

Medic ˈmēdik the Iranian language of
ancient Media

medic ˈmedik a plant of the genus
Medicago; a person engaged in
medical work

melange ˌmeˈläⁿzh to print colors on
top of woolen yarn

melange ˈmäˌläⁿzh a mixture or medley

melon ˈme·län a yellow powder
formed on heating various cyano-
gen compounds

melon ˈmelən a soft-fleshed sweet-
flavored fruit with a hard rind such
as muskmelon or watermelon; a
small reddish or chestnut brown
wallaby extensively distributed in
Australia and New Guinea

mere ˈmir exclusive of anything else

mere ˈmerē a Maori war club

meringue məˈrɑŋ a mixture of beaten
egg whites and powdered sugar
baked at low temperature and used
as a topping

méringue māˈrɑŋ a popular Dominican
and Haitian ballroom dance with a
limping step

Meshed məˈshed Iran's fourth largest
city

meshed ˈmesht resembling a network;
interlaced

meta ˈmetə characterized by or being
two positions in the benzene ring
separated by one carbon atom

meta ˈmētə a column or post, in ancient Rome, placed at each end of
a racetrack to mark the turning
places

micrometer 'mīkrō͵mēdər a unit of length equal to one millionth of a meter

micrometer mī'krämədər a caliper having a spindle moved by a finely machined screw and used with a telescope or microscope to make precise measurements

millet 'milət an annual cereal and forage grass

millet mə̇'let a non–Muslim group in Turkey

mind 'mīnd the intellect or brain; to obey; to take care of

mind 'min a thin gold ornamental plate used by ancient Celts

minute 'minət a unit of time and angular measurement

minute mī:nyüt of very small size or importance

minutely mī'nyütlē with precision or exactly

minutely 'minətlē from minute to minute, or happening every minute

mire 'mēr a fixed mark due north or south of a meridian

mire 'mīr wet spongy earth; a bog or marsh

Mobile mō'bēl a large city in southwestern Alabama

mobile 'mōbəl movable

mobile 'mäbəlē the lower classes of a community; the masses

Mod 'mōd a meeting to study and perform Gaellic arts

mod 'mäd modern (by shortening)

Moi 'mōē a group of Veddoid or Indo-Australoid people living in the mountain uplands of Annam, Vietnam

moi 'mō'ē an Hawaiian ruling chief or sovereign

Mojo 'mō͵hō an Arawakan people of northern Bolivia

mojo 'mōjō a voodoo spell or amulet

Mole 'mō͵lā a people of the west central Sudan

mole 'mōl a congenital mark or discoloration on the skin; a burrowing mammal

mole 'mōlē a highly spiced meat sauce

Moline 'mōlēn a city in northwest Illinois

moline 'mōlən a cross having the end of each arm forked and recurved

molle 'mälē in music, lower by a half step; flat

molle 'mō͵ya a Peruvian evergreen tree; a small shrubby New Zealand tree

moly 'mälē molybdenum, a fusible polyvalent metallic element

moly 'mōlē a European wild garlic

Mon 'mōn the dominant native people of Pegu in Myanmar

mon 'män the usually circular badge of a Japanese family; a usually large plank boat resembling a canoe common in Melanesia

Montana män'tanə a state in northwestern U.S.; a sheep bred or raised in Montana

montaña män'tanyə a forested region of the eastern slopes of the Andes

moped 'mō͵ped a lightweight low-powered motorbike that can be pedaled

moped 'mōpd acted in a brooding, dull, or dejected manner

Moré mə'rā a people of the west central Sudan

more 'mōr of larger size or extent

morné mȯr:nā in heraldry, a lion without teeth, tongue, or claws

morne 'mȯrn gloomy or dismal

mot 'mō a pithy or witty saying; an epigram

mot 'mät a grove or clump of trees, especially in open prairie country

mouth 'mau̇th an opening through which food passes into an organism

mouth 'mau̇ẖ to swage the top of a metal can to receive the cover

mow 'mō to cut down or off
mow 'maú a stack of hay or straw

Mura 'mūrə an Indian people of northwestern Brazil
mura 'mùrə a rural community in Japan

murid 'mú·rēd a Sufi disciple in Islam
murid 'myùrəd relating to a very large family of relatively small rodents including the house mouse and common rats

Mus 'məs a genus of rodents including the common house mouse
mus 'myūz bridging groups that join central atoms or ions; the plural of the 12th letter of the Greek alphabet

musar 'myü.zör a 12th century ballad singer of Provence
musar 'mü.sör a 19th century Jewish religious-ethical movement

Muter mü'ter a nomadic Bedouin people in Arabia
muter 'myüdər more unable to utter articulate sounds; less able to speak

Group I

macerate
mediate
misuse
moderate
multiply
murid

N

nadir 'nādər the lowest point
nadir 'nä.dir a Malayan light-draft fishing boat

Nama 'nämə one of a Hottentot people of southwestern Africa
Nama 'nāmə a genus of blue-flowered perennial herbs

nana 'nɑnə a child's nurse or nurse-maid
nana 'nə'nä a pineapple; mint
nana 'nānə dwarfish, especially of genetic variants of economic plants

nance 'nänsā a type of tree of the genus Brysonima, or its fruit
nance 'nɑns an effeminate male

Natal nə'tɑl a province in the eastern part of the Republic of South Africa
natal 'nād³l relating to birth; relating to the buttocks

Nice 'nēs a seaport city on the southeast coast of France; a grayish-blue color (also called Quimper)

nice 'nīs refined, cultured, pleasant, or satisfying

nonage 'nänōj a condition of not being of the required legal age to enter into some particular transactions
nonage 'nänij the ninth part of a decedent's movable goods, sometimes payable to the clergy

none 'nən not any
none 'nōn the canonical ninth hour

nudge 'nəj to touch or push gently; to prod lightly
nudge 'nùj to annoy with persistent complaints, criticism, or nagging; a pest

number 'nəmbər a numeral, digit, or integer
number 'nəmər more devoid of sensation

nun 'nən a woman belonging to a religious order, especially under vows of poverty, chastity, and obedience

nun ˈnün the 14th letter of the Hebrew alphabet

Nut ˈnüt in Egyptian religion, the goddess of the sky

nut ˈnət a hard-shelled dry fruit or seed; a perforated block of metal with an internal screw thread for attachment to a bolt

Group I

nacre

O

object ˈäbjikt something visible or tangible

object əbˈjekt to oppose or protest

officiate əˈfishē‚āt to perform a prescribed or traditional ceremony

officiate əˈfishēət a body of officials

Olive ˈōˈlēvā an Indian people of northeastern Mexico

olive ˈälēv or ˈäləv a plant of the genus Olea, or its oblong drupaceous fruit

ombre ˈämbər a European grayling; a three-handed game played in Spain

ombre ˈämːbrä shaded, especially in fabrics with a dyed or woven design

oner ˈōnər a heavy blow with a fist (slang)

oner ˈwənər one of a kind

ore ˈōr a natural usually unrefined mineral that can often be mined

öre ˈərˈə a Danish and Norwegian unit of value equal to 1/100 krone; a Swedish monetary unit equal to 1/100 krona

Oriental ːōrēːentᵊl relating or situated in the Far East

Oriental ‚ōre‚enˈtäl a native or inhabitant of Uruguay

os ˈäs a bone; a mouth

os ˈōs an esker, a long narrow often sinuous ridge of debris deposited between ice walls by a stream flowing within a stagnant glacier

outward ˈaútwərd toward the outside

outward ˈaútˌwȯrd a detached hospital ward; a ward outside the original bounds of a borough

overage ːōvərːäj too old

overage ˈōvərij excess or surplus

Group I

obdurate
obliterate
obstinate
officiate

P

pace ˈpās a rate of motion or performance

pace ˈpāsē with all due respect

Pala ˈpäˌlä a language mentioned in the Boghazkeui inscriptions

pala päˈlä an ivory tree affording an inferior quality of indigo

pala ˈpälə an impala

Pali ˈpälē an Indic language found in the Buddhist canon

pali ˈpälē a steep slope in Hawaii; an Indian timber tree

pali ˈpä.lī upright slender calcareous processes surrounding the central part of the calyculus of some corals

Palladian pəˈlādēən relating to wisdom or learning

Palladian pəˈlädeən relating to the classic architectural style based on Andrea Palladio's work

pallas ˈpaləz loose outergarments worn by women of ancient Rome

pallas ˈpäyəs Incan princesses

palled ˈpald acted as a pal to someone

palled ˈpȯld covered with a shroud; lost strength

palsy ˈpȯlzē a condition characterized by uncontrollable tremoring of the body or one or more of its parts

palsy ˈpalzē having or giving the appearance of having a high degree of intimacy

Palus ˌpaˈlüs wines from vineyards planted in the rich alluvial soil of southwest France

palus ˈpāləs any of several upright slender calcareous processes surrounding the central part of the calyculus of some corals

pan ˈpan a shallow container; to rotate a camera in any direction; to wash earth deposits in search of precious metal

pan ˈpän a betal palm leaf; a card game resembling rummy

panaché ːpanəːshä comprised of several foods

panache pəˈnash an ornamental tuft or tufts on a helmet; an heroic flourish of manner

pane ˈpān a window or door section

pané ˌpaˈnä food prepared with bread crumbs; breaded

papa ˈpäpə a father; a potato; a bluish New Zealand clay used for whitening fireplaces

papa pəˈpä a parish priest of the Eastern Orthodox Church

papa ˈpä.pa a baboon; a king vulture

papa ˈpäpȯ any of several American shrubs or trees of the genus Asiminia

Papio ˈpäpē.ō a genus of typical baboons

papio ˈpäpyō a young food fish of Hawaiian waters

parison ˈparə.sän even balance between members of a sentence

parison ˈparəsən a gob of glass partially shaped into an object

Passé ˌpäˈsä a member of an Arawakan tribe of northwestern Brazil

passé paˈsä past one's prime; no longer fashionable; a ballet movement in which one leg passes behind or in front of the other

passe ˈpäs in roulette, the numbers 19–36 when a bet is made on them

pastel ˌpaˈstel pale and light in color; delicate

pastel ˈpastel a woad plant, of the mustard family

pata ˈpətə a land grant engraved on metal; a gold plate tied on the forehead in ceremonies of investiture

pata ˈpətä a long straight gauntlet-hilted two-edged sword

pate ˈpāt the top of the head

pâte ˈpät plastic material for pottery

paté pəˈtä a cross with arms narrow at the center and expanding toward the ends

pâté päˈtä a spread of finely mashed seasoned and spiced meat

patte ˈpat a decorative band, strap, or belt to fasten garments

patté ˌpaˈtä in heraldry, having arms of a cross narrow at the center and expanding toward the ends

pave ˈpāv to cover with material making a firm level surface for travel

pave ˌpəˈvā in jewelry, a setting of stones placed close together so as to show no metal between them

peaked ˈpēkt pointed
peaked ˈpēkəd looked pale, wan, or sickly

Peba ˈpäbä a member of the Peban tribe of northeastern Peru
peba ˈpebə a small armadillo having nine moveable bands of scutes and ranging from Texas to Paraguay

peer ˈpir a person of equal standing; a member of one of the five ranks of the English peerage
peer ˈpēər a urinator

pension ˈpenchən a fixed sum paid regularly to a person, usually following retirement from service
pension päⁿsːyôⁿ or ːpäⁿsēːôn a payment for room and board; to receive board and lodging at a fixed rate

perfect ˈpərfikt constituting a form of the verb that expresses an action or state completed at the time of speaking or at a time spoken of; relating to a note in mensural notation equaling three rather than two of the next lower denomination
perfect pərˈfekt to bring to a state of supreme excellence (seldom ˈpərfikt)

perpend pərˈpend to reflect on or ponder
perpend ˈpərpənd a brick or large stone reaching through a wall and acting as a binder

pia ˈpīə the delicate and highly vascular membrane of connective tissue investing the brain and spinal cord (**pia mater**, by shortening)
pia ˈpēə a perennial herb of East India, Australasia, and Polynesia cultivated for its large starch-yielding root

piano pēˈänō in music, softly or quietly
piano pēˈänō a stringed percussion instrument

pic ˈpik a motion picture or photograph (slang)
pic ˈpēk the top of a hill or mountain; in piquet, the scoring of thirty points before one's opponent scores a point

Pila ˈpīlə the type genus of the family Pilidae comprising the apple snails and dextral shells
pila ˈpīlə heavy javelins of a Roman foot soldier
pila ˈpēlə a communal fountain

pili pēˈlē a nut of any of various trees of the genus Canarium
pili ˈpēlē a perennial grass of worldwide distribution that is used as forage in southwestern U.S.
pili ˈpīˌlī a hair or a structure resembling a hair

pinite ˈpēˌnīt a compact mineral that is essentially muscovite
pinite ˈpīˌnīt fossil wood

piqué ˈpēkā a durable ribbed cotton, rayon, or silk clothing fabric; inlaid, as a knife handle; a glove seam; a ballet movement
pique ˈpēk to stimulate by wounding pride or inciting jealousy or rivalry

pirr ˈpir a gust of wind or a flurry
pirr ˈper to blow with a whiz; to speed along

piscine pəˈsēn a stone basin with a drain located near the church altar for disposing of water from liturgical ablutions
piscine ˈpiˌsīn having the characteristics of a fish

pita ˈpēdə the century plant; the yucca
pita ˈpētä any of several small South American deer

placer ˈplāsər a person that places something
placer ˈplasər a deposit containing a valuable mineral

Planes ˈplāˌnēz a genus of small pelagic crabs
planes ˈplānz makes smooth or even; trees of the genus Platanus; soars on wings or skims across water

plaque ˈplak an ornamental brooch; an inscribed identification tablet; a film of bacteria-harboring mucus on a tooth
plaqué plaːkā a seal fixed directly to the face of a document

plat ˈplat a detailed plan of an area; a small tract of land
plat ˈplä a dish of food

platy ˈplād·ē consisting of plates or flaky layers
platy ˈplad·ē a small stockily built fish native to southern Mexico

plebes ˈplēbz first-year cadets at a military or naval academy
plebes ˈplē.bēz common peoples of ancient Rome

poise ˈpȯiz easy composure or manner marked especially by assurance and gracious dignity
poise ˈpwäz an absolute measure of viscosity

policize ˈpälə.sīz to act in a politic, diplomatic, or crafty manner
policize ˌpōˈlēsīz to govern by means of police

poll ˈpōl voting at an election; to cut off the head, horns, or treetops
poll ˈpäl a college or university degree without honors

polos ˈpōlōz games played by teams of players mounted on horseback, on bicycles, or swimming, the object of which is to drive a ball through goalposts
polos ˈpä.läs a high crown or headdress of cylindrical shape

pose ˈpōz to put or set in place or in a given position
posé ˈpōzā a ballet movement in which the dancer steps from one foot to the other with a straight knee

potty ˈpäd·ē a small child's pot for voiding
potty ˈpäti haughty or supercilious in bearing or speech

pram ˈpräm a small lightweight nearly flat-bottomed boat usually with a squared-off bow
pram ˈpram a baby carriage; a milk carrier's handcart

Precis ˈprēsəs a widely distributed genus of chiefly tropical nymphalid butterflies
précis prāˈsē a brief summary of essential points, statements, or facts

predicate ˈpredəkət the part of a sentence or clause that expresses what is said of the subject
predicate ˈpredə.kāt to affirm, declare, or proclaim

present prēˈzent to make a gift or donation
present ˈprezᵊnt existent; now

prima ˈprēmə the first or leading person or item
prima ˈprīmə the word at which reading is to be resumed after an interruption

primer ˈprimər an elementary instruction book
primer ˈprīmər a device to ignite an explosive charge

proceeds prōˈsēdz moves forward from a point
proceeds ˈprō.sēdz a total amount brought in

process ˈprō.ses to subject to a particular method, system, or technique
process prōˈses to move along; to go

produce prōˈdyüs to bring forth; to give being, form, or shape to
produce ˈprō.düs agricultural products and goods

product ˈprädəkt something produced
product prəˈdəkt to lengthen out

prosthesis ˈprästhəsəs the addition of a sound or syllable to a word, especially by prefixing

prosthesis präsˈthēsəs an artificial device to replace a missing part of the body

pud ˈpəd an animal's paw or child's hand

pud ˈpüd a penis

pugh ˈpü an expression of disgust or disdain

pugh ˈpyü a long-handled hooked prong for pitching fish

punto ˈpən·tō to hit, in fencing

punto ˈpüntō the ace of trumps, as in ombre

pussy ˈpüsē a catkin of the pussy willow; a cat

pussy ˈpəsē full of or like pus

put ˈpət a blockhead or dolt; to hit a golf ball

put ˈpüt to place

putter ˈpüd·ər a person who puts or places something

putter ˈpəd·ər a golf club

Group I

passement
pave
permit
pignorate
ponderate
prayer
precedent
preponderate
presage
prima
progress
proportionate

Q

quart(e) ˈkär|t a fencer's parry or guard position; a sequence of four playing cards of the same suit

quart ˈkwôr|t a U.S. liquid measure equal to two pints or ¼ gallon

Quiche ˈkē.chā an Indian people of south central Guatemala

quiche ˈkēsh a baked custard pie

quinate ˈkwi.nāt composed of sets of five

quinate ˈkwī.nāt a salt or ester of quinic acid

quite ˈkwīt to a considerable extent

quite ˈkētā a series of passes made by a matador to attract the bull away from a horse or fallen picador

---

R

Rabat rəˈböt the capital of Morocco

rabat ˈräbət a polishing material made from potter's clay

rabat ˈräbē a short cloth breast-piece worn by clergymen

rabat rəˈböt to rotate a plane about

a trace into coincidence with another plane

rabbi ˈrä.bī a Jew qualified by study of Jewish civil and religious law to expound and apply it

rabbi ˈrɑbē a short cloth breast-piece worn by clergymen

ragged ˈrɑgəd roughly unkempt
ragged ˈrɑgd persecuted in petty ways

Rainier ˌrəˈnēr the highest mountain in Washington state (14,410 feet), and fifth highest mountain in the 48 contiguous United States
rainier ˈrānēr wetter or more showery

Raja ˈrɑjə a genus of skates
raja ˈrɑjə an Indian prince or king

Rama ˈrɑmə a Chibchan people of southeastern Nicaragua
Rama ˈrɑˌmɑ either the sixth, seventh (the most famous), or the eighth incarnation of Vishnu

Rana ˈrɑnə a nearly cosmopolitan genus of frogs
rana ˈrɑnə an Indian prince

rape ˈrōp an annual herb of European origin; illicit sexual intercourse without the consent of the victim; an outrageous violation
rape rɑˈpɑ a highly seasoned hash used in the Middle Ages

raven ˈrāvən a large glossy black bird
raven ˈrɑvən to devour eagerly or greedily

rayon ˈrɑˌɑn a synthetic textile fiber made from modified cellulose
rayon rɑːōⁿ a ray or beam; a radius

Reading ˈrediŋ a city in southeast Pennsylvania
reading ˈrēdiŋ mentally formulating written words or sentences

real rēˈɑl a former monetary unit of several Spanish American countries and Spain
real ˈrēl actual, true, or objective

reason ˈrezən a horizontal timber over a row of posts supporting a beam
reason ˈrēzən an explanation or justification; to think; the power of comprehending

recollect ˌrekəˈlekt to recall or remember something
recollect ˌrē·kəˈlekt to gather together again

recreate ˈrekrēˌɑt to refresh after toil
recreate ˌrēːkrēːɑt to form anew or again

redial ˌrēˈdī(ə)l to remanipulate a dial, as on a telephone or television
redial ˈrēdēəl pertaining to a larva produced within the sporocyst of many trematodes

refuse rəˈfyüz to decline to accept; to replace a fuse in; to remelt
refuse ˈreˌfyüs a useless part of something

regale rəˈgōl to entertain
regale rəˈgōlē a royal prerogative; symbols indicative of royal status

relent rəˈlent to become less severe; to slacken
relent ˈrēˌlent loaned money again to a borrower

relievo rēˈlēvō a mode of sculpture in which forms and figures are distinguished from the surrounding plane surface
relievo rəˈlēvō a game in which members of one team are given time to hide, then are sought by those of the other team

repent rəˈpent to feel regret or contrition
repent ˈrēpənt creeping

repetition ˌrepəˈtishən the act of repeating something that has already been said or done
repetition ˌrēˌpəˈtishən to again make a request for something

repress rəˈpres to restrain
repress ˈrēːpres to press again

res ˈrɑs in law, a particular thing
res ˈrɑz second notes in the diatonic scale

resaca rə'sɑkə the dry channel or the former often marshy course of a stream
resaca rə'zäkə a rebounding billow

resent rē'zent or rə'zent to feel, express, or exhibit indignant displeasure
resent rē'sent transmitted by means of a repeater; sent again

reserve rē'zərv to keep in store for future or special use
reserve 'rē.sərv to furnish or supply again or anew

reside rə'zīd to have one's residence or abode
reside rē'sīd to install new or different siding on a structure

resole 'rē.sōl to put a new sole on a shoe
resole 're.zōl a fusible resin soluble in alkali and alcohol

resoluble rə'zälyəbəl able to be resolved
resoluble rē:sälyəbəl able to be dissolved into solution again

resound rə'zaûnd to become filled with sound; to become renown
resound re:saûnd to sound again

résumé :re|z|ə:mä a condensed statement
resume rə'züm to begin again

retiré rə:tē:rä a ballet movement
retire rə'tīr to withdraw from activity

rheum 'rüm a watery discharge from mucous membranes of the eye or nose
rheum 'rēəm an Asiatic herb

rig 'rē an ancient Irish king
rig 'rig to furnish with apparatus or gear; to equip

rima 'rīmə a long narrow aperture; a cleft or fissure
rima 'rēmä a breadfruit

rissole rə'sōl minced meat or fish covered with pastry and fried in deep fat
rissolé 'risəlē browned by frying in deep fat

Rite 'rīt the liturgy, especially an historical form of eucharistic service
rite 'rīt a ceremonial act
rite 'rīd·ē undistinguished achievement in academic requirements for graduation

river 'rivər a watercourse
river 'rīvər a person who splits blocks of wood

robin 'räbən a large North American thrush; a small European thrush
robin 'rōbən a toxalbumin similar to the toxic abrin and ricin

Rochet 'rōshä a fourth growth red wine from Medoc, France
rochet 'rächət a European gunard (fish) that is chiefly red; a close-fitting white ecclesiastical vestment resembling a surplice

rose 'rōz a flower; a perfume; a moderate purplish red color
rosé rō:zä a table wine made from red grapes

rote 'rōt mechanical repetition of a pattern
rote 'rət the noise of the surf crashing on the shore

rouge 'rüzh a powdery cosmetic
rouge 'rüj scrimmage in an English type of football

rower 'rōər a person who rows a boat
rower 'raûər a person who naps cloth by hand

rows 'rōz propels a boat with oars; continuous lines or strips
rows 'raûz noisy disturbances; heated arguments

rugged 'rəgd covered with a blanket or rug
rugged 'rəgəd hardy, robust, vigorous

Rum ˈrüm a term originally applied by Moslems in medieval times to peoples of the Byzantine empire

rum ˈrüm a blue dye resembling indigo obtained from an East Indian shrub

rum ˈrəm an alcoholic liquor prepared from fermented molasses

Group I

read

rearward
rebel
recast
record
regenerate
regress
reiterate
replicate
reprise
research
reset
resuse
rissole
routed

S

---

sabia ˈsōbēə a tropical Asiatic shrub

sabia səbˈyä a Brazilian thrush

said ˈsed expressed in words

said ˈsäid an Islamic chief or leader

sake ˈsōkē a Japanese alcoholic beverage made from fermented rice

sake ˈsāk enhancement of an object or group

sal ˈsöl an East Indian timber tree

sal ˈsɑl salt

Saliva ˈsäləvə a people of the Orinoco valley, Venezuela

saliva səˈlīvə a viscid secretion in the mouth

salve ˈsɑv a healing ointment

salve ˈsɑlv to save from destruction

salve ˈsɑl‚vē an exclamation of greeting; hail

salver ˈsɑvər a person who salves or cures

salver ˈsɑlvər a tray for serving food and beverages

San ˈsän a race of nomadic hunters of southern Africa now chiefly confined to the Kalahari dessert

san ˈsɑn a sanatorium (by shortening)

sang ˈsɑŋ produced musical tones with the voice

sang ˈsəŋ a Persian harp of the Middle Ages

Santal ‚sənˈtäl a member of a Kolarian people in southeastern Bihar and adjacent Bengal

santal ˈsɑntᵊl a crystalline compound derived from flavone and obtained from red sandalwood and cam wood

santon ˈsɑntən a saint in Muslim countries

santon säⁿtōⁿ a small clay image usually of a saint

sapo ˈsä‚pō a toadfish

sapo ˈsä‚pō a sodium soap, such as castile soap

Sara səˈró a people of the Carolinas tentatively assigned to the Siouan language family

Sara ˈsärə a people of the Shari river in central Africa

sardine sär‚dēn any of several small or immature clupeid fishes

sardine ˈsär‚dīn a deep orange-red variety of chalcedony

sat ˈsɑt rested in a position in which the body is essentially vertical and supported chiefly on the buttocks

sat 'sət eternal and immutable existence, in Hinduism

sate 'sāt to cloy with overabundance
sate ˌsä'tā an Indonesian and Malaysian dish of marinated, bite-sized pieces of meat

satiné 'sɑtᵊn.ā a timber tree of Brazil and the Guianas
satine 'sɑ.tēn a smooth durable lustrous fabric usually made of cotton

saucy 'sɑsē smart or trim, as a ship or automobile
saucy 'sɑisē. marked by impertinent boldness or forwardness

scat 'skät a three-handed card game played with 32 cards
scat 'skɑt to go away quickly; an animal fecal dropping; singing with meaningless syllables instead of words

scena 'shɑnə a scene or accompanied dramatic recitative in an opera
scena 'sēnə the structure of an ancient Greek theater behind the orchestra facing the cavea

second sə'känd to remove a person temporarily from one position for employment elsewhere; to lend someone temporarily to another organization
second 'sekənd next to the first in value or degree

secrete sə'krēt to produce or generate in the manner of a gland
secrète sə'kret a 17th century steel skullcap worn under a soft hat

seer 'sēər a person who sees
seer 'sir a person who predicts events or developments; a prophet

semis 'semēz semifinished metal; trucking rigs
semis sə'mē a scattering repetition of small design motifs to produce an overall pattern

Separate 'sepərət a member of a group favoring revivalism and emotionalism in religion
separate 'sepə.rāt to divide, sever, or detach

Sere 'sārā one of a Negroid people in eastern Sudan
sere 'sārā in Hebrew, a vowel point written below its consonant
sere 'sir dried up or withered

sett 'set a Scottish tartan pattern
sett 'sät a banker or rich merchant in India

severer sə'viər or sē'viər more strict or uncompromising in judgment or discipline
severer 'sevər.ər a person who divides or breaks up into parts

sew 'sō to fasten with stitches of thread or filament
sew 'sü to become grounded, as a ship

sewer 'sōər a person who fastens by stitches of thread or filament
sewer 'süər a conduit to carry off waste material

shames 'shɑməs the sexton of a synagogue; the candle used to light the other candles in a Hanukkah menorah
shames 'shāmz covers with contempt; dishonors or disgraces

shove 'shəv to cause to go by the application of force
shove 'shōv a thin wooden bung for casks or a thin flat cork for stopping a wide-mouthed bottle

shower 'shōr a person who exhibits or demonstrates
shower 'shaůər a rainfall of short duration; a party given by friends to present a person with gifts

sika 'sēkə any of several deers of the eastern Asiatic mainland closely related to the Japanese deer
sika 'ṣikə a flea which is common in the West Indies and South America

simile ˈsiməlē a figure of speech comparing two unlike things, as "a heart as cold as stone"
simile ˈsēmə,lō a musical direction to continue whatever has been previously directed

sin ˈsin a transgression of religious law; a serious offense
sin ˈsēn the 21st letter of the Hebrew alphabet

singer ˈsiŋər a person who produces musical tones with the voice
singer ˈsinjər a person who singes, as a textile worker with cloth

sis ˈsēz plural of the seventh tone of the diatonic scale
sis ˈsis sister (by shortening)

Siva ˈsevä one of the supreme deities of Hinduism
siva ˈsēvə a western Polynesian gesture dance with vocal accompaniment

skene ˈskēnē the structure of an ancient Greek theater behind the orchestra facing the cavea
skene ˈskēn a bronze double-edged dagger used in Ireland

skied ˈskēd glided over snow or water on skis
skied ˈskīd hit a ball high in the air; rose precipitously

skiver ˈskivər to skewer or impale
skiver ˈskīvər a thin soft leather made of the grain side of a split sheepskin

slaver ˈslāvər a person engaged in the trade of persons held in servitude
slaver ˈslavər or ˈslävər to let saliva dribble from the mouth (rarely ˈslāvər)

sliver ˈslivər a splinter or fragment
sliver ˈslīvər a loose soft untwisted strand of textile fiber produced by a carding machine and ready for drawing or roving

slouch ˈslau̇ch a person devoid of energy; to stoop one's head and shoulders
slouch ˈslüch a pipe through which an engine takes up water

slough ˈslü a marshy place
slough ˈsləf something shed or cast off
slough ˈslau̇ to strike heavily

SOB :e.sō'bē a son-of-a-bitch
sob ˈsäb to cry or weep; a noise made while weeping

Sol ˈsäl the sun
sol ˈsäl gold as used in alchemy; a fluid colloidal system; the sunny side or section of a bullfight arena
sol ˈsōl the fifth tone of the diatonic scale in solmization

sola ˈsōlä an East Indian shrubby herb the pith of which is used to make hats and toys
sola ˈsōlə an unduplicated bill of exchange

Solea ˈsōlēə the type genus of Soleidae, a family of flatfishes comprising the typical soles
solea sō'leə a raised part of the floor in front of the inner sanctuary in an Eastern Orthodox Church

son ˈsən the male offspring of human beings
son ˈsōn a folk song of Cuba, Mexico, and Central America; a Latin American ballroom dance

soufflé su:flō an entree or dessert made with white sauce and eggs
souffle ˈsüfəl a blowing sound heard when monitoring internal body parts

sous ˈsü of subordinate rank
sous ˈsau̇s the space outside the white ring of an archery target
sous ˈsüs the smallest pieces of money

sow ˈsō to plant or scatter seed
sow ˈsau̇ an adult female swine

spier ˈspīˀrē a person that watches in a furtive or stealthy manner
spier ˈspīrē a fixed and often architecturally treated screen

spiry ˈspīər rising in a slender tapering form to a point
spiry ˈspiər curving or coiling in spirals

springer ˈspriŋər a person or animal that moves by leaps or bounds
springer ˈsprinjər a person who sets a trap or ensnarement

Squalid ˈskwāləd relating to the Squalidae, a family of sharks having a spine in each dorsal fin
squalid ˈskwäləd marked by filthiness and degradation, usually from neglect (seldom ˈskwōləd)

statist ˈstātəst an advocate of concentrating all economic controls and planning in the hands of a highly centralized government
statist ˈstatəst a person who collects statistics

stingy ˈstinjē reluctant to part with something
stingy ˈstiŋē having a sting

stipes ˈstīps short stalks or supports
stipes ˈstī.pēz the second basal segment of a maxilla of an insect or crustacean

stipulate ˈstipyə.lāt to specify as a condition or requirement of an agreement or offer
stipulate ˈstipyələt furnished with stipules, the leaflike or membranous appendages that arise at the base of a leaf

subject ˈsəbjəkt something that forms an underlying theme or topic
subject səbˈjekt to bring under control or domination; to reduce to submission

sup ˈsüp in mathematics, a least upper bound
sup ˈsəp to eat supper or the evening meal

suppliance ˈsəplēəns a supplication or entreaty
suppliance səˈplīəns the act or process of supplying

supply səˈplī to provide or furnish
supply ˈsəplē in a limber or compliant manner

sura ˈsùrə the fermented juice of various East Indian palms
sura(h) ˈsürə a section or chapter of the Koran

swinger ˈswiŋər a person or thing that sways to and fro
swinger ˈswinjər a person that singes or scorches the pinfeathers off, as of poultry

---

Group I

satiate
stilly
subordinate
subsequence
syndicate

--- T ---

tain ˈtān thin tin plates
tain ˈthȯn one of a class of Irish epic tales, the central theme of which is a marauding expedition for cattle

tales ˈtālz narratives of events
tales ˈtālēz persons added to a jury from those in a courthouse

tali 'tā.lī ankles, especially of human beings

tali 'tālē a gold piece tied about a bride's neck by the bridegroom in India that is worn during his life

tally 'tólī in a tall manner

tally 'talī a reckoning or recorded account of something

Tampan 'tampən a native or resident of Tampa, Florida

tampan 'tam.pan any of various argasid ticks, especially the chicken tick

Tan 'dän a boat-dwelling people whose boats form compact colonies in the river, especially at Canton and Foochow, China

tan 'tan to covert skin into leather; a brownish color

Tang 'tän having characteristics of the Tang dynasty in China

tang 'tan a sharp distinctive flavor; the extension of a knife blade that connects with the handle

tangi 'tanē a lamentation or dirge that accompanies a Maori funeral rite

tangi 'tän.gē a narrow gorge

Tangier tan'jir a major Moroccan seaport near the Strait of Gibraltar; a strong orange color

tangier 'tanēər having a sharper or more distinctive flavor

Tanka 'dän'gä a boat-dwelling people whose boats form compact colonies in the river, especially at Canton and Foochow, China

tanka 'tänkə a Japanese fixed form of verse of five lines

tap 'tap a light usually audible blow or rap

tap 'tap malarial fever

tapa 'täpə a coarse cloth made in the Pacific islands from pounded bark of a variety of plants

tapa 'täpä a snack or appetizer

Tapé .tä'pā an Indian of a former Tupian tribe dwelling on the headwaters of the Uruguay River

tape 'tāp a narrow limp or flexible strip or band

tarry 'tarē to linger, dawdle, or procrastinate

tarry 'tärē covered with tar

Tat 'tät an agricultural people living in scattered groups throughout Transcaucasia

tat 'tät a coarse fabric stretched on a frame and used for withering tea leaves

tat 'tat to make delicate handmade lace

Tatu 'tätü a genus of armadillos

Tatu 'tätü an Indian people of the Eel river valley in northwestern California

taw 'tȯ a marble used as a shooter; to convert skin into white leather

taw 'täf the 23rd letter of the Hebrew alphabet

taxes 'taksəs pecuniary charges imposed by a public authority

taxes 'tak.sēz manual restorations of displaced body parts, as reductions or a hernia; reflex movements by a freely motile and usually simple organism

taxis 'taksəs a manual restoration of displaced body parts, as the reduction of a hernia; a reflex movement by a freely motile and usually simple organism

taxi(e)s 'taxēs chauffeur-driven automobiles available on call to transport passengers usually within a city for a fare (by shortening)

tear 'tir a drop of fluid secreted by the lacrimal gland near the eye

tear 'tar to divide or separate forcibly

terrace 'terəs a raised embankment with the top leveled; a gallery or portico

terrace təˈrɑs a light-colored volcanic tuff resembling pozzolana

Thais ˈtīz natives or inhabitants of Thailand

Thais ˈthāəs a widely distributed genus comprising marine shells with a rough thick shell

theoric thēˈòrik relating to an ancient Greek public spectacle

theoric ˈthēərik an early astronomical device for calculating positions of celestial bodies

thou ˈthau̇ the person being addressed

thou ˈthau̇ a thousand of anything

Thule ˈtülē belonging to the Eskimo culture extending over arctic lands from Alaska to Greenland about A.D. 500–1400; a settlement in northwest Greenland

Thule ˈthülē the northernmost part of the habitable world

tier ˈtir a row, rank, or layer of articles

tier ˈtīər a person who fastens, closes openings, or binds articles

tierce ˈtirs any of various units of liquid capacity, especially one equal to 42 wine gallons; the tone two octaves and a major third above a given tone

tiercé ˈtir:sā in heraldry, divided into three parts of different tinctures or bearing different coats of arms

ting ˈtiŋ a high-pitched sound, as made by a small bell

ting ˈdiŋ an ancient Chinese ceremonial vessel

tinged ˈtinjd slightly shaded or discolored

tinged ˈtiŋd made a high-pitched sound, as made by a small bell

titi ˈtī.tī a tree found in the southern U.S.

titi ˈtə̇ˈtē a small South American monkey

titi ˈtē.tē a New Zealand blue-footed petrel

toilé twä:lā a closely worked solid pattern in lace making that is contrasted with a net ground

toile ˈtwȯl a cloth consisting of various fibers

ton ˈtən a unit of U.S. weight equal to 2000 pounds

ton ˈtōⁿ the prevailing fashion or mode

tonal ˈtənᵊl the force that acts on the mass of a ton to accelerate it equal to one foot per second squared

tonal ˈtōnᵊl relating to the principle of organizing musical chords and notes in recognition of key relationships

tone ˈtōn a vocal or musical sound; a color quality or value

tone ˈdōnē a fishing or coastwise trading boat of India

tonite ˈtō.nīt a blasting explosive consisting of pulverized gun cotton impregnated with barium nitrate

tonite təˈnīt on this present night or the night following this present day (simplified spelling of tonight)

toots ˈtüts sounds a note or call suggesting the short blast of a wind instrument

toots ˈtu̇ts a woman or girl (slang)

tout ˈtau̇t to solicit patronage or canvass for customers

tout ˈtüt winning in a game everything in sight; to proclaim loudly

tower ˈtōər a person or animal that pulls a barge or boat; a person that smoothes ceramic ware

tower ˈtau̇ər a high vertical structure

traject ˈtra.jekt a place for passing across; a crossing route

traject trəˈjekt to transmit light through space or a medium

transform tranzˈförm to change completely or essentially in composition or structure

transform 'trɑnz.fȯrm the substitution of one configuration for or the alternation of a mathematical expression into another in accord with a mathematical rule

travail trə'vāl physical or mental exertion, especially of a painful or laborious nature

travail trə'vī a primitive vehicle used by the Plains Indians of North America

tref 'trāv a homestead or hamlet acting as a single community

tref 'trōf ritually unclean according to Jewish law

trite 'trīt stale or hackneyed

trite 'trī.tē a notation in ancient Greek music

Triton 'trītᵊn one of a class of minor sea divinities or partly human monsters, as the mermaid

triton 'trītᵊn any of the very large marine gastropod mollusks

triton 'trī.tän the nucleus of the tritium atom; *trinitrotoluene* (TNT or dynamite)

tuberose 'tü.brōz a Mexican bulbous herb commonly cultivated for its spike of fragrant white flowers

tuberose 'tübə.rōs resembling a short thickened fleshy stem or root

tun 'tən a large cask

tun 'tùn a period of 360 days used as the basis of the Mayan calendar

Tush 'tùsh a member of the Georgian people north of Tiflis

tush 'tùsh buttocks (slang)

tush 'təsh a long pointed tooth; a tusk

Group I

terminate
tooth
transplant
transport
treen
trefle
triply

U

Ulva 'əlvə a genus of green seaweeds

Ulva 'ülvä a people of Nicaragua and Honduras

umph 'həmf an expression of skepticism or disgust

umph 'ùmf personal charm or magnetism, spirit, or sex appeal

uncrooked :ən'krùkt not turned or bent from a straight line

uncrooked :ən'krùkəd honest or reliable

underage 'əndər'oj less than mature or legal age

underage 'əndərij a shortage or deficit

unionize 'yünyə.nīz to form into a labor union

unionize :ən'īə.nīz to cancel or destroy an equivalent number of oppositely charged ions

unPolish :ən'pōlish not characteristic of Poland or its people

unpolish :ən'pälish to make dull; to remove or deprive of polish

unwind :ən'wīnd to uncoil, disentangle, or straighten out

unwind :ən'wind to deflate or remove the wind from

upwind :əp'wīnd to roll or coil upward

upwind :əp'wind in a position toward the direction from which the wind is blowing

used 'yüzd employed in accomplishing something
used 'yüst accustomed; experienced

user 'yüzər a person who uses alcoholic beverages or drugs
user 'ü.zər the exercise of a right to the enjoyment of property

Uta 'yüd·ə a large genus of iguanid lizards
uta 'üd·ə a skin infection occurring in Central and South America

Group I

ultimate
unable
uncleanly
use

V

vale 'vāl a low-lying area usually containing a stream
vale 'v|älā a salutation on leave-taking

vat 'vɑt a large vessel, tub, or barrel
vat 'vät a temple or other religious monument

vice 'vīs evil conduct
vice 'vīsē in place of

vide 'vīdē see (to direct a reader to another item)
vide 'vēd a musical direction indicating a passage to be omitted

Viola vī'ōlə a genus of leafy stemmed herbs or undershrubs, including the pansy and violet
viola vē'ōlə a musical instrument of the violin family (seldom vī'ōlə)

violet 'vīələt a plant of the genus Viola; a reddish blue color
violet 'vīə.let a tenor viol having usually seven strings

violist 'vīələst a person who plays the viol
violist vē'ōləst a person who plays the viola

vise 'vīs a two-jawed tool for holding work
visé 'vē.zā a visa

visto 'vē.stō in music, very quick
visto 'vis.tō a vista

viva 'vēvə an expression of good will or approval
viva 'vīvə an oral examination

vole 'vōl a rodent closely related to lemmings and muskrats
volé vō'lā a ballet step that is executed with the greatest possible elevation

volte 'vɑlt or 'vōlt a gait in which the horse moves sideways and turns around a center
volte 'vōltā an early French dance with pivots and high springs

Group I

vitiate

W

Wagnerite 'vägnə.rīt an adherent of Wagner's theory of operatic composition

wagnerite 'vägnə.rit magnesium fluorophosphate

wall 'wȯl the external layer of structural material surrounding an object

wall 'wəl to roll the eyes so as to show the white

whoo 'wü an expression of sudden excitement, astonishment, or relief

whoo 'hü the cry of an owl

wicked 'wikəd of evil character

wicked :wikt having a wick, as a lamp

winder 'wīndər a worker or machine that winds yarn or thread

winder 'windər something that takes the breath away, as a hard blow

with the fist or a fast run

winds 'wīndz twists, coils, or curls

winds 'windz natural air movements

won 'wən gained victory in a contest

won 'wȯn the basic monetary unit of South Korea since 1962

woodward 'wu̇.dwərd toward a wood

woodward 'wu̇.dwȯrd an officer charged with guarding a forest

wound 'wünd an injury to the body

wound 'wau̇nd encircled

Group I

winged
worsted

Y

ya 'ya an expression of disgust, contempt, defiance, or derision

ya 'yä scholarly transliteration of the Hebrew tetragrammatron that constitutes a divine proper name, such as Jehovah

yang 'yän the masculine and positive principle in Chinese cosmology that interacts with its opposite yin; a Siamese gurjun balsam tree

yang 'yaŋ a cry of the wild goose

Z

Zemi 'zāmē a Naga people found chiefly in the Barail area of the Assam-Myanmar frontier region

zemi zə'mē an object believed to be the dwelling place of a spirit and to possess magical potency

Appendix: Unusual Groupings

Homophones

Four or more 1-syllable words

aer - air - are - e'er - ere - err - eyre - heir
ai - ay - aye - eye - I
ades - aides - AIDS - aids

ba - baa - bah - bas
baaed - baud - bawd - bod
Baal/baal - bael - bail - bale
bahr - bar - barre - Bhar
bai - buy - by - bye - 'bye
bait - bate - bete - beth
bans - bonds - bons - bonze
baos - boughs - bouse - bows
baule - bole - boll - Bolle - bowl
bawn - Bon - Bonn - bonne
beau - bo - boo - bow
beurre - birr - buhr - bur(r)
bold - boled - bolled - bowled
brae - braies - bray - brey
braes - braise - brays - braze - breys - brys

calk - cauk - caulk - cawk
can - cann - Cannes - khan
cart - carte - kart - quart(e)
cat - cot - cotte - Kot - xat
cay - kay - quai - quay
cees - C's - psis - seas - sees - seize - sis - Szis
ceil - ciel - seal - seel
cense - sents - scents - sense
cepe - cyp - seep - sipe
cere - sear - seer - sere
choux - shoe - shoo - shu
cite - cyte - sight - site

clews - clous - clues - cluse
coal - cole - Ko(h)l - kohl
cor - core - corps - khor
cough - Kaf - kaph - koff
crews - cruise - crus - cruse -krewes - Krus
croes - Cros - Crows/crows - croze

dak - dhak - doc - dock
daos - dauws - dhows - dowse - taos
dew - do - doux - due
does - dos - doughs - doze

eau - oe - oh - owe
ewe - yew - you - yu
ewes - use - yews - youse

faun - fawn - Fon - phon
fraise - frays - fraze - phrase

gnu - knew - new - Nu/nu
gray - greige - grès - griege
grease - Greece - gr(i)ece - gris(e)

hays - haze - he(h)s - heighs - heys
heigh - hi - hie - high
heugh - hoo - Hu - who - whoo
Ho/ho - hoe - Hoh - whoa
hoos - hoose - whos - who's - whose

knap - nap - nape - nappe
knot - nat - naught - naut - not

lacks - lacs - Lak(h)s - laks - lax
lais - lase - lays - laze - leas - leis
Lak(h)s - lochs - locks - lox
leud - lewd - lood - looed

lieu - loo - Loup/loup - Lu

ma'am - malm - Mam - mom
main - Maine - mane - mein
maize - Mayes - Mays - maze
mal - mall - maul - moll
meuse - mews - mus - Muse/muse
mho - mo - mot - mow
mohr - Moor/moor - mor - more -
   mower

nicks - nix - Nyx - Pnyx

oar - o'er - or - ore
oui - we - wee - whee

pa - pah - pas - paw
packs - PACS/pacs - pacts - Paks -
   Pax/pax
pall - pawl - pol - poll
peak - peek - peke - pique
peer - pier - Pierre - pir - pirr - pyr
picks - pics - Picts - pyx
plait - plat - Platt - Platte/platte
plait - plate - Platt - played
praise - prase - prays - preys
psis - scyes - sighs - size

raise - rase - rays - raze - rehs - res -
   reys - rigs
re - Ree/ree - rhe - rig
reams - reems - rhemes - R(h)eims -
   riems

Rhone - roan - rohun - rowan
rhos - roes - Ros - rose - rows
right - Rite/rite - wright - write
road - rode - roed - rowed
roos - roux - rues - ruse

Sacs/sacs - sacks - sacques - sax - Saxe
sann - son - sun - sunn
sault - sew - Sioux - sou - sous - sue -
   suite
schih - she - shea - sidhe
seau - sew - so - sow
Seoul - sol - sole - soul
sewer - soar - sore - sower
sewn - son - sone - sown
suit - suite - sute - tzut

tailles - Tais/tais - Thais - ties - tyes -
   Tyighs
their - there - there're - they're
toad - tode - toed - towed

WAACS - wacks - WACS - wax -
   whacks
ware - wear - weir - wer - where -
   where're
wats - watts - whats - what's
way - Wei - weigh - whey
weal - weel - we'll - wheal - wheel
whew - whoo - woo - Wu
whins - winds - wins - winze - wynns

Three or more 2-syllable words

actin - actine - acton
aerie - aery - airy - Eire
aerie - eerie - Eire
ama - amah - amma
ameen - amine - ammine
antae - ante - anti - auntie
armer - armoire - armor
arras - arris - heiress
attar - odder - otter
aural - oral - orle
Axel - axil - axle

Baatan - bataan - Batan - baton
baetyl - beadle - beetle - betel - bietle
bailee - bailey - bailie
bailer - bailor - baler
baleen - baline - Bilin
barry - berry - bury

bases - basis - basses
bayou - bio - byo
bb - beebee - bibi
Beni - ben(n)e - benny
berley - burley - burly
boarder - bordar - border
bootee - booty - buddhi
borough - burro - burrow
bouché - bouchee - boucher
Britain - Briton - britten

caama - cama - comma - kaama -
   Kama/kama
caapi - copje - copy
cachou - cashew - cashoo
caffa - Kafa - Kaffa
caller - choler - collar
capa - cappa - kappa

cape - kepi - KP
carab - Carib - carob
carat - caret - carrot - karat
carbeen - carbene - carbine
caries - carries - Carys - karris
carman - carmen - carmine
carol - carrel - Karel - kerril - keryl
carry - Cary - karri - kerrie - Kerry
casket - casquet - casquette
cedar - ceder - cedor - cedre - seater - seeder
cellar - sellar - seller
censer - censor - senser - sensor
ceres - Seres - series
ceresin - Saracen - sericin
cerous - cirrus - scirrhus - serous
champagne - champaign - champain
chauffeurs - chauffeuse - shofars
Chile - chili - chilly
choral - chorale - coral
cider - citer - sider - sighter
cirrhus - cirrus - seeress
cited - sided - sighted
citrene - citrin - citrine
clamber - clammer - clamor
coaly - coly - Koli
cobble - coble - Kabul
coccal - cockal - cockle
cocky - kaki - khaki
coda - cota - Kota
coddle - cottle - katel
comics - comix - kamiks
coolie - cool(l)y - coulee
Cora/cora - corah - kora
coscet - cosset - cossette
cotter - Kadir - quatre
courant - currant - current
crawley - crawlie - crawly
crewman - crumen - Kruman
crotal - crotale - crotyl
cuckoo - cucu - kuku
curdle - curtal - kirtle
cyan - Cyon - (s)cion - Sion
cycle - Seckel - Sicel - sickle
cygnet - signate - signet
Cyon - psion - (s)cion
cypress - Cypris - Cyprus

dalli - dally - dolly
daughter - dodder - dotter
deasil - decile - decyl - desyl
decan - Deccan - dekan

Dewar - dewer - doer - dour - dur
dhoti - doty - dudie
dieing - dyeing - dying
diker - duiker - dyker
docile - dossal - dossil
dooley - dooly - duly

endue - undo - undue

faded - fated - feted
farci - farcy - Farsi
faro - farrow - pharaoh
feral - ferrule - ferule
filar - filer - phylar
flaven - flavin - flavine
florin - flourene - flourine
forcene - forescene - foreseen
forcite - forecite - foresight
frater - freighter - phrator

gaiter - gater - gator
gala - Gal(l)a - galla - gallow
galley - gallie - gally
gaufre - gofer - goffer - gopher
gaufre - goffer - golfer
ginny - jinni - jinny
glacis - glassie - glassy
grader - grater - greater
grisly - gristly - grizzly
gumbo - gumboe - gum-bow

hackee - hackie - hacky
hallo - hallow - halo - hollo
heater - heder - heeder
holey - Holi - holy - wholly
howel - Howell - howl
human - humin - Yuman
humbles - umbels - umbles

idle - idol - idyll

knotty - naughty - noddy

laager - lager - logger
laurel - lauryl - loral - lorel
leachy - lichi - Litchi
leader - lieder - liter
leaver - lever - levir - liefer
lewder - looter - loutre - luter
liar - lier - lyre
liens - lions - Lyons

Mahri - Maori - Mari - marri
maizer - maser - mazer
Malay - mele - melee

Mali - mal(l)ie - molle - molly - moly
mare - Mayer - mayor
marischal - Marshall - marshal(l) -
    martial
marquees - Marquis/marquis - marq-
    uise
marry - mere - merry
medal - meddle - metal - mettle
meddler - medlar - metal(l)er
mini - Minni - minnie
missal - missel - missile
moirés - morays - mores
Moonie - moony - muni
Mossi - mossie - mossy

nitrile - nitryl - nytril
nodous - nodus - notice - Notus

oater - Oder - odor
ox-eyed - oxhide - oxide

paddy - patty - paty
paean - paion - peon
pairle - parrel - peril
palate - palette - pallet - pallette
Paris - parous - Parus
parol - parole - pyrrole
patens - patents - pattens - Pattons
Paya - pia - pyre
pedal - peddle - petal
plainer - planar - planer
platan - platen - platten
pleural - plural - plurel
polar - poler - poller
pomace - pumice - pummice
Psylla/psylla - Scilla/scilla - Scylla
Pteris - teras - terrace

quidder - quitter - quittor

rabat - rabbet - rabbit - rabot
racket - rackett - racquet
raiser - raser - razer - razor
rea - Rhea/rhea - ria - rya
reader - reeder - rhetor
Reading - redding - retting
ready - Reddi - reddy

regal - regle - riegel
reiter - rider - righter - writer
retard - retarred - ritard
riband - ribband - ribboned

Sacae - Sakai - sockeye
saeter - satyr - Seder
sandhi - sundae - Sunday
saran - serein - serin
sari - saury - sorry
saurel - sorel - sorrel
sawder - sodder - solder
scissel - scissile - Sicel - sisal - sisel -
    syssel
scissel - scissile - sizzle
senate - senit - sen(n)et - sinnet
sewer - soor - suer
solan - Solen/solen - solon
sordid - sorted - sworded
souma - Suma - summa
stealer - steeler - stelar
steelie - steely - stelae - stele
stolen - stollen - stolon

tailer - tailor - talar
talkie - talky - tawkee
taxes - taxis - Taxus
tearer - terrar - terror
teeter - titar - titer
termen - termine - termon
terrene - terrine - tureen
testae - teste - testee
tooter - Tudor - tutor
triptik - triptych - tryptic
troolie - truli - truly

unsold - unsoled - unsouled

vairé - vary - very

waded - waited - weighted
wader - waiter - weighter
wailer - waler - whaler
weather - wether - whether
wedding - wetting - whetting
whirley - whirly - wurley
windroad - windrode - windrowed

Three or more 3-syllable words

accidence - accidens - accidents
acetic - ascetic - Ossetic
aerial - areal - ariel
allision - elision - Elysian

alluded - eluded - eluted
allusion - elusion - illusion
area - aria - eria
Austria - Ostrea - ostria - Ostrya

Barbary - barberry - barbery
barrier - berrier - burier

cadalene - Catalan - Catalin
calabar - calabur - caliber
ceresin - Saracen - sericin
Cereus - serious - Sirius
chorea - Correa/correa - keriah - Korea
cirrhosis - psorosis - sorosis
confidant - confidante - confident - confitent
Cyclamen - cyclamin - cyclamine

deviser - devisor - divisor

emission - immission - omission
Eurya - urea - Uria

ileum - ilium - illium

manakin - mannequin - mannikin

parasite - parisite - pericyte
Paridae - parity - parody
populace - populous - Populus

reciting - re-siding - resighting - resiting
rhodeose - roadeos - rodeos

ternary - ternery - turnery

unceded - unseated - unseeded
uncited - unsided - unsighted
unfaded - unfated - unfeted
uranous - Uranus - urinous

All 4, 5, and 6-syllable words

Acacian - acaciin
Acadian - Akkadian
acclamation - acclimation
acephalous - acephalus
Aceria - Assyria
acrogenous - acrogynous
Adelea - Adelia
adventuress - adventurous
Alectrion - Alectryon
allegation - alligation
allegator - Alligator/alligator
alliterate - illiterate
allocator - allocatur
all together - altogether
amaretto - amoretto
Ambassadeur - ambassador
America - Amerika
amygdalin - amygdaline
androgenous - androgynous - androgynus
annunciate - enunciate
antecedence - antecedents
aplanatism - aplanetism
apophasis - apophysis
araneous - Araneus
Arianism - Aryanism
aureolin - aureoline
autonomous - autonymous

basilican - basilicon
Bougainvillaea - Bougainvillia

Caecilian - Sicilian
caliginous - kaligenous

calumniation - columniation
Camptosaurus - Camptosorus
censorial - sensorial
cerulean - c(o)erulein
cessionary - sessionary
Chamaeleon - chameleon
chlorogenin - chlorogenine
Chrysochloris - chrysochlorous
Cilicia - Silicea
Colombia - Columbia
Colombian - Columbian
comedia - commedia
commissariat - commissariot
compellation - compilation
complementary - complimentary
confectionary - confectionery
confirmation - conformation
consensual - consentual
continuance - continuants
conventical - conventicle
corydalis - Corydalus
covariance - covariants
cynicism - Sinicism
cynocephalous - Cynocephalus/cynocephalus
cytology - sitology

deprevation - deprivation
diaphane - diaphony
diverstisement - divertissement

ectocarpous - Ectocarpus
enterocele - enterocoele
enumerable - innumerable

ephemeris - ephemerous
escaladed - escalated
euonymous - Euonymus/euonymus
expatriate - ex-patriot

geophilous - Geophilus

heterogenous - heterogynous
heteronomous - heteronymous
hypogenous - hypogynous

ideogram - idiogram
ideograph - idiograph
impartable - impartible
impassable - impassible
infirmation - information
installation - instillation
intercession - intersession
interdental - interdentile
interosseous - interosseus
interpellate - interpolate

Jacobean - Jacobian

leptocephalous - Leptocephalus
leptodactylous - Leptodactylus

macrocephalous - Macrocephalus
martineta - martinete
menology - monology
micropterous - Micropterus
miliary - milliary
millenary - millinary
monogeneous - monogynous
myatonia - myotonia

overflour - overflower
overmeddled - overmettled

papagallo - papagayo
paragnathous - paragnatus
pentamerous - Pentamerus

periodic - periotic
perpetuance - perpetuants
phenology - phonoloy
physocarpous - Physocarpus
pluripotence - pluripotents
pneumatophorous - Pneumatophorus
polydactylous - Polydactylus
positivest - positivist
precedential - presidential
precipitance - precipitants
projicience - projicients
pterocarpous - Pterocarpus

sarcophagous - sarcophagus
sarcophilous - Sarcophilus
single-seated - single-seeded
stationary - stationery
subhyalin - subhyaline
superepic - superepoch
synechological - synecological

talkee-talkee - talky-talky
technology - tecnology
tetrastichous - Tetrastichus
tetravalence - tetravalents
theocracy - theocrasy
topography - typography
topology - typology
trachycarpous - Trachycarpus

unaffected - uneffected
unamendable - unemendable
uncomplementary - uncomplimentary
unerupted - unirrupted
unexercised - unexorcised
uniparous - uniporous

veracity - voracity
viviparous - Viviparus

wistaria - Wisteria

Homographs

Please refer to the appropriate word-grouping in the Homograph section of this dictionary to determine the pronunciation of each word in that word-grouping.

Three or more words

As/as
August/august
comes

Concord/concord
Even/even
fine

fourchette
grave
Guara/guara
lather
Mobile/mobile
Mole/mole
nana
Pala/pala
papa

Passe/passé/passe
pate/pâte/paté/pâté
pili
Rabat/rabat
salve
slough
sous
titi

Homophones and Homographs

All words that are both homophones and homographs. To recall the pronunciation of each word shown below, please refer to its underlined companion in the Homograph section of this dictionary.

aba
abaisse
aloe
anti
Arkansas
arras
As
aspirate
ate
ate
atta
axes
aye

ballet
ban
bar
bare
barre
bases
basis
bass
baule
bene
Beni
berg
Bern(e)
beurre
bin
bole
bombé
bombe
Bon
bon
bore

borne
bouché
boule
bow
bow
Brut

cala
cape
Cassia
cassia
cat
cave
cay
cay
cete
cham
chamar
chap
chap
chil
chose
choux
choux
classes
close
coax
coax
coif
colon
come
commit
connex
connex
coop

coupe
couped
crotal
crotal
crus

dah
desert
dine
do
do
does
dom
dos
dos

eve
ewe

file
filé
flageolet
flower
formal
forme
forte
forte
frater
fray
frette
frappe
fur

gallant
gally
gaufre
gene
genet
ger
gill
gill
gimel
glace
goût
grave
graves

hache
hale
halo
Hamburg
headward
here

kaki
Kasha
kate
Kin

Lais
lais
Lak(h)s
laks
laser
lat
lax
laze
lead
lied
lied
lien
lien
lira
lis
lower
lunger

male
Mam
mane
manes
mare
maria
matte
mere
mere
mind
mire
Mod
mod
Mojo
mole
molle
moly
Mon
morné
morne
mot
mow
mow
Mus
mus

nance
Nice
nice
none

nun
nun
Nut
nut

oner
ore

Pali/pali
pan
pan
pane
passé
pate
pâte
patte
peak
peak
peer
Pila/pila
piqué
pique
pirr
pirr
planes
plat
poise
poll
poll
pram
present
primer
put

quart(e)
quiche

rabat
Reading
real
reason
res
res
rheum
rig
Rite/rite
robin
rose
rote
rows
rows
Rum/rum

rum

sake
sal
salver
sang
sang
satiné
saucy
scat
second
seer
sere
sett
sett
sew
sew
sewer
sewer
shames
shower
sin
sin
sis
sis
slough
slough
Sol/sol
son
son
sous
sous
sow
sow
spier
spier
sup
suppliance
sura
sura(h)

tales
Tampan
tang
tangi
tarry
taxes
taxes
taxi(e)s
taxis
taw
tear

tear   tun
terrace   Tush/tush
Thais
Thule   vale
tier   vice
tier   vise
ton   volé
ton   volte
tonal
tone   whoo
tower   whoo
travail   winds
tref   winds
                              won

Annotated Bibliography

The following books and articles were consulted in preparing this volume. The terms **homophone** (bona fide, Group I, and Group II), **homograph** (bona fide and Group I), and or **homonym** used in these annotations are defined in the table on p. 2 and the narrative on p. 1 of this dictionary.

Anderson, James G. *Le Mot Juste: A Dictionary of English and French Homonyms* (revised by L. C. Harmer). New York: Dutton, 1938. A listing of French and English words that are similar in spelling, meaning, and or pronunciation, such as **abscond** (English)/**abscondre** (French). 383 pp.

Baillairge, Charles P. Florent. *Vocabulary of English Homonyms.* Quebec: C. Darveavy, 1891. A mixture of homonyms, homophones (bona fide, Group I, and Group II), and homographs without segregation. Proper names, places, rivers, and words such as **a loft/aloft** are included. 190 pp.

Barrett, Bryon S. *Book of Homonyms: With Copious Exercises on Homogenous and Homophonous Words.* New York: Pitman, 1908. The book is written from a "practical rather than a theoretical viewpoint," and contains compound and hyphenated words, uses of the apostrophe and figures, and rules for spelling, formation of plurals, and contractions. Approximately 600 words are included, reflecting a mixture without segregation of "homophonous" words (words pronounced alike but spelled differently) and "homogenous" words (words somewhat alike in pronunciation or spelling, with different or similar meanings, such as **affect, effect, effects, in effect,** and **effective**). Numerous proper names are included. 192 pp.

Basil, Cynthia. *How Ships Play Cards.* New York: Morrow, 1980. An illustrated children's book containing 13 homonyms. 32 pp.

_____. *Nailheads and Potato Eyes: A Beginning Word Book.* New York: Morrow, 1976. An illustrated children's book containing several homonyms. 32 pp.

Behrens, June. *What Is a Seal?* LaPuente, CA: Jay Alden, 1975. An illustrated children's book of homonyms. 32 pp.

Bilucaglia, Marino. *Gli Omonimi nella Lingua Inglese (The Homonyms in the English Language).* Milan: Istituto Editoriale Cisalpino, ca. 1968. A book of English homonyms translated into Italian. 159 pp.

Bossom, Naomi. *A Scale Full of Fish and Other Turnabouts.* New York: Greenwillow Books (Division of Wm. Morrow & Co.), 1979. An illustrated children's book containing 20 homonyms. 24 pp.

Bostick, Charles W. "Homophones Pairs," *Word Ways.* Vol. 10, No. 1, Feb. 1977, p. 26.

Brandreth, Gyles. *More Joy of Lex: An Amazing and Amusing Z to A and A to Z of Words.* New York: Morrow & Co., 1982. An assemblage of oddities, puns, and word amusements in the English language. 287 pp.

Bridges, Sir Robert Sheldon. *On English Homophones.* (Society for Pure English Tract No. II.) Oxford, England: Clarendon Press, 1919. England's poet laureate from 1913 to 1930 makes a broadside indictment of Daniel Jones' system of phonetic spelling and pronunciation. Sir Robert's arguments are: (1) Homophones are a nuisance and are mischievous; (2) They are exceptionally frequent in the English language; (3) They are self-destructive and tend to become obsolete (although he admitted that this argument was difficult to prove); (4) Nonetheless, their loss impoverishes the language; and (5) This impoverishment is proceeding at an accelerated pace due to the general prevalence of the Southern English standard of speech encouraged by Mr. Jones' theory of fanatic phoneticism which is causing "the mauling of words." 48 pp.

Carruth, Gorton, David H. Scott, and Beverly J. Yerge. *The Transcriber's Handbook: With the Dictionary of Sound-Alike Words.* New York: Wiley, 1984. Numerous bona fide homophones and homographs, Group I and Group II homophones, and often confused words such as **laboratory/lavatory** are contained in the Dictionary section, pp. 22–274. 519 pp.

Cerutti, Bruno Augusto. *Dizionario degli Omofoni Inglesi (Dictionary of English Homophones).* Milan: Casa Editrice Ceschina, 1967. English homophones are translated into Italian and incorporated into illustrative English sentences. 1,277 pp.

Cook, Olive Marie. *Sparks for Sparkle: A Book of Homonyms and Double-Duty Words.* Upland, IN: A. D. Freese & Sons, 1963. The intended audience for this book includes persons who enter advertising jingle contests and complete such phrases as "Brand X peanut butter is great because. . ." 129 pp.

Dictionary of American Regional English, Volume I, Introduction and A–C. (Frederic G. Cassidy, chief editor). Cambridge, Mass.: Belknap Press of Harvard University Press, 1985. 903 pp. + clvi pp.

Dictionary of American Regional English, Volume II, D–H. (Frederic G. Cassidy, chief editor). Cambridge, Mass.: Belknap Press of Harvard University Press, 1991. 1175 pp. + xv pp.

Durso, Mary Wilkes. *Mastering Confusing Words: A Basic Approach to Meaning and Spelling.* New York: Wiley, 1965. Several bona fide and Group II homophones and confusing words such as **defer/differ.** 245 pp.

Ellyson, Louise Withers. *A Dictionary of Homonyms: New Word Patterns.* Mat-'tituck, NY: Banner Books (Amereon Ltd.), 1977. This volume claims to be the first serious and complete dictionary of English language homonyms. Homonyms, homophones (bona fide and Group I), and homographs are intermixed, such as **sew, so, sow** (to plant), and **sow** (a female pig). Numerous proper names are included. "Bruisers" (near-homonyms or words that are so much alike as to be easily confused, such as **accidence/accidents, adieu/ado, assay/essay, bauble/bubble,** and **bellow/below**) are included in a separate section. 166 pp.

Espy, Willard R. *An Almanac of Words at Play.* New York: Clarkson N. Potter, 1975. Several bona fide homophones are on pp. 15, 131–132, and 315–316. 360 pp.

————. *The Game of Words.* New York: Grosset & Dunlap, 1972. Several bona fide homophones are reflected on pp. 126–132. 279 pp.

————. *Say It My Way.* Garden City, NY: Doubleday & Co., 1980. A few bona fide homophones are included on p. 87. 219 pp.

Franklyn, Julian. *Which Witch? Being a Grouping of Phonetically Compatible Words.* Boston: Houghton Mifflin, 1966. Homophones (bona fide, Group I, and Group II) are intermixed with homographs. Numerous proper names are included. Groups of homophonic words are arranged in illustrative sentences or paragraphs, such as "skill with the adze adds virtue to the man." 198 pp.

Games. Published monthly at PO Box 10145, Des Moines, Iowa, 50340, often provides several homophones and homographs. The publisher is PSC Games Ltd. Partnership, 810 7th Avenue, New York, NY 10019 (212-246-4640).

Gilliéron, Jules, and Mario Roques. *Études de Géographie Linguistique: L'Atlas Linguistique de la France (Studes of Linguistic Geography: According to the Linguistic Atlas of France).* Paris: Honore Champion, 1912. In this work, Gilliéron introduces the doctrine that two words of different origin which become homonyms by regular sound changes may interfere (due to ambiguity and confusion) with one another to such as extent that one is ultimately excluded from the vocabulary of a particular dialect. 155 pp. plus maps.

Gilman, Mary Louise. *3000 Sound-Alikes and Look-Alikes.* Vienna, VA: National Shorthand Reporters' Association, 1986. The volume contains bona fide homophones, homonyms, and confusing words like **abduct/adduct.** 60 pp.

Gwyne, Fred. *A Chocolate Moose for Dinner.* New York: Windmill Books/Simon and Schuster, 1976. An illustrated children's book of several bona fide homophones and homonyms. 47 pp.

_____. *The King Who Rained.* New York: Windmill Books and E.P. Dutton, 1970. An illustrated children's book of 19 homonyms and homophones. 40 pp.

_____. *A Little Pigeon Toad.* New York: Simon and Schuster Books for Young Readers, 1988. An illustrated children's book of thirteen bona fide homophones and seven homonyms. 47 pp.

_____. *The Sixteen Hand Horse.* New York: Windmill/Wanderer Books, 1988. An illustrated children's book containing six bona fide homophones and sixteen homonyms. 47 pp.

Hanlon, Emily. *How a Horse Grew Hoarse on the Site Where He Sighted a Bare Bear: A Tale of Homonyms.* New York: Delacorte, Press, 1976. An illustrated children's book containing several bona fide homophones. 32 pp.

Hanson, Joan. *Homographic Homophones: Fly and Fly and Other Words That Sound the Same But Are as Different in Meaning as Bat a Bat.* Minneapolis: Lerner, 1973. An illustrated children's book of 26 homophones. 32 pp.

_____. *Homographs: Bow and Bow and Other Words That Look the Same But Sound as Different as Sow and Sow.* Minneapolis: Lerner, 1972. An illustrated children's book of homographs (bona fide and Group I). 32 pp.

_____. *Homonyms: Hair and Hare and Other Words That Sound the Same but Look as Different as Bear and Bare.* Minneapolis: Lerner, 1972. An illustrated children's book of 26 homophones. 26 pp.

_____. *More Homonyms: Steak and Stake and Other Words That Sound the Same but Look as Different as Chili and Chilly.* Minneapolis: Lerner, 1973. An illustrated children's book of 26 homophones. 32 pp.

_____. *Still More Homonyms: Night and Knight and Other Words That Sound the Same but Look as Different as Ball and Bawl.* Minneapolis: Lerner, 1976. An illustrated children's book of 26 homophones. 32 pp.

Harder, Keith C. "The Relative Efficiency of the 'Separate' and 'Together' Methods of Teaching Homonyms." *Journal of Experimental Education,* Sept., 1937, pp. 7–23. An abstract of Harder's doctoral dissertation at Iowa State University in which he tested two methods of teaching the spelling of homonyms (actually homophones): (1) presenting each pair of words (such as **dear** and **deer**) together simultaneously; and (2) presenting the words separately with a three- to four-day interval between exposure to each word. He concluded that pupils learned to spell by either method and the range of differences in learning between the two was small.

Harrison, Jim. *Confusion Reigns: A Quick and Easy Guide to the Most Easily Mixed-Up Words*. New York: St. Martin's Press, 1987. This volume contains a mix of bona fide homophones, homonyms, and easily confused words like **ablution/absolution** and **flounder/founder**. 119 pp.

Hobbs, James B. *Homophones and Homographs: An American Dictionary*. Jefferson, NC: McFarland, 1986. The first edition of this volume contains 3,625 bona fide homophones, 602 bona fide homographs, numerous Group I homophones and homographs, Groups I and II homophones, unusual groupings, and an annotated bibliography. It served as the prototype for this second edition. 264 pp.

Hodges, Richard. *A Special Help to Orthographie or the True-Writing of English*. Ann Arbor: Edwards Bros., 1932. A mixture of bona fide homophones and confusing words like **beholden/beholding, valley/value** are included. 27 pp.

Hunt, Bernice Kohn. *Your Ant Is a Which: Fun with Homophones*. New York: Harcourt Brace Jovanovich, 1975. An illustrated children's book containing several bona fide homophones. 32 pp.

Kilpatrick, James Jackson. *The Ear Is Human: A Handbook of Homophones and Other Confusions*. Kansas City, KS: Andrews, McMeel & Parker, 1985. A mix of bona fide homophones and confusing words like **appraise/apprise** are included. 119 pp.

Kirtland, Elizabeth. *Write Is Right: A Handbook of Homonyms*. New York: Golden Press, 1968. Contains 1,650 homonyms and homophones (bona fide and Group I, such as **mucous/mucus**). Numerous obsolete and archaic words, proper names, and suffix-extended words such as **dyeing/dying** are included, plus a homonym quiz containing 108 exercises. 128 pp.

Klasky, Charles. *Rugs Have Naps (But Never Take Them)*. Chicago: Childrens Press, 1984. An illustrated children's book containing several homonyms. 31 pp.

Klepinger, Lawrence. *Write English Right: An ESL Homonym Workbook*. New York: Barron's Educational Series, 1993. An instruction book offering English-as-a-second-language students a method to unravel complexities surrounding numerous English homophones. 160 pp.

Kreivsky, Joseph and Jordan L. Linfield. *The Bad Speller's Dictionary*. New York: Random House, 1987. A large listing of frequently misspelled and often confused words, including numerous "look-alikes," almost "look-alikes," "sound-alikes," and almost "sound-alikes." 186 pp.

————. and ————. *Word Traps: A Dictionary of the 7,000 Most Confusing Sound-alike and Look-alike Words*. New York: Collier Books—Macmillan Publishing Co., 1993. A compendium of about 2,000 bona fide homophones, ten homographs, several Type II homophones, and numerous other confusing words, such as *haircut* and *haricot*. 319 pp.

Kruger, Gustav. *Synonymik un Wortgebrauch der Englischen Sprache (Synonyms and Word Usage of the English Language)*. Dresden and Leipzig: C. A. Koch, 1897. Contains mostly English synonyms (such as **tall, large, great, big,** and **hug**) translated into German. 1,528 pp.

Kudrna, Charlene Imbior. *Two-way Words*. Nashville: Abingdon, 1980. An illustrated children's book of twelve pairs of bona fide homophones and twelve pairs of homonyms. 32 pp.

Lecky, Prescott. *The Playbook of Words.* New York: F. A. Stokes, 1933. An illustrated children's book of homonyms. 36 pp.

The Lincoln Library of Essential Information, 18th edition, Vol. I. Buffalo, NY: Frontier Press, 1949. Several bona fide homophones are reflected on pp. 67–69.

Longman, Harold S. *Would You Put Your Money in a Sand Bank?: (Fun with Words).* Chicago: Rand McNally, 1966. An illustrated children's book containing several bona fide homophones and homonyms. 46 pp.

McGraw-Hill Dictionary of Scientific and Technical Terms. (Sybil P. Parker, editor). 3rd edition. New York: McGraw-Hill, 1984. A reference work containing 98,500 scientific and technical terms. 1,781 pp.

McLenighan, Valjean. *One Whole Doughnut, One Doughnut Hole.* Chicago: Children's Press, 1982. An illustrated children's book of fifteen pairs of bona fide homophones. 30 pp.

Maestro, Giulio. *What's a Frank Frank?: Tasty Homograph Riddles.* New York: Clarion Books, 1984. An illustrated children's book containing several bona fide homophones. 64 pp.

Manchester, Richard B. *The Mammoth Book of Word Games.* New York: Hart Publishing, 1976. Several homophones are reflected on pp. 38–39, 88–89, 449, 456, and 458. 510 pp.

Menner, Robert J. "The Conflicts of Homophones in English." *Language* 12 (1936), pp. 229–44. Professor Menner critiques and refines the doctrine (advanced by Jules Gilliéron from 1902 to 1921) that two words of different origin which become homonyms by regular sound changes may interfere (due to ambiguity and confusion) with one another to such an extent that one is ultimately excluded from the vocabulary of a particular dialect.

Murdoch, John. *The Dictionary of Distinctions in Three Alphabets.* London: 1811. The book consists of three sections called "alphabets": (1) "Words the same in sound, but of different spelling and signification; with which are classed such as have any similarity in sound, proper names not excepted." This section includes homophones (bona fide and Group I), near-homophones (such as **adapt/adept/adopt** and **clef/cliff**), obsolete and archaic words, dialects (such as dropping an *h* to make homophones like **eddy/heady** or **hitch/itch**), and names of cities and countries; (2) "Showing how one orthography has a plurality of pronunciations, and varies in sound or meaning according to the circumstances of accentuation or connection" (such as a **vast/avast**); and (3) "Which points out the various changes, in sound and sense, produced by the addition of the letter *e*, whether final or medial" (such as **bar/bare**, or **bar/bear**).

Newhouse, Dora. *The Encyclopedia of Homonyms: 'Sound-alikes.'* Hollywood, CA: Newhouse Press, 1976. Contains homophones (bona fide, Group I, and Group II), archaic and obsolete words, dialects, proper names, and places. 238 pp.

————. *Homonyms: Sound-alikes—Homonimos: A Bilingual Reference Guide to the Most Mispronounced, Misspelled, and Confusing Words in the English Language.* Los Angeles: Newhouse Press, 1978. This volume is an updated and expanded version of Newhouse's *Encyclopedia of Homonyms* containing about 3,500 English words that are translated into Spanish. Includes homophones (bona fide, Group I, and Group II), homonyms, obsolete and archaic words, dialects, foreign coins and measures, geographic locations, and suffixes. 247 pp.

Ogata, Hideo and Roger Julius Inglott. *A Dictionary of English Homonyms: Pronouncing and Explanatory.* Tokyo: Maruzen, 1942. Approximately 2,900

English words are translated into Japanese, including homophones (bona fide, Group I, and Group II), obsolete and archaic words, dialects, proper names, countries and nationalities, foreign coins and weights, and suffixes. 271 pp.

The Oxford English Dictionary, 2nd edition. J. A. Simpson and E. S. Weiner, compilers. Oxford: Clarendon Press, 1989. Volumes I–XX. This classic reference was a useful arbiter in deciding several technical issues that arose during the compilation of the second edition of this book.

Paxson, William C. *The New American Dictionary of Confusing Words.* New York: Signet, 1990. A dictionary of approximately 2,000 commonly confused words and terms, such as **ectomorph, endomorph**, and **mesomorph**. A few bona fide homophones are included. 311 pp.

Phythian, B. A. *A Concise Dictionary of Confusables: All Those Impossible Words You Never Get Right.* New York: John Wiley & Sons, 1990. A dictionary of frequently confused words, such as insidious/invidious, maladroit/malaprops, perpetrate/perpetuate, and repairable/reparable. A few bona fide homophones are included. 198 pp.

Powell, David. *Look-alike, Sound-alike, Not-alike Words: An Index of Confusables.* Washington, DC: University Press of America, 1962. A particularly useful source of bona fide homophones and homographs (plus confusing words). 185 pp.

Raith, Josef von. *Englische Dictate mit Homophonen (English Dictation with Homophones).* Stuttgart: Ernst Klett, 1970. Contains about 375 homophones with numerous illustrative sentences, paragraphs, exercises, and examination questions. 61 pp.

The Random House Dictionary of the English Language. 2nd Edition, unabridged. (Stuart B. Flexner, editor in chief). New York: Random House, 1987. 2478 pp. + xlii + 32 pp. of maps.

Raymond, Eric S. (ed.). *The Hacker's Dictionary.* Boston: MIT Press, 1991. A comprehensive compendium of computer terminology and slang, illuminating many aspects of hacker tradition, folklore, and humor. 433 pp.

Rockey, Denyse. *Phonetic Lexicon of Monosyllabic and Some Diasyllabic Words, with Homophones, Arranged According to Their Phonetic Structure.* London: Heyden & Son, 1973. Developed from material compiled during Rockey's years of professional work in speech and hearing clinics, this volume has a practical clinical orientation. Seventy-nine tables, each in a matrix format of 19 columns and 40 lines (monosyllabic and diasyllabic only), contain 7,754 words positioned according to their initial, medial, and final sound. Approximately 3,500 homophones are listed, including proper names, letters of the alphabet, colloquialisms and slang, common abbreviations, contractions, acronyms, foreign words adopted by English, obsolete and archaic words, dialect, and technical words. 250 pp.

Sage, Michael. *If You Talked to a Boar.* Philadelphia: Lippincott, 1960. An illustrated children's book of 24 homophones. 31 pp.

Schmidt, Jacob Edward. *English Speech for Foreign Physicians, Scientists, and Students.* Springfield, IL: Chas. C. Thomas, 1972. This book was designed "to knock down the barricades and widen the bottlenecks of communication between visitors and natives of the United States." A 78-page section includes approximately 890 words containing a mixture of homonyms, homophones (bona fide and Group I), homographs, and other closely associated but confusing words like **exalt/extol/exult**. 237 pp.

Scholastic Dictionary of Synonyms, Antonyms, Homonyms. New York: Scholastic Book Services, 1965. 220 pp.

Shipley, Joseph Twadell. *Playing with Words.* Englewood Cliffs, NJ: Prentice-Hall. Several homophones are reflected on pp. 73–75 and 119. 186 pp.

Sieron, Martha. *Dictionary of Confusing Words.* Miami, FL: M. Sieron, 1986. A mixture of bona fide homophones and homographs, plus confusing words like **ablate/oblate** and **accrue/ecrue**. 431 pp.

Snow, Emma. "My List of Homophonenous [sic] Words." *The Association Review.* American Association to Promote the Teaching of Speech to the Deaf: 1903. Contains a list of homophonous words that cause frequent confusion among lip-readers, being relatively difficult to distinguish visually, such as **back, bank, bag, bang,** and **pack.**

Terban, Marvin. *The Dove Dove: Funny Homophone Riddles.* New York: Clarion Books, 1988. An illustrated children's book containing several bona fide homographs. 64 pp.

_____. *Eight Ate: A Feast of Homonym Riddles.* New York: Clarion Books, 1982. An illustrated children's book containing several homonyms. 32 pp.

_____. *Funny You Should Ask: How to Make Up Jokes and Riddles with Wordplay.* New York: Clarion Books of Houghton Mifflin Co., 1992. An illustrated book of several homophones, "almost homophones," and homonyms (which are mis-identified as homographs). 64 pp.

_____. *Hey, Hay!: A Wagonful of Funny Homonym Riddles.* Boston: Clarion Books of Houghton Mifflin Co., 1991. An illustrated book of 214 homophones, including several proper names. 64 pp.

Tester, Sylvia Root. *Never Monkey with a Monkey: A Book of Homographic Homophones.* Elgin, IL: Child's World, 1977. An illustrated childrens' book containing several homonyms. 32 pp.

_____. *What Did You Say? A Book of Homophones.* Elgin, IL: Child's World, 1977. An illustrated children's book of 32 homophones. 30 pp.

Thomas, Jonathan. *English as She Is Fraught.* London: Wolfe, 1976. A collection of numerous homonyms, homophones, and double entendres — many of which are off-color or have sexual overtones. Illustrated. 95 pp.

Townsend, William Cameron. *A Handbook of Homophones of General American English.* Waxhaw, NC: International Friendship. 1975. Numerous bona fide homophones and homographs, plus closely associated words like **abase/a base.** 121 pp.

Tyschler, Iosif Solomonovich. *Slovar' Omonimov Sovremennogo Iazya Angliiskogo (Dictionary of Contemporary English Homonyms).* Saratov, U.S.S.R.: Saratov University Press, 1963. Contains English homophones and homonyms translated into Russian. 231 pp.

Van Gelder, Rosalind. *Monkeys Have Tails.* New York: David McKay Co., 1966. An illustrated children's book containing several bona fide homophones and homonyms. 48 pp.

Waite, C. B. *Homophonic Vocabulary: Containing More than 2,000 Words.* Chicago: C. V. Waite, 1904. Over 2,000 words that are common to nearly all Indo-European languages are included. For example **alcohol** (English, Spanish, Dutch); **alkohol** (Danish, German, Norwegian, Swedish); **alkogol'** (Russian — the **g** is a guttural **h**); and **alcool** (French, Italian, Portuguese). 162 pp.

_____, and C. V. Waite. *Homophonic Conversations: In English, German, French, and Italian.* Chicago: C. V. Waite, 1903. The principal words of almost every sentence and phrase in this book have a similar sound and meaning in at least three of the four languages selected. For example: **At what hour** (English); **À quelle heure** (French); **A che ora** (Italian); **um wieviel Uhr** (German). 137 pp.

Wallace, Viola. *Wordwise.* New York: Vantage Press, 1968. Contains approximately 1,670 "homophones," 140 "heteronyms," 730 "homographs," and 290 "accent shifts." 262 pp.

Webster's New International Dictionary of the English Language 2nd Edition Unabridged. (William A. Neilson, Thomas A. Knott, and Paul W. Carhart, editors). Springfield, MA: G & C Merriam Co., 1949. 3,210 pp.

Webster's Third New International Dictionary of the English Language Unabridged. (Philip B. Gove, editor in chief). Springfield, MA: G & C Merriam Co., 1981. 2,765 pp.

Wentworth, Harold and Stuart Berg Flexner. *Dictionary of American Slang, 2nd Supplemented Edition.* New York: Thomas Y. Crowell Publishing, 1975. 766 pp.

White, Mary Sue. *Word Twins.* New York: Abingdon Press, 1962. An illustrated children's book of 30 homophones. 32 pp.

Whitford, Harold Crandall. *A Dictionary of American Homophones and Homographs.* New York: Teachers College Press, 1966. Contains over 800 homophones (bona fide and Group I) and approximately 220 homographs (bona fide and Group I), including proper names, foreign countries, suffixes, and 40 oral and written exercises. 83 pp.

Williams, Edna Rees. *The Conflict of Homonyms in English.* New Haven, CT: Yale University Press, 1944. Professor Williams' 1936 Yale doctoral dissertation deals with the loss or change in form or status of certain words due to their being homonyms. 127 pp. and seven maps.

Williams, Stephen N. *The Dictionary of British and American Homophones.* London: Brookside Press, 1987. A particularly useful volume containing numerous bona fide homophones and a few homographs. 503 pp.

Wolpow, Edward R. "Humorous humerus." *Word Ways.* Vol. 14, No. 1, Feb. 1981, pp. 55 and 64.

Word Ways: Journal of Recreational Linguistics. Published quarterly at Spring Valley Road, Morristown, NJ, 07960, (A. Ross Eckler, editor and publisher, 201-538-4584). This periodical frequently provides several homophones and homographs.

Zviadadze, Givi. *Dictionary of Contemporary American English Contrasted with British English.* Atlantic Highlands, NJ: Humanities Press, 1983. Contains several bona fide homophones and homographs. 460 pp.